AN INTRODUCTION TO HEGEL'S METAPHYSICS

IVAN SOLL
Foreword by Walter Kaufmann

THE UNIVERSITY
OF CHICAGO PRESS
CHICAGO AND LONDON

Standard Book Number: 226–76794–9 *(clothbound)*
226–76795–7 *(paperbound)*

Library of Congress Catalog Card Number: 75–85447

THE UNIVERSITY OF CHICAGO PRESS, CHICAGO 60637
The University of Chicago Press, Ltd., London

To Sandra, wife and midwife

CONTENTS

FOREWORD

This book is my intellectual grandchild. It has other ancestors, and I have other offspring, but I am proud of it without always agreeing with it. And, of course, it does not always agree with me.

The book's father, Ivan Soll, majored in philosophy at Princeton, and after a year's graduate work at Harvard and another year on a Fulbright at Munich he returned to Princeton for his doctorate. He wrote both his B.A. thesis (on Sartre) and his Ph.D. dissertation (on Hegel) with me, but by the time he completed the latter he was teaching at The University of Wisconsin—Hegel among other subjects. And since he got his degree he has done further work on Hegel, some of it in Paris where he spent a leave of absence.

Our approaches to Hegel are similar in many ways —above all, sympathetic and critical at the same time. But Soll deals with problems that are not discussed in comparable detail in my *Hegel*, and his orientation is less historical than mine.

My book aimed to show how Hegel and his philosophy were very different from the prevalent conceptions of the man and his system. Hegel's personality and development, the nature and aim of his *Phenomenology*, his *Logic*, and his system, and his attitude toward history were moved into the center. Balancing this concern with the whole phenomenon of Hegel, my commentary on the long preface to the *Phenomenology* involved some more microscopic work. My hope was to make a new beginning and to lay the foundations for further studies.

Good monographs on Hegel's aesthetics and his political philosophy, his philosophy of religion and his philosophy of nature are still sorely needed. Hegel's metaphysics is easily as important as any of these subjects, the more so because he has so often been seen as above all a metaphysician, if not the arch-metaphysician of all time. There is thus a special need for the present *Introduction*.

Soll's Hegel *is* a metaphysician, but not a proponent of the kind of metaphysics that was associated with his name during the heyday and in the wake of British Idealism. The Hegel encountered in the following pages is concerned with the relation of truth to human activity, with Kant's thing-in-itself, with subjectivity and objectivity, and with what Hegelians call the good and the bad infinite.

In one important respect this book stands in the tradition of Anglo-American Hegel scholarship. It is not an essay in the history of ideas, and there is little concern with influences or comparisons. Thus Royce's conception of Hegel's relation to pragmatism is criticized in these pages, but Dewey's debt to Hegel is not discussed. But anyone interested in that question is sure to find Soll's study extremely helpful.

In the second chapter, where Hegel's rejection of Kant's thing-in-itself is discussed, the treatment of the same problem by Fichte, Schelling, and Schopenhauer is not brought in. Soll's central aim, of which he never loses sight, is to show how Hegel dealt with some fundamental problems that continue to be of great interest to philosophers. In this way important questions are opened up in a fruitful manner that invites further reflection and research.

The style is exceptionally clear and straightforward, unencumbered both by Hegelian jargon and by current fads. Rarely have such metaphysical complexities been treated with such lucidity. This is a welcome departure from the tradition of paraphrasing obscure texts and, when the original becomes too dark for paraphrase, taking refuge in quotations. Thus this *Introduction* is a fine guide into Hegel's metaphysics and theory of knowledge.

The discussion of the celebrated section on master and slave in the *Phenomenology* is especially illuminating. It makes an important point that I had overlooked in my account, and after reading Soll's dissertation I therefore added a note to the Anchor Books paperback edition of my *Hegel* (1966, p. 137), citing him. (In the following pages I am still charged with having overlooked this point.)

The final section in this Introduction deals with "Passion in the *Logic*," with my conception of the dialectic as "the logic of passion," and with Royce's earlier use of the same phrase. As long as Soll has given so much attention to the provenance of this phrase, it would be stuffy to eschew further clarification.

The phrase "the logic of passion" came to me when I was a student, and it was with some disappointment that I encountered it in Royce a little latter, in 1942. While this was nothing like Scott's finding that Amundsen had reached the south pole a month before him, it was a fly in the ointment. Royce had used the phrase in an altogether different sense and had not applied it to Hegel. Hence I did not consider it necessary to mention Royce years later when I explained in *From Shakespeare to Existentialism*, at the end of the chapter on "The Young Hegel and Religion," in what sense "the dialectic of Hegel's *Phenomenology* is a *logic of passion*," and how "Hegel's own development illustrates the logic of passion." But in my *Hegel* I included some discussion of Royce's use of the phrase, leaning over backwards to be fair to him. Now Soll says that "Kaufmann fails to make clear that, when Royce uses the phrase . . . he does not use it to mean what Kaufmann does." Did I really lean over that far?

The final point in Soll's book is that I wrongly denied that the dialectic of Hegel's *Logic* is also a logic of passion. But it is only in the final paragraph of the book that Soll tries all too briefly in a few lines to persuade us of "the passion of the *Logic*." As usual, his point is worth thinking about because he calls attention to something interesting. For all that, the differences between the logic of the *Phenomenology* and that of the *Logic* remain remarkable, and the reader will have to decide for himself whether my way of putting the matter is really more misleading than Soll's.

Considering the traditional view of Hegel, it would have been a regression and some cause for disappointment if this *Introduction* denied the presence of passion in the *Phenomenology*. That the author moves in the opposite direction and insists on finding quite as much passion in the *Logic* comes as a rather delightful surprise. Most important, this is one of the very few books in English that will prove really helpful to students who are wrestling with Hegel's metaphysics.

WALTER KAUFMANN

PREFACE

"You see, at that time and in those portraits I felt that what I had to say was fairly hard to understand. It's like Hegel. Hegel was a very interesting man, but there aren't many people who want to take the trouble to read him. He's up there where he is for the few people who want to give themselves that trouble and will go in search of whatever nourishment is there."

I told him these applications of Hegel were very impressive. How much of him had he read?

"None," he said. "I told you there weren't many people who wanted to take the trouble to go that far. And I don't either. I picked up my information on the subject from Kahnweiler."

From *Life with Picasso*,*
by Françoise Gilot and Carlton Lake

Hegel had a grand conception of philosophy. He conceived its task to be the attainment of a knowledge which is *absolute*, that is, without limitation. However, since some of his most important, immediate, philosophical predecessors had placed striking limitations upon man's cognitive capacities, Hegel had to rebut their restrictions in order to make his conception of the philosophical task tenable.

Hegel's heroic, if somewhat quixotic, attempt to restore the traditional grandeur of philosophic ambition, his reasoned rejection of that increasingly popular and powerful opposition to such ambition which had culminated in Immanuel Kant's *Critique of Pure*

* Copyright 1964, McGraw-Hill, Inc. Used with permission of McGraw-Hill Book Company.

Reason, is the central theme of this book. I believe that in Hegel's struggle to overcome the limitations placed upon human knowledge by his predecessors lies a major motivation of his philosophic method and a key to its comprehension. His struggles against the claims that man can have knowledge only of things as they appear to him, not as they are in themselves; that knowledge is only subjective, not objective; and that knowledge of the infinite or unconditioned is impossible, are traced in chapters 2, 3, and 4.

Regarding these issues, Hegel views Kant as his most formidable opponent, and Hegel's defense of absolute knowledge is, in large measure, directed against Kantian criticisms. Being primarily interested in the motivations of Hegel's method, I have not attempted to corroborate or criticize Hegel's interpretation of Kant, but have rested content with uncovering that interpretation and the nature of its influence on Hegel.

Hegel not only awarded philosophy the exalted task of attaining absolute knowledge, but also placed this philosophic task in an exalted position with respect to human endeavor in general. He presented the philosophic task of attaining absolute knowledge or truth as the ultimate task of all human endeavor; he thus presented philosophy as the ultimate form of all human activity. This general theory of human activity is traced in chapter 1.

I have focused upon three of the four books which Hegel actually wrote and published: the *Phenomenology of the Spirit,* the *Science of Logic* and the *Encyclopedia of the Philosophical Sciences.* The fourth, the *Philosophy of Right,* because it is restricted to social and political problems, is not as important for an investigation of Hegel's general conception of philosophy. These books form the core of Hegel's philosophy: they are more reliable than the many volumes compiled from students' notes of Hegel's lectures on the history of philosophy, the philosophy of history, aesthetics, and the philosophy of religion; they represent a more mature position than the *Jugendscriften* (which Hegel never even tried to publish) and his early articles in the *Critical Journal of Philosophy*.

Although I firmly adhere to the methodological principle that the texts which Hegel actually wrote and published are to be taken more seriously than the *Zusätze* (secondhand student reports of Hegel's verbal commentaries on these texts), I have made use of *Zusätze* where they clarify and do not contradict the texts actually written by Hegel.

Since I have sought to reveal the basic goals and concerns which motivate Hegel's philosophic exertions, I have paid special attention to his prefaces and introductions, for, not surprisingly, they contain the best statements of his initial problems and his general philosophic program.

It has become commonplace to contrast sharply the *Phenomenology* (1807) with Hegel's later writing in the *Science of Logic* (vol. 1, part 1, 1812; vol. 1, part 2, 1813; vol. 2, 1816) and the *Encyclopedia* (1817; rev. ed., 1827; 3rd rev. ed., 1830). And Hegel's admirers have often sworn allegiance to one while neglecting the other. On the Continent the general trend has been to study the *Phenomenology*, but to neglect the *Logic* and the *Encyclopedia*; in the English-speaking world this trend has been reversed. There are indeed differences between the *Phenomenology* and the later work, but I have stressed their often overlooked continuity and presented them as elements of a single philosophic enterprise.

Rather than following the complete detailed development of the *Phenomenology* or of the *Logic*, I have focused on certain sections in each which are crucial for understanding Hegel's overall conceptions of these works and his general philosophic program. This program, though ultimately unfulfilled and occasionally ignored by Hegel, supplies a useful framework for more complete and detailed studies of his individual works.

All translations of quotations from Hegel, unless otherwise noted, are my own. However, I have consulted and occasionally profited from Sir James Baillie's translation of the *Phenomenology*, Walter Kaufmann's superior translation of the Preface to the *Phenomenology*, W. H. Johnston and L. G. Struther's translation of the *Science of Logic*, and William Wallace's translation of the *Encyclopedia* version of the *Logic*. Where the original German text has been translated rather freely, or explains some stylistic oddity of my translation, or more clearly supports one of my interpretations, I have inserted it in brackets.

I have used as texts: Johannes Hoffmeister's 1952 edition of the *Phänomenologie des Geistes*, Georg Lasson's 1934 edition of the *Wissenschaft der Logik*, and Friedhelm Nicolin and Otto Pöggeler's 1959 edition of the *Enzyklopädie der philosophischen Wissenschaften im Grundriße* (1830). I have made reference to the page numbers in these editions, except in the case of the *Encyclopedia*—where I have referred instead to the short, numbered sections into which the body of the book is divided. As my text for the *Zusätze* to the *Encyclopedia*, which are not included in the Nicolin and Pöggeler edition, I have had to use the older *Jubiläumsausgabe* (1927–30) edited by Hermann Glockner. References are made to the number of the section and the *Zusatz* (e.g., *Enc.*, sec. 41, Z 2). In general I have resorted to the *Jubiläumsausgabe* only where more recent and superior *Philosophische Bibliothek* editions did not exist or were unobtainable.

Paradoxically, the commentaries I have criticized most are the ones I have generally found to be best: Josiah Royce's *Lectures on Modern Idealism*, John N. Findlay's *Hegel: A Re-examination*, and Walter Kaufmann's *Hegel: Reinterpretation, Texts, and Commentary*. Interpretations which are neither plausible nor clear enough to consider seriously are not worth criticizing.

I want to thank Professor Walter Kaufmann, teacher, advisor and friend, who inspired, encouraged, and carefully criticized this study.

AN
INTRODUCTION
TO
HEGEL'S
METAPHYSICS

ABBREVIATIONS

The following nonstandardized abbreviations are used in the footnotes. For details, consult the Bibliography (page 153).

Enc.	Hegel's *Encyclopedia of the Philosophical Sciences*, 1830 ed.
Findlay	J. N. Findlay's *Hegel: A Re-examination*.
G	Glockner edition of Hegel's works, *Jubiläumsausgabe*.
Kaufmann	Walter Kaufmann's *Hegel: Reinterpretation, Texts, and Commentary*.
Logic	Hegel's *Science of Logic*.
PG	Hegel's *Phenomenology of the Spirit*.
Royce	Josiah Royce's *Lectures on Modern Idealism*.
Z	*Zusatz*

1 ~ PHILOSOPHY, TRUTH
AND HUMAN ACTIVITY

Hegel's method is best approached by asking what he was trying to accomplish with it. Since his is a method for philosophy, it is naturally designed to achieve whatever it is that he thought philosophy seeks to achieve. What then does Hegel take to be the goal of philosophy? His answer in its most general form is as straightforward as it is unilluminating; the goal of philosophy is the truth. In 1817 Hegel dedicated the first edition of the *Encyclopedia of the Philosophical Sciences* to "this interest in knowing the truth."[1] Ten years later, in the preface to the second edition he still insists: "In general, that toward which I have worked and am still working in my philosophical endeavors is the scientific knowledge of the truth."[2] And in the introduction to the same work: "Philosophy shares, to be sure, its objects with religion. Both have the truth for their object."[3] In the *Science of Logic* the real interest of philosophy is equated with "the interest in what the true [das Wahre] . . . is."[4]

But this general statement of purpose does not seem to be exclusive enough; do not the natural sciences, mathematics, and even subscientific, unsystematic natural curiosity have truth for their object? Philosophy seems to share this object not only with religion. Yet Hegel would admit this expanded community of pur-

1. p. 22.
2. p. 3.
3. *Enc.* (see Abbreviations), sec. 1.
4. *Logic* (see Abbreviations), 1:51.

3

pose and even continue to expand it somewhat beyond the limits set for it by common sense and ordinary linguistic usage.

The magnificently ambitious, if quixotic and unfulfilled, program of the *Phenomenology of the Spirit* required ordering all the forms of consciousness (*die Gestalten des Bewußtseins*) in a single, ascending series, beginning with ordinary sense perception (*die sinnliche Gewißheit* and *die Wahrnehmung*) and working up to the philosophical consciousness which Hegel here terms "absolute knowledge" (*das absolute Wissen*). But also included in the series are such apparently nonepistemological and only partially epistemological forms as the master-servant relation, the conflict between human and divine law as exemplified in Sophocles' *Antigone*, the moral world view of Kant's ethics, and various forms of art and religion.

The book is remarkable in its scope. As Walter Kaufmann says: "To organize such a wealth of material—indeed, in a sense 'everything'—in the framework of one story is an astonishing feat."[5] No less remarkable is the limited means used to organize this wealth of material; the story is allowed but a single plot-line. The *Phenomenology* displays, however, not merely a linear succession of forms of consciousness but also a progression; the series ascends according to some more or less vague standard. Kaufmann suggests that the arrangement is made according to the relative maturity of the forms, and that "this does not mean that what comes later is always better and more attractive. Early childhood has its unsurpassable charm, youth in some respects is never

5. Kaufmann (see Abbreviations), p. 146.

eclipsed."[6] Yet this maturity cannot be equated simply with what comes later in time, for the development of the stages in the *Phenomenology* deviates radically from their order of appearance in history. But likewise, a person's maturity is not a direct function of his age. The process of maturation is not merely that of aging, and, although maturation does not imply improvement in every way, it suggests improvement in at least some ways.

The arrangement of the forms of consciousness included in the *Phenomenology* in a linear progression is of a piece with Hegel's view that, in some broad sense, they are all engaged in the same endeavor, but with varying degrees of success. Since the most mature or successful form of consciousness is philosophy or absolute knowledge, and the object and goal of philosophy is the truth, all the stages of the *Phenomenology* leading up to this form of consciousness can be considered as also seeking the truth but as being less adequate to the task.

But the notion of seeking the truth has a distinctly epistemological flavor, and it might seem that to view the *Phenomenology* in this way is to represent it as being merely an epistemological work. And certainly it is more. Although the first and last stages, sense perception and philosophy, are easily recognized to be epistemological, that is, as ways or modes of knowing, this is not true of some of the intervening stages already mentioned. If, like Josiah Royce, one were to approach the stages of the *Phenomenology* with a pair of putatively exclusive and exhaustive categories, with the be-

6. Ibid., p. 149.

lief that each stage, each form of consciousness, can be labeled either *theoretical* and *epistemological* on the one hand, or *practical* and *ethical* on the other, some stages would be classified as practical rather than theoretical, for they seem to be ways of acting in the world rather than ways of knowing the world.

However, Royce overstates this point when he claims that in the *Phenomenology* Hegel operates "rather by means of a reducing of the thinking process to pragmatic terms than by means of a false translation of real life into the abstract categories of logic."[7] It is just as one-sided to ignore the theoretical and epistemological aspect of the work as it is to ignore the practical. To ask which aspect is "reduced" to the other is unimportant, if not unanswerable. That Hegel denies any hard and fast distinction between epistemology and ethics, between theory and practice, between knowing and doing, is a crucial aspect of his philosophy. But this denial is not made by asserting either that all knowing is only a kind of doing or that all doing is only a kind of knowing. It is rather part of the following program: different ways of behaving are not to be compared merely with one another, nor are different ways of knowing to be compared merely with one another. We must make a more comprehensive comparison which also includes and reveals relationships between ways of knowing and ways of behaving, a more complete synthesis and systematization in which each way of relating to the world, each "form of consciousness," has its place in relation to each of the others.

In suggesting that all the stages of the *Phenome-*

7. Royce (see Abbreviations), p. 145.

nology are more or less adequate ways of seeking the truth I am not suggesting that these stages are merely epistemological. I want rather to stress that, for Hegel, not only does philosophy share its goal with religion (by his own admission) and with mathematics, the natural sciences, and ordinary curiosity (because of his too general formulation of philosophy's object as "the truth"), but that, as evidenced by the program and plan of the *Phenomenology*, sense perception, science, ethical codes, artistic activity, political behavior, and religion and philosophy are all considered different forms of the same endeavor. And given this vast community of aim and activity, the goal of philosophy is not merely the goal of philosophy alone but also the goal of all human activity. Moreover, this common activity tends to be described by Hegel in terms of seeking the truth, even where the particular form of consciousness considered is least obviously epistemological but rather prima facie pragmatic.

SELF-CONSCIOUSNESS

Both the fusing and relating of modes of acting and knowing, and the use of the quest for truth as the synoptic framework of all human activity are well illustrated in section B of the *Phenomenology*, titled "Self-Consciousness."[8] This is by far the best known and most influential part of the *Phenomenology*. It has been singled out for admiration by many, including Marx and, if imitation be a form of admiration, Sartre. Among the recent interpreters of Hegel to the English-speaking world, Findlay finds that the *Phenomenology* becomes

8. See Appendix.

"more lucid and illuminating" at this point and says that this section "has been *deservedly* admired"; while Kaufmann considers it the most interesting section next to the preface.

In the preceding section, "Consciousness," the first in the book, Hegel had treated three forms of consciousness which are all plainly epistemological.[9] The first, "sense-certainty" (*die sinnliche Gewißheit*), is, to quote Findlay's nice formulation, "the state of mind in which, in Russellian terms, we enjoy a direct acquaintance with some object which we *app*rehend without seeking either to *com*prehend or describe."[10] This object is not even the colored patch so popular with sense datum theorists, but is describable only as a *this, here, now.* The breakdown of this view, for reasons to be discussed later,[11] leads to the next form of consciousness, "Perception" (*Wahrnehmung*). Here the object of consciousness is no longer the directly presented particular of sense but the physical object, as Hegel puts it, "the thing" (*das Ding*). In turn, this view proves in-

9. Although only section A is titled "Consciousness," every stage in the entire *Phenomenology* is a form of consciousness (*Gestalt des Bewußtseins*). In the introduction to the *Science of Logic* Hegel says: "In the *Phenomenology of the Spirit* I have given an example of this method applied to a more concrete object, to consciousness." (1:35). And later in the *Logic* with reference to this passage: "It has been remarked in the introduction that the *Phenomenology of the Spirit* is the science of consciousness" (1:53). Similarly, the whole book is the *Phenomenology of the Spirit*, yet "Spirit" is also the title of section BB. An analogous use of one term to designate both whole and proper part occurs in the *Logic*; "being" *(Sein)* is the name of the first category, the generic name of the first three categories, and the name of the entire first third of the *Logic*.

10. Findlay (see Abbreviations) p. 88.

11. See Chap. 3, "Two Kinds of Universality."

adequate and is replaced by the "Understanding" (*Verstand*), in which the objects of consciousness are not observable physical things but forces and laws, themselves unobservable but productive of the observable world, the explanatory constructs of physical theory. Consciousness then realizes that these unobservable forces and laws, these constructs of physical theory, are not only the objects but also the products of the understanding. Consciousness, in having had these constructs as its objects, had actually had itself for an object. With the realization of this fact, consciousness becomes self-consciousness.

Since the three stages of "Consciousness" are all plainly epistemological, neither the relating of knowing and acting nor the use of truth as the goal of all human endeavor can be demonstrated by them. Because the stages are epistemological, Hegel's tendency to describe the object of each of these forms of consciousness as "the truth" is neither remarkable nor illustrative of any supraepistemological, all-encompassing use of this idiom. And there is no relating of knowing and acting simply because there is no acting. If these two features of the *Phenomenology* are not demonstrated here, neither are they contradicted. The monolithically epistemological character of this section does, however, contradict Royce's assertion that in the *Phenomenology* "theoretical problems always appear as also life problems."[12]

In "Self-Consciousness," on the other hand, the plainly practical character of some of the stages makes possible the demonstration of these two points. Also manifest are the looseness of the argument (even

12. Royce, p. 152.

though Kaufmann rightly considers these transitions "among the most plausible in the whole book," and Findlay speaks of their "obscure but powerful 'logic' ") and the book's typically irregular structure.[13]

There is a general introductory section called "The Truth of Self-Certainty" followed by "A: Independence and Dependence of Self-Consciousness; Mastership and Servitude" and "B: Freedom of Self-Consciousness."

As the title of the introductory section suggests, the general characterization of self-consciousness is made in an epistemological idiom, that is, in terms of knowledge and truth. The previous stages of the *Phenomenology* are described as those in which "the truth is for consciousness something other than itself," and the dialectical process which revealed their inadequacy as that in which "the concept of this truth disappears."[14] Self-consciousness is then contrasted with its predecessor: "What did not come about in these earlier relationships will henceforth be the case, namely a certainty which is the same as its truth, for certainty is itself the object, and consciousness is itself the truth."[15]

Notice that in these quotations "the truth" of a form of consciousness is simply its object and is contrasted to the conscious subject rather than to falsity. However, "truth" is also used in contrast to falsity. In dialectically disappearing, "consciousness"—which takes its object to be external to itself—"shows itself rather not to be in

13. See Appendix
14. *PG* (see Abbreviations), p. 133.
15. Ibid.

the truth," whereas, "with self-consciousness we have thus entered the native domain of the truth."[16] To identify the objects of consciousness and self-consciousness as their "truths" is of a piece with characterizing each as a "form of knowledge" (*Gestalt des Wissens*). Both locutions are epistemological.

In self-consciousness the external world apprehended by consciousness does not completely vanish but merely loses its "otherness" (*Anderssein*), its character as an independent reality. It is recognized as being only an aspect (*Moment*) of self-consciousness, a product of abstraction unable to exist by itself. If the external world were not preserved as an aspect of self-consciousness, but completely annihilated and ignored, the resulting form of consciousness would produce only "the tautology, I am I."[17] This contentless self-contemplation would hardly be an advance, a more adequate way of knowing the truth. Since self-consciousness is supposed to be an advance over consciousness, Hegel denies that true self-consciousness can be achieved by completely blotting out the external world. The external sensible world must appear to self-consciousness, yet the "essence" or "truth" of self-consciousness is to remove any external object, to maintain its "unity with itself," to have only itself for an object. Paradoxically, the external world must be both preserved and destroyed.

Self-consciousness attempts to resolve this paradox by preserving this world but removing its external character. Self-consciousness attempts to do this by making

16. *PG*, p. 134.
17. Ibid.

the world its own, by taking possession of it. Thus, self-consciousness manifests itself as "desire" (*Begierde*).[18]

The epistemological quest for truth, with a sudden twist, expresses itself as desire, which, being the spring of all action, catapults the spirit from theory to practice. We take possession of things by using them for our own purposes. This entails changing them and *acting* upon them.

The action initiated by desire changes, uses, and possesses the external world but not merely for the benefits ordinarily associated with these activities. The immediate goals of desire and the behavior implementing it are viewed rather as manifestations of the basic drive of self-consciousness to negate the external world and have only itself for an object. In this respect Hegel's theory resembles other theories of behavior which view the vast variety of human activity as the varying expression of a single drive. Like Nietzsche's "will to power" and the "pleasure principles" of Mill and Freud, the desire of the self-conscious spirit to negate the external world furnishes the ultimate explanatory principle for a theory of all behavior. All the stages of self-consciousness are to be viewed as different attempts to negate or deny the reality of the external world.

It is the broadness of such concepts as *denial* and *negation* that enables Hegel to make the transition from theory to practice. If one is threatened by the apparition of a dragon, as the self-sufficiency of self-consciousness is threatened by the apparition (*Erscheinung*) of the external world, one may, without stirring, simply deny the reality of such apparitions. If, however, such appari-

18. *Begierde* has overtones of inordinateness, greed and carnal desire.

tions persist, as the external world continues to appear to self-consciousness, one may be tempted to slay the dragon by sword. Both the skeptical scholar and the swordsman can be said to "negate" the threat.

The transition to the practical realm is also aided in a similar fashion by the duality of the German word "*Selbstbewußtsein.*" As Walter Kaufmann points out: "While being self-conscious often means being unsure of oneself and embarrassed, *selbstbewußt sein* means just the opposite: being self-assured and proud. Of course, the primary meaning in both languages is the same: self-awareness. But while this sense is most important, the other connotations are relevant."[19] What Kaufmann calls the primary meaning is relied upon in the initial, epistemological characterization of self-consciousness; there the truth and essence of self-consciousness is to be aware only of itself. But when self-consciousness expresses itself as agent, the external world becomes not only a threat to its epistemological self-sufficiency but also a threat to the self-assurance and confidence of the agent. Also, "*die Gewißheit seiner selbst,*" *Self-Certainty*, is used both epistemologically and to mean self-assurance.

This negation of the world through action is still, interestingly enough, described in terms of truth: "Self-consciousness, certain of the nothingness of this other, sets this nothingness up as its *truth*, destroys the independent object and thereby achieves self-certainty, true certainty, as the certainty which has accrued to it in an objective manner."[20] It was previously noted that where

19. Kaufmann, pp. 152–53.
20. *PG*, p. 139.

a form of consciousness is discussed epistemologically, as a way of knowing, Hegel speaks of its object as its truth. In discussing a form of consciousness which is prima facie a way of acting, Hegel further extends the use of this idiom and speaks of its objective or goal as its *truth*. With this extension the notion of seeking the truth becomes flexible and imprecise enough to serve as a synoptic framework in which all forms of human activity can be placed.

But the negation of the world through action inspired by desire is doomed to failure. Even where action is successful and desire satisfied, the external world is not negated, for desire, though it may capture, use, and even physically destroy its objects, requires the presence of these objects for its expression and satisfaction. The satisfaction of desire reveals the dependence of desire on objects external to it.

Self-consciousness expresses itself as desire *in order* to do away with the external world, but instead, by requiring such a world to overcome, it insures the continued existence of such a world and, in turn, the continuance of desire.

This suggestion that desire inevitably contains the seeds of its own frustration has been taken up by Jean-Paul Sartre in his *Being and Nothingness*, a book heavily indebted to the *Phenomenology* and particularly to section B. However, unlike Hegel, Sartre attributes this fundamental futility not merely to a particular mode of human activity, but to all human endeavor. Accepting Hegel's thesis that the ultimate drive and motivation of human behavior is the urge to become completely self-sufficient, autonomous, independent of anything external by being both subject and object of consciousness, Sartre proceeds to argue that this is an unattainable goal, and man a "useless passion." Hegel, on the contrary, allows for the fulfillment of this drive but only after the spirit has endured the entire course of the *Phenomenology*. One might describe Sartre as a pessimistic Hegel, or Hegel as an optimistic Sartre.

Although the description of desire and its inevitable downfall seems to be made with reference to the external world in general, Hegel, in the course of this presentation, baldly asserts rather than argues that the object of desire is not the external world in general but that part of it which has life: ". . . the object of immediate desire is a living thing."[21] Findlay suggests that self-consciousness in the form of desire has "a more adequate exemplification of itself where a phenomenal object is living: a living thing has something of the perpetual direction toward self which is characteristic of the self-conscious subject and therefore serves to mirror the latter."[22] This gloss supplies somewhat of a justification for Hegel's assertion, but not one to be found in Hegel. To be sure, Hegel claims that the external object "has, like consciousness, gone back into itself" and "has become life through this reflection."[23] But there is no mention here of this external object serving as a mirror for self-consciousness.[24] Findlay glosses over the startling absence in the text of any justification for this claim, which is really made ad hoc, to introduce the

21. *PG*, p. 135.
22. Findlay, p. 94.
23. *PG*, p. 135.
24. Hegel does, however, use such an argument later in discussing the master-slave relationship.

discussion of certain types of interpersonal behavior which follows. To parody a phrase of Findlay's, the "logic" at this point is infinitely more obscure than powerful. It is the desire to include certain topics rather than any kind of "logic" which here dictates to the dialectic. And this pattern is not atypical.

To further set the scene for a discussion of interpersonal behavior Hegel makes the object of desire not just a living thing but another self-consciousness. Findlay again explains this move in terms of self-consciousness seeking an adequate mirror: ". . . the one clear outcome is that self-consciousness cannot be adequately mirrored in an object incapable of itself 'negating' what is external. . . . Another self is, in short, the only adequate mirror of my self-conscious self: the subject can only satisfactorily see itself when what it sees is another self-consciousness."[25] Unlike the previous move, this one is argued, but not in the way Findlay suggests. Desire is only truly satisfied by the negation of its object, and, since desire cannot bring this about through its own action on this object (as Hegel argued earlier), desire can be satisfied only if this object negates itself. Then, with extreme opacity this ability to negate is identified with self-consciousness, and Hegel concludes: "Self-consciousness achieves satisfaction only in another self-consciousness."[26]

Findlay's interpretation is too epistemological. If one were to describe the attainment of life and self-consciousness by the object of self-consciousness in terms of his mirror metaphor, it would be well to remember

25. Findlay, p. 94.
26. PG, p. 139.

that self-consciousness is here expressing itself as the desire to destroy through action. What self-consciousness seeks in the hall of mirrors is not an accurate image of itself to contemplate but a flawed pane whose destructibility affords an escape route to independence.

After generally delineating the basic drive of self-consciousness as the attempt to achieve self-sufficiency by negating everything external to itself, Hegel exemplifies this drive in a variety of more specific forms.

THE LIFE AND DEATH STRUGGLE

As the result of the preceding development, "the other is also a self-consciousness; individual confronts individual."[27] We are now in the social sphere, but in an antisocial way. Each of these individual self-consciousnesses tries to negate the other by killing it and must risk its own life to do so. They engage in a "life and death struggle" which is the direct consequence of the general character of each self-consciousness to negate whatever is external to it.

But by referring to the realization of the drive toward self-sufficiency and self-certainty as its *truth*, even this struggle is discussed as a kind of seeking after truth: "They must enter this struggle, for they must lift their self-certainty to the *truth*. . . . The individual who has not risked his life can, of course, be recognized as a *person*, but he has not achieved the *truth* of this recognition as an independent self-consciousness."[28] Even where least expected, the goal remains "the truth."

The reasons for the failure of this attempt to achieve

27. *PG*, p. 143.
28. *PG*, p. 144.

true self-consciousness through the death of the other and the transition to the next stage are only obscurely indicated by Hegel. Kaufmann suggests that the life and death struggle gives way to the master-slave relationship because "the loser prefers servitude to death."[29] But why should the winner bent upon the death of the other allow his victim this option? Findlay is vague on this question: "To carry on this struggle till it results in the death of one of the parties will, however, remove a necessary condition of self-consciousness."[30] Although Findlay never tells us what this condition is, his suggestion that the struggle is abandoned because the murdering *winner* finds his victory somehow unsatisfactory seems sound.

Royce attributes this unsatisfactoriness to "the fact that killing a man proves nothing, except the victor, in order to prove himself to be the self, needs still another man to kill."[31] Royce's explanation of this transition is essentially an application of Hegel's argument for the inevitable frustration of desire in general.[32] And although it is applicable, there is no textual evidence that Hegel actually invokes this argument here.

As I have tried to show, Hegel arrives at the conclusion that self-consciousness must have another self-consciousness as its object, not by stressing its epistemological need for an adequate mirror, but by stressing its need to negate the external world. However, in making the transition from the life and death struggle to the master-servant relationship, Hegel uses this con-

29. Kaufmann, p. 153.
30. Findlay, p. 96.
31. Royce, p. 177.
32. See Chap. 1, "Self-consciousness."

clusion by giving it an epistemological twist. Suddenly, at the very beginning of section IV A, the second self-consciousness is asserted to be necessary for the assurance and autonomy of the first, not because it can be destroyed, but because this assurance and autonomy require a *witness*: "Self-consciousness exists in itself and for itself because it exists as such for another self-consciousness, that is, it exists only by being recognized."[33] The other suddenly becomes, not a threat and obstacle to self-realization, necessary only as something to destroy, but an accomplice to be preserved. "Each is the other's *means* (*Mittel*) through which it mediates (*vermittelt*) and unites with itself, and each . . . exists for itself only through this mediation (*Vermittlung*). They recognize themselves as mutually recognizing each other."[34] The need for a witness, though itself merely postulated and not justified, enables Hegel to make this transition.

The other has now been deemed necessary both because of its vulnerability and its awareness; self-consciousness requires both a mortal enemy to destroy and a witness to whom it can demonstrate its willingness to risk its life in mortal combat. But where the enemy is the only witness, victory insures lack of recognition. And since victory is meaningful only when recognized by another, victory becomes impossible. Hegel speaks of death as the "natural negation of life . . . which remains without the required significance of recognition."[35] Since killing the enemy also destroys the

33. *PG*, p. 141.
34. *PG*, p. 143.
35. *PG*, p. 145.

witness, a way must be found to negate the other while preserving his ability to witness. So the victor makes the vanquished his vassal instead of his victim.

It is not, as Kaufmann claims, that the loser prefers servitude to death, but rather that the winner prefers a servant to a corpse. And the assurance of even the successful head hunter is flawed not, as Royce claims, just because "even head hunting implies dependence upon one's neighbor who is good enough to furnish one more head for the hunter,"[36] but also because the successful head hunter's potential admiring public is constantly shrinking.

MASTER AND SERVANT

The two self-consciousnesses are now related as master and servant. This relation is the result of attempts by self-consciousness to achieve two sometimes conflicting goals, the negation of everything external to it, and recognition. It seems at first that the master has solved both of these problems. Since desire requires external objects for its satisfaction, it cannot successfully negate the external world. The servant, as a self-consciousness, tries to negate the external world by changing it through work, but although work can change the world, it cannot completely negate or destroy it. For him the world is an autonomous entity with which he must cope. But the master, by setting the servant to work for him, derives "enjoyment" from this world without having to cope with it, without having to experience its "autonomy" (*Selbständigkeit*) . Thus, he succeeds where desire failed, negates the external world, and becomes "the

36. Royce, p. 177.

purely negative power for which the thing is nothing." The servant also furnishes him with the recognition required by self-consciousness.

Then, in a sharp reversal, which deeply influenced Karl Marx, the servant emerges as the higher realization of self-consciousness. There are three arguments offered for this conclusion. First, since each serves as the object or "truth" of the other, the inferior one (the servant) has the superior one (the master) for an object and thus has a higher truth: "For the master the inessential consciousness is the object which constitutes the truth of his self-certainty. . . . For servitude the essence is the master; thus its truth is the independent consciousness existing for itself."[37]

This is outrageous; one might analogously argue that the loser of a chess game knew more about chess than the winner because the loser could observe the superior play of the winner, while the winner could observe only the inferior play of the loser.

Secondly, since the servant "felt the fear of death, the absolute master," and, because of it, "trembled throughout, making all that was stable in him shudder," he has the independent consciousness not only for his object but also *in himself*, because, "this pure universal movement [the trembling], the absolute dissolving of all that is enduring [the shuddering], is however the simple essence of self-consciousness."[38] This is certainly more poetically impressionistic than philosophically impressive, more of a metaphor than an argument.

37. *PG*, pp. 147–48. Findlay's misplaced mirror metaphor seems to fit this passage better than the ones to which it is applied.
38. *PG*, p. 148.

Thirdly, although the enjoyment of the master is a "pure negation of the object," which produces "unalloyed self-reliance, [*Selbstgefühl*]," Hegel argues: "This satisfaction is, for that very reason, itself only evanescent, for it lacks the *objective* side or *continued existence* [*Bestehen*]. Work, on the contrary, is restrained desire, arrested evanescence; work, in other words, shapes and forms [*bildet*]."[39] The fleeting enjoyments of the master do not last, but the servant, because he does not and cannot completely negate the objects he works on, creates something enduring (*ein Bleibendes*).

The downfall of desire was its failure to do away with external objects, but now this same failure is cited as responsible for the success of the servant. Does not the continued existence of the external object limit the practical independence and epistemological autonomy of the servant, just as it limited desire? It does not, for the servant having given form to the object by working on it, recognizes himself in the object and thus removes its external character.

One extremely plausible interpretation of the ascendancy of the servant, and one attractive to Marxists, is also offered by Kaufmann: "The servant comes to live by his own work and thus becomes self-reliant and independent, while the master comes to rely on the servant's labor and thus becomes dependent."[40] And Royce says, "Unfortunately, however, for the master, the master becomes dependent upon the slave's work."[41] But as

39. *PG*, pp. 148–49.
40. Kaufmann, p. 153.
41. Royce, p. 178.

sensible as this way to argue the superiority of the servant would have been, Hegel himself does not, in fact, use it.

The ensuing transition from the master-servant relationship to the next form of consciousness, *stoicism*, is again inadequately described by the commentators. Findlay's interpretation is: "The slave's labour is also a more genuine overcoming of material externality than the master's idle round of vanishing enjoyments. But, since for the slave all rational direction lies outside himself in the master, his self-assertion will be necessarily degraded to self-will (*Eigensinn*), and his intelligence to a relatively hidebound skill or aptitude (*Geschicklichkeit*). It is only in an attitude that can rise *above* the whole master-slave distinction that self-consciousness can be adequately realized."[42] The passage to which Findlay refers[43] is not even relevant and must be strangely read to make it yield an explanation of a transition it does not discuss. The passage occurs immediately after the servant discovers himself in the products of his work. Hegel nowhere says that this "rediscovery of its own mind and significance (*seinen eigenen Sinn*) in work" is necessarily degraded to mere capricious obstinacy (*Eigensinn*)[44] and skill because this work is externally directed by the master. Findlay's gloss is suspiciously incoherent and paradoxical; should not the master's external direction prevent all caprice and obstinacy on the part of the servant rather than produce it?

42. Findlay, p. 96.
43. The last paragraph in IV. A, pp. 149–50.
44. *Sinn* means both mind and significance; *Eigensinn* means both caprice and obstinacy; all these meanings are relevant.

Hegel actually argues only that unless the work and rediscovery are accompanied by absolute fear, this degradation occurs: "If consciousness forms without the prime absolute fear, it is only its own mind and significance in a vain way."[45] But as was plainly stated in Hegel's second argument for the ascendancy of the servant, the servant does experience absolute fear.[46] Hegel is not describing the servant's inevitable failure, but one of the necessary conditions of his actual success. No transition is being discussed here.

Moreover, the fact that the servant obeys orders, the very fact which Findlay claims to be responsible for the servant's failure, is here cited as another necessary condition for his success: "For this reflection [self-discovery] both the elements [*Momente*] of fear and *service* in general, like that of giving form, are necessary. . . . Without the discipline of service and obedience, fear remains formal and does not spread itself over the known actuality of existence."[47]

Both Kaufmann and Royce view the transition to stoicism as occurring simply with the servant's *recognition* of his own superiority and independence. Kaufmann says, "The transition to the first of these outlooks is easy to follow: the attitude of the servant who, despite his status, feels essentially self-reliant and independent may be characterized as stoicism."[48] Royce says, "Let this essential character of the slave,—the fact that he, as worker, is the only true man in this primitive society —let this fact come to his own consciousness, and the

45. PG, p. 150.
46. See above.
47. PG, p. 149.
48. Kaufmann, p. 153.

self becomes transformed from slavery to a higher phase of consciousness. This new phase is represented . . . by stoicism."[49]

But Hegel gives reasons for the *inadequacy* of the servant's independence and autonomy, even where they are recognized by the servant. In this transition the servant's independence is not merely recognized but also rejected and replaced. In short, there is more of a transition than Royce or Kaufmann indicate.

The basic drive of self-consciousness is to become its own object, to collapse the distinction between consciousness and its object. The servant's failure to complete this unification is the inadequacy which initiates the transition. The servant's self-consciousness recognizes itself in two ways—in the master and in the objects it works on. In each it sees itself; in the master, it sees itself as a consciousness; in the artifact, it sees itself objectified in the form it imparts to the *object*. "The repressed self-consciousness [the servant], in the activity of forming, becomes its own object [in the sense that it is embodied] in the form of the fashioned object. At the same time it sees in the master being for itself [*Fürsichsein*, here roughly synonymous with self-consciousness] as a consciousness."[50] But for the servant, the master and the artifacts, that is, consciousness and object, are separate and distinct: "But in the servant's consciousness as such, these two elements, itself as an independent object and this object as a consciousness, fall asunder and thus its own essence falls asunder."[51]

49. Royce, p. 178.
50. *PG*, p. 151.
51. Ibid.

Where consciousness is not identical with its object, there is no true *self*-consciousness. Although the servant cannot know it, "the thinghood which the form receives through work is nothing other than [*keine andere Substanz als*] consciousness."[52] A transition must be made to a new form of consciousness which is able to recognize and thus bring about this identity between subject and object.

The servant recognizing himself in his artifacts approaches this identity, but to the extent that he still admits the separation of artisan and artifact, of consciousness and object, he falls short.

STOICISM

Stoicism is viewed as a denial of the external world and correspondingly of the subject-object distinction. This denial is accomplished by withdrawing from the life of action, from the servant's attempt to effect the external world by acting on it, to a life of *thought*. Action, be it the crude destruction of desire and war or the constructive creation of work, never succeeds in doing away with the need for an external object and thus with the subject-object distinction.

Action was originally resorted to by the self-conscious spirit when mere contemplation failed to accomplish this very task.[53] Now it seems that with the failure of action, the spirit in desperation hopelessly *reverts* to contemplation. But this is not so.

The transition from action to thought is not merely

52. Ibid.
53. See Chap. 1, "Self-consciousness."

a return from action to contemplation in general. *Thought (Denken)* is distinguished from other ways of knowing the world, in particular from knowing by means of sense perception, and thus from the stages in Section A, "Consciousness": "The object comes to thought not in sensible representations or figures [*in Vorstellungen oder Gestalten*] but in concepts [*Begriffen*] . . ."[54]

Unlike sense-certainty, perception, and understanding, thought is not an attempt to know an external world. When one thinks concepts, no reference is made to anything external. For concepts are not only objects of the thinking consciousness but also its products. Furthermore, the fact that concepts belong to the thinking consciousness and are not external to it is immediately obvious: "What is represented sensuously, as existing and having a shape, has as such the form of being something other than consciousness; but a concept . . . is not like a representation, where one has first to recollect that it is one's own representation, but the concept is for me immediately *my* concept."[55] Hegel is arguing that the mental images produced by perception of the external world and by sensuous imagination are similar. When one entertains such an image, one must ask oneself whether it is one's own product or that of the external world, whether it is imagination or perception. But when one considers an abstract, non-sensuous concept, there is no comparable alternative. If it is a concept, it must have been produced by me. Thus the

54. *PG*, p. 152.
55. *PG*, p. 152.

stoical thinker cannot help but recognize that unity of consciousness and object of consciousness which escaped the servant.

Although stoicism is a new form of consciousness, it does mark a return to an epistemological mode of fulfilling the basic drive of self-consciousness. As illustrated by the preceding development, this drive can be expressed positively as the attempt to have only oneself for an object and thereby to achieve *autonomy* or *self-sufficiency*. It can also be expressed negatively as the attempt to negate the external world and thus become *independent* of it.

For Hegel both the positive and negative expressions are essentially equivalent, and, correspondingly, both the idea of independence and that of autonomy are expressed by Hegel's term—*Selbständigkeit*. To negate the external object is to remove the possibility of having anything but oneself for an object. Put another way, it is to negate the distinction between subject and object.

The basic drive is couched in terms broad enough to be given both epistemological and practical interpretations, and, contrary to Royce, Hegel does not opt for one or the other. This suspension of decision is deliberate and enables Hegel to move from an epistemological stage to a practical one and back to another epistemological one by viewing them as successive attempts to fulfill the same basic drive.

The autonomy and independence sought by the spirit are equated with freedom *(Freiheit)*. Because the stoic is a thinker thinking his own thoughts, self-contained and autonomous, he is free. Because the external world plays no part in this thinking of abstract concepts, he is as a thinker independent of it: "In thought I am free, because I am not in another but remain simply myself."[56]

The stoic has a position in the external world of practical affairs; he may be a master like Marcus Aurelius or a servant like Epictetus, "on the throne or in chains,"[57] but his worldly position is irrelevant to his freedom. Since the external world is not the object or "truth" of the thinking consciousness, "the freedom of self-consciousness is indifferent toward its position in the natural world [*das natürliche Dasein*]"[58]

The servant can become a stoic while outwardly remaining a servant, yet it is misleading to describe this transition as the mere recognition of an independence already possessed by the servant. First, the servant before the transition already recognizes his particular kind of independence when he recognizes himself in the products of his labor. Secondly, the independence of the stoic has a radically different basis from that of the servant; the former is the result of a certain kind of action, while the latter is the result of withdrawing from all action. The independence that the stoic recognizes is not the same one which the servant possessed.

The sort of freedom which a man may possess while in chains is not obvious and contradicts ordinary common sense. Freedom is a notion usually associated with action, and to consider a man free whose range of actions is severely restricted seems strange. Hegel is able to consider the stoic slave free, first, because of the

56. Ibid.
57. *PG*, p. 153.
58. Ibid.

equation of freedom with autonomy and self-sufficiency, and second, because autonomy can be epistemological as well as practical. The stoic's freedom is
actually epistemological autonomy.

Royce, committed to the rigid view that Hegel is a
pragmatist who in every case reduces thought to its
practical significance, is forced to claim: "Stoicism,
however, is here viewed in its practical, and not in its
theoretical aspects as a doctrine of the world. Practically, stoicism is the attitude of the man who regards
all things with which he deals as necessarily subject to
his own reason, whether he can control them physically
or not."[59] It takes more than a little stretching to consider only practical and not at all theoretical the renunciation of the importance of all overt physical activity as
a means to freedom and truth. To be sure, the stoic
seeks freedom, but in a peculiarly theoretical manner.
The stoic "regards all things with which he deals as
necessarily subject to his own reason," but only because
he refuses to deal with anything but his own thoughts. If
there is any "reduction" in Hegel's discussion, it is not
the "reduction" of stoicism from a theoretical to a practical view, but the reduction of freedom from a normally
practical concept to a peculiarly theoretical and epistemological one. The only sense in which stoicism is presented as "practical" is the trivial one in which all
theoretical views involve *mental activity*. This hardly
makes Hegel a pragmatist; he is in this particular section
rather somewhat of an antipragmatist.

With sharp sociological and psychological insight
Hegel says that, "stoicism, the freedom which goes back

59. Royce, pp. 178–79.

into the pure universality of thought, could appear as a general form of the world spirit only in a time of general fear and servitude but also of general education which had taught men to think."[60] The point seems to be that the frustration of the freedom to act results in the search for a type of freedom immune to such frustration. Where the capacity for abstract thought exists, freedom, outwardly thwarted, is sought in thought. Hegel seems to suggest that the stoic's freedom is what Freud might call a substitute gratification. However, this suggestion, interesting and true as it may be, is not completely consonant with the genesis of stoicism in the *Phenomenology*. Although stoicism arises from servitude rooted in fear, it does not arise because the servant is not allowed to act freely, but because all action proves ultimately futile.

Although in the *Phenomenology* stoicism is associated with a particular kind of worldly milieu and rejected as an inadequate form of consciousness, its concept of freedom as autonomy or self-sufficiency is never rejected by Hegel. In so far as the stoical consciousness *thinks*, it resembles the last stage and goal of the *Phenomenology*, "absolute knowledge," the philosophical consciousness within which Hegel's *Logic* unfolds. The unity of subject and object achieved by a thinker thinking his own thoughts, this epistemological autonomy, is as characteristic of the ultimate philosophical consciousness as it is of the stoical consciousness. And freedom is claimed for the philosophical contemplator of concepts, as it was for the stoic, on the basis of epistemological autonomy.

60. *PG*, p. 153.

Later, in the *Encyclopedia*, in passages reminiscent of the stoic's rejection of action, freedom is still found only in thought: "In logic, thoughts are understood to have no content except that which belongs to and is produced by thinking. Thus, the thoughts are pure thoughts. Thus, the spirit remains with itself and so is free, for freedom is just this: to remain with oneself in its other, to depend on oneself, to determine oneself. In all impulses and appetites (*Trieben*) I begin with an other, with something which is external to me. In this case we speak of dependence. Freedom is only present where there is no other for me, which is not myself."[61] Empirical knowledge—because it requires an external object and is therefore not autonomous—is branded unfree: "While this sensible world [*dies Sinnliche*] is and remains for empiricism something given, empiricism is a doctrine of bondage [*Unfreiheit*], for freedom consists precisely in my having no absolute other opposed to me, but in my depending on a content which I am myself."[62]

Stoicism is not, as Royce suggests,[63] rejected because its freedom is sought in thought rather than in overt action. The self-sufficiency of conceptual thought as the source of freedom is rejected neither at this point nor later. To be sure, Hegel says, "Freedom in thought has only pure thought as its truth which is without the fulfillment of life and therefore only the concept of free-

61. *Enc.*, sec. 24, Z2. See also *Enc.*, sec. 23.
62. *Enc.*, sec. 38, Z.
63. "The dialectical defect of the stoic's position is that the actual world of the stoic's life—the world of activity of desire, of interest—is meanwhile going on in its own accidental way. The self in order to attain independence has resigned all definite plans of control over fortunes" (Royce, p. 179).

dom, not living freedom itself.[64] But the immediately following explication makes clear that what is required to fulfill the concept of freedom is not to abandon thought and return to overt action, but to fill in the general concept of pure thought with a detailed and determinate content of particular thoughts: "However, since individuality should show itself to be alive by acting, or grasp the living world in a system of thought by thinking, there must lie *in thought itself* the contents of the good for action and the contents of the true for thought, so that there is no ingredient other than the concept . . . in all that exists for consciousness."[65]

The autonomy of thought is not to be rejected but saved, and this can only be done if the thinking subject produces not only the general conceptual form of his object but also its specific content. Even if the stoic acts, this action must be directed and determind by *thought*. His failure does not lie in his desertion of action for thought, but in his inability to derive from thought explicit directives for both. It is not action per se which the stoic has neglected but the specificity of both action and thought.

Since the stoical consciousness needs a content and cannot itself provide one, it must accept and depend upon one *given* to it from without. Thus, its autonomy and freedom are lost. The autonomous last stage of the *Phenomenology*, on the contrary, is able to provide its own content, that is, the determinate development of Hegel's *Logic*, and thus maintain its autonomy and freedom.

64. *PG*, p. 153.
65. *PG*, p. 154.

The stoic's wisdom is limited to the knowledge that truth, goodness, and freedom reside in thought. His true but trivial generalizations, that one should know the truth, think thoughts, do the good, and seek virtue and wisdom, make him an uplifting bore. When Polonius asks Hamlet what he is reading, Hamlet answers, "Words"! Hegel's stoic resembles a Hamlet without irony, a man who says and knows only that the book contains words.

SKEPTICISM

Skepticism seeks to correct the inadequacies of stoicism. Since stoicism's fault was not that it sought freedom in thought, there is no return to action. Instead, skepticism is "the realization of that of which stoicism is only the concept—and the actual experience of what *freedom of thought* is."[66] The downfall of the stoic's independence was caused by his need for a specific content and his inability to provide one himself. The skeptic does not, however, solve the problem of content by providing one; instead he explicitly denies the necessity and reality of any specific content. The "remaining determinateness," which the stoic, unable to produce, had to accept as an external given, is for the skeptical consciousness "completely inessential."

Although, in contrast to the ultimate stage of the *Phenomenology*, neither stoicism nor skepticism provides its own specific content, there is a difference between them: what the stoic *ignores*, the skeptic *denies*. Stoicism places no importance on its worldly position;

66. Ibid.

skepticism goes a step further and explicitly denies the reality of this world. Skepticism makes explicit what was implicit in stoicism.

In its negation of the external world skepticism resembles desire and work. But while those attempts to negate through *action* fail, "this polemical course against the manifold independence of things is successful, because it turns against them as an already completed, free self-consciousness, more precisely, because it contains *thought*.[67] Unlike negation through action, denial through thought does not require the presence of the objects it negates. Yet, although the skeptic denies the manifold reality of the external world, he finds himself behaving as if it were real. The skeptical consciousness is schizoid; it contains two conflicting conceptions of itself: "It admits to be an entirely accidental, individual consciousness—a consciousness that is empirical, conforms to what has no reality for it, obeys what has no significance for it, and does and makes real what has no truth for it. But even as it considers itself individual, accidental, animal life, and lost self-consciousness, it also makes itself, on the contrary, general and self-identical, for it is the negativity of all individuality and all distinction."[68]

Hegel also claims that the skeptic's "words and deeds constantly contradict each other" because "it pronounces absolute disappearance, and the pronouncement exists . . .; it pronounces the nullity of seeing, hearing, etc., and it itself sees, hears, etc.; it pronounces the nullity of ethical realities, and acts according to them

67. *PG*, p. 155.
68. *PG*, p. 157.

[*macht sie selbst zu den Mächten seines Handelns*]."[69]

Although Hegel does not develop this line of thought more fully, he certainly supplies stimulus for further reflection. It might be noted that the three arguments offered, despite their obvious similarities, make slightly different points. The first ("It pronounces absolute disappearance, and the pronouncement exists") shows that the actual utterance of a certain skeptical position—that nothing exists—is self-defeating. In this respect it resembles utterances like "I am mute" and "I do not exist."[70] Of course, the skeptic, by not stating his position, could escape this difficulty.

The second argument ("It pronounces the nullity of seeing, hearing, etc., and it itself sees, hears, etc.") is, in one sense, more basic, for it finds fault with those skeptics who, regardless of whether or not they state their positions, continue to perceive the external world, though they deny the reality of both this world and the perception of it. To refrain from perceiving the world is, even for a skeptic, most probably impossible and, at least, much more difficult than simply refraining from stating one's skepticism.

The third argument ("It pronounces the nullity of ethical realities, and acts according to them.") refers to the fact that those skeptical of the validity of moral codes and principles usually follow them anyway. The skeptic can certainly avoid this pitfall by acting amorally; Hegel only argues that, as a matter of fact, they do not.

69. Ibid.
70. It resembles a negative form of A. J. Ayer's version of the *Cogito ergo sum* argument. See Ayer, *The Problem of Knowledge*, pp. 44–52.

However, the general criticism that the skeptic's deeds contradict his words is only obliquely and incompletely exemplified in these three arguments. We are offered the two highly specialized and easily avoidable activities of obeying moral precepts and actually stating the skeptical position, and the very general, if not universal, perception of the external world, which is only dubiously a "deed." The best case for the claim that the skeptic's deeds contradict his words is not made by any of these three arguments, but it is a consequence of the last. The skeptic betrays himself, not only in his philosophical garrulity and moral conventionality, but in the entire range of his normal practical activity, his ordinary reactions to an environment whose existence he denies.

Hegel suggests this more general and forceful objection in describing one of the skeptic's two conceptions of himself as "a consciousness that is empirical" which "conforms to what has no reality for it." We find this more general statement of the manner in which the skeptic's deeds contradict his words in the middle of what seems to be a separate objection.[71] This is not surprising if we give up the idea that the contradiction between the skeptic's words and deeds and his conflicting conceptions of himself are separate points. Their relation is close and simple; the conflicting conceptions arise as the result of the discrepancy between word and deed. One of the skeptic's conceptions of himself is based on his words, that is, his skeptical doctrine; the other on his betrayal of this doctrine in action.

Much the same objection, that the skeptic betrays

71. See Kaufmann, p. 154.

himself in his ordinary and inevitable reaction to the physical environment, is made more clearly in David Hume's *Dialogues Concerning Natural Religion* (1779). There, Cleanthes says to Philo, "Whether your skepticism be as absolute and sincere as you pretend, we shall learn by and by, when the company breaks up; we shall then see whether you go out at the door or the window, and whether you really doubt if your body has gravity or can be injured by its fall, according to popular opinion derived from our fallacious senses and more fallacious experience."[72] Attempting to exit through the door betrays a belief which the skeptic denies having. A point is made of the fantastic difficulty involved in remaining true to this position: "In reality, Philo, continued he, it seems certain that, though a man, in a flush of humour, after intense reflection on the many contradictions and imperfections of human reason, may entirely renounce all belief and opinion, it is impossible for them to persevere in this total skepticism or make it appear in his conduct for a few hours."[73]

Hegel's charge is not merely that the skeptic is inconsistent, but that the willingness to maintain this inconsistency shows a lack of seriousness and sincerity. Also this point is more clearly expressed by Hume: "I shall never assent to so harsh an opinion as that of a celebrated writer [Antoine Arnauld] who says that the skeptics are not a sect of philosophers: they are only a sect of liars. I may, however, affirm (I hope without offence) that they are a sect of jesters or railers."[74] For

72. Hume, *Dialogues Concerning Natural Religion*, p. 7.
73. Ibid., p. 7.
74. Ibid., p. 12.

both Hegel and Hume, the skeptic appears to be like a man who professes asceticism at a banquet. However, Hegel views the skeptic not so much as a liar or jester but as a self-deceiver—what Sartre would consider a case of *mauvaise foi*.

As I have repeatedly tried to show, Royce's thesis that Hegel *everywhere* reduces theory to its practical implications is false. However, the rejection of skepticism follows a roughly Roycean pattern.[75] Although the theory is not reduced to its practical implications, these implications are treated as an integral part of the skeptical position. While Hegel does not make the questionable claim that all theories amount to nothing more than

75. Ironically, Royce fails to point out the pragmatic basis of the very transition capable to some extent of supporting his thesis. Of skepticism, he says, "The result of a thorough-going adoption of this point of view is that life gets the sort of vanity which has been well suggested to our own generation by Fitzgerald's wonderful paraphrase of the Omar Khayyam stanzas" (pp. 179–180). Of the transition from skepticism to the next stage, "The Unhappy Consciousness," he says only, "That the consciousness of the Omar Khayyam stanza is unhappy we shall all remember. And that this unhappiness results from scepticism concerning the worth of every concrete human life, is also obvious" (p. 180). But skepticism falters and becomes an unhappy consciousness just because it cannot completely convince itself that life is in vain and acts instead as if life were worth something. Royce has inverted Hegel here.

Just for the record, Omar Khayyam, far from holding concrete human life to be worthless, finds it to be the only thing of worth. For example, Quatrain XXIII:

Ah, make the most of what we yet may spend,
Before we too into the dust descend,
Dust into Dust, and under Dust, to lie,
Sans Wine, Sans Song, Sans Singer and—sans End!

(Also quatrains II, III, VII) Khayyam is skeptical of any afterworldly reward (XII) and of philosophy because it does nothing to change life (XXII, XXV, XL). The shortness of life is lamented (XIV, XVI, XVII) not because of its vanity, but because of the unique worth of its sensual joys (X, XI).

their practical implications, he sensibly believes that theories do have practical implications, and that to hold a theory seriously and sincerely involves *living* in accordance with it, as well as mouthing it.

Although it seems obvious that being a Buddhist involves more than learning to recite the Four Noble Truths and the Eightfold Path, and being an ascetic more than clever tabletalk, it has not generally been quite so clear that being a skeptic involves any more than the mastery of certain destructive arguments. For this reason, calling attention to the impossibly rigorous behavioral directives involved in skepticism is worth doing.

The same sort of thesis constitutes perhaps the general theme of the philosophy of Søren Kierkegaard, one of Hegel's most prominent and vehement critics. Kierkegaard constantly calls attention to the extremely rigorous and usually ignored implications for life involved in being a Christian. Kierkegaard's point about being a Christian is essentially Hegel's point about being a skeptic: it is much easier said than done.

THE UNHAPPY CONSCIOUSNESS

When the skeptical consciousness becomes aware of the contradiction it contains, it becomes "The Unhappy Consciousness," which through a profusion of rather specific allusions is related to medieval Christianity. In its insistence on the unimportance and unreality of worldly existence Christianity resembles stoicism and skepticism. Each has the negation of the physical world as a goal. While stoicism tries to achieve this goal by ignoring the physical world, and skepticism by denying that it exists, Christianity unhappily accepts the fact of its existence and looks forward to the fulfillment of its goal, independence from the physical world only in an afterlife (*Jenseits*). Emerging from the self-deception of stoicism and skepticism, the unhappy consciousness faces the fact of its present failure, and hopes instead for future success in an eternal world. But since this other world is defined only negatively as being beyond this one, as a *Jenseits*, "the hope to unite with it must remain a hope, that is, without fulfillment in the present."[76] Adumbrating Nietzsche and Freud, Hegel considers the otherworldliness of Christianity both as a response to failure and an insurance against success.[77]

The unhappy consciousness miserably aware of its physical existence and environment tries to negate them and thus become free from them by renouncing the sensual world and its pleasures. But asceticism fails to achieve its end because

> These [animal functions], instead of being done naturally as something which, in and of itself, is inconsequential and can acquire no importance and essentiality for the spirit, become, since they are viewed as the enemy in his proper form, the object of serious effort and precisely the most important thing. Since, however, this enemy creates himself even in defeat, consciousness is fixated by it and, instead of becoming free of it, constantly dwells upon it and is aware of being constantly defiled. At the same time, this content of its effort is, rather than something essential, the lowest, rather than

76. *PG*, p. 161.
77. See Chap. 4, "Bad Infinity and the Beyond."

something universal, the merest particular. Thus we see a personality, as unhappy as it is pitiful, limited to itself and its petty deeds, and brooding over itself.[78]

This is essentially the same criticism of asceticism offered by Gautama, the Buddha,[79] and also anticipates some of Nietzsche's remarks on chastity: "Chastity is a virtue in some, but a vice in many. They abstain but the bitch, sensuality, leers enviously out of everything they do. . . . And how nicely the bitch, sensuality, knows how to beg for a piece of spirit when denied a piece of meat. . . . And this parable too I offer you: not a few who have wanted to drive out their devil have themselves entered into swine.[80]

The unhappy consciousness, because it honestly faces the problematic existence of the external world rather than trying to ignore or deny it, is an advance over stoicism and skepticism. But its two attempts to solve the problem after facing it, asceticism and otherworldliness, are no more successful than either stoicism or skepticism. With the failure of the unhappy consciousness to negate the physical world and attain the autonomy

78. *PG*, pp. 168–69.

79. The spirit of Hegel's and the Buddha's criticism is neatly captured in the Zen story, *Muddy Road*: "Tanzan and Ekido were once travelling together down a muddy road. A heavy rain was still falling. Coming around a bend, they met a lovely girl in a silk kimono and sash, unable to cross the intersection. 'Come on girl,' said Tanzan at once. Lifting her up in his arms, he carried her over the mud. Ekido did not speak again until that night when they reached a lodging temple. Then he could no longer restrain himself. 'We monks don't go near females,' he told Tanzan, 'especially not young and lovely ones. It is dangerous. Why did you do that?' 'I left the girl there,' said Tanzan. 'Are you still carrying her?' " In *Zen Flesh, Zen Bones*, ed. Paul Reps, p. 18.

80. *Thus Spoke Zarathustra*, part 1, "On Chastity," in *The Portable Nietzsche*, trans. Walter Kaufmann, pp. 166–67.

and independence which we have seen to be the elusive goal of all the forms of self-consciousness, the spirit moves on to the third, large section of the *Phenomenology*, "Reason." The spirit returns to forms of consciousness which—like those in Section A, "Consciousness"— appear to be epistemological rather than practical.

However, as I have stressed in this exposition of "Self-consciousness," the task of the spirit is formulated so as to allow for both epistemological and practical attempts at fulfillment. The spirit's goal of practico-epistemological autonomy does not clearly emerge until self-consciousness is attained, for its introduction depends on the notion of self-consciousness. Yet this goal is neither relinquished with the transition from "Self-consciousness" to "Reason" nor later in the *Phenomenology*. This is not surprising, for, just as the stages of the *Phenomenology* occurring after the section titled "Consciousness" are still forms of consciousness, the stages occurring after the section titled "Self-consciousness" are still forms of self-consciousness.[81] Given this goal, it is again not surprising that the remainder of the *Phenomenology* exhibits that alternation of modes of knowing and of acting so typical of the section titled "Self-consciousness."

Certainly, it is interesting and worthwhile to attempt to construct a general theory of human behavior which encompasses both endeavors, to know and to act. Merely because both Hegel and the pragmatists make such an attempt, we should not conclude with Royce that Hegel is a pragmatist. There are obvious ways of relating thought and action other than reducing

81. See Appendix.

the former to the latter: what we think and know influences how we act, and experience gathered in action helps determine what we think and know. Tracing relationships of this sort in no way bizarre or objectionable and can be fruitful. But Hegel, as we have seen, does more than this; he considers all the different forms of knowing and acting, all the exertions of the human spirit, as expressions of the same basic drive, the drive toward autonomy and self-sufficiency. In this lies the real "reduction" of the *Phenomenology* and the root of the book's linear development.

We have seen how the concept of *autonomy* easily and naturally runs into that of *freedom*, and how freedom, usually a practical concept, is released from its binding associations with action and also equated with epistemological autonomy. Freedom acquires that practico-epistemological duality characteristic of the basic goal of the spirit and, in fact, becomes *synonomous* with this goal. The spirit seeks freedom (in its expanded sense).

Yet the efforts of the spirit culminate in philosophy, and the goal of philosophy and thus of the spirit in general was not said to be freedom but *truth*. However, this is only a superficial inconsistency. Just as the concept *freedom* was expanded by 'epistemologizing' it, the concept of truth is expanded by 'pragmatizing' it. As I have pointed out,[82] this expansions involves two major steps: (1) in addition to its normal use as the contrary of falsity, truth is also used as synonym for the *object* of consciousness and opposed not to falsity but to the conscious subject. What the subject knows or is

82. See Chap. 1, "Self-consciousness."

conscious of is for Hegel its "truth." (2) When the form of consciousness is active rather than contemplative, its object (*Gegenstand*) is really an objective or goal. Once the object of a form of consciousness has already been identified as its "truth," it is but a small additional step also to identify the objective of an activity as its "truth."

The spirit can now seek truth both through contemplation and through action. The concept *truth* acquires that same practico-epistemological duality characteristic of *autonomy, self-sufficiency,* and *freedom*, which enables it to join them as an alternative expression for the general goal of human endeavor.

There remains one difficulty. Although truth comes to share this practico-epistemological character with autonomy, self-sufficiency, and freedom, it does not seem to have any other conceptual similarity to them, while they seem to be roughly synonomous with each other in Hegel's philosophy. If truth is not somehow identified conceptually with these other expressions of the basic goal, then despite his efforts to give each of them the prerequisite duality Hegel is still guilty of offering two different things as the one basic goal of the human spirit.

However, Hegel does try to identify truth with freedom and autonomy. We have seen how he argues that freedom is found only in conceptual thought.[83] He also argues that truth is to be found only in conceptual thought because only there is consciousness autonomous and free. It remains to be seen how freedom, even in the sense of epistemological autonomy, is argued

83. See Chap. 1, "Stoicism."

to be necessary for knowing the truth. In other words, why must genuine knowledge be self-knowledge? To answer that only self-knowledge is autonomous and thus free is to beg the question. What must be shown is why only knowledge which is autonomous and free is truly knowledge.

Hegel's arguments to this end are motivated and to some extent justified by his attempt to resolve the problem of knowing things as they are in themselves, Kant's onerous legacy to his philosophic successors. In the next chapter I shall discuss Hegel's struggle with this problem.

2 ~ THE PROBLEM OF
THE THING-IN-ITSELF

Hegel stresses the fact that philosophy's goal is the goal of all human endeavor and characterizes this goal very generally as the truth. Yet he ranks the various forms of human activity; and philosophy, as evidenced by its terminal position both in the *Phenomenology* and the *Encyclopedia,* emerges as the highest form of this common endeavor—the fullest realization of truth. With this exalted position come more rigorous requirements. The philosopher, like everyone else, seeks truth, but the philosopher cannot be satisfied with anything less than the highest form of truth.

By characterizing the object of each form of consciousness as its truth, Hegel subtly reinforces and draws upon his thesis that each form of consciousness, despite its inadequacies, has some degree of success and contains some degree of truth. But although each has truth as its object, each has it in a different form. Philosophy "is different from other ways of becoming conscious of this one and the same content only in form,"[1] and philosophy's task is more precisely to seek "the true form in which the truth exists."[2] The sublime truth of philosophy is identified throughout Hegel's works as "the absolute-truth"[3] or more often simply as *the absolute (das Absolute)*: "The history of philosophy is the history of the discovery of thoughts about the absolute,

1. *Enc.,* sec. 6.
2. *PG*, p. 12.
3. *Logic*, 1:41.

which is its object."[4] For philosophy, "the principle in which alone the interest of the matter seems to lie is the interest as to what is the truth, the absolute ground of everything."[5]

Since philosophy's goal is nothing less than "the highest truth,"[6] truth without any of the limitations characteristic of the other forms of knowledge, it is not surprising that philosophy requires a special method of its own. Philosophy is the final form of a relentless drive toward truth which can accept no limitation to its scope or to its certainty. Therefore, Hegel, along with his thesis about the community of all human endeavor, can still emphasize the inadequacy of philosophic methods borrowed from other disciplines, such as mathematics and the empirical sciences. He can claim to offer "a new reworking of philosophy, presented according to a method which is still going to be recognized, I hope, as the only true one, the only one identical with its content."[7]

Other methods are rejected for philosophy because they are incapable of attaining absolute truth. Implicit in this rejection and the search for a new and adequate method is the belief that absolute truth, complete, necessary, free of all limitation, is an attainable or at least tenable goal. Since Immanuel Kant had denied the possibility of such absolute, unlimited knowledge in his *Critique of Pure Reason* (1781), Hegel's entire program and conception of philosophy depended upon re-

4. *Enc.*, Preface, p. 10.
5. *Logic*, 1:51.
6. *Logic*, 1:31.
7. *Enc.*, Preface, 1st ed., p. 20.

futing Kant's limitation of reason. More specifically, Kant had claimed that we can know things only as they appear to us, but never as they really are in themselves. Hegel could not accept this restriction of knowledge and devoted a great deal of his time and energy to removing it. This problem assumed tremendous importance for Hegel.

Ascertaining the relative importance for Hegel of various philosophers is a reasonable and fruitful undertaking, but only if the complexity of this question is realized and no simplistic linear ranking sought. It is not difficult to select with some accuracy a group of the most important influences; certainly Plato, Aristotle, Spinoza, and Kant would be included. But it would be difficult to rank them, for, not surprisingly, each influenced him in a different way and on different issues. Hegel probably derived more of his terminology from Aristotle than from anyone else, yet his idea of the dialectic was inspired more by Plato and Kant, and his central concepts of freedom and infinity stem from Spinoza.

Individual commentators have emphasized different influences; Josiah Royce[8] and Richard Kroner[9] trace the relationship to Kant. G. R. G. Mure devotes a third of his *Introduction to Hegel* to discussing the relevant parts of Aristotle's philosophy. Henry Alonzo Myers devotes his *Hegel or Spinoza* to a comparison and contrast of the two. These varied approaches complement rather than conflict with one another.

Walter Kaufmann, in a more varied and balanced

8. *Lectures on Modern Idealism*
9. *Von Kant bis Hegel.*

approach, traces many of the influences on Hegel and then soundly suggests that the apportionment of space in Hegel's *History of Philosophy* is indicative of the relative importance for Hegel of the various philosophers.[10] By this criterion Kant runs a poor third to Plato and Aristotle, each of whom is given over twice as much space as Kant.

Although this apportionment is indeed "surprising but revealing," it is also misleading if taken as the only index of Kant's importance for Hegel. (Kaufmann does not claim that it is.) This particular bit of evidence has the attraction of being comprehensive and quantitative, but a consideration of the *Phenomenology, Science of Logic,* and *Encyclopedia* furnishes evidence which, though not as neat, is still relevant and modifies the picture derived solely from the *History of Philosophy.*

In these works a philosopher's importance cannot be measured solely by the amount of explicit reference made to him. Since the *Phenomenology* relies on allusion rather than explicit reference, counting the rare references which do occur is extremely unreliable. In both the *Science of Logic* and the *Encyclopedia,* where more abundant references form a more reliable index, Kant's is the name mentioned most often.[11] Still, statistics of this sort furnish only a purview of Kant's importance for Hegel.

Hegel's estimation of Kant's stature and importance appears clearly in a footnote to the *Science of Logic:* "I am calling attention to the fact that I often take the

10. Kaufmann, sec. 66, pp. 278–81.
11. Based on the *Personenregister* at the back of the *Kritische Ausgabe,* edited by J. Hoffmeister.

Kantian philosophy into consideration in this work (which could appear superfluous to many), because no matter how its smaller details and the particular parts of its development may be regarded in this work and elsewhere, it constitutes the basis and point of departure of the modern German philosophy."[12]

In any case, it is not important to argue whether Kant was the single greatest influence on Hegel. It is more interesting to see exactly how, rather than how much, Kant influenced Hegel. Kant's denial of the possibility of knowing things-in-themselves (*Dinge-an-sich*) poses one of the major problems for both the *Phenomenology* and the later system. This problem haunts Hegel's philosophy, which is, to a large extent, an attempt to solve it.

Following the famous "Preface" to the *Phenomenology* there is a shorter "Introduction" in which the problem of knowing things as they are in themselves is the major theme. The "Introduction" (unlike the "Preface" which was added later) was written immediately prior to the main body of the work and reveals the concerns with which Hegel approached that undertaking:

> It is natural to suppose that, before philosophy enters upon its subject proper, namely the actual knowledge of what truly is, it is necessary first to understand knowledge, which is considered the tool with which one masters the absolute, or the medium through which one catches sight of it. . . . This concern necessarily transforms itself into the conviction that the whole undertaking to gain for consciousness a knowledge of that which

12. *Logic*, 1:44.

is in-itself [*was an sich ist*] is absurd in its conception, and that between knowledge and the absolute a barrier falls which completely separates them. For if knowledge is the tool with which to master the absolute, it is immediately apparent that the application of a tool to something does not leave it as it is for itself but undertakes to form and change it. Or if knowledge is not the tool of our activity but to some extent a passive medium through which the light of truth reaches us, we do not receive it as it is in itself, but as it is through and in this medium. In both cases we use a means which immediately brings about the opposite of its end; or rather the absurdity is that we use a means at all. It seems, of course, that this difficulty can be remedied by knowing how the tool works, for it would then be possible to subtract from the notion of the absolute which we receive by means of the tool the part which belongs to the tool, and thus receive the pure truth. But this improvement would, in fact, only bring us back to where we were before. If we take away from a formed thing what the tool has done to it, then the thing—here, the absolute—is again exactly what it was before this now obviously superfluous effort. . . . Or if the examination of knowledge, which we now represent to ourselves as a medium, taught us the law of its refraction, it would be of no use to subtract the refraction from the result, for knowledge is not the refraction of the ray, but the ray itself through which the truth contacts us. With this removed, only the bare direction or the empty place would be indicated to us.[13]

Although Kant is not explicitly mentioned, and the metaphors of the tool and the medium replace the Kant-

13. *PG*, pp. 63–64.

ian terminology, Hegel is referring to Kant's denial of
the possibility to know things as they are in themselves.
The absence of explicit reference is not unusual in the
Phenomenology, and there is an obvious kinship between this passage and passages in the *Science of Logic*
and the *Encyclopedia* which clearly refer to Kant or the
"Critical Philosophy." For example: "A major viewpoint of the *Critical Philosophy* is that, before one attempts to know God, the essence of things, etc., one
must first investigate the capacity of knowledge itself, to
see whether it is able to accomplish such tasks. One
must first become acquainted with the *instrument*, before one undertakes the work which is to be accomplished by means of it. Otherwise, if the instrument
were inadequate, all efforts would be wasted and in
vain."[14]

There also is an obvious reason for the metaphorical
presentation. At this point Hegel does not try to refute
Kant's denial directly. Instead, he suggests that this
denial draws support from *unexamined* and *misleading*
metaphors: "In fact, this fear of error assumes something, indeed quite a lot, as true, and supports its
scruples and conclusions on what should itself be examined for its truth beforehand. It unquestioningly represents [*setzt Vorstellungen voraus*] knowledge as a tool
and a medium and presupposes a distinction between
ourselves and this knowledge."[15]

Hegel admits that the metaphors of the tool or the
medium, once accepted, lead inexorably to the conclusion that we cannot know things as they are in them-

14. *Enc.*, sec. 10.
15. *PG*, pp. 64–65.

selves. But he denies that we must, or even should, accept these models for knowledge. He is adamant both about the unacceptability of the consequences of these metaphors and the complete lack of any justification for their use.

Knowledge limited to phenomena, the knowledge offered by Kant, is spurned. For Hegel, this kind of knowledge is not only ultimately unsatisfying, but does not even deserve to be called knowledge. In the *Phenomenology* he says,

> This fear of error principally presupposes that the absolute stands on one side, and that knowledge, on the other side, by itself and separated from the absolute, is still something real, or that knowledge, which being outside of the absolute is also outside of the truth, is still true knowledge. This assumption reveals what calls itself the fear of error to be rather the fear of the truth.
>
> This conclusion follows from the fact that the absolute alone is true, or the true alone is absolute. It can be denied by making a distinction allowing knowledge which does not, as science requires, know the absolute to be true knowledge also. [Or one might consider that] knowledge in general, though unable to grasp the absolute, is still capable of another truth.[16]

Here, Hegel is content to point out that salvaging a limited truth, like the use of the tool and medium metaphors, depends upon ideas and distinctions which are never examined. The need for conceptual analysis is stressed: "But we see immediately that such aimless talk stems from a murky distinction between an abso-

16. *PG*, p. 65.

lute truth and some other kind of truth, and 'absolute,' 'knowledge,' etc., are words which presuppose meanings which first have to be obtained."[17] If these words and distinctions are not first analyzed and their use justified, one can, he argues, just as well blindly ignore them as blindly accept them.

Hegel asserts that one has even *more* right to ignore them than to accept them, for they produce "only an empty appearance of knowledge, which disappears immediately when science arrives." This is a heuristic point: *in the absence of any justification either for accepting or rejecting these metaphors*, one should ignore them and try to develop the science which knows things as they are in themselves. If one succeeds, the metaphors and the limitation of knowledge which follows from them will be rejected or, as Hegel puts it, "will immediately disappear." If on the contrary, one uncritically accepts the impossibility of absolute knowledge, no such effort will be made.

In the *Science of Logic*, knowledge limited to phenomena is rejected not only because it rests on unanalyzed concepts and strangles philosophic progress, but also because it is a notion which crumbles upon examination. It poses as a kind of knowledge but really is not.

Since . . . this knowledge knows itself to be only knowledge of appearances, it admits to be unsatisfactory. Yet, it is assumed at the same time that things, though not rightly known in themselves, are still rightly known within the sphere of appearance, as though only the kinds of objects were different, and one kind, namely things in themselves, did not fall within knowledge, but

17. Ibid.

the other kind, namely appearances, did. How would it be to attribute accurate perception to a man, with the proviso that he was not able to perceive truth but only untruth? As absurd as that would be, a true knowledge which did not know its object as it is in itself would be equally absurd.[18]

Things as they are in themselves and things as they appear to us are not merely two kinds of objects; the former are things as they truly are, the latter are things but not as they truly are. Thus, to know things only as they appear to us and not as they are in themselves is to know things but not as they truly are. Hegel doubts whether this can be considered knowledge at all. Again the heuristic motive is operative: accepting the false consolation of this pseudoknowledge dulls our drive for genuine knowledge.

It might seem that Hegel, without any justification, denies that things appear to us as they truly are. But Hegel has not, in the preceding argument, even committed himself to this view. He asserts only that, *if* the distinction between things in themselves and things as they appear is accepted, then appearances are contrasted with the things as they are in themselves, that is, with things as they truly are. The falsity of appearances is only argued to be a consequence of the very distinction Hegel tries to refute.[19]

Given the distinction between things as they are in themselves and things as they appear to us, and their

18. *Logic*, 1:27.
19. Since empiricism does not contrast appearances with things as they really are, Hegel never charges it with not *seeking* genuine knowledge, even though it uses the appearance of things as its basis.

respective truth and falsity, Hegel's refusal to consider knowledge of appearances to be truly knowledge is not idiosyncratic. Hegel argues that, if what is 'known' is not true, it is not really known. Essentially the same point is made by A. J. Ayer when he claims that a necessary condition for knowledge is that "what one is said to know be true."[20] And as Ayer is quick to add, this is a common sense view: "For while what is true can be believed, or disbelieved, or doubted, or imagined, or much else besides being known, it is, as we have already noted, a fact of ordinary usage that what is known, in this sense, cannot but be true."[21]

Unlike Ayer, Hegel does not support this particular point by explicitly appealing to common opinion or ordinary linguistic usage. Yet, in discussing the general problem of knowing things as they are in themselves he does consider common opinion and usage.

After characterizing the current and unacceptable view as one in which "thought, in its relation to the object, does not come out of itself toward the object, which remains, as a thing in itself, simply something beyond thought [*ein Jenseits des Denkens*]"; Hegel candidly admits that "these views of the relation between subject and object express the determinations which constitute the nature of our ordinary conscious-

20. *The Problem of Knowledge* (Edinburgh, Penguin Books, 1956) p. 35.
21. Ibid, p. 12. The sense of knowing that Ayer refers to is knowing that something is the case, which he is careful to distinguish from knowledge in the sense of acquaintance, and Hegel, in talking about knowing things, seems rather to be discussing the latter. But the difference between them is diminished if it is remembered that Hegel does not make such a distinction, and that much of our knowledge by acquaintance can be easily translated into knowledge that something is the case.

ness."[22] The subject-object distinction which leads to
the Kantian limitation of knowledge is here said to have
a basis in ordinary thought, not to justify it, but merely
to explain its prevalence. Hegel admits that this distinction is widely accepted, but he still maintains that it is
an unexamined "prejudice," unfit for philosophy. The
implications are clear: popularity is not a sufficient criterion for philosophical truth; popular notions must be
subjected to analysis and criticism.

Although Hegel does not consider ordinary opinion
and usage the ultimate arbiter of philosophic problems,
he occasionally draws supplementary support from this
quarter. This procedure may seem arbitrary, inconsistent, and even dishonest. What right does Hegel have
to use only that part of ordinary opinion and usage
which confirms his theories and to reject the rest? However, as long as ordinary opinion and usage are used only
as *supplementary* sources of philosophical enlightenment, Hegel's occasional appeal to them is quite consistent with his rejection of their ultimate authority. In
fact, this procedure itself follows the dictates of good
common sense. Ordinary opinion and usage, like the
theories and idiom of any great, extraordinary philosopher, are to be used selectively and in conjunction with
other considerations. Rejecting parts of ordinary opinion and usage is more like occasionally rejecting the
opinion of a generally reliable adviser than it is like
rejecting unpleasant experimental data.

The sharp separation of subject and object, knower
and known, thought and its object, may have roots in
ordinary opinion and usage, but the Kantian limitation

22. *Logic*, 1:25.

of knowledge which results from this separation does
not. In the *Logic*, an attack of an admittedly popular
belief is unabashedly followed by: "On the other hand,
however, one can appeal to the characteristic *ideas of
ordinary logic*; it is assumed that definitions, for example, do not contain determinations which fall only in
the knowing subject, but determinations of the object,
which constitute its most essential and inmost nature."[23] In the *Encyclopedia*, this same confidence in
the ability of thought to know things in themselves is
claimed to be even more extensive: "All incipient philosophy, all of the sciences, even the daily deeds and
drives of consciousness live in this belief."[24]

Consequently Kant's theory runs counter to common
sense: "It has been said that things in themselves are
quite different from what we make out of them. In particular, the Critical Philosophy has gained acceptance
for this divorce between thought and thing despite the
conviction of the entire previous world that their agree-
ment was a matter of course."[25]

This common belief is said to be "of the greatest importance" and the task of philosophy to be a return to
the ordinary and—in this instance—sound view: "The
business of philosophy consists only in explicitly bringing to consciousness what, in retrospect, has prevailed
in human thought for ages. Philosophy therefore advances nothing new; what we have here brought out
through reflection is already the immediate prejudice of

23. *Logic*, 1:32.
24. *Enc.*, sec. 26. The reference to the beliefs implicit in our everyday
activity echoes the criticism made of skepticism in the *Phenomenology*.
See above, Chap. 1, "Skepticism."
25. *Enc.*, sec. 22, Z.

everyone."[26] Despite the unrestricted formulation of the passage, Hegel's open condemnation of many common sense views makes it clear that he is here presenting not a description of philosophic method in general, but only of proper procedure in one instance.

In an even more contemporary tone, ordinary *usage*, not just ordinary *opinion*, is invoked: "In general, it lies at the very basis of the use of such forms as the concept, the judgment, the inference, the definition, the division, etc., that they are forms not only of self-conscious thought, but also of the objective world."[27] Since Hegel later criticizes some of these same forms,[28] the appeal to ordinary usage, like the appeal to ordinary belief, must be viewed merely as an added inducement to be dissatisfied with Kant's position and to examine it critically.

The fact that Kant's limitation of knowledge, which contradicts common sense, is based on metaphors and distinctions that are rooted in common sense, shows that common sense, far from being faultless, may have implications that it cannot itself accept. It supports the demand that philosophy analyze ordinary belief in order to bring these implications and inconsistencies to light.

That Hegel would resort to ordinary opinion and usage despite his reservations about this approach is another indication of the great importance he placed upon the problem of knowing things as they really are in themselves. As we have seen, Kant's limitation of knowledge seems completely to undermine the quest for ab-

26. *Enc.*, sec. 22, Z.
27. *Logic*, 1:32.
28. See, e.g., *Enc.*, sec. 31.

solute truth, which, for Hegel, was the ultimate goal of both philosophy and the human spirit.

Kant's view had to be criticized in order to make Hegel's philosophic program tenable. Therefore, it is not surprising to find that Hegel devotes much space and effort to this problem in the introductory sections of the *Phenomenology, Science of Logic* and *Encyclopedia.* To gain sympathy for his program Hegel first had to silence the predictable Kantian objections to any talk of knowing things as they really are. Or, as Hegel says in the "Introduction" to the *Logic,* because this limitation of knowledge "obstructs the entrance to philosophy," it must be "sloughed off before philosophy."[29]

The problem posed by Kant's limitation of knowledge loomed large for Hegel not only because of the unpalatable consequences of Kant's view but also because of its prevalence in the philosophical world. The already mentioned appraisal of Kant as "the basis and point of departure of the modern German philosophy" is immediately justified by reference to the currency of Kant's limitation of reason: "The philosophizing which is widest spread among us does not get beyond the Kantian results, that reason cannot possibly know a true content, and with regard to absolute truth must be referred to faith."[30]

Hegel prefaces the *Encyclopedia* by a compressed historical *Vorbegriff* in which he limns the development of philosophy preceding him in terms of those problems and positions most relevant to his own thought. Because the *Vorbegriff* functions as an introduction to

29. *Logic,* 1:25.
30. *Logic,* 1:44.

Hegel's System and is much shorter than Hegel's other account of this same development in his lectures on the *History of Philosophy*, it is more selective than the lectures and better indicates what aspects of Hegel's predecessors most influenced and disturbed him. The *Vorbegriff* has the further advantage of being actually written by Hegel; the *History of Philosophy* was compiled from students' lecture notes.

The entire presentation is permeated by the concern about whether thought is capable of knowing things as they really are. Hegel indicates the importance of this concern by titling each of the *Vorbegriff*'s three sections an "attitude of thought to objectivity" (*Stellung des Gedankens zur Objectivität*). This historical introduction is divided into "Metaphysics," "Empiricism," "Critical Philosophy," and "Immediate Knowledge," which are then condensed into three sections by somewhat arbitrarily grouping "Empiricism" and "Critical Philosophy" together.

The section on metaphysics certainly is meant to refer specifically to modern rationalism (Descartes, Leibniz, Spinoza, etc.), but not only to modern rationalism. The defining characteristic of "Metaphysics" is the pre-Kantian confidence in the power of thought to know reality: "The first attitude . . . contains the belief that through reflection truth is known, that what the object truly is is brought before consciousness."[31] As we have seen, this characteristic is generally attributed to "all incipient philosophy" as well as all of science and ordinary activity. But this widespread view has its "most explicit development, and the one nearest to us, in former

31. *Enc.*, sec. 26.

metaphysics, as it was among us before Kant."[32] How far back in time this metaphysics extends is unimportant; it is essentially pre-Kantian.

Hegel's perspective is different from our present one. We tend to view the rationalist confidence in reason as having been undermined by the British empiricists led by Hume and then somewhat restored by Kant. Hegel, on the contrary, sees Kant as further developing the criticism of reason which the empiricists had only begun. For Hegel, Kant's limited restoration of reason was so limited as to be no restoration at all. This may partially explain why Empiricism and Critical Philosophy are grouped together.

Empiricism, "which instead of seeking truth in thought [*Gedanken*], goes to fetch it from experience,"[33] still seeks a truth which, for it, is the only truth there is. Unencumbered by the distinction between knowledge of appearances and knowledge of things in themselves, it considers the experiential knowledge it seeks to be the only and therefore absolute truth. Hegel saw empiricism, not so much as a criticism of all metaphysics, but merely as a different kind of metaphysics, one which held that reality was revealed in experience, and not in abstract thought. The empiricists are criticized for not realizing that their view "itself contains metaphysics"; Hegel calls this "the basic deception of scientific empiricism."

The crushing blow to metaphysics was administered not by empiricism but by Kant: "In common with empiricism the Critical Philosophy takes experience to be

32. *Enc.*, sec. 27.
33. *Enc.*, sec. 37.

the only basis for knowledge, which, however, it does not allow to count as truth, but only as knowledge of appearances."[34] Empiricism only set up the destruction of metaphysics and absolute knowledge which was carried out by Kant.

In this presentation Kant certainly overshadows his predecessors; metaphysics is characterized as essentially pre-Kantian, empiricism as proto-Kantian. And Kant is allotted more than twice as much space as the other two combined.[35]

Hegel also thought that Kant's limitation of knowledge had played a crucial role in the development of a post-Kantian, Romantic rejection of reason—exemplified by Jacobi. Although, like Hegel, Jacobi was unsatisfied by the limited knowledge offered by Kant, unlike Hegel, he completely swallowed Kant's limitation of reason. Thus he was forced to claim that reality could be known in a nonconceptual way. Since the criticism of absolute knowledge that Jacobi accepted represented thought as a means to truth that only made truth inaccessible, he tried to reach truth without thought or any other self-defeating means (*Mittel*). He sought to know truth directly. Hence Hegel calls this section "Immediate Knowledge" (*Das Unmittelbare Wissen*).

34. *Enc.*, sec. 40.
35. Reading Kaufmann's section 66 (pp. 278–81) will remove any inclination to deplore Hegel's provincialism in this matter. Kaufmann argues that Berkeley and Hume would have been given even less consideration in England at that time, and that the later English interest in Berkeley and Hume was initiated by English admirers of Kant and Hegel.

It is also interesting that this apportionment reverses the emphasis in the *History of Philosophy*, where Greek philosophy is given twice as much space as modern philosophy. Perhaps the existence of both treatments alleviates the radical appearance of each.

The consequent reliance on direct intuition, inspiration, ineffable insight, edification, and feeling is often attacked vehemently by Hegel, especially in the "Preface" to the *Phenomenology*. However, what interests us here is not the details of the attack, but the fact that Hegel viewed one major theme and malaise of post-Kantian philosophy to be the result of *accepting* Kant's limitation of conceptual knowledge to phenomena.[36]

Although Kant's doctrine is held to be largely responsible for the subsequent flight from reason to faith and mysticism, Hegel respects Kant more than his romantic successors: "But one immediately begins in this philosophizing with what, for Kant, was a result, and thereby cuts away beforehand the preceding exposition out of which that result came, and which is philosophical knowledge."[37]

Kant's position, wrong and pernicious as it might be, is at least presented as the result of a demonstration, which itself displays philosophical merit and serious effort. Hegel finds the wide, uncritical acceptance of Kant's doctrine suspicious. For those who find conceptual thought too taxing, the doctrine of its metaphysical futility offers a tempting excuse to give it up. Intellectual sloth explains the mysterious popularity of an apparently unpalatable view: "The Kantian philosophy thus serves as a pillow for intellectual indolence which soothes itself with the idea that everything has

---

36. Hegel is concerned only with what he considered one major trend in post-Kantian philosophy, not with all of it. Post-Kantian idealism (Fichte and perhaps Schelling) was exempted from this particular criticism. See *Logic*, 1:28, quoted early in Chapter 3.

37. *Logic*, 1:44.

been already proved and done away with."[38] In the *Phenomenology* Hegel views the arguments for "the impotence of science" based upon unexamined metaphors to amount to "subterfuges" *(Ausreden)*, which are motivated by the desire "to free oneself from the effort of science and, at the same time, to give oneself the appearance of a serious and passionate striving."[39] Surely Kant's successors, and not Kant himself, are being criticized here.

But laziness and pretense aside, it is the rejection of thought's ability to know ultimate reality, common to both Kant and his successors, which seemed to Hegel the major contemporary philosophical issue. He says of the opposition of thought and its object: "Around this opposition revolves the interest of modern philosophy."[40] More elaborately: "Around its nature and validity revolve the interest of the philosophical standpoint of our present time and the question about truth and the knowledge of truth."[41] And this obsession seems justified by the gravity of the issue: "It is the sickness of our time to despair of ever knowing more than something subjective."[42]

THE THING-IN-ITSELF AND KANT'S PHILOSOPHY

Sometimes Hegel's generally sympathetic approach to the history of philosophy and his great respect for Kant lead him to consider this problematic and pernicious doctrine not to be an essential part of Kant's phi-

38. Ibid.
39. *PG*, p. 65.
40. *Enc.*, sec. 22, Z.
41. *Enc.*, sec. 25.
42. *Enc.*, sec. 22, Z

losophy. In an early essay on *The Difference between
the Fichtean and Schellingian Systems of Philosophy*
(1801) he relies on Fichte's distinction between the
spirit and the letter of Kant's philosophy to divide the
wheat from the chaff: "The Kantian philosophy had
required that its spirit be separated from its letter, and
that the purely speculative principle be lifted out of the
rest which belonged to argumentative [*raisonnieren-
den*] reflection *or could be used for it*."[43] We have seen
with what contempt Hegel considered the post-Kantian
use of the *Ding-an-sich* doctrine. The desire not to
blame Kant for the sins of his successors was probably
one motive for adopting Fichte's distinction.

Another was the belief that Fichte had indeed successfully winnowed Kant's philosophy. Hegel continues: "In the principle of the deduction of the categories this philosophy is genuine idealism, and it is this
principle that Fichte lifted out in purer, more rigorous
form and called the spirit of the Kantian philosophy."[44]

First and foremost among the chaff is the *Ding-an-
sich* doctrine: "That things-in-themselves (which are
nothing but the empty form of opposition [of subject
and object] objectively expressed) are hypostasized and
set up as absolute objectivity, like the things of the dogmatic philosophers, . . . and only with more pretension
called 'Critical Philosophy'—these conditions lie at
most in the form of the Kantian deduction of the categories, not in its principle or spirit."[45]

While it is sound procedure to admire a great phi-

43. G (*See* Abbreviations), 1:33.
44. G, 1:33–34.
45. G, 1:34.

losopher selectively, distinguishing the valuable elements in his thought from the worthless ones, the true theses from the false, and the valid arguments from the fallacious, one should not confuse the procedure with the question of what the philosopher "really meant" or felt was most important. Since the confusion of evaluation and interpretation often results in apologetics, the more a philosopher is revered, the more likely is this confusion. The distinction between the spirit and the letter of Kant's philosophy is a misguided attempt to emphasize his greatness by subtly disassociating him from what seem to be his less fortunate doctrines. What is found to be inferior is said to be not essential, not really meant, or only the letter and not the spirit of the philosophy. These idioms cloak the entry of indirect and unjustified apologetics.

Typically, what the apologist finds to be the superior essence or spirit of the revered philosophy is his own view; old icons are refurbished only to serve as mirrors: "In that deduction of the forms of the understanding the principle of speculation, the identity of subject and object, is expressed most distinctly."[46] An already devious apologetics can serve as an even more devious summoning of support from respected sources.

I am not suggesting that these general tendencies are peculiar to Fichte and Hegel or that they need be conscious strategies. They are to be viewed rather as omnipresent pressures to which any historian of philosophy might succumb without ever becoming aware of their presence. These pressures are understandably strongest where the commentator feels his own work to be the

46. Ibid.

extension or fulfillment of the other man's philosophy, and Fichte held his task to be the completion of what Kant had started.

Hegel, who early in his career adopts from Fichte this manner of discussing Kant, does not continue to use it. In the Preface to the first edition of the *Science of Logic* (1812) Hegel still blames the "decline of metaphysics" and the "strange spectacle of a cultured people without metaphysics" on "the exoteric teaching of the Kantian philosophy—that understanding dare not transcend experience."[47] However, no contrast between an exoteric and an esoteric teaching is developed, and Hegel seems here to be referring primarily to the popularity and influence of this particular doctrine. Furthermore, in the Introduction to the same work the insistence on the subjectivity of knowledge is called Kant's "chief thought" (*Hauptgedanken*). And in the *Encyclopedia* Kant's position is epitomized in terms of this doctrine. Despite a continuing respect for Kant, Hegel clearly finds him responsible for a good part of the "sickness of our time."

THE "PHENOMENOLOGY" AND THE PROBLEM OF THE THING-IN-ITSELF

Removing the limitation of knowledge posed by the *Ding-an-sich* doctrine was for Hegel a necessary propaedeutic to philosophy, and thus his introductions are permeated with this problem. There is one introduction of which this is true that has not yet been considered—the entire *Phenomenology*.

Although the *Phenomenology* was originally con-

47. *Logic*, 1:3.

ceived as the first part of a *System of Science,* to be followed by a second part containing a logic, philosophy of nature, and philosophy of the spirit, Hegel's conception soon changed. The logic, intended to be the first third of the second part, grew so large that it had to be published in three separate volumes.[48] But there was a stronger reason why Hegel never referred to any or all of his later work as the second part of the System. After all, he did eventually publish an *Encyclopedia of the Philosophical Sciences*[49] which in one condensed volume contains everything originally planned for the second part of the System. Yet the *Encyclopedia* is presented not as the second part of the System, but as the entire System.

This happened because Hegel came to consider the *Phenomenology* an *introduction* to his system of philosophical science rather than its first part. This change of view is not radical and involves only a slight shift of emphasis and terminology. Even as the first part of the System the *Phenomenology*'s function was to prepare the way for the second part.

The prevalent doubts about the possibility of knowledge of things-in-themselves is mentioned by Hegel at the very beginning of the Introduction to the *Phenomenology* and traced to several unexamined metaphors and an equally unexamined distinction between the knowing subject and its object. Although attention is called to the uncritical way in which the metaphors and the corresponding distinction had been accepted, no refutation is offered in the Introduction itself. However,

48. 1812, 1813, 1816. In the critical edition edited by Lasson there are about 900 pages of text.
49. First Edition, 1817.

given these prevalent doubts, the possibility of a science that can know things as they really are had to be demonstrated. The entire course of the *Phenomenology* is offered as such a demonstration.

Starting with the ordinary view that the conscious subject is separate and distinct from its object, Hegel tries to show how the spirit is forced to reject one form of consciousness after another until this separation is completely overcome in the last stage, "Absolute Knowledge." According to Hegel, the denial of knowledge of things-in-themselves rests on the separation of the knowing subject from its object. Therefore, the rejection of this separation in the course of the *Phenomenology* undermines the view that knowledge of things-in-themselves is impossible, and provides a justification of a philosophic science which claims to know things as they really are.

In the *Science of Logic* Hegel repeatedly confirms this interpretation of the *Phenomenology*'s major function:

In the *Phenomenology of the Spirit* (Bamberg and Würzburg, 1807) I have presented the consciousness in its forward movement from its first immediate *opposition of itself and its object* all the way to absolute knowledge. This path goes through all forms of the relation of consciousness to its object and *has the concept of science as its result*. This concept requires therefore . . . no justification here, because it has already received one there. This concept is incapable of any *justification* other than this production of it by consciousness, for consciousness resolves all its own forms in this concept as in the truth.[50]

50. *Logic*, 1:29 (my italics).

This justification is clearly associated with the removal of the subject-object distinction:

> The concept of pure science and the deduction of it are assumed in the present treatise inasmuch as the *Phenomenology of the Spirit* is *nothing other* than the deduction of it. Absolute knowledge is the truth of all modes of consciousness, because, as that development made clear, only in absolute knowledge has the separation of the object and the certainty of oneself completely resolved itself.[51]

It is concluded that pure science "presupposes liberation from the opposition of consciousness," which is later described as the opposition between an "independent subjective being and a second such being, an objective one."[52]

Although Hegel himself says that the *Phenomenology* is "nothing other than" the justification or deduction of science by means of the removal of the opposition between subject and object, he was well aware that the book contained an abundance of material which was not relevant to this end. In a section of the *Encyclopedia* which gives added support to this interpretation of the overall function of the *Phenomenology*,[53] he adds:

> It was impossible to restrict it to the formal aspects of bare consciousness, for the standpoint of philosophical

51. *Logic*, 1:30 (my italics).
52. *Logic*, 1:42. This passage repeats and reenforces the one on page 30.
53. Sec. 25. The introduction is seen as being necessary to combat the idea that thought is "only subjective and has an enduring opposite in the objective."

knowledge is at the same time the most concrete and richest in content. Arising as a result, it presupposed the concrete forms of consciousness, such as morals, ethics, art, and religion. In the development of what at first appears to be limited to the formal aspects of consciousness, there is at the same time the development of the content or objects of the special branches of philosophical science. . . . The presentation thereby becomes more complicated, and what belongs to the more concrete branches of philosophy is put, in part, into that introduction.[54]

Although Hegel confesses and tries to justify the inclusion of material extraneous to the major function of the *Phenomenology*, he in no way repudiates his general conception of the book. In fact, if he had not retained this conception, there would have been no need to justify these elements, which are extraneous only in relation to what he regarded to be the general function of the book.

TRUTH, FREEDOM, AND THE THING-IN-ITSELF

I argued in the first chapter that Hegel views all human endeavor as the varied expression of one basic drive, which encompasses both theoretical and practical endeavor, both attempts to know and attempts to act. But as the one goal of the basic drive Hegel seemed to offer two different things: truth and freedom. He gives the normally epistemological concept of truth an additional practical interpretation, and the normally practical concept of freedom an additional epistemological interpretation, giving each the practico-epistemological

54. *Enc.*, sec. 25.

duality requisite for the goal of this corresponding dual drive. But although each was made eligible, it still seemed that two candidates were being endorsed for one position.

I claimed that this apparent inconsistency was relieved by Hegel's identification of truth and freedom, but I was able to present only part of the mechanism of this identification. Hegel argued that freedom is found only in conceptual thought, because, since the objects of conceptual thinking are the subject's own thoughts, the subject does not rely on any external objects and thus becomes self-sufficient, autonomous, and independent.[55]

To complete the identification, truth also must be linked to the autonomy of conceptual thought, and thus to freedom. Then the concepts of truth and freedom will have been identified with each other by identifying each with the bridge concept of autonomy or self-sufficiency. The concept of autonomy is able to serve as a bridge between the normally practical concept of freedom and the normally epistemological concept of truth only because it is broad enough to be interpreted both epistemologically (as knowledge which requires no external object, i.e., self-knowledge) and practically (as independent action). If truth can be somehow linked and limited to self-knowledge, then it can be identified with freedom through the bridge concept of autonomy.

But why is autonomy, even in the epistemological sense, necessary for truth? In other words, why must genuine knowledge be, in some sense, self-knowledge?

For Hegel, genuine knowledge has to be knowledge

55. See Chap. 1, "Stoicism."

of things as they really are in themselves, not merely knowledge of appearances. Since the opposition of the knowing subject and its object is held to be responsible for the limitation of knowledge to appearances, genuine knowledge is possible only where this opposition has been overcome. Only where knowledge has no external object, that is, where it is self-knowledge, is truth attainable. The spirit, in seeking truth, must seek autonomy, and to seek autonomy is to seek freedom; to seek freedom and truth is to have but one goal. Hegel's identification of truth and freedom is of a piece with his rejection of the limitation of knowledge to appearances.

HEGEL'S ARGUMENTS AGAINST THE LIMITATION OF KNOWLEDGE

The entire *Phenomenology*, by "deducing" a final form of consciousness in which the opposition of subject and object is overcome, removes the objection to knowledge of things as they are in themselves. But the entire *Phenomenology*, viewed as a single argument to this end, is a grotesque, unwieldy demonstration involving many steps, most of which are of dubious relevance and validity. In the *Science of Logic* and the *Enclyclopedia* Hegel offers more manageable and direct criticisms of the Kantian position.

Since the limitation of knowledge is the result of "a major viewpoint of the Critical Philosophy, that before one attempts to know God, the essence of things, etc., one must first investigate the capacity of knowledge itself, to see whether it is able to accomplish such tasks,"[56] Hegel attacks this viewpoint. He claims that

56. *Enc.*, sec. 10.

the plan to examine knowledge before using it is based on a false analogy with tools: "If one does not want to fool oneself with words, it is easy to see that other instruments can be investigated and criticized without using them in the particular work for which they are designed. But the investigation of knowledge can only be performed by an act of knowledge."[57] This so-called 'tool' can be investigated only cognitively.

In the *Phenomenology* Hegel had merely noted the uncritical acceptance of the tool metaphor. Now the metaphor is critically examined and an important disanalogy pointed out. Both the plan to examine knowledge before using it and the tool metaphor on which it rests are rejected simultaneously. The plan is not only based on an inappropriate metaphor, but is also internally inconsistent. Since knowledge must be used to examine knowledge, the plan to examine knowledge before using it is paradoxical. It amounts to "wanting to know before one knows" and is "just as absurd as the wise resolution of that scholastic who wanted to learn to swim before venturing into the water."[58]

Knowledge can be examined only in use; the analysis and criticism of certain concepts cannot precede but must accompany their use. Much the same point was neatly put by Otto Neurath and adopted by Willard Van Orman Quine as the motto of one of his books: "We are like sailors who must rebuild their ship on the open sea, without ever being able to take it apart in a dock and reconstruct it out of the best components."[59]

57. Ibid.
58. Ibid.
59. Neurath, "Protokollsätze," in *Erkenntnis,* 3:206 (my trans.); Quine, *Word and Object.*

Hegel, like Neurath and Quine, denies neither the need for an examination of knowledge nor its possibility; he denies only the possibility of a *preliminary* examination: "Of course the forms of thought should not be used unexamined, but the examination is already a knowing. Therefore, the activity of the thought-forms and their critique must be united in knowing."[60]

THE CONCEPT OF THE THING-IN-ITSELF

Hegel also directly examines and criticizes Kant's notion of an unknowable thing-in-itself. The thing-in-itself is not supposed to be "posited and determined by the thinking self-consciousness"; it is supposed to "remain foreign and external to thought."[61] But as Hegel points out, "it is easy to see that such an abstraction as the thing-in-itself is itself only a product of thought."[62] The thing-in-itself, which is opposed to concepts, is really just another concept. We know this because the thing-in-itself is an abstraction, and all abstractions are concepts and thus products of thought.

If the abstract character of the thing-in-itself betrays it to be only another concept, its completely abstract character shows it to be a rather dubious concept: "The *thing-in-itself* . . . expresses the object, as it is in abstraction from everything that it is in relation to consciousness, in abstraction from all determinations of feeling and from all determinate thoughts about it. It is easy to see what is left over—the *complete abstractum*, the total void, determined only as *a beyond*; the negative of rep-

60. *Enc.*, sec. 41, Z1.
61. *Logic*, 1:45.
62. Ibid.

resentation of feeling, of determinate thought, etc."[63]
Hegel suggests that the thing-in-itself is a suspiciously
vacuous concept. One cannot say what it *is*; one can
only say what it *is not*.

Essentially the same sort of criticism was used much
later by Gilbert Ryle to attack the Cartesian concept of
mind.[64] Ryle charged that the mind and mental processes had been defined solely as the negations of their
physical counterparts, that minds were described only as
not in space, *not* in time, *not* subject to causal laws, and
so forth. Since Ryle considered this theory of mind a
"para-mechanical hypothesis," Hegel might be said to
have considered the *Ding-an-sich* theory a "para-phe-
nomenal hypothesis." In each case the philosopher is
attacking what he considers to be a spurious dualism,
created by the artificial introduction of a pseudoentity
whose entire conceptual content is to be the negative or
opposite of its counterpart.

Hegel also attacks the alleged unknowability of the
thing-in-itself.[65] He again asserts the thing-in-itself to
be a product of the abstracting process of thought, and
identifies its completely abstract character with the
equally undetermined, abstract concept of Kant's (and
Fichte's) nonphenomenal self, whose only characteristic, according to Hegel, is to be identical with itself.[66]

63. *Enc.*, sec. 44.
64. *The Concept of Mind*, chap. 1, "Descartes' Myth."
65. *Enc.*, sec. 44.
66. "Kant clumsily said that 'I' *accompany* all my representations, also
my feelings, desires, actions, etc. . . . But 'I' in the abstract, as such, is
the pure relation to itself, which is abstracted from representation, feeling
and from every condition, as from every particularity of nature, talent,
experience, etc." (*Enc.*, sec. 20.).

The thing-in-itself is only this vacuous self-identity (*leere Identität seiner selbst*) of the nonphenomenal ego externalized and viewed as an object. Hegel's argument is that both the thing-in-itself and the noumenal self amount to nothing more than bare self-identity. Thus, there is nothing more to knowing them than being acquainted with and understanding the simple concept of self-identity. Far from being impossible, this is rather common and easy.

A second, similar argument for the knowability of the thing-in-itself follows from its completely negative character. Since the thing-in-itself is defined solely as the negation of all phenomenal qualities, Hegel argues that its conceptual content amounts to nothing more than the abstract concept of negation. In this case, not only is negation a familiar and easily comprehended concept, but it is ironically also listed by Kant as one of the necessary and universal categories of the understanding. "The negative determination, which this abstract identity receives as an object, is also included among the Kantian categories and is just as well known as that vacuous identity. Hence, only with astonishment can one read the so often repeated dictum that one cannot know what the thing-in-itself is. There is nothing easier to know than this."[67]

It might be objected that Hegel cannot advance both arguments, for although the thing-in-itself may be reducible to self-identity or to negation, it cannot be reducible to both. Hegel does not discuss this difficulty here, but he no doubt considered abstract self-identity

67. *Enc.*, sec. 44.

to result from the negation of all conceptual content and thus to be roughly equivalent to negation. And he actually argues along these lines in the equation of *Being* and *Nothing* in the first transition of his *Logic*. Hegel offers two different formulations of what, for him, is basically the same analysis because he feels that each of them clearly illustrates the knowability of the thing-in-itself.

Hegel's criticism of the notion of an unknowable thing-in-itself should be distinguished from several different but similar and more usual criticisms which have been falsely attributed to him.[68] A standard criticism of Kant's philosophy is that although the categories of the understanding are not supposed to apply to things-in-themselves, the latter are said to exist and to be the causes of our sensations. This entails applying the categories of existence and causality to them. It is further argued that if we know that the things-in-themselves exist and are causes, we know something about them, and thus they are, at least to some extent, knowable.[69]

These arguments are like Hegel's reduction of the thing-in-itself to negation in showing certain categories of the understanding to be applicable to the thing-in-itself. But Hegel's position is much more radical. He asserts not only that the thing-in-itself is at least partially knowable, but that since it is nothing more than the concept of negation or self-identity, it is completely knowable. Moreover, Hegel simply never uses the argu-

68. See Walter Stace, *The Philosophy of Hegel*, pp. 43–49.
69. For a defense of Kant against these arguments see A. C. Ewing, *A Short Commentary on Kant's Critique of Pure Reason*, (1938), pp. 187–95.

ments from the attribution of existence or a causal character to the thing-in-itself.[70]

Hegel further criticizes Kant's theory by posing the dilemma that either the categories are applicable to things-in-themselves, or the categories cannot be applicable to the understanding. For if the categories are really applicable to the understanding, then the categories are applicable to it as it really is—as a thing-in-itself.

> The critique of the forms of the understanding has had the result that these forms have no applicability to things-in-themselves. . . . But if they are allowed to remain valid for the subjective reason and experience, then the critique has not changed them, but allows them to remain valid for the subject in the same way that they formerly would have been valid for the object. . . . If they cannot be determinations of the thing-in-itself, still less can they be determinations of the understanding, to which at least the dignity of a thing-in-itself should be allowed.[71]

Hegel is *not* arguing here that Kant's categories are the actual determinations of the understanding; on the contrary, he denies their adequacy. He is merely calling attention to what seems to be an inconsistency in Kant's philosophy.

70. Yet Hegel would probably have endorsed these criticisms. In a letter to Schelling he makes a similar criticism: "If substance and accidents are corollaries, then it would seem to me that the concept of substance would not be applicable to the absolute ego—only to the empirical ego" (in Kaufmann, p. 304).

71. *Logic*, 1:27.

3 ~ SUBJECTIVITY AND OBJECTIVITY

Among the unexamined ideas held responsible in the *Phenomenology* for the unjust limitations philosophers had placed upon human knowledge are "the objective and subjective."[1] In these terms the limitation which philosophers had placed upon human knowledge amounts to the assertion that knowledge is merely subjective and not objective. Although Hegel considered the assertion that knowledge is subjective to be often just another formulation of the assertion that there is no knowledge of things-in-themselves, he realized that the two doctrines, though closely connected, were distinct, and he rejected them both.

One obvious way to do away with the philosophical embarrassment of the unknowability of any object as it exists independent of the knowing subject, that is, as a thing-in-itself, is to adopt some form of subjective idealism which denies the existence of anything "objective" and asserts that all reality and all knowledge of reality is in some sense "subjective." In this manner one can deny the existence of an unknowable thing-in-itself by holding that all we know, and all there is, is subjective. This flight from the Kantian dilemma of not being able to know ultimate reality is different from that romantic acceptance of the inadequacy of reason and reliance on direct, nonconceptual intuition that Hegel criticizes in the preface to the *Phenomenology* and in the section titled "Immediate Knowledge" in the *Vorbegriff* to the *Encyclopedia*. The subjective idealist does not reject

1. PG, p. 65.

82

the adequacy of reason, but rather ascribes to it, and to the ultimate reality it successfully knows, a subjective character.

Although Hegel distinguishes post-Kantian idealism from post-Kantian romanticism, he finds both unacceptable. For Hegel, reason must be retained as the way to truth, but not at the cost of making both reason and truth subjective:

> Transcendental idealism, carried more consistently to its logical conclusion, recognized the emptiness of that ghost of the thing-in-itself which the Critical Philosophy left behind—this abstract shadow, divorced from all content—and had as its goal to destroy it completely. This philosophy also made a beginning of letting reason produce its own determinations out of itself. But the subjective attitude of this attempt did not allow it to be carried to completion.[2]

Since Hegel wanted to show that reason could know an ultimate and *objective* reality, he rejected the subjective idealism of Fichte as well as the romantic intuitionism of Jacobi.

Even Kant, in spite of his doctrine of the thing-in-itself, is classified as a subjective idealist because he held that thought is subjective.

> The Critical Philosophy . . . like the later idealism, gave, as previously mentioned, because of its fear of the object, an essentially subjective meaning to the logical determinations. In doing this, it remained burdened with the object it fled, and a thing-in-itself, an endless impulse, remains as a beyond.[3]

2. *Logic*, 1:28.
3. *Logic*, 1:32.

Kant is said to have argued that "the categories have their source in the unity of self-consciousness, and that, for this reason, knowledge, in fact, comprehends nothing objective by means of them."[4] Hegel concludes, "If only this aspect is considered, Kant's critique is merely a subjective (shallow) idealism."[5]

But Hegel considers more than this aspect of Kant's philosophy. He attempts a full-scale analysis of the concepts, "subjective" and "objective," in conjunction with a thorough examination of Kant's use of them.

The need for conceptual analysis is stressed throughout Hegel's philosophy and especially in the *Vorbegriff* to the *Encyclopedia*. A large part of Hegel's respect for Kant is due to Hegel's belief that Kant had at least to some extent, tried to examine the concepts used uncritically by his rationalist and empiricist predecessors:[6] "The Critical Philosophy subjects the worth of the concepts of the understanding used in metaphysics—and also in the other sciences and ordinary thought—to examination."[7] And the fact "that the determinations of the old metaphysics were subjected to examination" is "without a doubt an important step."[8]

But because Kant's analysis is limited to distinguishing what is subjective from what is objective, Hegel

4. *Enc.*, sec. 46.
5. *Ibid.*
6. "This metaphysics . . . examined neither the content and worth of the determinations of the understanding nor . . ." (*Enc.*, sec. 28). "Scientific empiricism . . . uses the metaphysical categories of matter, force, not to speak of unity, plurality, universality, infinity, etc. . . . and uses those categories and their relations in a fully uncritical and unconscious manner." (*Enc.*, sec. 38.)
7. *Enc.*, sec. 41.
8. *Enc.*, sec. 41, Z1.

finds it inadequate: "This critique, however, does not deal directly with the content and the specific mutual relationships of these determinations of thought, but only considers them with respect to the contrast between *subjectivity* and *objectivity*."[9] Hegel does not object to this question per se; he objects only to the pursuit of this question to the exclusion of all others. He also thinks that Kant's major critical tools, the concepts "subjective" and "objective" are themselves desperately in need of examination.

HEGEL'S ANALYSIS OF SUBJECTIVITY AND OBJECTIVITY

Hegel's analysis of "subjective" and "objective" is interlaced with his exposition of Kant.[10] Hegel explicitly derives the first sense of these terms from the "linguistic usage of ordinary life" (*Sprachgebrauch des gemeinen Lebens*). In this common view, what is "present outside of us and reaches us through perception" is objective. "Subjective" means belonging to the perceiving subject, and, correspondingly, "objective" means belonging to its external object. In this sense, thought is subjective. Kant, by arguing that substance, cause and effect, and so forth, are categories of the understanding, produced by the knowing subject rather than presented to it as external data, had denied that they are objective in this sense.

Yet Kant's argument for the subjectivity of sub-

9. *Enc.*, sec. 41. And in the second *Zusatz* to this section: "Kant's examination of the determinations of thought suffers in an essential way from the defect that they are not considered for their own sakes but only to learn whether they are subjective or objective."

10. The most thorough discussion is in *Enc.*, sec. 41, Z2, from which the following quotations are taken.

stance, cause and effect, etc. is accompanied by, and even depends upon, an assertion of their universality and necessity. Kant had argued that all human experience *must* be experience of substances connected by relations of cause and effect, and that this universality and necessity can be accounted for only if these features of experience are unvaryingly imposed by the subject on the data it receives from the external world rather than being features of the world as it exists independently of being perceived. Because of the universality and necessity of these "categories of the understanding" Kant had, according to Hegel, called them objective: "However, Kant nevertheless called thought—more precisely what is universal and necessary—*objective*, and what is only felt, *subjective*."[11] In this second sense, what is objective is contrasted not to the knowing or perceiving subject, but to what is "particular" and "accidental."

In contemporary English the presence of roughly the same two sets of meanings for "objective" and "subjective" creates a danger of equivocation and confusion. For instance, a popular, if misguided, way of arguing for the relativity of ethical and aesthetic evaluations depends upon sliding from the first to the second sense of "subjective" that Hegel distinguishes. From the unobjectionable and seemingly innocuous assertion that all evaluations are subjective in the sense that they arise in a subject, one can easily slide to the more problematic view that they are subjective in the sense that they are not amenable to intersubjective debate, confirmation, or criticism. All opinions, judgments, evaluations, and thoughts are subjective in the trivial sense

11. *Enc.*, sec. 41, Z2.

of being in some way ascribable to a personal subject. Yet there is still a question about the subjectivity or objectivity of judgments recognized as emanating from a personal subject. This is a question about their intersubjectivity, their independence from the caprice, carelessness, and prejudice of any particular subject or subjects.

Although Hegel, following Kant, links the second sense of objectivity with universality and necessity, not with intersubjectivity, this distinction between being independent of any subject at all and being independent of any particular subject is operative in Hegel's distinction between the two senses of "objective." The categories of the understanding, though originating in the thinking subject, are objective because they are claimed to be found in *every* thinking subject. This can be described as their universality and necessity, but it amounts to the fact that the categories of the understanding are not just characteristic of some particular knowing subjects, but of all: they are intersubjective. The second set of meanings for "subjective" and "objective" seems no less a part of ordinary usage than the first. It also seems quite distinct from the first.

Hegel defends Kant's use of "objective" in this second way, but not by appealing to "ordinary linguistic usage." Hegel claimed that Kant had introduced this second sense of these terms into the language and was responsible for whatever limited currency it enjoyed in more sophisticated circles:

> The here mentioned determination of the distinction between the subjective and the objective, established by Kant, is found today in the linguistic usage of more

highly cultured consciousness. For example, it is demanded of the judgment of a work of art that it be objective and not subjective, and by this is understood that it should not proceed from the particular feeling and mood of the moment, but should keep in sight the universal view, grounded in the essence of art. In the same sense, in a scientific undertaking an objective interest can be distinguished from a subjective one.[12]

The second way to use the term is argued to be an advance over the first, not merely an acceptable addition to it. But it would be pointless to argue that one of two sets of meanings for the same words is superior unless there is some shared function in respect to which they can be compared and contrasted. It is hard to imagine arguing the relative merits of using "fit" in the sense of a sudden seizure and using "fit" in the sense of appropriateness, since the contexts in which the two meanings would furnish viable alternative interpretations are rare. In order to show that one of the two sets of meanings for "objective" and "subjective" is superior, Hegel must show that both, though distinct from each other, can serve as the answer to the same question.

Indeed, Hegel's argument for the superiority of Kant's usage relies on the implicit claim that the use of "objective" in either sense serves to designate what is independently real and enduring. Kant's use of "objective" is argued to be a superior way of designating what the ordinary use of "objective" also tries to designate, and therefore to be an improvement *evolving from*

12. *Enc.*, sec. 41, Z2.

ordinary usage, not simply an unjustified departure from it.

> The previously mentioned linguistic usage [the ordinary one] appears to be turned topsy-turvy by this [Kantian usage], and Kant has therefore been accused of linguistic confusion, but with great injustice. The following is more nearly the case. To the common [*gemeinen*] consciousness the sensuously perceivable things which confront it (e.g. this animal, this star, etc.) appear to be what is independent and enduring. Thoughts, on the contrary seem not to be independent but dependent on something else. But in fact what is sensuously perceivable is what is really dependent and secondary, and thoughts are, on the contrary, what is truly independent and primitive [*das wahrhaft Selbständige und Primitive*]. In this sense Kant called what is contained in thought (what is universal and necessary) "objective," and, indeed, with complete justification.[13]

Since Kant's new use of these terms retains and better fulfills some of their previous functions, his revision is not merely the gratuitous introduction of ambiguity and linguistic confusion. Hegel suggests that the philosophic use of terms should be based upon their ordinary use.

But he also insists that "ordinary linguistic usage" should supply only the roots of philosophic usage. The German *gemein*, like the English *common*, means popular and general, but also vulgar and low. When Hegel refers to ordinary (*gemein*) usage or the consciousness it expresses, the deprecatory connotation is stressed.

13. Ibid.

Although Hegel emphasized the importance of considering ordinary usage, philosophy is supposed further to develop and refine it, not just to revert to it. These philosophic developments and refinements themselves take root in the language, though in the case at hand their growth seems limited to the "more highly cultured" circles. Hegel's general view is that philosophy is nourished by general liguistic usage and, in turn, nourishes it.

Yet there is a third sense of "subjective" and "objective" which stems from Kant's *Ding-an-sich* doctrine and counters his second sense by reaffirming the subjectivity of thought: "But furthermore the Kantian objectivity of thought is itself only subjective, since, according to Kant, thoughts, though universal and necessary determinations, are still only our thoughts and separated from the thing-in-itself by an impassable gulf. On the contrary, the true objectivity of thought lies in the fact that thoughts are not merely our thoughts, but at the same time the essence [*An-sich*]of things and of what is objective in general."[14] The concept of *independent reality* which linked the first two senses of "objective," is operative. Kant's denial of the applicability of the categories to the independent reality of things-in-themselves amounts to a denial of any true objectivity to them.

After locating both objective and subjective elements within experience and equating the objective element with the universal, necessary, a priori element, Kant had ultimately made both elements of experience sub-

14. Ibid.

jective in contrast to an unknowable, unthinkable, but objective thing-in-itself.

TWO KINDS OF UNIVERSALITY

Here, Hegel is content to conclude that their "three-fold meaning" shows that: " 'Objective' and 'subjective' are comfortable and current expressions, which nevertheless easily lead to confusion."[15] Elsewhere, he tends to opt for the second meaning in defending the objectivity of thought. This defense relies on an extension of the Kantian assertion of the universality of the categories of the understanding, an extension which depends upon an equivocation and reveals Hegel's misinterpretation of Kant's position.

Kant's point about the universality and necessity of the categories amounted very roughly to the assertion that *every* human consciousness *must* experience according to the same basic conceptual scheme. This scheme, which involves Kant's table of the categories of the understanding, is claimed to be universal because it is used by every experiencing subject. If this were in fact true of Kant's categories, they would be objective in the sense of being intersubjectively valid.

Hegel wants to argue the much stronger and more general thesis that all thoughts, not just Kant's limited list of categories, are objective because universal. But the sort of universality which he plausibly attributes to all thoughts is different from the sort Kant attributed to the categories and, more important, not of a sort to support the claim that thought is objective.

15. Ibid.

In making the transition from "sense-certainty" to "perception," early in the *Phenomenology*, and in introducing the *Encyclopedia*, much is made of the abstract, general or universal character of our concepts and words: ". . . the determination or form of thought is the *universal*, that is, the abstract."[16]

Hegel argues for the universal or abstract character of *all* thoughts and concepts in two ways. First, he appeals to the results of introspection:

> The determinations offered here and in the immediately following sections are not to be taken as [mere] assertions and as my opinions [*Meinungen*] about thought. But, since no deduction or proof can be given in this preliminary way, these determinations might [instead] be considered as factual data. Thus, everyone who has thoughts and observes them in his consciousness should find empirically that they have the character of universality and also of the determinations to be mentioned subsequently. Of course, a previous cultivation of our powers of attention and abstraction is required for this observation of the facts of our consciousness and our ideas [*Vorstellungen*].[17]

Secondly, Hegel appeals to the nature of language, which, he held, mirrors the nature of thought: "Since language is the work of thought, nothing can be said in it that is not universal."[18] The argument consists of trying to show that all locutions, even those that

16. *Enc.* sec. 20.
17. Ibid.
18. Ibid.

seem to refer only to a particular individual, really function as universals, that is, apply equally and indifferently to each member of a class of individuals.

We may attempt to use language to pick out or to refer to some particular thing of which we are aware through the senses, but, according to Hegel, this attempt is doomed to fail. The particular thing may be described by using nouns and adjectives such as "rose" and "red," but "rose" refers indifferently to any one of those many things which are roses, and "red" refers indifferently to any one of those many things which are red. That such descriptive concepts function in our language as universals, not as names of individuals, seems so obvious to Hegel that he hardly bothers to mention or argue for their universality.[19] Instead, he concentrates on those locutions that seem specially designed to refer to individual things—those that seem to pose the greatest problems for his thesis.

One way of limiting the general reference of "rose" to a particular rose would be to prefix a demonstrative to the description, for example, "this rose." It seems that by means of the demonstrative—"this"—language can refer to particulars, so Hegel must ask: "What is the *this?*"[20] "This" is analyzed into "the double form of its being as the *now* and *here.*"[21] In other words, by saying "this rose" I am referring to the particular rose present to me here and now, not to roses in general. When a speaker tries to specify a particular by using

19. However, "If I say 'anger,' 'rose,' 'hope,' for example, they are all familiar to me through sensation, but I speak this content in a universal way, in the form of thought." (*Enc.*, sec. 24, Z1.)

20. *PG*, p. 81.

21. Ibid.

"this," he does so by referring to its spatiotemporal position in relation to his own.

But both "here" and "now" are correctly used by the same speaker or by different speakers at different times and places. Any point in time is *now*, and any point in space is *here*, for someone properly located. "Now" is a universal which refers indifferently to every possible instant. "Here" is a universal which refers to every possible place.

Hegel felt that the universal character of these words and concepts had been generally misunderstood: "To the question, What is *now*? we answer, for example, now is night."[22] By using "now" we intend to refer to a particular time, and this answer identifies "now" with its intended referent. But the possibility of referring to any time as "now," is, for Hegel, proof that any such particular reference, though intended, can never actually be made.

The mistake of identifying a universal with one of the several particulars to which it indifferently applies is illustrated by pointing out its application to other particulars: "We write this truth [that it is now night] down. A truth cannot lose anything by being written down, and just as little by our preserving and keeping it. If *now, this noon*, we look again at the truth we have written down, we would have to say that it has become stale. . . . *Now* maintains itself but as something which is not the night; in the same way it maintains itself against the day, which it now is, as something which is also not the day, or generally as something negative."[23]

22. Ibid.
23. Ibid.

Analogously: "*Here* is, for example, the tree. If I turn around, this truth has vanished and turned into its opposite. Here is not a tree but rather a house. *Here* does not vanish but endures while the house, tree, etc. vanish. *Here* is indifferent to its being a house or a tree."[24]

What is true of *here* and *now* is also true of *this*; depending upon the speaker's spatiotemporal location anything can be a "this." And what is true of *this* is true of *that*. Similarly, anything might be referred to as "the individual" or even "this individual." The very locutions with which we try to refer to individuals are themselves universals: "When I say, 'the individual,' 'this individual,' 'here,' 'now,' all of these are universals. Everything and anything is an individual and a this."[25]

Since the specific reference of demonstratives is relative to the speaker, one attempt to salvage the use of demonstratives to identify particulars would be to refer them back to the particular subject who is using them: "Now is day, because I see it; here is a tree, for the same reason. . . . *This I* sees the tree and asserts the tree to be here; *another I* sees, however, a house and asserts, not the tree, but the house to be here."[26] Every speaker, however, refers to himself as "I": "*I* is only a universal like *now*, *here*, or *this*. . . . When I say 'I, this individual I,' I really say [i.e., refer to] 'every I.' What I say applies to everyone; everyone is [i.e., can refer to himself as] this individual I."[27] "Similarly, in saying 'I,' I mean myself to the exclusion of all others. But what I say ap-

24. *PG*, p. 82.
25. *Enc.*, sec. 20.
26. *PG*, p. 83.
27. *PG*, pp. 83–84.

plies to everyone; everyone says 'I' and means himself
to the exclusion of all others."[28] Again, Hegel argues,
the attempt to refer to particulars breaks down.

There is still another linguistic device with which
we seem to refer to particular individuals—proper
names. When I mention "Berlin," "G. W. F. Hegel,"
or "Socrates," I seem to refer in each case to a particular
thing and not to any one of a class of things. Surprisingly, Hegel does not even attempt to undermine the
apparently individual reference of proper names. Considering his previous arguments one might expect him
to have argued that often a proper name has been assigned to more than one particular and that theoretically all proper names could be assigned more than
once. In addition to the Berlin in Prussia there is a
Berlin, New Hampshire; many Greeks have been named
"Socrates"; and even if there has never been another
man named G. W. F. Hegel," there is nothing to
prevent the use of this name in the future.

Not only does the putative particularity of proper
names remain unassailed, but in these passages proper
names are not even discussed as threats to the theory
that language is universal and cannot successfully refer
to particulars. This omission is, if not justified, at least
partially accounted for by Hegel's attitude toward
proper names which briefly emerges in other passages.
In the preface to the *Phenomenology* Hegel criticizes
sentences in which "God" is the subject and various
predicates are attributed to him because, among other
reasons, the subject "God" has no conceptual content
or is only a name. He holds that proper names have no

28. *Enc.*, sec. 20.

conceptual content; in other words, that they are meaningless. In such sentences, "it is above all the name as name that designates the pure subject, the empty unit devoid of concept."[29]

In the *Logic* proper names are admitted to be exceptions to the otherwise universal character of language, yet the force of these exceptions is not removed by denying their particularity, but by denying their significance: "By using 'this' one intends to express something perfectly determinate. It is overlooked that language, as the work of the understanding, expresses only what is universal, except for the name of an individual object. However, the individual name is meaningless in the sense that it does not express a universal."[30]

Proper names, if indeed meaningless, do not pose a serious threat to Hegel's thesis that language expresses only what is universal, for language, although it contains proper names, can still be said to express nothing *meaningful* which is not also universal. It might be argued that the expression of meaningless names is only dubiously expression at all. To deny that proper names have meaning or are concepts is not implausible and has the advantage of calling attention to differences between proper names and other kinds of words.[31] However, the way in which the meaninglessness of

29. *PG*, p. 53.
30. *Logic*, 1:104–5.
31. A similar conclusion was reached by John Stuart Mill, who said, "A proper name is but an unmeaning mark . . ." (*A System of Logic*, chap. 2, sec. 5). More recent philosophers of language have also held that proper names have no meaning, e.g., Paul Ziff, *Semantic Analysis*, secs. 106 and 180.

proper names is supported in the passage just quoted introduces an objectionable circularity into Hegel's theory. The universal character of all the meaningful content in language is maintained only by asserting proper names to be meaningless, but proper names are only asserted to be "meaningless in the sense that [they do] not express a universal." The universal character of the meaningful content of language is maintained only by assuming it.

This *petitio principii* is slightly ameliorated by the fleeting suggestion of a separate reason for denying meaning to proper names. Hegel adds as an afterthought that "individual names can be assumed, bestowed, or even changed arbitrarily."[32] Although this germ of an idea is developed no further, it is an interesting suggestion. Anything can be given any conceivable name. Some names might seem strange or in some sense inappropriate; a boy might be named "Jane," or a child of either sex "Abracadabra." Yet, in assigning proper names one cannot be mistaken in the same straightforward sense as one can be in describing something. To name one's son "Jane" is merely peculiar, but to describe a window as "a horse" is mistaken. The complete interchangeability of proper names might be accounted for by arguing that all proper names have the same meaning—no meaning.

Let us temporarily forget the circulatory and incompleteness of Hegel's justification for the thesis that proper names have no meaning; let us suppose this thesis is correct. It still does not follow that proper names, though meaningless, cannot refer to particulars,

32. *Logic*, 1:105.

unless meaning and reference are equated. Indeed, Hegel's position is elusive because he does not distinguish between the question of what is the nature of the conceptual content of language and the question of what it is to which language can refer.

LANGUAGE AND "MEINUNG"

Throughout his discussion of the universal character of language Hegel sharply contrasts what we intend (*meinen*) to do with language and what the nature of language allows us to do. Simply to equate the German verb *meinen* with the English "to mean" is incorrect, and to translate the noun *Meinung* as "meaning" is worse.[33]

In English "to mean" can be a synonym either of "to signify" or of "to intend." Ambiguity is usually avoided because the presence of a personal grammatical subject generally indicates that the verb is synonymous with "to intend," and the absence of a personal subject indicates that the verb is synonymous with "to signify." "*Meinen*" can be synonymous with "to intend," but not with "to signify." Correspondingly, only persons—not words, concepts, propositions, theories, or behavior—can be the grammatical subjects of *meinen*. *Meinen* can also mean "to be of the opinion that," especially where opinion is contrasted with knowledge, that is, where it is unsupported.

A *Meinung* correspondingly belongs to a person, not to a word, concept, etc., and should be translated "opinion" rather than "meaning." In discussing *Mein-*

33. See Sir James Baillie's translation of the *Phenomenology*, 2d ed., pp. 152–53.

ungen Hegel is not discussing semantics but rather certain opinions which he holds to have no meaning or expression in language, and which therefore are sublinguistic and subsemantic.[34] The meaning of a word or concept is its *Bedeutung*, not its *Meinung*.

Since a *Meinung* is an opinion, *meinen* might be translated by the archaic verb "to opine" in order to retain a common root for both noun and verb. But to retain the morphological similarity of the German noun and verb is not an unalloyed virtue, for they differ semantically: although *Meinung* is never synonymous with *Absicht* (intention), *meinen* is sometimes synonymous with *beabsichtigen* (to intend). No single English verb can consistently be used to translate *meinen*.[35]

With the aid of a pun, Hegel further derogates *meinen* and *Meinungen* as being subjective in the sense of idiosyncratic: "What I merely opine (*Was ich nur meine*) is mine (*ist mein*), belongs to me as to this particular individual."[36] More disturbing than the casual use of a pun to make a point is the implicit confusion of different senses of subjectivity which Hegel himself distinguished. Certainly all my opinions, like all my thoughts, are mine in the trivial sense that *I* entertain them. They are subjective simply in being the opinions

34. In the *Enc.*, sec. 88, Hegel denies that there is any difference between two particular concepts by calling this difference "ineffable, mere opinion" (*das Unsagbare, die blosse Meinung*). *Enc.*, sec. 87; *Logic*, p. 77; *PG*, p. 88 also illustrate Hegel's attribution of ineffability to *Meinungen* and what we *meinen*.

35. I have evaded the problem in the following short quotations by using different words and indicating the occurrences of *meinen* in the original text.

36. *Enc.*, sec. 20.

and thoughts of an opining and thinking subject. But because my opinions are mine in this trivial sense, it does not follow that they cannot be shared by others, or that they are not amenable to intersubjective debate, confirmation, or criticism. To be mine is not necessarily to be only mine.

Hegel is trying to contrast opinions (*Meinungen*), which he claims to be particular and therefore inexpressible in language, with thoughts (*Gedanken*), which are universal and expressible: "If, however, language expresses only what is universal, I cannot say what I merely intend [*meine*]."[37] However, this fallacious argument for the idiosyncrasy and lack of intersubjectivity of *Meinungen* applies no less well to thoughts, for thoughts are subjective in the trivial sense of being the thoughts of some thinking subject. Yet thoughts are, according to Hegel, exactly what language can and does express.

The supposed lack of intersubjectivity which is held to render *meinen* particular and therefore inexpressible in language is not only ill argued but otiose. Our *Meinungen* are inexpressible for a different reason: according to Hegel, what we intend (*meinen*) is to refer to particulars, and, as we have seen, Hegel has independent arguments for the impossibility of linguistically referring to particulars.

This line of argument has further sweeping philosophic consequences. Since these particulars are presented to us in sensation and feeling, to deny the possibility of linguistically referring to particulars is also to deny the possibility of linguistically expressing what we

37. Ibid.

sense and feel. Hegel is thus attacking the foundation of any empiricism which views one of the most fundamental and unproblematic functions of language to be the reporting of the individual data of sensation.

For those of a certain mystical bent, what is ineffable is the highest, truest, and most real; the extralinguistic is the supralinguistic. For Hegel, on the contrary, ineffability is a defect; the extralinguistic is the sublinguistic: "And the *ineffable* [*das Unsagbare*] feeling and sensation is not the most excellent and true but the least important, the least true."[38] And "what is called the ineffable [das Unaussprechliche] is nothing but the untrue, irrational, the merely believed [*Gemeinte*]."[39] The excellence of the effable is not directly argued in these passages; it is simply stated.

It follows that we are to rejoice, not despair, that language does not allow the expression of the sensuous particulars which we intend to express. If what the "divine nature" of language rejects is shown to be unreal, untrue, and unimportant, then the possibility of linguistic expression serves as a welcome test of truth. Even in vainly attempting to express sensuous particulars, "I experience what the truth of sense-certainty, in fact, is . . . i.e., a universal."[40] An unsuccessful attempt to give linguistic expression to one of the forms of consciousness in the *Phenomenology* provides the nec-

38. Ibid.
39. PG, p. 88.
40. PG, p. 89. Also, p. 82—"Language is, as we see, the truer; in it we directly refute our *Meinung*. And since the universal is the truth of sense-certainty, and language expresses only this truth, it is impossible for us ever to express [*sagen*] a sensible being that we intend to express [*meinen*]."

essary impetus to *progress* to a higher form. For Hegel, the limits of language are laudable.

Even if we accept Hegel's central conclusion that our mental concepts and their linguistic correlates—thoughts and words—are universals, three major problems remain. (1) From the conclusion that words are universals, does it follow that language cannot be used to refer to particulars? (2) From the conclusion that thoughts are universals, does it follow that thoughts are in any sense objective? (3) Does Hegel consider the universal to be truer than the particular only because the former but not the latter is expressible in language?

1. *From the conclusion that words are universals, does it follow that language cannot be used to refer to particulars?* Let us temporarily dismiss the possibility of referring to particulars by means of proper names. Even if the thoughts and words at our disposal are all universals, it does not follow that we cannot think or speak of a particular individual, for the following reasons:

First, although each of the thoughts or words used applies to a whole class of things, a complex enough combination of universals may apply to only one thing.

Second, as P. F. Strawson has elaborately argued, individuals can be referred to by supplying both their spatial and temporal positions.[41] This second way of

41. *Individuals*, esp. pp. 15–30. Strawson's theory, in stressing the importance of the spatiotemporal framework for referring to particulars, approaches Hegel's analysis of *this* into *here* and *now*. But, of course, in affirming the possibility of referring to particulars with language, Strawson radically differs from Hegel.

referring to individuals is really based on the first. The concepts of meridian, parallel, hour, minute, second, and the ordinal and cardinal numbers are all universals. Yet by combining them in various ways reference can be made to unique spatiotemporal positions. And by combining these unique spatiotemporal positions with descriptions we can refer to particular individuals. For example, we can refer unambiguously to this particular red chair by identifying it as the red chair at a numerically specified longitude, latitude, and date. Put in a more Hegelian manner, the use of a spatiotemporal framework to identify individuals shows that there is a way to specify any *this, here,* and *now* which "cannot lose anything by being written down and just as little by our preserving and keeping it."[42]

Third, although by assigning numerical spatial and temporal coordinates it is theoretically possible to refer to an individual in a way which can be recorded and preserved *salve veritate*, Hegel's arguments suggest that our ordinary attempts to refer to individuals by using demonstratives like "this," "here," and "now" are still failures. According to Hegel, only those statements are true which are still true when reread after being written down and kept for any length of time. It is also suggested, though not actually stated, that a true statement should still be true if reread after being written down and carried to another place or given to someone else to read. In short, according to this criterion the truth of a statement must be independent of its context of utterance.

A great many statements normally considered unob-

42. PG, p. 81.

jectionable do not pass this test, for example: "This is a book," "Now it is noon," "Here is the library," "I am happy," "The book is red," "He is intelligent." Whether these statements are true or false depends upon the context in which they are uttered—the speaker, the place, the time, etc. Either we must go along with Hegel and consider all these statements whose truth is not independent of their context of utterance to be automatically false, or we must reject Hegel's criterion for the truth of statements. The latter alternative seems much more sensible.

However, to reject Hegel's criterion only to consider all such statements automatically true would be equally ridiculous. Calling attention to the context-dependent nature of certain statements—as Hegel does—only makes clear the inadequacy of any theory—like Hegel's own—which does not make a distinction between statement types and statement tokens[43] and implies that truth and falsity apply to statement types, not to tokens.

W. V. O. Quine, for instance, is led to reject any such theory because of the very same considerations.

> Strictly speaking, what admits of truth and falsity are not statements as repeatable patterns of utterance, but individual events of statement and utterance. For utterances that sound alike can vary in meaning with the occasion of the utterance. This is not only due to careless ambiguities, but to systematic ambiguities which are essential to the nature of language. The pronoun "I" changes its reference with every change of speaker;

---

43. If "the rose is red" is uttered or written at one time and then uttered or written at another time or by another person, two tokens of the same type have been uttered or written.

"there" changes its reference with every significant
movement through space; and "now" changes its reference every time it is uttered.[44]

Hegel's discovery of the universal character of the
words with which we attempt to refer to particulars led
him to conclude that statements which purport to refer to particulars fail to do so and are false. Although
his discovery does not warrant his conclusion, it does
have important implications for any theory of linguistic
reference. Hegel's discussion of demonstratives shows
that any statement which refers to particulars by means
of them does not do so simply in virtue of a meaning
which it possesses as a statement type in abstraction
from the various contexts of its use. Such statements,
contrary to Hegel's conclusion, do refer to particulars,
but only as individual instances of repeatable patterns
of utterances, as tokens of types, used in specific linguistic and nonlinguistic contexts.

2. *From the conclusion that thoughts are universals,
does it follow that thoughts are in any sense objective?*
Hegel's discussion of language and reference is really
an outgrowth of what for him was a more crucial task.
Since language is "the work of thought," to show the
universal character of words serves to show the universal
character of the corresponding thoughts. And from the
universality of thoughts he wants to argue for their
objectivity. If thought is objective, knowledge of
thought—which Kant allowed—is not merely subjective
and limited. It becomes knowledge in the fullest sense,
and Kant's limitation on knowledge is removed.

Kant had argued that certain categories of the under-

44. *Methods of Logic*, p. xi.

standing were universal in the sense that every human consciousness uses them; he argued that the categories were objective in the sense of being intersubjectively valid. Hegel argues for the universality not only of Kant's twelve categories of the understanding but of all concepts. He seems to be arguing a much stronger thesis than Kant, but the two theses cannot be so simply compared because Hegel has not really argued for the universality of all concepts in the same sense that Kant argued for the universality of the categories.

Hegel, as we have seen, argues that all concepts are universals in the sense that they refer indifferently to any and all members of a certain class. But even if all the concepts people use are universals, that is, class concepts, there is no guarantee that all people use the same concepts to refer to the same classes. There is no guarantee that everyone uses the same system of universals in thinking. For example, the words "beautiful," "good," "democratic," and "philosophy" are all universals in the sense Hegel has argued. It is no less true that any one of these words and its corresponding concept can be and is in fact used and applied differently by different people. It is a commonplace that people disagree violently about what particular things are to be classified as "beautiful," what particular actions are to be classified as "good," and what particular institutions are to be classified as "democratic." The fact that our concepts are universals, and not names of particulars, does not imply that they are also universal in the sense that their use is intersubjectively consistent, or even that it is amenable to intersubjective confirmation and criticism.

If Kant's claim that the same basic categories of the

understanding are used by every human consciousness were true, then they would be objective in the sense of being true of all subjects, that is, intersubjective. But even if all thoughts are universals, they need not be objective in this sense. Hegel confuses something's being a universal with its being universally true of all subjects.

3. *Does Hegel consider the universal to be truer than the particular only because the former but not the latter is expressible in language?* It is clear that, for Hegel, what can be expressed in language is for that reason more excellent, real, and true than what cannot be so expressed, and that what language can express is the universal. However, the greater reality and truth of the universal is not only based on its being expressible in language but is reinforced by other arguments. The just criticized claim for the objectivity of the universal, which is based on a confusion between being a universal and being universally true, is one such putative reenforcement.

Additional support is mustered by trading on the traditional distinction between essence and accident. According to this view, the substance or reality of a thing resides in its essence or inner nature, that which remains the same through the vicissitudes of accidental change; what does not endure through change is only accidental. Individual things come to exist and cease to exist; individual animals are born and die. What endures through this change is obviously not the individual thing but the species to which it belongs. Therefore, it is argued, the species is the essence and reality, and the individual is only accidental. The species is identified with the universal, for the universal refers indifferently to each member of the species; "animal" refers indifferently to each thing that is an animal. It follows that the universal is the enduring essence and, therefore, more true and real than the particular.

> A more specific example is that when we speak of a specific animal, we say, "it is [an] animal." We can point out a specific animal but not animal as such. Animal does not exist, but it is the universal nature of individual animals, and every existing animal is something much more concretely specific and special. But to be [an] animal, the species as the universal, belongs to the specific animal and constitutes its specific essentiality. If we subtracted from a dog its being an animal, it would be impossible to say what it was. Things in general have an enduring, inner nature and an external existence [*Dasein*]. They live and die, come to be and pass away; their essentiality, their universality is the species, and this is not to be understood merely as what they have in common.[45]

Hegel has identified thought with the universal. Thus in identifying the essence or inner nature of things with the universal, Hegel is identifying ultimate reality with thought and with what thought can grasp. Consequently, he is arguing against any denial that thought can know ultimate reality. He wants to show that the study of thought (the universal) and what thought can grasp is also the study of objective reality. Indeed Hegel adduces this traditional argument for the reality of the species in a *Zusatz* to support the position that

45. *Enc.*, sec 24, Z1.

"thoughts . . . can be called *objective* thoughts, including the forms which, to begin with, are considered in the ordinary logic to be only forms of conscious thinking. Logic [the science of thoughts] therefore coincides with metaphysics as the science of things grasped in thoughts, which are considered to express the essences of things in thought."[46]

46. *Enc.*, sec. 24.

4 ~ INFINITY

The view that philosophy attempts to attain an unrestricted or absolute knowledge is, for Hegel, tantamount to the view that philosophy attempts to know an absolute object or "the Absolute." The soundness of this identification is questionable[1] but unimportant, for Hegel supports the view that philosophy seeks to know the Absolute, not just by deriving it from the view that philosophy seeks absolute knowledge, but by appealing to history: "The history of philosophy is the history of the discovery of thoughts about the Absolute, which is its object."[2] In other words, he views philosophy as having been historically the search for a completely comprehensive and adequate metaphysics.

Hegel says not only that philosophy has "the Absolute" for its object, but also that it has "absolute objects."[3] He offers as examples the soul, the world, God, freedom, and spirit. But though these are indeed traditional philosophic concerns, why are they *absolute objects?*

Traditional metaphysical speculation about these objects had been criticized for being nonempirical by both the British empiricists and Kant: "In common with empiricism, the Critical Philosophy takes experience to be the only basis for knowledge."[4] Hegel agrees

1. The identification seems to rely on the unsound assumption that any knowledge must have an object to which can be ascribed all the characteristics ascribable to the knowledge itself. Crude knowledge is, for example, not necessarily knowledge of crude objects.
2. *Enc.*, Preface to the 2d ed., p. 10.
3. *Enc.*, sec. 10.
4. *Enc.*, sec. 40.

that these objects cannot be treated by any of the ordinary "empirical sciences," which take experience as their point of departure and then develop general laws and theories about it. However, the reason for this is not that these objects are not to be found in experience: "To be sure, they are not experienced through the senses, but whatever is in consciousness is experienced —this is even a tautology."[5] Rather, what puts these traditional philosophical objects beyond the reach of empirical science is that they "immediately present themselves as *infinite* [*unendlich*] in content."[6]

Hegel thought that he had deftly and conclusively countered the empiricist criticism that the objects of metaphysical speculation are not to be found in experience. Of course, he admits that they are not experienced through the senses, but suggests that this is also true of the general laws and theories produced by the empirical sciences.[7]

For Hegel, what seems to make traditional philosophical speculation peculiarly problematic is its attempt to know objects that are infinite. Furthermore, it is their infinite character that makes these objects "absolute." "Infinite" and "absolute" are used interchangeably. Hegel says that the "thought used in the philosophical way of knowing needs itself to be justified concerning . . . its ability to know absolute objects."[8] The need for such a justification is established in the immediately preceding paragraph: "What is usually

5. *Enc.*, sec. 8.
6. Ibid.
7. *Enc.*, sec. 7.
8. *Enc.*, sec. 10.

called a *concept* is to be distinguished from a concept in the speculative sense. It is in the former, one-sided sense that the assertion that the infinite could not be grasped by concepts is advanced, repeated thousands and thousands of times, and made into a prejudice."[9] The prejudice against conceptually grasping the infinite necessitates justifying the possibility of knowing the Absolute, for Hegel treats "infinite" and "absolute" as synonymous.

Hegel explicitly identifies these infinite and absolute objects as the objects of the pre-Kantian metaphysics,[10] and calls attention to Kant's attack on the metaphysical attempt to know them. Kant had considered metaphysical speculation to consist in an illicit extension of the categories of thought beyond their proper sphere of application. He had sharply distinguished the proper application of the categories to experience by the *understanding* (*Verstand*) from their improper or transcendent application beyond experience by *reason* (*Vernunft*).

UNDERSTANDING AND REASON

Hegel adopted and adapted Kant's distinction. Like Kant, he associated reason with metaphysical speculation, and understanding with less ambitious intellectual enterprises. But just as Hegel rejected the idea that the distinction between the objects of ordinary empirical inquiry and the objects of metaphysical speculation was that the former but not the latter were to be found in experience, he does not treat the distinction between

9. *Enc.*, sec. 9.
10. *Enc.*, sec. 30.

understanding and reason as depending upon whether or not the categories are applied to experience. Again, Hegel makes the distinction primarily in terms of infinity, not experience. Reason, but not understanding, has the infinite for its object.

Hegel acknowledges that this way of drawing the distinction is also derived from Kant: "Kant was the first to set forth distinctly the difference between understanding and reason. He defined the former as having the finite and conditioned for its object and the latter as having the infinite and unconditioned as its object."[11] Kant had held that reason requires, with respect to any judgment, to know the condition of that judgment, namely, the premise from which the judgment follows as a conclusion. Since the condition is itself a judgment, reason requires, in turn, to know its condition. Reason is not satisfied until the series is completed and knowledge obtained which is not conditioned by anything further. Reason seeks to know the completed series of conditions, the series of consequents and their grounds, of effects and their causes. Since this completed series of conditions is itself unconditioned, reason seeks to know the unconditioned. Since the series of conditions seems to be infinite, knowing the unconditioned is tantamount to knowing the infinite. Kant argues that an infinite series could never be experienced; he supports his contention that reason transcends experience by pointing to the unconditioned or infinite nature of its object. Kant also tries to show how traditional metaphysical concerns about the soul, the world, God, and

11. *Enc.*, sec. 45, Z.

freedom are all manifestations of reason's attempt to know the unconditioned or infinite.

Although Hegel rejects the Kantian claim that the objects of metaphysics are not to be found in experience, he accepts Kant's view that reason, in the service of metaphysics, seeks to know the unconditioned, and explicitly identifies the unconditioned (*das Unbedingte*) with the infinite (*das Unendliche*).[12]

Kant had declared knowledge of the unconditioned to be impossible and "criticized this application of the categories [of the understanding] to the unconditioned, that is, metaphysics."[13] Hegel considers this criticism and limitation of knowledge—in contrast to Kant's limitation of knowledge to phenomena and subjectivity—as "the second side of the critique of reason" which is "in itself more important than the first."[14] In order to rebut this limitation of knowledge to the finite and the corresponding criticism of metaphysics as the illicit attempt to know the unconditioned or infinite, Hegel had to show that the infinite could be known. He identifies the infinite with the truth[15] and thereby turns Kant's criticism into a challenge. The prejudice that the infinite cannot be conceptually grasped is thus made tantamount to the belief that the truth cannot be conceptually grasped. This prejudice had to be refuted, and reason, which claims to know the infinite, had to be defended.

---

12. *Enc.*, sec. 45.
13. *Enc.*, sec. 46.
14. Ibid.
15. *Enc.*, sec. 28, Z—"The truth is, however, what is in itself infinite." See also sec. 62 and *Logic*, 1:17.

It is to this end that Hegel *adapted* Kant's dichotomy between reason and understanding. Hegel identifies the Understanding with ordinary thought and its extension and refinement in the empirical sciences—and admits that it is unable to comprehend the infinite. This inability is explained by the understanding's use of categories which are meant to be opposites and contradictories of one another: "If the determinations of thought are encumbered with fixed opposites, i.e., if they are of a *finite* nature, then they are incommensurate with the truth, which is absolute [i.e., infinite] in and for itself. In this case the truth cannot enter into thought. Thought which brings forth only finite determinations and operates with them is called *understanding* (in the more exact sense of the word) ."[16]

INFINITY AS TOTALITY

To characterize understanding as operating with concepts and categories which are mutually exclusive and to identify this operation with ordinary thought is not particularly puzzling. Consider, for example, *large* and *small, round* and *square, odd* and *even.* But why should the fact that our ordinary conceptual scheme contains mutually exclusive categories make it unfit for grasping the infinite? To answer this problem we must examine Hegel's notion of infinity.

For Hegel, "a finite being is one which relates itself to something *else*; it is a content which necessarily stands in relation to *other* content, to the whole world."[17] Following Spinoza, Hegel holds that *to be*

16. *Enc.*, sec. 25. Note the implicit equation of the absolute, the infinite, and the truth.
17. *Logic*, 1:71 (my italics).

finite is to be limited by something else.[18] From this view it follows that "the whole world" or universe is infinite, for since it includes everything, there can be nothing *else* left to limit it. Hegel would undoubtedly consider any cosmology positing a finite universe to be *conceptually* impossible.

Hegel holds not only that the whole (*das Ganze*) cannot be finite, but also that anything less than the whole must be finite. Any "being" that is less than the whole of being, any "content" that does not exhaust all content, "necessarily stands in relation" to what remains. And to stand in relation to something else is, in Hegel's view, to be limited by it and thus to be finite.

In denying the possibility of infinite proper parts Hegel again follows Spinoza.[19] More important, he also completes his identification of *infinity* with *totality*. Now the whole, and only the whole, is infinite. In the *Science of Logic*, Hegel rejects one notion of infinity because "it is not the whole [*das Ganze*], but only one side of it ... It is thus the finite infinite."[20] In the *Encyclopedia*, the traditional objects of metaphysics, which Hegel characterizes as infinite, are also said to be "totalities" (*Totalitäten*).[21]

The Hegelian identification of infinity and totality is not only absent from the usual conception of infinity

---

18. Spinoza, *Ethics*, part 1, proposition 8. "[Substance] does not exist as finite, for (by Def. 2) it would be limited by something else of the same kind. . . ."

Definition 2, "A thing is called finite after its kind, when it can be limited by another thing of the same nature. . . ."

19. *Ethics*, part 1, proposition 13, note. ". . . and by a [proper] part of substance, nothing else can be understood than finite substance."

20. *Logic*, 1:33.

21. *Enc.*, sec. 30.

but is also in direct conflict with it. An infinite series is commonly defined as a series with no last number, and the natural numbers (1, 2, 3, 4 . . .) are often cited as a paradigm of such a series. But the series of the even natural numbers (2, 4, 6, 8 . . .) and the series of the odd natural numbers (1, 3, 5, 7 . . .) have no last members and, accordingly, are also infinite. Since the set of odd natural numbers and the class of even natural numbers are proper subsets of the class of natural numbers, they would not be considered infinite by Hegel. Yet they are generally taken to be infinite.

We can now see why Hegel asserts that the mutually exclusive categories—the "fixed opposites"—of the understanding cannot grasp the infinite. In a conceptual scheme composed of mutually exclusive categories the domain of each category is external to the domains of the others: each concept has a "content which necessarily stands in relation to other [conceptual] content." Given Hegel's view that to be related to something else is to be limited by it and thus to be finite, it follows that each concept is a set of mutually exclusive concepts is limited by the others and is thus finite. For example, if a number is odd, it cannot be even. Thus, in Hegel's view, *odd* would limit *even* and vice versa. Given Hegel's identification of infinity and totality, such concepts, each a discrete and proper part of its conceptual system, are finite and thus unable to grasp the infinite.

THE FAILURE OF TRADITIONAL METAPHYSICS

The understanding, which "tarries in finite thought-determinations, i.e., in still unresolved oppositions," is

said to have its "most distinct and proximate development" in "previous metaphysics as it was among us
before the Kantian philosophy."[22] Because traditional
metaphysics operates with the mutually exclusive categories of the understanding, it demands to know, with
respect to any of its objects (the world, God, the soul,
etc.) which *one* of a set of mutually exclusive categories
applies to it. Traditional metaphysics asks whether the
world is finite or infinite, simple or composite, and so
on,[23] and assumes that one and only one of any set of
putatively exclusive categories applies: "This is in general the strict *either—or*, and according to it, the world
is, for example, either finite or infinite but only one of
the two."[24]

Hegel terms this attitude "dogmatism": "This metaphysics became *dogmatism* because it had to assume, in
accordance with the nature of finite determination, that
of two opposed assertions . . . one must be true and the
other false."[25] And, "Dogmatism, in the narrower sense,
consists in holding fast to one-sided determinations of
the understanding to the exclusion of the opposed
[determinations]."[26]

Since the objects of traditional metaphysics were the
infinite objects of reason, the fact that "the thought of
the old metaphysics was finite thought" doomed this
metaphysics to failure: "But the objects of reason cannot be determined by such finite predicates, and the
endeavor to do this was the defect of the old meta-

22. *Enc.*, sec. 27.
23. *Enc.*, sec. 28.
24. *Enc.*, sec. 32, Z.
25. *Enc.*, sec. 32.
26. *Enc.*, sec. 32, Z.

physics."[27] The result was "merely understanding's view of reason's objects."[28]

Hegel argues that no concept that has a fixed opposite and is thus only *one side* or a *part* of a conceptual scheme can adequately characterize the objects of metaphysics, which are *totalities*: "The dogmatism of the metaphysics of the understanding [*Verstandesmetaphysik*] consists in holding fast to *one-sided* determinations of thought in their isolation; in contrast, [the proper method of] speculative philosophy contains the *principle of totality* and reveals itself by transcending the *one-sidedness* of the abstract determinations of the understanding."[29]

Although Hegel finds in pre-Kantian metaphysics a paradigm of the futile attempt to grasp the infinite by means of finite concepts, he also thinks that there is a timeless tendency to make this mistake: "This metaphysics is something in the past, however, only in relation to the history of philosophy. In itself it is really always present—[it is] merely understanding's view of reason's objects."[30] Since our normal mode of thought is the understanding, we naturally, albeit futilely, tend to apply it to the infinite objects of metaphysics.

KANT'S CRITIQUE OF TRADITIONAL METAPHYSICS

Hegel thought that Kant had rightly called attention to the failure of traditional metaphysics but had not correctly located the reasons for this failure. [As we

27. *Enc.*, sec. 28, Z.
28. *Enc.*, sec. 27
29. *Enc.*, sec. 32, Z.
30. *Enc.*, sec. 27.

possibility of metaphysics. Hegel, on the contrary, allows for the possibility of revising or replacing this scheme, and thus allows for the possibility of metaphysics.

Kant blames the failure of the metaphysics of the understanding (*Verstandesmetaphysik*) on the impossibly ambitious aims of *metaphysics*, while Hegel blames it on the inadequacy of the finite categories of the *understanding*. Given the failure of *Verstandesmetaphysik*, metaphysical pursuits need be rejected only if the understanding is uncritically accepted. And Hegel charges that Kant failed to examine the understanding critically: "The Kantian philosophy allows the categories and methods of ordinary knowledge to remain completely uncontested."[44]

JACOBI'S REJECTION OF CONCEPTUAL KNOWLEDGE

As we have seen, Hegel interprets Jacobi's philosophy of immediate knowledge and intuition as a response to Kant's limitation of conceptual knowledge to appearances.[45] He also interprets it as a response to the problem of knowing the infinite, given finite categories of thought. Before the Critical Philosophy,

> thought [*Denken*] was credited with stripping away the finitude from sensuous representations of the Absolute, according to the . . . prejudice of all times that one reaches the truth only through reflection [*Nachdenken*]. Now at last, . . . thought has been declared to perform *only* the activity of *making things finite*. In Supplement VII to the letters concerning Spinoza, Jacobi has presented this polemic most distinctly . . .

44. *Enc.*, sec. 60.
45. See Chap. 3, "Hegel's Analysis of Subjectivity and Objectivity."

and has used it in the fight against knowledge [*Erkennen*]. In this polemic, knowledge is considered only as knowledge of the finite, as a procedure in thought from *conditioned* to *conditioned*, along a series in which everything that conditions is also conditioned—by *conditioned conditions*. In accordance with this polemic, to explain or comprehend [*begreifen*] is to show something to be *mediated* by *another*, and all content is only *specific, dependent,* and *finite*. The infinite, truth, God, lies outside the mechanism of this context, to which knowledge is limited.[46]

Since Jacobi believed that all conceptual knowledge [*Erkennen*] used categories which were conditioned or "mediated" by their fixed opposites—and thus were finite and metaphysically ineffectual—he rejected conceptual knowledge in favor of direct intuition or "immediate knowledge."[47]

Like Kant and Hegel, Jacobi accepted the impossibility of grasping the infinite objects of metaphysics with finite categories. Like Hegel, but unlike Kant, he refused to limit knowledge to finite objects and thereby deny the possibility of metaphysical knowledge. But like Kant, and unlike Hegel, he accepted the finitude of all conceptual thought. Therefore Jacobi, unlike Hegel, was forced to find knowledge of the infinite outside conceptual thought.

THE MERITS OF THE UNDERSTANDING

Although Hegel considers the understanding's isolated, opposed, finite categories inadequate for meta-

46. *Enc.*, sec. 62.
47. *Enc.*, sec. 63.

physical speculation about infinite objects, he does not reject these categories *tout court*. He holds that infinite objects cannot be grasped by finite categories, but that finite objects not only can, but can only be grasped by finite categories. Juxtaposed to his criticism of the old metaphysics for trying to determine the objects of reason with finite predicates, we find: "To be sure, concerning finite things, it is the case that they must be determined by finite predicates. Here the activity of the understanding is in its proper place. The understanding, being itself finite, knows, however, only the nature of the finite."[48] And in arguing that "the laws of inference which really serve a major function of the understanding" are "unusable" for higher forms of truth, he admits that it is "unjust to disregard that they have their field of knowledge within which they must be valid."[49]

When McTaggart argues that Hegel shows the categories of the understanding to generate contradictions wherever they are applied, he disregards the important Hegelian distinction between the unobjectionable, and even necessary, application of finite categories to finite objects and their contradiction-generating misapplication to the infinite objects of metaphysics: "The examination of a certain category leads us to the conclusion that, *if we predicate it of any subject*, we are compelled by consistency to predicate of the same subject the contrary of that category."[50] McTaggart erroneously sug-

48. *Enc.*, sec. 28, Z.
49. *Logic*, 1:17–18.
50. *Studies in Hegelian Dialectic* (London, 1896), 2d ed., 1922, p. 1 (my italics).

gests that, for Hegel, all employment of these categories, even in ordinary nonphilosophical contexts, is illicit and that to employ them even in ordinary ways "we must contrive for a time to arrest the [contradiction-generating] dialectic movement."[51]

Hegel argues that the necessary function of the understanding, its peculiar virtue, is to make clear, precise categorizations and distinctions.

> First of all, the rights and merits of even that thought which belongs merely to the understanding [*dem bloß verständigen Denken*] must be conceded. They consist in the fact that without the understanding neither constancy nor precision is attained in either the theoretical or practical realms. First, in theory, knowledge begins by comprehending the objects present to it according to their precise differences. In the study of nature for example, matter, forces, genera, etc., are differentiated, and each is fixed in its isolation.[52]

Because the categories of the understanding are not infinite, they are not sufficient for philosophy. But because only they are definite, they are necessary for philosophy: "After the preceding exposition, the fact that finally even philosophy is unable to do without the understanding scarcely requires to be specially mentioned. The most crucial thing for philosophizing is that every thought is comprehended in its full precision, and that one does not rest satisfied with anything vague or indeterminate."[53]

51. Ibid., p. 11.
52. *Enc.*, sec. 80, Z.
53. Ibid.

Since only the understanding can make precise categorizations and distinctions, to reserve it no role in
philosophy is to abandon philosophy to feeling and intuition. In the *Vorbegriff* to the *Encyclopedia* this
abandonment of conceptual thought is discussed as the
"Third Attitude of Thought to Objectivity" and exemplified by Jacobi's philosophy. There, Hegel presents
the view as a natural but unsatisfactory response to
Kant's limitations of knowledge to appearances and to
finite objects.[54]

Earlier, in the preface to the *Phenomenology*, both
the popularity and unacceptability of the view that "the
Absolute is not supposed to be grasped conceptually
[*begriffen*] but felt and intuited,"[55] had been major
themes. There, rather than explicitly identifying the
view with Jacobi or any other figure, Hegel presents it
as a general tendency of the time, as "a notion and its
consequences that are as presumptuous as they are
widely accepted in our times."[56] And rather than sympa-
thetically tracing the motivation and genesis of this
view, Hegel devotes his energies to a polemic against it.[57]

In this attack on intuitionist philosophy Hegel elab-

54. See above, pp. 64–66, 127–28.
55. *PG*, p. 13. Hegel also refers to it as the view that "the truth exists
only *in*, or rather only *as*, that which is sometimes called intuition, sometimes immediate knowledge of the Absolute, religion, or being" (p. 12).
56. *PG*, p. 12. (Kaufman's translation, p. 374, my italics). Lasson
suggests that Hegel was referring to "Jacobi, the romantics, Schlegel, and
Schleiermacher."
57. However, in the following sentence Hegel adumbrates the clearer
Encyclopedia presentation of the view as a response to the problem of
knowing the infinite: "This prophetic talk . . . glances scornfully at determinateness (the *Horos*) and intentionally keeps its distance from the
concept and from necessity—identifying these with reflection, which
dwells in finitude" (*PG*, p. 15).

orately argues the indispensability of the understanding for philosophy. First, since the "analysis" of a notion involves differentiating its elements, and "the activity of differentiation [*Scheidens*] is the strength and work of the understanding,"[58] only the understanding can analyze our ordinary, subphilosophic notions and sensuous representations (our *Vorstellungen*). Hegel enthusisastically praises the understanding's capacity for analysis as "the most amazing and greatest, or rather the absolute power" and as "the enormous power of the negative."[59]

Second, Hegel associates the understanding (*Verstand*) with general intelligibility (*Verständlichkeit*), that is, with public accessibility. He argues that with the removal of the understanding's analyses, categorizations, and distinctions, philosophical truth becomes esoteric in the objectionable sense that no amount of intelligence and effort necessarily provide access to it. He laments the lack of the understanding's "development of the form whereby distinctions are determined with certainty and ordered in firm relationships," and then laments the consequences: "Without this development, science sacrifices general intelligibility and has the appearance of being an esoteric possession of a few individuals. . . . Only what is completely determined is also exoteric, comprehensible [*begreiflich*], and capable of being learned, and thus the possession of all."[60] Hegel is not merely trading on the similarity of *Verstand* and

58. *PG*, p. 29.
59. Ibid.
60. *PG*, p. 16.

Verständlichkeit. If philosophical truth is revealed only by a special intuition which not all men possess, this truth is, indeed, esoteric and not publicly accessible.

Hegel is well aware that the intellectual demands of philosophy are too rigorous for most people. Analysis requires "the seriousness, pain, patience, and work of the negative."[61] Trying to operate in the philosophical realm of abstract concepts (*Begriffe*) rather than with the usual notions and sensuous images (*Vorstellungen*) is, like "the attempt to walk on one's head," unusual, difficult and seemingly unnecessary.[62] But while Hegel finds it acceptable and predictable that philosophical truth be inaccessible to sloth and stupidity, he rejects any view on which philosophical truth may remain inaccessible to effort and intelligence.

Although reason (*Vernunft*), the mode of thought appropriate to philosophy, is different from understanding (*Verstand*), the ordinary mode of thought common to all, we must be able to reach reason through the understanding if philosophy is to be accessible to all: "The intelligible [*verständige*] form of [philosophical] science[63] is the path to science which is offered to all and made equal for all. To reach rational knowledge [*zum vernünftigen Wissen*] through the understanding is the justified demand of the consciousness that approaches science. For the understanding is thinking, the pure ego; and the intelligible [*das Verständige*] is that which is already known and common to both science and un-

61. *PG*, p. 20.
62. *PG*, p. 25.
63. In this passage, "science" refers to scientific philosophy, not the natural sciences.

scientific consciousness—that whereby unscientific consciousness can immediately enter science.''[64]

DILEMMA AND DIALECTIC

Hegel is faced with a dilemma: the determinate and finite categories of the understanding are both indispensable and unfit for philosophic knowledge of the infinite. He must, therefore, develop a method of philosophic thought which somehow retains the fixed distinctions and oppositions necessary for conceptually determining an object, and also transcends the finitude inherent in such distinctions and oppositions. In philosophical reason, which seeks to know the infinite, the understanding's finite categories must be both preserved and negated—or, to use a term favored by Hegel just because it possesses this double meaning, *aufgehoben.*[65] If, like Kant, we simply preserve these categories, reason becomes an illicit application of finite categories to the infinite. If, like Jacobi, we simply negate them, reason becomes mere intuition or belief.

This dilemma is one important source of the method Hegel uses in the *Science of Logic* and in the shorter *Encyclopedia* version of this logic. This method, the famous *dialectic,* consists in examining the understanding's pairs of putatively opposed categories and showing that these categories, ordinarily thought to be mutually exclusive, really involve each other. They are shown to be one-sided abstractions from a concrete whole to which each belongs. Kaufmann rightly says, "That is

64. *PG,* p. 17.
65. "*Aufheben* exhibits its true double meaning . . . it negates and preserves at the same time" (*PG,* p. 90). See also, *Logic* 1:93–95.

the heart of Hegel's *Logic*; that is the meaning of its much misunderstood dialectic."[66]

However, it is not yet obvious how this dialectical analysis of categories is in part a response to the dilemma posed by the metaphysical task of knowing the infinite and the necessity of using the determinate but finite categories of the understanding for this task. I shall try to make this more apparent.

ANALYSIS AND METAPHYSICS

First, what does the analysis of categories, whether dialectical or not, have to do with traditional metaphysical speculations about the nature of ultimate reality? In introducing the *Science of Logic*, Hegel laments at length "the remarkable spectacle of a cultured people without a metaphysics."[67] And in the *Vorbegriff* to the *Encyclopedia*, he promises to remedy this situation in a logic which "coincides with metaphysics."[68] How does the analysis of categories in the *Logic* coincide with metaphysics?

Kaufmann's answer is that Hegel simply replaced traditional metaphysical speculation with conceptual analysis.

> With Hegel, metaphysics ceases to be speculation about the nature of ultimate reality. He is fond of speaking of 'speculation' and 'speculative,' but as a matter of fact *he does not speculate about things of which we could say that the time for speculation is long past because we now look to the sciences for verifiable hypothe-*

66. Kaufmann, p. 194.
67. *Logic*, 1:4.
68. *Enc.*, sec. 24.

*ses. With Hegel, analysis of categories replaces specu-
lative metaphysics.* He gives metaphysics the new
meaning and content that it still retains with some of
the best philosophers of the twentieth century.[69]

Kaufmann's answer has two virtues: it rightly calls
attention to the often ignored predominance of conceptual analysis in Hegel's *Logic*, and it also rightly
denies the unwarranted charge that Hegel was vainly
and anachronistically competing with the natural sciences. However, to cease competing with the natural
sciences and to engage in the analysis of categories is
not necessarily to abandon the traditional metaphysical
quest for knowledge of ultimate reality

Hegel thought that metaphysics should not try to
compete with the natural sciences, but not because he
thought that the natural sciences had usurped the traditional metaphysical task of speculating about the nature of ultimate reality. Natural science could usurp the
place of traditional metaphysics only if both had the
same task, and for Hegel they do not. He holds that
the natural sciences, which use the finite categories of
the understanding, are adequate to their particular task
of knowing ordinary finite objects, while traditional
metaphysics has the different task of knowing absolute
or *infinite* objects.

This traditional metaphysical task is still the task of
Hegel's *Logic*. Hegel rejects the traditional means of
metaphysics (the finite categories of the understanding), but only because he retains its end—knowledge of
the infinite, absolute, "ultimate" reality of the world,
God, the soul, and freedom.

69. Kaufmann, pp. 195–96.

The analysis of categories in Hegel's *Logic* does not replace speculative metaphysics; this analysis *is in the service of* speculative metaphysics; or rather, it *is* speculative metaphysics.

In the Introduction to the *Science of Logic*, Hegel describes his *Logic* as "the account of God, as he is in his eternal essence before the creation of nature and any finite spirit."[70] Kaufmann calls this "perhaps the maddest image in all of Hegel's writing"[71] and sensibly rejects its suggestion that the *Logic* takes us back to a time before the creation of the world. However, what concerns us here is simply Hegel's conception of his *Logic* as "the account of God" and his removal of it from the sphere of the "finite."

This passage is echoed and somewhat clarified at the beginning of the *Encyclopedia* version of the *Logic*: "Being itself, the following determinations of being, and logical determinations in general can be viewed as definitions of the Absolute, as metaphysical definitions of God."[72]

The *Encyclopedia* passage makes clear that Hegel is using "God" as an alternative theological idiom for absolute metaphysical reality, much in the way that Spinoza did. It shows that Hegel views his *Logic* not simply as an examination of categories, but as an examination of categories with respect to their adequacy as characterizations or definitions of the absolute, infinite, ultimate reality of traditional metaphysics.

This conception of the *Logic* is further reenforced

70. *Logic*, 1:31 (Kaufmann's trans., p. 195).
71. Kaufmann, p. 195.
72. *Enc.*, sec. 85.

by Hegel's historical parallels. He associates each of the first three categories of the *Logic* (*being, nothing,* and *becoming*) with a historical view which attempts to use that particular category as a *complete characterization of ultimate reality*: "First the Eleatics, especially Parmenides, pronounced the simple thought of pure being to be the absolute and the one truth. . . . It is well known that in oriental systems nothingness, the void, is the absolute principle. In opposition to those one-sided and simple abstractions the profound Heracleitos stressed the higher, total concept of becoming, and said that . . . becoming is all."[73] The examination of each of these categories is associated with the historical attempt to define absolute reality solely by means of it.

DIALECTIC AND METAPHYSICS

But even if Hegel's analysis of categories is addressed to the traditional metaphysical task of characterizing ultimate reality, how is the *dialectical form* of Hegel's analysis relevant to this task? More precisely, how is the dialectic a response to the dilemma posed by the task of knowing absolute reality, which is infinite, and the necessity of using for this task the determinate but finite categories of the understanding?

The finitude of a category, and thus its inadequacy as a definition or characterization of the Absolute, which is infinite, consists in the category's having a fixed opposite, which limits it. For example, *being* is usually opposed by *nothing, immediate* by *mediate, something* by *something else . . . (Etwas* by *ein Anderes), finite* by *infinite*. Although the pattern of Hegel's dialectical

73. *Logic*, 1:68.

analysis changes from case to case, it repeatedly attempts to argue that categories which are ordinarily thought to be mutually exclusive opposites actually involve each other. Putatively opposed categories are shown to be actually one-sided abstractions from a concrete whole of which each is only a partial aspect.

But a category that is or describes only a partial aspect of the reality of the concrete whole from which it is abstracted cannot be an adequate definition of this whole. An adequate definition of a concrete whole must include all its partial aspects. Thus, a definition is required which includes categories ordinarily considered to be mutually exclusive—a definition that not only includes these finite, one-sided abstractions, but also removes their specious incompatibility. This is accomplished by introducing as a definition a more concrete category that contains these abstractions as necessary elements. For example, the first pair of categories in the *Logic*, *being* and *nothing*, are argued to be abstractions which, contrary to ordinary opinion, do not exclude each other, and they are superseded by *becoming*, which is called "the unity of being and nothing."[74]

The dialectic *preserves* pairs of putatively opposed categories as the necessary elements (*Momente*) of more concrete categories. But as necessary elements of a more concrete category their mutually exclusive character is removed or negated. These categories are both preserved and negated—they are *aufgehoben*.

74. The analysis of the categories *finite* and *infinite* furnishes another example of this pattern. See below, pp. 141–46. Although this pattern is repeatedly used, far from all the *Logic*'s analyses follow it. It represents Hegel's *initial conception* and *ideal* of dialectical form, from which his actual analyses diverge more and more in the course of the *Logic*.

Since for Hegel the finitude of a category consists in its being excluded and thus limited by an opposed category, the removal of the mutually exclusive character of categories by the dialectic is also the removal of their finitude. Thus, the dialectic is, at least in part, a philosophic method addressed to the dilemma posed by the necessity of using the finite categories of the understanding to comprehend the infinite reality of metaphysics. The dialectic resolves this dilemma by retaining these categories while removing their finitude.

If we ignore Hegel's description of his *Logic* as the analysis of various definitions of the absolute or infinite reality of traditional metaphysics, if we ignore Hegel's insistence that the traditional search for an adequate definition of this absolute reality is still *the* philosophic task, if we view his *Logic* as merely conceptual analysis and clarification for its own sake, we cannot account as well for the *dialectical form* of this analysis, that is, for its repeated denial of the putatively opposed character of various pairs of concepts. If we ignore the traditional metaphysical motivations of Hegel's dialectic, we make it more contemporary, but only at the cost of making it less comprehensible.

The *Logic* develops by repeating, albeit in a complicated and irregular way, this dialectical pattern. Categories in which speciously incompatible abstractions are preserved as compatible and necessary elements are themselves preserved and reconciled with their putative opposites in even more concrete categories. The *Logic*, at least in its general conception, is supposed to present a series of progressively more adequate characterizations of absolute reality. Hegel says that each category subsequent to *being* and *nothing* "is to be viewed only as a *more precise determination* and *truer definition* of the Absolute."[75]

BAD INFINITY AND THE BEYOND

Since the infinity of the Absolute is a presupposition of the *Logic* and a motivation of its method, it is not surprising that in the *Logic* itself *infinity* is one of the categories considered as a definition of the absolute: "Infinity as a simple concept can be viewed to begin with, as a new definition of the Absolute."[76]

But although Hegel insists that absolute reality is infinite, he also insists that this reality cannot be adequately defined by the concept of infinity as it is ordinarily understood. Ordinarily *finite* and *infinite* are held to be mutually exclusive opposites; ordinarily infinity is held to be "the negation of something else, of the finite."[77] But, paradoxically, *infinity*, like any other concept, is finite if excluded and limited by an opposing concept: "The infinite thus delineated is one of a pair, but as only one of a pair it is itself finite. It is not the whole but only one side of the whole; it has its limit in what is opposed to it; thus it is the finite infinite."[78] Hegel calls this finite infinite "the bad infinite, the infinite of the understanding."[79] It is the infinite, but "not yet in its final truth."[80]

As with the earlier categories of being, nothing, and

75. *Enc.*, sec. 87.
76. *Logic*, 1:125.
77. *Logic*, 1:127.
78. *Logic*, 1:133.
79. *Logic*, 1:128. See also p. 125.
80. *Logic*, 1:135.

becoming, Hegel associates the category of the bad infinite with an entire metaphysics based upon it. The conceptual scheme in which the (bad) infinite is separated from the finite is identified with a metaphysics in which "there are two worlds, an infinite and a finite."[81] There is the finite world that we presently occupy, a *Diesseits*, and an infinite world beyond it, a *Jenseits*. The infinite world is "separated from" (*abgesondert*) and "placed over" the finite world, and each "is given a different place."[82]

No names are mentioned, but Hegel's language strongly echoes his discussion of Kant's notion of the thing-in-itself, his discussion of Kant's ethical theory in the section of the *Phenomenology* titled "Morality," and his discussion of the Christian world view in the section of the *Phenomenology* titled "The Unhappy Consciousness." In Hegel's philosophy the concept of a *Jenseits*, a beyond, is the leitmotiv which links Kant, Christianity, and the concept of the bad infinite.

Elsewhere, Hegel says that Kant's thing-in-itself is "simply something beyond thought" (*schlechthin ein Jenseits des Denkens*)[83] and is "determined only as a beyond" (*bestimmt nur noch als Jenseits*).[84] Here, he describes the metaphysics of the bad infinite as containing: "the finite as the determinate being of this present place and time [*das hiesige Dasein*] and the infinite, which, though taken to be the *in-itself* of the finite, is nevertheless a beyond [*ein Jenseits*] in the dim,

81. *Logic*, 1:128.
82. Ibid.
83. *Logic*, 1:25.
84. *Enc.*, sec. 44.

unreachable distance outside which the finite is located and remains."[85] In this passage, Hegel not only characterizes the bad infinite, like Kant's thing-in-itself, as a *Jenseits*, but also directly links the bad infinite with the thing-in-itself.

In the section of the *Phenomenology* titled "Morality," Hegel argues that Kant's ethical theory, because it depends heavily upon the postulation of a second noumenal world of things-in-themselves in addition to the ordinary phenomenal world of our experience, depends in an objectionable way on a world which is essentially a *Jenseits*. He argues that, since for Kant an action is moral only when it results from duty prevailing against sensual inclination, the removal of the conflict between sensual inclination and morality is paradoxically the removal of moral action. "This moral consummation in which the battle betwen morality and sensuality has ceased," "this harmony of morality and sensuality," is also the destruction of morality and thus cannot be allowed to occur, to become "present." For this reason, moral consummation is "dishonestly displaced . . . beyond [*jenseits*] consciousness at a foggy distance at which nothing can be precisely distinguished or comprehended."[86]

Hegel thinks that the noumenal world functions in Kant's ethical theory as a ruse, as an infinitely remote repository for the fulfillment of a morality which is em-

---

85. *Logic*, 1:128.
86. *PG*, pp. 438–39. Hegel typically turns ambiguity to his advantage. *Verstellen* can mean either to *displace* or to *dissemble*. As he did with *aufheben*, Hegel utilizes the several connotations of *verstellen* simultaneously. I have attempted to retain the dual connotation by translating *verstellen* as *to displace dishonestly*.

barrassingly also the annihilation of that morality. Since this world is essentially a *Jenseits*, by definition it is never present but always *beyond* the place and time at which we are. It is like *tomorrow* in the sense in which tomorrow never comes. To place an event in this world is merely a devious way of postponing it indefinitely.

> Therefore, this consummation is only a dishonest displacement of the matter, for morality would, in fact, abandon itself in this consummation, for morality is only consciousness of the absolute purpose as the purpose in opposition to all other purposes. Thus, morality is the *activity* of this pure purpose—conscious of the interference of sensuality, of its battle with and opposition to sensuality, and of lifting itself above sensuality. That this consciousness is not serious about moral consummation is immediately made clear when it dishonestly displaces this consummation to infinity, i.e., asserts that morality is never consummated.[87]

Hegel, in his discussion of the "Unhappy Consciousness," characterizes the Christian idea of an afterlife much in the same way that he characterizes Kant's noumenal world. In this afterlife, ordinarily referred to in German as *Jenseits*, goals frustrated on earth are supposed to be fulfilled. But because it is by definition an "unreachable beyond [*das unerreichbare Jenseits*], which flees, or rather has already fled, every attempt to grasp it,"[88] the hope it offers is spurious: "Where it is sought it cannot be found, because it is supposed to be

87. *PG*, p. 439.
88. *PG*, p. 164. In the *Logic* the bad infinite is described as an "empty flight" (1:135) and as "the Unreachable" which is "supposed to be unreachable" (1:138).

a beyond, the kind of thing which cannot be found."[89] Christian afterlife offers the false promise of reward in a tomorrow which by definition is always one day distant.

Hegel considers the bad infinite, Kant's noumenal world of things-in-themselves, and the Christian afterlife each to be essentially a *Jenseits*, and he treats the Kantian and Christian cosmologies as variants of the same basic metaphysic of the bad infinite, in which there are two worlds. He rejects the bad infinite as a definition of the absolute and infinite reality of metaphysics because it is only a finite infinite. But this rejection is reenforced by his distaste for what he takes to be self-deception and even dishonesty in both the Christian and Kantian postulations of a transcendent world. Even as Hegel rejects the bad infinite, he insists on the great philosophical importance of finding a true infinite: "*What alone matters* is not to take for the infinite that which by its very determination is made into something particular and finite. For this reason we here directed our thorough attention to this distinction; *the basic concept* [*Grundbegriff*] *of philosophy, the true infinite*, depends upon it."[90]

The limitation of the *infinite* by an opposed *finite* must be removed by removing their independent and opposed character and preserving them as interdependent elements in a higher category, which is—having removed the opposition limiting the infinite—*the true infinite*. In this process, the *independent reality* of both the finite and the bad infinite, which is also finite, is denied, and they are shown to be merely one-sided ab-

89. Ibid.
90. *Enc.*, sec. 95 (my italics).

stractions from a more concrete whole. Thus Hegel says that they are shown to be "something untrue, something *ideal*,"[91] and that "this ideality of the finite is the *main point* [*Hauptsatz*] *of philosophy*."[92]

It should now be clear that the need for a category which can adequately characterize the *infinite* reality of metaphysics is one of the major motivations of Hegel's *Logic* and its dialectical method.

PASSION IN THE LOGIC

Walter Kaufmann finds Josiah Royce's phrase "logic of passion" to be a felicitous expression for the spirit of the dialectic in the *Phenomenology*. Kaufmann has in mind the *Phenomenology's* passionate attempt to push each form of consciousness, each world view, as far as possible, finally exhausting it and revealing its errors and limitations. He says, "Goethe was not only close to the spirit of the dialectic of the *Phenomenology* but probably influenced it profoundly when he wrote in his great *Bildungsroman*, *Wilhelm Meister*: 'Not to keep from error is the duty of the educator of men, but to guide the erring one, even to let him swill his error out of full cups—that is the wisdom of teachers.' "[93]

It is true, as Kaufmann says, that Royce makes much the same point about the dialectic as a general method not limited to Hegel: "Without erring, and transcending our error, we, as sometimes suggested by the Socratic irony, simply cannot become wise. . . . Error is not a mere accident of the untrained intellect, but a

91. *Enc.*, sec. 95.
92. Ibid (my italics).
93. Kaufmann, p. 170.

necessary stage or feature or moment of the truth as it is in itself."[94] But Kaufmann fails to make clear that, when Royce uses the phrase "logic of passion" a few pages later, he does not use it to mean what Kaufmann does. For Kaufmann, the *Phenomenology's* dialectic is itself a passionate procedure—this logic of passion is a passionate logic. Royce, on the other hand, is merely claiming that our emotions or passions are often contradictory or dialectical; his idea of a logic of passion is merely a logic modeled upon the contradictory character of our passions.

Royce is trying to explain the genesis of the "so-called dialectical or antithetical method." He argues that interest in the correctness of such a method could not arise unless one "had cases of apparently dialectical or antithetical thinking before his mind," and also that "the idealists believed themselves to be in possession of such cases."[95] He cites the "rapid and contradictory changes of popular opinion and social action" of the age—for example, "the outcome of the Revolution [of 1789, which intended to secure individual freedom] was a military despotism"—as "the first class of *illustrations.*"[96] Then he cites our emotions as a second class of illustrations of contradiction: "Of course this obvious instance of the revolutionary tendencies awakened the reflections of our philosophers. But the instance did not stand alone. All the greater emotions are dialectical. The tragedies of the storm and stress period, and of the classical and romantic literature, are portrayals of this

94. Royce, p. 79.
95. Ibid.
96. Pp. 81–82 (my italics).

contradictory logic of passion. . . . The fascination and power of Byron are due to his *contradictions*. Because of the loftiness of his emotional demands upon life he finds only triviality and failure."[97]

Royce then contrasts the passions or "passive emotions" to the "active will" and asserts that the will *better* illustrates the dialectic: "It is easy to say that all such phenomena express precisely the unreasonableness of the emotions. But a closer view shows that this dialectical tendency belongs rather to the active will than to the mere emotions."[98]

Royce cites the passions or emotions only as one of several illustrations of contradiction and as one of several models for the dialectical method, in which contradiction is a crucial element.

In discussing the virtues of the dialectic, Royce, like Kaufmann, points to the pedagogical worth of embracing and then transcending erroneous views. But unlike Kaufmann, Royce does not insist that these views be *passionately* embraced in order to reveal their error. To use Goethe's words, Royce asserts that "not to keep from error is the duty of the educator of men," but neglects to mention that one should "swill his error out of full cups."[99]

Kaufmann says only that "logic of passion" is "a fine phrase" and "a very suggestive phrase." However, by not making clear that what the phrase suggests to him

97. Pp. 82–83 (my italics).
98. P. 83.
99. Royce actually cites Goethe's *Wilhelm Meister*, but only for its contradictions: "There is a glory in winning all by abandoning all. Wilhelm Meister, like Saul, sets out to seek asses and finds a Kingdom" (p. 83).

is not what Royce meant by it, he undermines the originality of his own excellent suggestion that the *Phenomenology* not only uses a logic modeled on passions (emotions) but is itself a passionate logic.

Unfortunately, while Kaufmann thinks it enlightening to view the *Phenomenology* as a logic of passion, he fails to see passion in Hegel's *Logic*: "The dialectic of the *Logic* is somewhat different from the dialectic of the *Phenomenology*: one could not possibly call it a logic of passion."[100] I want to argue, however, that Hegel's *Logic* is a "logic of passion" in exactly that sense of the phrase suggested by Kaufmann.

In support of his position, Kaufmann cites Hegel: "The system of Logic is the realm of shadows, the world of simple essences [*Wesenheiten*], freed from all sensuous concretion. . . . Here it pursues tasks remote from sensuous intuitions and aims, from feelings. . . ."[101] Kaufmann concludes:

> Hegel still confronts us as another Odysseus: in the *Phenomenology* we follow his Odyssey, the spirit's great voyage in search of a home where it might settle down; in the *Logic* we are asked to follow him into a realm of shadows. There we moved in a world where the passions had their place; here the passions are left behind. We are to contemplate Concepts and categories—and see them as one-sided abstractions and mere shadows that are not what they seem.[102]

Admittedly, the *Logic* deals with abstract concepts rather than passions or emotions. But the treatment of

100. Kaufmann, p. 194.
101. *Logic*, 1:41 (Kaufmann's translation, p. 194).
102. Kaufmann, p. 194.

abstract concepts in the *Logic* is like the treatment of concrete forms of consciousness in the *Phenomenology*, just in that respect which makes the dialectic of the *Phenomenology* a passionate procedure. The passion of the *Phenomenology* consists in its completely unreserved embracing of each form of consciousness in turn —in its attempt to find in each a completely adequate way of relating to the world. Similarly, the passion of the *Logic* consists in its attempt to find, in each abstract category considered, the basis of a complete cosmology, an entire metaphysics, an adequate "definition of the absolute." In both the *Phenomenology* and the *Logic*, the passion of Hegel's dialectic lies in its attempts to find in each successive category or form of consciousness the ultimate answer to ultimate problems.

APPENDIX

Contents of the
Phenomenology of the Spirit

Preface
Introduction

BIBLIOGRAPHY

Ayer, A. J. *The Problem of Knowledge*. Edinburgh and New York: Penguin Books Inc., 1956.

Ewing, A. C. *A Short Commentary on Kant's Critique of Pure Reason*. 2d ed. London: Methuen, and Chicago: University of Chicago Press, 1950. Paperback reprint, Chicago: Phoenix Books.

Findlay, John N. *Hegel: A Re-examination*. London and New York, 1958. Paperback reprint, New York: Collier.

Hegel, Georg Wilhelm Friedrich. *Enzyklopädie der philosophischen Wissenschaften im Grundriße* (1830). Edited by Friedhelm Nicolin and Otto Pöggeler. Hamburg: Felix Meiner, 1959. Translated by William Wallace, part 1 as *The Logic of Hegel* (2d rev. ed., Oxford, 1892), part 3 as *Hegel's Philosophy of Mind* (Oxford, 1894).

―――. *Grundlinien der Philosophie des Rechts*. Edited by Johannes Hoffmeister. Hamburg: Felix Meiner, 1955. Translated by T. M. Knox as *Philosophy of Right* (Oxford, Oxford University Press, 1942).

―――. *Hegels theologische Jugendschriften, nach den Handschriften der Kgl. Bibliothek in Berlin*. Edited by Herman Nohl. Tübingen: Verlag von J. C. B. Mohr, 1907. Translated by T. M. Knox as *Early Theological Writings*, with an introduction and fragments translated by Richard Kroner (Chicago: University of Chicago Press, 1948).

―――. *Phänomenologie des Geistes*. Edited by Johannes Hoffmeister. Hamburg: Felix Meiner, 1952. Translated by J. B. Baillie as *The Phenomenology of Mind* (2 vols. London: George Allen & Unwin, and New York: Macmillan, 1910; 2d rev. ed., in one vol., ibid., 1931). Preface translated by Walter Kaufmann in *Hegel* (see below).

―――. *Sämtliche Werke: Jubiläumsausgabe*. 20 vols. Edited by Hermann Glockner. Stuttgart: Fromann, 1927–30. Supplemented by a very useful 4-vol. *Hegel-Lexikon* (1935–39; 2d rev. ed. in 2 vols., 1957).

———— *Die Vernunft in der Geschichte*. Edited by Johannes Hoffmeister. Hamburg: Felix Meiner, 1955.

————. *Wissenschaft der Logik*. Edited by Georg Lasson. 2 vols. Hamburg: Felix Meiner, 1923. Translated by W. H. Johnston and L. G. Struthers as *Science of Logic* (2 vols., London: George Allen and Unwin, 1929).

Hume, David. *Dialogues Concerning Natural Religion* (1779). New York: Hafner Publishing Company, 1948.

Kant, Immanuel. *Kritik der reinen Vernunft* (*Original-Ausgabe* A, 1781; B, 1787). Edited by Raymond Schmidt. Hamburg: Felix Meiner, 1930. Translated by Norman Kemp Smith as *Critique of Pure Reason* (1929; rev. ed., 1933; reprinted, London: Macmillan, and New York: St. Martin's, 1958).

————. *Prolegomena zu einer jeden zukünftigen Metaphysik* (1783). Edited by Karl Vorländer. Leipzig: Felix Meiner, 1926. Translated by Lewis White Beck as *Prolegomena to Any Future Metaphysics* (New York: Library of Liberal Arts, 1950).

Kaufmann, Walter A. *From Shakespeare to Existentialism*. Boston: Beacon Press, 1959. See especially chaps. 7, 8, and 9, "The Hegel Myth and Its Method," "The Young Hegel and Religion," and "Hegel: Contribution and Calamity."

————. *Hegel: Reinterpretation, Texts, and Commentary*. Garden City, N.Y.: Doubleday, 1965.

Khayyam, Omar. *The Rubaiyat*. Translated by Edward Fitzgerald, 1851. Reprinted, Garden City, N.Y.: Doubleday, 1952.

Kroner, Richard. *Von Kant bis Hegel*. 2 vols. Tübingen: Mohr, 1921.

Marcuse, Herbert. *Reason and Revolution: Hegel and the Rise of Social Theory*. Oxford, 1941. 2d ed., New York, 1955. Reprint, New York: Beacon Paperback, 1960.

McTaggart, J. M. E. M. *Studies in the Hegelian Dialectic*. Cambridge: At the University Press, 1896.

Mure, G. R. G. *An Introduction to Hegel*. Oxford: At the Clarendon Press, 1940.

Myers, Henry Alonzo. *The Spinoza-Hegel Paradox*. Ithaca: Cornell University Press, 1944.

Neurath, Otto. *Erkenntnis*. Leipzig: Felix Meiner, 1932.

Nietzsche, Friedrich. *The Portable Nietzsche*. Edited and translated by Walter Kaufmann. New York: Viking Press, 1954.

Quine, Willard Van Orman. *Methods of Logic*. New York: Holt, 1950.

———. *Word and Object*. Cambridge, Mass.: M.I.T. Press, 1960.

Reps, Paul, ed. *Zen Flesh, Zen Bones*. Garden City, N.Y.: Doubleday, 1961.

Royce, Josiah. *Lectures on Modern Idealism*. New Haven: Yale University Press, 1919. Paperback reprint, ibid., 1964.

Ryle, Gilbert. *The Concept of Mind*. New York: Barnes and Noble, 1949.

Sartre, Jean-Paul. *Being and Nothingness*. Translated by Hazel Barnes. New York: The Philosophical Library, 1956.

Spinoza, Baruch. *Ethics*. Translated by R. H. M. Elwes. New York: Dover Publications, 1951.

Stace, W. T. *The Philosophy of Hegel: A Systematic Exposition*. London, 1924. Paperback reprint, New York: Dover Publications, 1955.

Strawson, P. F. *Individuals: An Essay in Descriptive Metaphysics*. London: Methuen, 1959.

Ziff, Paul. *Semantic Analysis*. Ithaca, Cornell University Press, 1960.

INDEX

Absolute: absolute knowledge, 4, 5, 31, 71, 111; absolute objects, 111, 112, 136; absolute power, 132; absolute reality, 136, 138–41 passim, 145; absolute truth, 47–48, 54–55, 61; the Absolute, 47–48, 51–52, 111, 112, 127, 131 n. 55 137, 138, 141

Abstraction: from concrete whole, 134, 139, 145–46. Abstract character of all thought, 92; abstract character of Hegel's *Logic*, 149–50; abstract nature of the thing-in-itself, 77–78

Accident, 35, 86; and essence, 108–9

Action, 12, 26, 29–37 passim, 43, 45, 144. *See also* Theory and practice

Aesthetic evaluations, 86–87, 88

Antinomies, 121–24

Aristotle, 49

Arnauld, Antoine, 38

Art, 4, 7, 73, 88

Asceticism, 41–42

Aufheben, 134, 139, 143 n

Aurelius, Marcus, 29

Autonomy, 14, 20, 28–33 passim, 42–46, 74–75. *See also* Independence; Self-sufficiency

Ayer, A. J., 36 n, 57

Being, nothing, becoming, 80, 138–39, 141–42

Berkeley, George, 64 n

Buddhism, 40, 42

Byron, 148

Christianity, 40–42 passim, 141–46 passim

Concepts (*Begriffe*), 27, 77, 113, 128, 131 n. 57, 133, 149–50

Conceptual analysis, 54–55, 58, 84–85, 97, 132, 135–38, 140

Consciousness: forms of, 4, 6, 8 n, 10, 102, 150; sec. A of *Phenomenology*, 8–9, 27, 43; use of term in *Phenomenology*, 8 n

Contradiction, 4, 35, 116, 122, 123, 129–30, 147–48

Descartes: 62; Cartesian concept of mind, 78

Desire (*Begierde*), 12, 14, 15, 18, 20, 26

Dialectic, 16, 130, 134–35, 138–41 passim, 146–50

Dogmatism, 119, 120

Eleatics, 138

Empiricism, 32, 56 n, 62, 63, 102, 111

Epictetus, 29

Esotericism, 132–33

Essence: 90, 110, 123, 137, 149; and accident, 108–9

Ethics, 6, 7, 73; Kant's, 4, 141–46 passim; skeptical rejection of, 35–37; ethical evaluation, 86–87

External object or world: affecting it through action, 26; attempt to know it, 27; its negation by self-consciousness, 11–17 passim, 20, 22; as object of empirical knowledge, 32; skeptic's denial of, 34–36; stoic's independence of, 29

157

158 ~ INDEX

Ewing, A. C., 80 n

Fear, 21, 24
Fichte, 65 n, 67, 68, 78, 83
Findlay, J. N., 7, 10, 15–17, 18, 23
Freedom: identity of with truth, 44–46, 73–75; as object of metaphysical speculation, 111, 115, 136; stoic concept of, 28–34 passim. *See also* Autonomy; Independence
Freud, 12, 31, 41

God, 96, 111, 114, 119, 122, 136, 137
Goethe, *Wilhelm Meister*, 146, 148

Hamlet, 34
Hegel:
  Difference between the Fichtean and Schellingian systems of philosophy, 67
  Encyclopedia of the Philosophical Sciences: 3, 32, 47, 50, 53, 59, 61, 69, 75, 134, 137; *Vorbegriff* of, 61–66 passim, 82, 84, 131, 135
  History of Philosophy, 50, 62, 64 n
  Phenomenology of the Spirit, 50, 61, 102; A. "Consciousness," 8–9, 27, 43; its dialectic, 146–50 passim; general program, 4–7; Introduction, 51–55; as introduction to Hegel's system, 69–70; VI. C. "Morality," 141–46 passim; overall function of, 71–73; Preface, 62, 82, 131; C. (AA) "Reason," 43; B. "Self-consciousness," 7–46 passim; A. I. "Sense-certainty, the this, and opinion," 92–103 passim

Science of Logic, 3, 50, 53, 55, 59, 61, 69, 75, 97, 134, 135, 137
Heracleitos, 138
Hume, David; 64; *Dialogues Concerning Natural Religion*, 38, 39

Idealism: post-Kantian, 65 n, 83; subjective, 82, 84; transcendental, 83. Ideal as untrue, 146
Immediate knowledge, 62, 64–66, 127
Independence, 14, 28–29, 43–46 passim. *See also* Autonomy; Freedom
Ineffability, 65, 102–3, 108
Intersubjectivity, 86–87, 91, 101, 107, 108
Intuition, 64, 131, 134

Jacobi, 64, 83, 127–28, 131, 134
Jenseits (beyond, afterlife), 12, 41, 57, 77, 83, 125, 141–46

Kant: ethical theory of, 4, 141–46 passim; as idealist, 83–84; importance of, for Hegel, 48–51; on metaphysics, 111–13 passim, 120–27; spirit and letter of, 67–68; on subjectivity and objectivity, 82–91; things-in-themselves, 43, 46, 48–81 passim, 142–43; treatment of, in *Vorbegriff* to *Enc.*, 62–66 passim, 84; on understanding and reason, 113–16; on universality and necessity, 91, 106–8

Kaufmann, Walter, 4–5, 8, 10, 20, 22, 24, 49–50, 64, 134–38 passim, 146–50 passim
Khayyam, Omar, 39 n

THE INNER WORLD OF CHOICE

FRANCES G. WICKES

❧❦❧

THE INNER WORLD
OF CHOICE

HARPER & ROW, PUBLISHERS

NEW YORK, EVANSTON
AND LONDON

For quotations from the Collected Works of C. G. Jung, translated by R. F. C. Hull, acknowledgment is made to Bollingen Foundation, publishers of this edition in the United States of America.

FIRST EDITION

B-N

LIBRARY OF CONGRESS CATALOG CARD NUMBER: 63–7613

Contents

੬ঙ ৡৡ

v

IN MEMORY OF CARL G. JUNG

"The man who speaks with primordial images speaks with a thousand tongues. . . . He transmutes personal destiny into the destiny of mankind, thus evoking all those beneficent forces that have enabled mankind to find a rescue from every hazard and to outlive the longest night."

Contributions to Analytical Psychology, p. 248

Acknowledgments

❧ ❦

I wish to express my gratitude to the many persons whose generosity has contributed so significantly to this book. I am indebted especially to the individuals who have allowed me to make use of case material, to the publishers who have granted permission to reprint selections from their books, and especially to William McGuire of the Bollingen Foundation, and to M. Eleanor Stone, custodian of the Library of the Analytical Psychology Club. I am indebted also to Monica McCall, and to Edith Noss for her assistance in preparing the manuscript. And my special thanks go to Muriel Rukeyser for her sustained interest in the manuscript and her invaluable research on source material.

Foreword

⋅≈§ ξ≈⋅

This remarkable book, composed by a remarkable woman at the age of eighty-seven, is the consummation of some forty years of practice and reflection devoted to guiding individuals out of the distressful states of mind in which they came to her for help.

Frances G. Wickes became famous in the twenties, near the start of her dauntless and singularly successful career in psychotherapy, when an ever-expanding circle of readers took *The Inner World of Childhood* to their hearts as the product of an unusually astute, penetrating, and humane intelligence, one that was in such close touch with the multifarious trends and turns of a child's fabulous imaginations that the discernment of their meanings seemed to come to her without a struggle as a gift of grace. And now, in the sixties, at the termination of her career, we find her wondrous intuitions, abundant, subtle, sharp, and fresh as ever, operating on a deeper level in this richest of her written works, *The Inner World of Choice*.

As its title tells us, the author is still preoccupied with the interior, experiential aspect of the development of personalities, with covert being and becoming rather than with overt action and achievement; but now the time span of her concern includes maturity as well as childhood, and whereas in her first book the influence of Jung was in the offing, here his shaping hand is everywhere, seen or unseen. As maker and propounder of personological principles and concepts he is the writer's trusted rock of explicit theoretical reference; and as discriminator of the better from the worse, he is her implicit and almost all-pervasive source of inspiration. In fact, this last book, completed

for his sake and in his name, constitutes a testifying tribute to the charismatic power of his thought. As consequence of her seasons of training and her subsequent friendship through the years with the "Wise Old Man" of Zurich and of her appreciative inward understanding of the significance and use of his ideas, Frances Wickes is certainly as qualified as anybody in America to show, as she does here, with attention focused in each instance on what is most salient and crucial, how the seminal intellections of the Master may be most fruitfully applied at timely moments in the therapeutic process.

In her own nature and endowments, however, Frances Wickes is an "original," whose rare degree of special talents—manifestations of the "feminine principle" in pure form—are copiously displayed in this volume, the choicest parts of which consist of terse, dramatic presentations of occasions for decision arising in the course of psychological maturation. In their concreteness, vividness, intimacy, and power to generate suspense, these short short stories surpass anything of this genre that Jung has published and they can be read with wonder, relish, and much personal profit without getting entangled in the proffered web of Jungian abstractions. That is to say, to derive enjoyment and illumination from these abbreviated case reports, the reader does not have to be a Jungian therapist or even congenially at home with Jungian terminology.

Each of the recounted episodes is a micro parable insofar as it exhibits in narrative form the better of two possible choices in a confounding situation; and it is a micro myth to the extent that it contains the essential components of a fundamental type of conflict which, however different in its manifest specific features, will be experienced, consciously or unconsciously, by virtually every human being, and furthermore, by portraying a beneficent solution of that conflict, provides a model of choice for whoever in a similar dilemma has the wit and courage to be invited by it. The mythic quality of these narratives of dispositional antitheses and syntheses is intensified by the tone of the author's metaphors and quotations and by the aphoristic manner in which she communicates her judgments. Hers is the voice of an authentic seer.

The author's numerous case stories are embedded in chapters devoted to extensive, though necessarily indefinite, expositions of the elusive Jungian concepts in terms of which the various types of conflict are defined, concepts such as: conscious and unconscious, animus

or anima, persona and shadow, extraversion and introversion, superior function and inferior function, self (ego) and Self, masculine principle and feminine principle, thinking and feeling. Dispositional clashes are also represented by such opposites as: power *vs.* love, social (especially parental) pressures *vs.* the individual's own path, superficiality *vs.* depth, personal *vs.* superpersonal.

Some of these types of conflict are linked to the ages of life in which they usually occur in Western cultures; but no invariable chronological sequence is proposed. Too much depends on chance, environmental factors, and individual capacities and peculiarities, on whether, for example, a personal problem is permanently solved when it comes up in adolescence, or, after being sidetracked, reappears in a new guise, or persists unchanged to burden the years of adulthood. Theoretically and ideally considered, however, the temporal relations of the choice-points that the author so graphically describes are consonant with the general conception of genetically determined cycles of personological transformation, somewhat analogous to the largely predetermined series of somatic transformations. The phases of each successive cycle in which the author is evidently most interested are these: (1) the maintenance of an established system of values and of action (commonly implanted by the parents), which, if prolonged beyond its limited season of utility and fruitfulness, will not uncommonly result in zestless repetition, rigidity, stagnation, apathy, and discontent; (2) the emergence of a new potentiality, value, opportunity, or challenge, which, being opposed by the established system, generates (3) an internal conflict, a conflict, the author insists, that should be faced and settled by a conscious choice for which the chooser takes personal responsibility. As a rule, only a choice that favors the embracement and incorporation of the new potentiality will result in (4) a beneficial enlargement and reconstruction of the self, a virtual rebirth, that is attended by an illuminating extension of consciousness. In other, briefer terms, the successive phases are as follows: a restricted sameness (*thesis*) punctuated by a birth of novelty (*antithesis*) that endangers the stability of the existing ego system and thus initiates a state of conflict, temporary or protracted, of which the happiest issue is a unifying *synthesis* which establishes a new level and circumference of being. Illustrations of different versions of this sequence are plentiful in the pages that await the reader.

According to the Jungian hypothesis or assumption to which the au-

thor wholeheartedly subscribes, each transition phase in the progressive unfoldings of the self is (theoretically and ideally) marked by the constellation of an "archetype," the emergence of which is made known to those who are prepared to understand its meaning by the appearance in a dream, fantasy, or vision of a mythic image or mythic imagent (imaged event), which in many instances represents either the salient features of the person's present situation or the choice that will advance his personality to the next level of its developmental history. These archetypes—carriers of generations of primitive mentations and experiences, ancient personifications of internal and of external powers, gods of our distant forebears—are conceived to be the directors and stage managers of the interior serial drama that each of us is destined to live out, wittingly or unwittingly, as it proceeds.

In addition to the multiplicity of absorbing case stories, supplemented by an abundance of illuminating and sagacious comments, in conjunction with explications of the dynamic meanings of the concepts illustrated by the described experiences, we find in *The Inner World of Choice* an implicit set of values—the components of an individual philosophy of life or faith—that is amply exemplified by the conflict-settling decisions which are set forth as right, good, or, at least, better than their alternatives.

This set of values is founded first of all on a firm allegiance to the above-discussed conception of individual development, that is, on a belief in the existence in every person of a galaxy of potentialities for growth marked by a succession of personological evolutions in interaction with environments. These potentialities and their unfoldings constitute the major determinant of a person's destiny, one which may be blocked, impeded, or facilitated both by circumstance and by the choice, or the choice of choices, that the person makes at each transition point. The choices that are preferred by Frances Wickes are those that are consonant with this determinant of destiny, those that go with the grain of maturation rather than against it, since this is nature's way, the way to completion, the way to the ultimate expression and fulfillment of the total Self. Ripeness, wholeness, unity are all. Progression toward this end, as portrayed by the author, is achieved, for the most part, by periodic incorporations of previously excluded constituents of the Self: the repressed inferior function, the anima, the shadow, the superpersonal archetype; and, consequently, for the author, novelty, change, and creativity are values of a high

order. And since, as she views them, these fresh potentialities and opportunities for further growth are emergents from the lower, unconscious strata of the psyche, Frances Wickes is a faithful and forceful advocate of everything that is "inner"—introversion, inner experience, the inner reality, inner-directedness—and of upsurges from below, be they gales of emotion or demons of the imagination, and, of course, of courage, courage to face the worst and risk a new experiment in living.

For Frances Wickes, it seems that a balancing and guiding function is constantly fulfilled by a substantial body of uncelebrated common sense oriented by her vision of creative love as *summum bonum*. Onto a limb of Oriental inwardness growing from a trunk of primitive mythology, she has grafted, what was in her heart from the beginning, a branch of the essence of Judaeo-Christianity, the love of God and man. Is it not with this sound sense and sensibility and with these cherished ideals hovering in her head that she interprets the significance and estimates the vital value of the archetypal symbols that are constellated in the course of inner life? In any case, at the conclusion of this book there has remained in the mind of one reader a vivid vision of the world's tumultuous sea of troubles and in the middle of it all, immune to its diabolisms, a green and granite island of fearless sanity, serenity, and blessedness.

HENRY A. MURRAY

Cambridge, Massachusetts

Introduction

∽§ ইॐ

Modern man is unaware of the myth that lives itself within him, of the image, often invisible, that dynamically impels him toward choice. Yet, all unconsciously, he lives out, through his often unacknowledged desire, the myth which manifests itself in his way of meeting both inner and outer events.

Myth is not invented; it is experienced. It formulates itself from an urge to understand what has happened in the dark mystery of the past and what may happen in the unknown and unknowable future. It records the psychic history of a man or of a nation. To know the myth is to know the man. It is also to know the god worshiped by him in secret, the god of his dominant desire, his cherished value or his greatest fear, for that god rules the life that lives itself in his unconscious and strangely dominates the choices he believes are made by his conscious will.

As psychic history, myth tells of man's search for understanding of the mysteries of his own life and his experience of the world in which he finds himself. Such narrative has been handed down to us, not because of its historical accuracy, but because of its numinous, dynamic quality. It is true in a nonfactual, living way that brings man nearer to the meaning of his life. "The hollow man speaks more than he says, but the living man tells us the old, old tales of our creation and the songs of our dancing; and he tells us why we are small or mighty. We Indians must talk with the man who hears the voice of the Great Spirit."[1] For the living man speaks in myth, poetry —also in legend, which is not the story of a man, but of a quality

---

[1] Said by Mountain Lake of the Taos Pueblo, in conversation with the author.

that he embodied and that made him "small or mighty." The legend has evolved long after the hero has died, yet, since the elemental force that his legendary life made manifest is an attribute of every man, it awakens response in the minds and hearts of the hearers.

From his first gropings toward consciousness, childhood man used a mysterious image-creating potential in his effort to find answers to his first questions, whence? how? why? whither? As if in answer, vague forms emerged from the mists of his unknowing. They moved before the eye of his spirit, and the perceptions of their movements were woven into myths. Everywhere and every while, in answer to the question whence? there arose images of a dawn state, a "time before there was a time," when the first act of creation took place, the creation of light. Then images of unknown dimly perceived beginnings, which had been before light, slowly grouped themselves about the eternal question, whence? Symbols of self-begetting wholeness, of undifferentiated hermaphroditic unity, from which all life was born and to which all life returns, centered in the image of the original mother, the Great Mother.

> There was something formless yet complete
> That existed before heaven and earth;
> Without sound, without substance,
> Dependent on nothing, unchanging.
> All pervading, unfailing.
> One may think of it as the mother of all things.[2]

There was earth; there was sky; there was wind, the breath proceeding from the oneness, moving on darkness, bringing forth light; there was silence, creating the word. "Mankind asks about the origins of life, and immediately life and soul fuse into one as living psyche, power, spirit, motion, breath and the life-giving Mana. This One who stands at the beginning is the creative force contained in the uroboric unity of the World Parents, from whom it blows, begets, gives birth, moves, breathes and speaks."[3]

Then came differentiation. The creative urge, arising out of the void of solitude and silence, split apart the original undifferentiated

---

[2] Tao Teh Ching, XXV, in Waley, *The Way and Its Power*, p. 174. (Full details on any work cited in footnotes will be found in the Bibliography, p. 313.)
[3] Erich Neumann, *The Origins and History of Consciousness*, p. 22.

unity, and from the division came two, through whose union the creative urge could become manifest. "The one produced the two; the two became the three, and out of the three evolved the ten thousand things."[4]

As man became aware of the diverse ways in which these primordial forces manifested themselves, it indeed seemed as though the ten thousand things assailed him. Every stone or tree, every animal, every natural force—wind, fire, sun, moon—had its separate daemonic being. So too had dynamic emotions and psychic energies. Love and hate, fear and courage, inertia and swift movement, craft, cunning, credulity and, at the last, wisdom took on personality as gods and goddesses. These images were woven into man's psychic pattern. He did not recognize them as inborn potentials but, since they could possess and dominate him, he saw them as outer forces, gods who ruled with the same mysterious power as did sun and moon, darkness and light.

Energies arising from the secret springs of his being exerted unacknowledged power over his actions and chose for him in ways he could not comprehend. Nor, for that matter, does modern man comprehend the strength of the unconscious motives that choose for him. He may no longer see them as gods, but as qualities of his fellow man. In this way he manages to remain ignorant of the part that he himself plays in his own choices, and of the forces of the unconscious that choose for him, often against his ego-acknowledged purpose.

The gift of consciousness man fought for and fought against, or, one might say, a power within fought for him against his own desire for nondemanding unconsciousness. Necessity, a blind urge for life, an inborn desire as mysterious as the movement of the sunflower toward the sun, moved him to seek understanding. And a knower beyond his knowing spoke from within his psyche. This knower we later come to know as the Self.[5]

In the deeper layers of the psyche are all the materials and potentials from which consciousness is formed. They are inherent in the psychic structure. They are the *a priori* realities of psychic life, which exist before personal experience brings forth consciousness. In this vast amorphous region, they exist as dynamic forces, demiurgic energy

---

[4] After the Tao Teh Ching, XLII.

[5] Whenever the Self is spoken of with transpersonal meaning, the word is capitalized.

that moves into consciousness as thought substance to be formed into concept, or as emotional motivation from which feeling, with all its positive or negative possibilities, can evolve.

One cannot know the motive of one's choice or perceive the nature of what one chooses without an awareness of the action of eternal potentials that move both in the individual psyche and in the collective psyche of mankind and may be constellated in image form as archetypes.

Archetypes are pre-existent, not as definitive images but as deposits of man's innumerable reactions to typical experiences.

The form of these archetypes is perhaps comparable to the axial system of a crystal, which predetermines as it were the crystalline formation in the saturated solution, without itself possessing a material existence.[6]

Archetypes become constellated as images through man's own experience of a situation that innumerable men have faced before him, such as the encounter with the opposing or enveloping power of the Mother, the Father, the Monster; the challenge of fording the stream, of bridging the abyss. The archetypal world is a magnetic center underlying the world of images. This world of images is the world of early man, of the child, of the still unawakened adult. Most powerful is the image of the god—that is, the secretly worshiped power which holds dominion over his inner life. This may be very good or very evil, for the ancient gods of cruelty, brutality, and lust for power may arise as forces man must reckon with as existent within himself and determining his choices. He meets this unknown god on every level and, as he becomes himself created and transformed by his inner and outer life experiences, this god image also is transformed: a new god tells him of his own life's meaning, a new urge to consciousness impels him forward.

To trace the history of a man or a people we study these god-forming images. The beliefs, the passions that are the dynamism of man's inner life, the forces that impel toward life or death, move not only in the psyche of individual man, but in the life and death of societies. One cannot enslave a man or a nation until one has destroyed the god image that rules him. When his god image is captured, his power of choice is destroyed.

---

[6] C. G. Jung, "Psychological Aspects of the Mother Archetype," as quoted in Jacoby, *The Psychology of C. G. Jung*, p. 57.

The more clearly man can discern the essential meaning of the archetype appearing in relation to the time and place where he stands, the more the individual can be said to choose his own way. Slowly he discovers that underneath the conflict runs a purposive creative force, that works for him or against him as he enters or evades the conflict. This creative purpose must be experienced by each man for himself through the increasingly conscious encounter with the factors, primordial and present, that move in his own psyche. Only so is it given living reality.

The transpersonal images of the unconscious are timeless. They are primordial, fundamental and basic. They are potent factors in the emergence of consciousness. We see their action not only in myth but in the dawn of individual consciousness. Modern man may suddenly find himself confronted by the same image that overcame archaic man. It may reappear in any era and in any circumstance of life. How he meets it determines not only the form in which it will reappear but also its power to dominate or quicken his spirit. This encounter reveals the era in which his inner life is lived. We do not realize how much destiny is determined by inner time. There are no protective boundaries of time in the inner world until man has built them for himself. A troglodyte and a modern scientist may sit side by side in the subway, each unaware of the far different psychic subways in which they are traveling. The modern scientist may also be unaware of the ancient god living within him—a god capable of murder and destruction even of the world.

The symbols that are activated within the personality move in their own world of reality. They involve intensities of psychic energy and produce potent affects.

We must realize that the unconscious is not bound by our concepts of logic and of cause and effect. It fashions an image that reveals the transpersonal behind the personal, so releasing a hitherto unknown potential of psychic energy; or this image may show how an opposing force may act in a compensatory role and, if accepted, restore balance to an ego that has fallen under the domination of a ruling image. The fact that the image enters the psyche shows its reality in terms of active existence. Its power to attract, repel or fascinate may be so great as to becloud or even to usurp the reality of the outer world.

Great individuals manifest the meaning of these inner realities in the life of the world. But whether we are great or small, we must face

the typical situation that the archetype embodies. These images move in us as our psychological ancestry, our spiritual heritage. Severed from this continuity, man is hung up in the immediate with nothing under his feet. His adaptation—and he must adapt—lacks the integrating power of the greater memory and the greater will. In the encounter of consciousness with the unconscious, tensions are produced—conflicts out of which new awareness comes. This energy often finds its expression without regard to the demands or controls of consciousness. It activates elements or entities within the psyche that live a life of their own, enacting a drama where they choose their own parts. William James describes this drama as the relatedness or lack of relatedness of a multiplicity of selves within the psyche. Jung names and defines these entities: the ego, the persona, the shadow, the anima, the animus—all as factors that may move toward wholeness or may act in defiance of the integration of the personality if they assume a central role that is not their own. Since they will appear so often in this volume as creatures who consciously or unconsciously choose for us, I venture to redefine them.

The ego is the central figure of the conscious personality. It is the "I" of whom we are aware in our waking life. It is also the "I" who in most of our dreams perceives the movement of the actors. It develops from inner and outer experience, moving toward the activation of inner images in introversion and toward action in extraverted experience. Its choices of what it accepts or rejects seem to be governed by a mysterious instinctive process operative from the beginning, a process which Erich Neumann has called centroversion, a power invested in the germ of life through which it selects that which agrees with its own nature. Even in the embryonic stage, the central germ chooses, somatically at first, then with increasing consciousness as the ego comes into being. The human child is more at the mercy of parental choice and environmental custom, yet, even in childhood, this power of centroversion resides within the self. As life develops, choices must be made in the worlds both of personal and transpersonal experience. In this greater world "ego consciousness evolves by passing through a series of 'eternal images' and the ego, transformed in the passage, is constantly experiencing a new relation to the archetypes."[7] This is true historically and personally. The degree of development might be said to depend upon "the degree of permeability of the ego to the archetypal experience."

---

[7] Neumann, *op. cit.*, p. xvi.

But the ego must meet the outer world; it must adapt to the demands of daily reality. It must develop in ways acceptable to its environment and to society. It must put on a good face, a mask used by the ego, more or less successfully, to cover inner reactions and to present to the world a picture of itself that it desires others to see. This mask, known as the persona, may suitably or unsuitably portray the real nature of the ego. The persona has acquired a bad name, but it is as necessary as clothing. Without its protection man may become a nuisance to himself and to society. A man, finding the world unsympathetic toward his gauche self-revelations, dreams:

I am at a large gathering. I notice everyone avoids with disgust an unattractive creature who occupies the center of the room, waving its head about to attract attention. It has a thin skin through which you can see its innards working. It is a turtle that has come out without its shell. I think, how indecent of it.[8]

It is only when the persona denies the truth of the inner man that it becomes a secret enemy of the ego. Then the ego identifies with the ideal image that it believes to be identical with its own reality.

When the ego looks into the mirror held up by the persona, it beholds only its own shining face; but if an invisible hand turns the mirror inward, the ego perceives its own dark brother, the shadow. If the ego continues to look, it will see the actions of this blood brother who thrives on all the negative, because neglected, elements that the persona has repressed from consciousness. If the ego continues to look, it will see not only these neglected elements but the values they contain hidden in their own darkness. Still facing the shadow, the ego can discern images of other entities over whom the shadow has exerted control. Jung says, "Whoever builds up too good a persona has to pay for it in irritability." He speaks of visiting an elderly man who was so above criticism that "I began seriously to think of how I might better myself. But on the fourth day his wife consulted me. Well—I learned . . . from it."[9] In the conveniently private chamber of domesticity, the shadow had been let out for exercise and had brought with him a neglected creature, an inner woman whom Jung has called the anima, the man's own feminine side. The shadow presented her to his virtuous ego—so above criticism!—as an embodiment of negative unfeeling qualities which, since

---

[8] For further elaboration, see my book, *The Inner World of Man*, p. 67, from which this dream is taken.

[9] *Two Essays on Analytical Psychology*, Dodd, Mead edition, p. 209.

they could not originate in a saintly sage, must belong to his wife. This was proved by the irritation that she so frequently caused him and clearly showed that the reprehensible characteristics were ones that *she* must face. By the simple method of projecting these unsavory problems upon her, he could peacefully return to his spiritual heights. Had he instead faced the shadow as his own, he might have freed the inner woman from its power and found within himself qualities of feeling and creative impulse well worth cultivating.

This inner woman, the anima, lives in every man. She is the creative feminine component of his own being, to which he must become consciously and responsibly related if he would become whole.

In woman there lives an inner man, the animus, an embodiment of her own inborn masculine traits to which she must become consciously related. Otherwise, from his stronghold in the unconscious, he will dominate her thinking so that she falls under the spell of his absolutism.

The masculine and feminine principles seek union in the individual psyche. In their harmonious interplay they act as mediators between conscious and unconscious. From their marriage a child is born. With each beginning, each dawning of a new possibility or awakening of a latent potential, the image of the child may appear as herald of a potential future and of a change in the personality which, though only a possibility, can be brought into reality by a willing choosing ego. The child may come as an outcast, a neglected or forgotten element of the self, yet still a savior because, if accepted, he will bring us nearer to the truth of our being. In its god form the child is daemonic, violent and brutelike, or full of numinous light, but its coming is frequently accompanied by an uprush of vital energy. It has an element of wonder and surprise, as childhood itself has in its original connection with the unconscious.

We shall meet this child in every discussion of conscious choice. It must not be confused with an image of childhood. It is the child as an expression of the preconscious aspect of the psyche. Yet it shares a quality that children also possess, the quality of direct expression. Children's lives are not yet overgrown by concealment and subterfuge, by convention and conciliation. They are very near to the unconscious, to the wisdom of thoughts that blow through them, to dreams that we have learned to forget; near to love and fear, to generosity and cruelty—to the direct experience of opposites. They are near to

the images of the unconscious and to a preknowledge of things that must later become consciously known through individual experience. In almost every chapter of this book a child has interrupted to say, "Oh, yes, I know about that," and out of strange distances thoughts beyond their knowing come and are gone again, thoughts born of an ancient wisdom. We can no more keep children out of a book about life than we can keep them out of our own lives if we want to let wholeness in; if we want to know the livingness of life and more about the nature of our own myth of being and becoming, and of the slow emergence of consciousness from the vast sea of the unconscious. For in children images move as they did in early man.

The image of the child who comes in dream or fantasy shows us most clearly the quality of that which is emerging into life and will choose without our consent unless we face it as an inner potential and seek to understand its nature. In its transpersonal daemonic form it stands in the right of its eternal being, cradled in its own essential meaning, changeless but eternally reborn. The Christ child lives on as immortal child when the Christ has become the crucified God. Through its presence in the psyche it reveals "how silently, how silently the gift of love is given." The daemonic child, embodiment of energy, is born in full strength. Hercules in his cradle battles the snakes. As destructive force, the child, Kullervo, cruel, vengeful, strong beyond the strength of man, tears up the mighty forest trees, and kills the child who annoys him. All these children are images of forces that may arise within us. We meet them as we move on the pathway of choice. They offer a possibility of transformation if the ego will accept and deal with them as elements that may become active within the self.

In the coming of the child, we discern that meeting of the personal and the transpersonal which the wholeness of life demands. In transpersonal form he is an incarnation of evil or a hero element that dares move forward through darkness into new day. But it is the ego who, through growing awareness and act of will, chooses which child shall become director of his destiny.

Deeper than the personal life is the transpersonal, where man knows himself not only as an individual particle, complete in his own psychic wholeness, but also as a part of the human stream, part of the eternal plan in which the mysterious inner god becomes manifest and man encounters a Self greater than his own individual self.

There is no individuation[10] in its true meaning of self-realization and wholeness without consciousness of man's dual dependence upon the factors of the personal and archetypal worlds.

The more we study this mysterious relation of consciousness to the unconscious, the more we realize that, from the beginning, a dynamic power acts, not only to protect the growing ego consciousness, but also to enrich and enlarge its boundaries through the integration of the unconscious non-ego forces. The Self, the developing center of gravity of both ego and non-ego, acts as both the dynamis and the goal of the process.

Here, from the beginning, is the action of a power invested in the ego yet greater than the ego; a dynamic directive force beyond and behind ego choice. In childhood this connection with the non-ego power comes in flashes. It is not continuous or even assimilated into consciousness, yet it has its part in the integration of non-ego powers into the growing ego. Each choice man makes leaves a small deposit for or against the process of ego integration and fortifies or weakens the ego for the ensuing encounter with the unknown.

When we reach a crossroad in our life journey, all the choices that we have made and forgotten, as well as those to which we have given conscious loyalty, enter into the moment when choice becomes decision.

---

[10] We must not confuse the individual and the individualist. Jung says, "The individualist is only the distilled egotistic essence of an egoist—a man who has failed to individuate." (Said by Jung, quoting from himself, in conversation with the author.)

THE INNER WORLD OF CHOICE

CHAPTER 1

The Gift of Choice

᪌᪐᪑

Man was created for the sake of choice.[1]

The more one sees of human fate and the more one examines its secret
springs of action, the more one is impressed by the strength of unconscious motives and by the limitations of free choice.[2]

THE ART OF LIVING is, in its essential meaning, a development and
transformation of the power of inward choice. It is of all creative arts
the most difficult and the most distinguished. Its products are fashioned in the workshop of the soul whose windows open upon inner
and outer worlds. If the door between these worlds be locked, transforming energy is imprisoned, and awareness, that precursor of new
consciousness, becomes bereft of its mobility, its power of quick
response.

> Man! swinging-wicket set
> Between
> The Unseen and Seen[3]

needs both worlds, for each act of creation is born of a subtle interchange, or clashing encounter, of inner and outer.

Truly this art is one of rare distinction. It involves

---

[1] Hebrew saying.
[2] Jung, "The Psychology of the Transference," p. 177.
[3] Francis Thompson, "Any Saint," in *Works*, Vol. II, p. 47.

> A condition of complete simplicity
> (Costing not less than everything),[4]

a humility that holds the sense of the real within the heart, a courage that dares the leap into the unknown, and an acceptance of the dignity of human life that comes from a reverence and respect for the potential existing in each individual. Thus it comes to pass that this artist is not primarily concerned with concrete objective expression though, when form and pattern are perceived by inner vision, there may arise a compelling desire to express its meaning objectively. For the artist seeks to reveal to himself and, through himself, to others a world within man that cannot be expressed in three-dimensional form.

A work of art can never be wholly objective, for spirit, shaping and reshaping, moves within the creator, changing, transforming, expressing its own dimensions, moving in a world of eternal meanings. Spirit, entering into the simplest act of love, here also creates its own dimensions in human form. It steps out of time into eternity, for an act of awakening and awakened love lives on long after the actor has become spirit or earth. All decision and choice rests primarily upon our openness to the transforming spirit, upon awareness of its messages and a simultaneous awareness of the outer situation and our own involvement in it.

God says, "Choose what you will and pay for it."[5] We choose; we try to bargain with this mysterious god, secretly expecting him to give back our money if we do not like what we have chosen. But in merciless wisdom, he—this inmost "Wholly Other"—exacts full payment, through which new consciousness may be born and a step toward wholeness taken. Hardened by defeat, confronted by his own weakness, tempered by the very injustice of life, man is thrown back upon himself and begins to see the nature of and the reasons for his choices. The payments then become the means of his learning how to choose.

Refusal of inward choice and its creative power makes of life a repetitious round, a treadmill of duty or a merry-go-round of meaningless activity. Man is bound to the wheel of fate until consciousness of his God-given power of choice dawns upon him. Then he glimpses the paradoxical nature of the force that has both bound

---

[4] T. S. Eliot, "Little Gidding," in *Four Quartets*, p. 39.
[5] Spanish proverb.

him and given him power to break the bonds *if* he will choose the pain entailed in the struggle and accept the perils of freedom to be encountered on the spiral way that sweeps upward from the broken wheel.

A man dreams:

I am driving a high old-fashioned car with very large heavy wheels. It is filled with chattering laughing people. A man is bound to the rear left hand wheel. At every turn of the wheel he shrieks in torment. The others do not hear, but each cry pierces through me as an actual knife thrust so that, inwardly, I am a bleeding mass of wounds. We pass an intersection and a sudden blinding light streams upon the car. Simultaneously I know I am both the man driving the car and the one bound to the wheel. A mysterious act of choice takes place within me; I *will* to become this man. My energy flows into him. The wheel now seems to turn of itself but, as it turns, the man makes a mighty struggle and, though the chains cut into his flesh, he breaks them. Car and occupants vanish. I am completely alone.

What had bound the dreamer to this wheel? He could find no answer to his question till another dream came to him.

I am driving a hand car through a long dark tunnel. The roof is so low that I have to crouch in a way that cramps every muscle. I feel that I will smother if I do not soon come out into the open; but the tunnel goes on and on, stretching endlessly into the same dreary darkness. As I wake, gasping for breath, I see the hand car. On each side is painted, "B & O R R."

Meaning dawned upon him. The Baltimore & Ohio was the family railroad on which they traveled with passes of inherited prestige. The family fortune, traditions, conventions were indissolubly linked to this road. No member of the family had ever thought of running off these tracks any more than would one of the cars start off into the open on its own initiative.

All this man's early choices had been determined by those iron tracks laid down so long ago. Of this he was totally unconscious. Things that looked like free decisions were only changes of switches. He was indeed bound to the wheel by chains of adherence to the laws that had enslaved him from his childhood. Tormented by his own desires and innate predispositions, his ego will drove the car of his

self-destruction till the light of sudden consciousness gave him power of individual choice and freed him from the wheel.

"I am alone." Alone with his doubts, his fears, his uncertainties, wounded by his former bonds, unsustained by the conviction of his own infallible rightness, suffering the agonies of self-revelation and doubt. Alone with himself. In such aloneness man slowly learns, through the healing power of the Self, how to vanquish the enemy who has bound him to the wheel.

As man reaches the same point on a new level of the spiral's sweep, he may encounter an old situation. The same images arise and he is offered new choice, or perhaps an opportunity to confirm an earlier one. Shadow selves, early fears, secret greeds are not vanquished by a single encounter or overcome by a single choice. Over and over they must be met at each turn of the spiral way. But as horizons widen and things are seen in new proportion, it is our own choice that decides whether we will go forward to new heights or turn back to lower levels.

This is the spiral way that the artist in life must travel. If he goes forward, he becomes increasingly aware of possibilities, inner and outer, that choice offers in his discovery of the essential meaning of his life. "To know the seeds, that is divine indeed."[6] They are the small beginnings, the movement of life below the surface, the unborn potentials awaiting birth into consciousness. "Pear seeds grow into pear trees, nut seeds grow into nut trees: God seeds into God"[7] and self seeds, implanted by the mysterious force of life, grow into the unique individual who can accept and fulfill the part destined for him in the eternal drama of choice.

The words of Plotinus come to us here:

As the actors of our stages get their masks and their costumes, robes of state or rags, so a Soul is allotted its fortunes, and not at haphazard but always under a Reason: it adapts itself to the fortunes assigned to it, attunes itself, ranges itself rightly to the drama, to the whole Principle of the piece: then it speaks out its business, exhibiting at the same time all that a Soul can express of its own quality, as a singer in a song. . . . But these actors, souls, hold a peculiar dignity: they act in a vaster place than any stage: the Author has made them masters of all this world.[8]

---

[6] *I Ching*, Vol. I, p. 73.
[7] *Meister Eckhart, A Modern Translation*, p. 75.
[8] *The Enneads*, p. 176.

This "vaster place" is where the great drama of life is enacted. It is here that man, through slowly achieved mastery in the microcosmic world, perceives the vaster world of which it is a manifestation. Here he may play the part that he discovers is assigned to him by destiny.

And the words of Jung:

. . . we know that there is no human foresight or wisdom that can prescribe direction to our life, except for small stretches of the way. . . . Fate confronts [us] like an intricate labyrinth, all too rich in possibilities, and yet of these many possibilities only one is [our] own right way.[9]

And he also says: "The x in the calculation is predisposition."

Predisposition, the unknown factor that is to be found, is the already existing potential or tendency implanted in the germ of the personality. Unrecognized, this x gives to certain objects or situations a power of magnetic attraction or repulsion whose force is often quite beyond our understanding. While it remains a factor moving in the unconscious, it makes us creatures of circumstance. Accepted and unmasked, it may suffer transformation and reveal itself as of the essence of our being. Often it is the factor that we are most reluctant to discover; it shows us how we ourselves are responsible for our fate. Jung says:

If you accept the fact that fate is really created by your own self, then you are in the current, and then, even if the external situation is bad, you have the spring flowing within. Then you can say with the exalted, the soul becometh joyful, for you are in the river of life; you are joyful, you are lifted up by the river.[10]

Yet the part and the ultimate meaning of the part are veiled in the cloud of unknowing; only purity of intention, inner integrity, willingness to venture into life risking the chance of mistake and disaster, can give man courage to choose his own experience as the destined part reveals itself to him.

A man woke feeling that he had been—or was he still?—in a strange land, far distant in time and place. A dream enclosed him.

Gigantic forms rise dimly about me. Ghost presences move among the shadows that are like stage sets. They have three

---

[9] *Two Essays on Analytical Psychology* (Coll. Works, 7), pp. 47–48.
[10] "Zarathustra." (Seminar notes, privately circulated. Permission to quote given by Dr. Jung to the author.)

dimensions, though they move like drifting shadows. A very old man is seated at a table. He hands me a paper. I see that on it is written a role that I am to play. I exclaim, "Not this! I will play it badly." He answers, "How you play it is your concern." On waking I cannot remember the part assigned; only the words of the old man remain distinct. "How you play it is your concern." But the part is unknown. I feel that some new situation is awaiting me, some change of fortune that I must meet with a conscious choice of the way that I will play the to-be-given role. I have a sense of preknowledge, of a coming to pass, which I do not want.

He tried to forget the dream. He told himself that, since he could not remember the given part, the dream could have no meaning for him. But it haunted him, for he had been where strange distance in time and place is an element of the eternal drama that is played in the unconscious.

Here, a truth that is two thousand years old is still the truth today—in other words, it is still alive and active. Here too we find those fundamental psychic facts that remain unchanged for thousands of years and will still be unchanged thousands of years hence. From this point of view, the recent past and the present seem like episodes in a drama that began in the gray mists of antiquity and stretches all through the centuries into a remote future. This drama is an "Aurora consurgens," the dawning of consciousness in mankind.[11]

Did he want the dawning of new consciousness in a world where eternal truths move in changing form, as their unchanging essence becomes embodied in the choices of man?

The sensible thing to do was to forget the whole thing and concentrate on the business of his known life. It was only a dream. But it refused to be forgotten. Again he saw the old man and heard the words, "How you play it is your concern." Awe fell upon him, for he had been in the presence of one of the great archetypal images, the Wise Old Man, an unknowable force that can reveal the role in which man's life is cast, but not the way he shall play it. God himself can do nothing against man's choice of how he will play his part in the drama of human destiny. Not until, in a moment of transformation, this man's unwillingness became willingness, could he know

---

[11] Jung, *Psychology and Alchemy* (Coll. Works, 12), p. 456.

himself to be part of a life greater than any he had heretofore envisioned. Yet all that his newborn willingness could do was to hold him in a state of quickened awareness that enabled him to listen with the inner ear, to see with the inner eye, and in this way to perceive the forces moving in small beginnings within himself that might show him how to play his allotted role.

The premonition contained within the dream took on reality as he went forward. A change came into his life and he was called upon to play a part that his ego would never have chosen, and in which he would have failed, had he sought oblivion of the message of the dream.

> If I drink oblivion of a day,
> So shorten I the stature of my soul.[12]

A day! *the* day when we "know" within ourselves that we have come face to face with decisive choice. If we evade it, we shorten the stature of our soul and close the door on willingness and awareness. Then we misplay our part in the Divine Comedy enacted in that vaster place greater than any stage erected by human hands. Here all humanity is upon the stage; but the unseen actors are those forces of good and evil rising from a world below the stage erected by human consciousness, and compelling the actors to their several parts.

Like the dream within the dream, there is a drama within the drama—the no-less-divine drama of man's personal life where he may become increasingly conscious of the archetypal forces that act as directors of the human play. Their clash, their opposition, produces conflict, and out of conflict energy is born.

These energies *are* the universe. The images man has made of these energies become the gods, the tutelary deities acting upon him and, through him, upon life. If he can perceive them and can understand their action in his own life, they interpret for him the nature and purpose of his choices. If he is blind to their presence, deaf to their voices, they become agents of doom. It is the man who listens to the creative voice of dawning awareness, daring to look upon the daemonic forces of the unconscious, who comes at last to the fulfillment of his destiny through acceptance of the part given, and a knowledge of the x, the predisposition which must be brought into conscious relation with the forces of creative energy in inner and outer worlds.

---

[12] George Meredith, *Modern Love*, XII.

In this way, man creates in himself the role chosen for him by the greater creative forces; for creative energy moves in a world of contradiction—good and evil, despair and belief, the power of destruction and the power of rebirth, move side by side, and the divine force which man actually encounters in life does not hover above the daemonic, but penetrates it.[13]

Through his own choice of entering this world of contradictions, and with increasing consciousness creating his role within himself, man comes to the freedom defined by Jung: "Freedom of will is the ability to do gladly that which I must do."

The role is given. It is "that which I must do"; but the gladness which makes it freedom is man's own choice.

The role is given. It may be that of king or servitor, sovereign or slave.

To the king are allotted his robes of state, his mask of sovereignty, his stage settings of magnificence. Yet inwardly he may play his part as slave: slave to his will to power, to his greed, to his fears, to his avarice or his lusts. Any of these inner rulers may have power to enslave him. Outwardly he may exert the choices of life or death over his subjects, but behind the kingly mask is the face of the slave who forfeited to these inner rulers the divine gift of choice through which he might have ruled the kingdom of his inner world.

In like manner, the one to whom the rags and the mask of slavery are given may play his role with knowledge of his kingship in the kingdom of his own soul. Here he exerts freedom of choice over his thoughts, his compassions, his truth of being. In this inner kingdom he is ruler, and his subjects are obedient to him. In each role "the soul sings out its own part as singer in a song." The role is allotted, the song is the choice of the soul.

Man wins the right to this choice of what he inwardly creates by an act of bringing to consciousness something hitherto a possession of the unconscious, withheld by an ancient god. Choice is not only a gift but a theft, an act of primal disobedience, through which man steals from God something of His daemonic omnipotence. Prometheus stole the divine fire, the creative flame; he who consciously accepts his right to individual choice steals an attribute of God. Through this theft he brings upon himself the punishment of consciousness, of responsibility, of self-awareness, and of self-judgment. Yet this theft is also a gift, for the inborn creative spark, which makes

---

[13] Martin Buber, "Religion and Reality," in *Eclipse of God*, p. 31.

the theft possible, is the potential of divinity implanted in man in the act of creation; and the punishment, which is also the gift, is that he must now enter upon a way of transformation, a journey through darkness into light.

It is this potential of choice which is the supreme gift of the God of Being and Becoming. At every shift in the eternal drama of transformation, there is offered the divine gift of choice.

CHAPTER 2

Choice of Consciousness

❧ ❦ ❧

Becoming conscious is of course a sacrilege against nature, it is as though
you had robbed the unconscious of something.[1]

I DREAMED THAT THE WORLD outside is all waves. Angels told me
to die of my own accord. But God said, "Don't do that." If you
die of your own accord when angels tell you, you step out on the
waves and don't get anywhere. But if you die when God tells
you, he takes you and cleans away all your ghosts, and you can
walk out on the water and come back and live all over again.

I dreamed that I have died in my sleep but now I must be reawakened to die while I am awake and conscious.

The first is the dream of a five-year-old child; the second is the
dream of a man of fifty. These two dreams have a profound kinship
in that they both deal with the divine gift of choice in its relation to
the eternal mystery of death and rebirth.

This choice between life and death is ever-recurrent. In varying
forms it appears whenever a new adaptation is needed or a new potential is ready to be born. For the child, it is the death of the old
wish-fulfilling dream world and an acceptance of the world of conscious experience. This is the birth of the ego that must now meet
earthly reality through which it can consciously develop and separate
itself from the unconscious. For the man who has attained his ego
goal, it is a voluntary acceptance of the death of his ego life in order
that he may be reborn into the greater reality of the Self. Through

---

[1] Jung, "Zarathustra."

10

every phase of existence, choice between life and death—the yea-saying or the nay-saying—is always present in the daily event as well as in those crises when we stand at the crossroad of a decision which may alter the pattern of our lives.

In the child's dream the death counseled by the angels is not suicide—except as every choice that denies life to emerging consciousness is suicidal. "Own accord" means passive acquiescence in the old unconscious ways that refuse to accept the reality of earthly life. This is the death counseled by the angels. The concept of angels—the child's own—as winged creatures who can do no wrong corresponds to primitive belief. Their voices are those of childlike innocence so often mistaken for the voice of the spirit. Heraclitus says, "It is death to the soul to become water," that is, to lose one's individual form and become dissolved in the flux of fantasy, or to wander about in life without a sense of its real meaning or a consciousness of one's own responsibility.

We all know those maddeningly innocent people who seem always to be listening to angel voices, who never have an evil intent, who wander into circumstances of disaster where things "just happen" to them, or who produce disaster for others without "meaning any harm" and regard in hurt amazement the exasperation they stir up in others. These are the people who die (at ninety, perhaps) before they are really born into our wicked world where they must know evil as well as good and must acknowledge the meaning of what they do.

Acceptance of reality means staying with your feet on the good earth of human experience. Consciousness involves definite effort. You have to pull yourself up and ask, "Now why did I do that? What, or who, lives in me and acted or spoke or imagined?" Angelic unawareness would be beatific innocence were it not for the fact that the unconscious is always moving, bringing things to pass that you do not choose to perceive in time to prevent the disaster that "happens." The god voice is always warning, suggesting, revealing. Thoughts come to you; feelings arise; emotions engulf you; but instead of making them conscious so that you can see their meaning, you let them carry you where they will, and so you become flotsam tossed about by waves of impulse and emotion. You are of course innocent. Yet, in this drifting, you may happen upon a leviathan. He doesn't know about the angels; he just swallows you up.

Such persons may be angelically or unconcernedly daemonic. They

are never quite human. The idea that man is a little higher than the angels because he has the gift of choice is told in a Hebraic legend.

A Hasid asked Rabbi Zusya: "Concerning Abraham receiving the three angels, it is written: 'And he took curd and milk and the calf which he had dressed, and set it before them; and he stood *above* them, under the tree, and they did eat.' It is not strange that here the man stood 'above' the angels?"

Rabbi Zusya expounded: "When a man eats in a state of consecration, he redeems the holy sparks which are imprisoned in food. But the angels are not aware of this service unless the man has told them of it. That is why it is written of Abraham that he 'stood above them.' He let the consecration of the meal descend on them."[2]

Consciousness stands above innocence and, through its intervention, releases the creative element contained in matter. The angels can become aware of the meaning of this ritual meal only through Abraham's act, for the release of the divine spark is an act of conscious choice that makes man a creature standing above "unconscious emanations"—even those of God. Release of the spark makes of the simplest meal an act of communion.

A Gnostic myth defines the God who warns the child against angelic voices. He is the God of Light who divided the darkness of unconsciousness from the light of conscious perception. The demiurge, creator of the visible physical world, created man, the highest animal, without the gift of consciousness. But on the seventh day, the day of contemplation, the God of Light looked down on this instinctual, unchoosing creature made by the demiurge, and perceived his incompleteness; so He sent Christ, his son, in the form of a serpent to tempt man to choose for himself whether or not he would remain an obedient child, or would, through his own choice of disobedience, steal from God a knowledge of good and evil that would forever close to him the gates of the garden of innocent unknowing and drive him into the earth life of human experience. Through this choice, man started on his long journey in quest of consciousness.

This God of Light who sent the serpent to offer the gift of choice says to the child who would innocently blunder into disaster, "Don't do that." He comes like a stranger who taps the sleepwalker upon the shoulder and says, "Look where you are going. Don't you know

---

2 Martin Buber, *Tales of the Hasidim*, Vol. I, p. 248.

that way can't possibly get you anywhere? For heaven's sake, see what you are really doing before you get too far off on those beautiful waves. Come back to earth and see what life is about and what part you are meant to play in it."

There are times in every life when, passionately convinced of our own righteousness and feeling justified in our accepted way of dogmatized respectable living, we hear the voice of this unknown God saying, "Don't do that. For you it is not right." We may have been taught it is right, self-sacrificing or conventionally good and proper, but this inner voice says, "For you it is death." Or there are times when, caught by blind desire to proceed with an unconcern—that we prefer to call trustful obedience—an intuition of the evil contained in the situation or existing in the desired object rises in us. The angelic voices tell us that to distrust is disloyal or disobedient or uncharitable; we must not even look on evil; and, besides, it is easier to go ahead and follow blind impulse without all the trouble of evaluating the situation and choosing our own right way. It is nicer to listen to angel voices that tell us everybody is good and lovely and we shall be taken care of by a kind God who likes us to be obedient children. So again we "step out on the waves" and don't "get anywhere."

The rabbi of Kobryn once looked at the heavens and cried: "Angel, little angel! It is no great trick to be an angel up there in the sky! You don't have to eat and drink, beget children and earn money. Just you come down to earth and worry about eating and drinking, about raising children and earning money, and we shall see if you keep on being an angel. If you succeed, you may boast—but not now!"[3]

An angel must content himself with unawareness of the reality of human experience if he wants to retain his halo untarnished.

But the God who separated light from darkness desires man to become conscious. He waits for him to struggle through his early experiences, to reflect upon them, to discover the meaning of his mistakes and, through a sequence of choices that involve him in failure or success, to come to a consciousness of the reality of his life. When man is for a moment silent and ready to listen, the God who speaks through the voice of the Self tells him to die.

The death that the angels counsel is the living death of the once-born, who never come to a life of consciousness nor to the knowledge

---

[3] *Ibid.*, Vol. II, p. 161.

of death that is rebirth. The death God counsels is the death of unconscious life and a rebirth into a life of conscious choice.

To every thing there is a season; and a time to every purpose under the
heaven: a time to be born, and a time to die; a time to plant and a time
to pluck up that which is planted; . . . a time to get, and a time to lose;
a time to keep, and a time to cast away; . . . a time to keep silence,
and a time to speak. . . . *That which hath been is now; and that which
is to be hath already been.*[4]

There is a time and a purpose in dying "when God tells you." The
time is when one phase of life has reached its completion and is out-
grown, and the germ of new being is ready for birth within the psyche;
the purpose is the rebirth of which Christ spoke when He said to
Nicodemus that man must "be born of water and of the Spirit."[5]
"That which hath been is *now.*" We are aware that things once
known in childhood are moving in the present. With each return of
the image comes new recognition of its meaning and we hear its
voice speaking the truth of the moment as an opportunity for bringing to birth something that has already existed in the unconscious.

This voice, speaking out of the silence of the Self, brings with it
the astonishing conviction: *this thing is true*; it lives within me. ("I
live; yet not I, but Christ liveth in me."[6]) We know in a new and
different way something that we have already known with our ego
mind. We know it now with our heart and soul. It *is.* This is the
voice heard by the prophets who bore "the burden of the valley
of vision."[7] Also, it is the voice of the new man who is prophet
of our individual destiny. He exists in each one of us and, in dream,
vision or flash of insight, shows us the truth of our being. He stands
at the crossroads of decision and, if we ask, will tell us the path that
is our right way, which we may choose yet which is already chosen
for us.

This voice can be silenced. Then death becomes the living death
of those who have all they want to have and know all they want to
know, and so have died to the life of transformation.

Even these "innocent" dead may come to life through some sudden intervention of circumstance or disaster, through achieving suc-

---

[4] Ecclesiastes 3:1–15. My italics. All scripture citations are from the King
James Version, unless otherwise noted.
[5] John 3:5.
[6] Galatians 2:20.
[7] Isaiah 22:1.

cess and finding it valueless, or through a failure that confronts them with the sudden knowledge that they are already middle-aged and have not got anywhere. They have listened to angel voices, and dreamed their life instead of living their dream. Yet the awakening voice of disaster or disillusionment again offers choice between life and death. Upon this choice depends what happens to the ghost life.

"He takes you and cleans away all your ghosts"—the daydreams that never were given body by being made into reality, the thoughts and feelings that kept you from living your own life, the potentials rejected by the ego in its concentration upon its chosen form of adaptation. Most potent are the ghosts of the unlived past—ghosts of the things one did not do, commitments one did not make, choosing instead the provisional life that did not demand decisive choice. These ghosts haunt the crossroads, reiterating that it is too late, or too soon, or not possible now; but when "God takes you and cleans away all your ghosts," you accept the here and now and try to see what you can make of your life in spite of limitations and past mistakes. Then you can "step out on the waves" and "come back to live all over again."

You come back to the same old life; but the old is now the new because a new concept reanimates and transforms it. Now when you journey on the waves, you understand that these waters are waters of life: you see beneath the surface the deeper forces moving. The fantasies, the dreams, the visions, the intuitions of truth that arise within you are no longer ghost whispers blowing through you as wailing or singing wind blows through a windharp; they are real living experiences that speak their meaning in both inner and outer life. The voice we now hear is that of the Living Word that moves upon the waters of life. Good and evil are realities, and we accept the burden of choice.[8]

The man of fifty who dreamed, "I have died in my sleep but now I must be reawakened to die while I am awake and conscious" was a

---

[8] The interpretation of the dream which is given here was not made by the small dreamer. No child could be aware of the profound meaning contained within an archetypal dream. Yet the dream lived itself within her through her direct approach to experience, her almost uncanny, often disconcerting insight into her own motives and those of others. She also faced her own acts and their buried impulses with astonishing candor. This quality, or predisposition, of direct approach, a will to consciousness, continued to be a dominating factor. In this way she lived the dream and unconsciously interpreted it. Since this dream has a universal message, it belongs to anyone who is touched by its meaning. We are therefore warranted in making this interpretation.

scientist and very awake to the claims of his scientific life. He had lived consciously and effectively, also creatively, in his chosen world. He had married, begotten children, achieved prestige in his field. No angel voices had lured him from his accepted reality. In fact, he had done all the things that the rabbi of Kobryn had demanded of the angel. He had "come down to earth" and fulfilled what his ego had told him was the "trick" of earth life. In his chosen world, he was awake and conscious. His wife and children could, perhaps, speak of another world where the burden of consciousness was projected upon them, a realm of feeling and of irrational perception that must never be allowed to intrude upon the intellectual, scientific, rational world that demanded all his concentrated effort. He had acquired a wife to act as housekeeper to his feelings, to feed them and keep them tidy, and also to keep other people's feelings from intruding upon him with preposterous demands. Lately, a conviction had come to him that his family had failed him. In an effort to impress them with a sense of their duty toward him and his work, his demands upon them increased. His irritation with them spread to a sense of irritation with life. Of what use was his success? Often his own thoughts, heretofore so eagerly pursued, bored him. The sterile finger of ego achievement had touched him with a sense of futility.[9]

---

[9] And here his wife had a dream. Women sometimes have this unpleasant way of interrupting, with a dream or fantasy, the flow of masculine thought, when it would be much more convenient for the husband if her unconscious would hold its peace. She dreamed that she was in their living room. She saw the rug moving. Something living buried beneath it was trying to get out. A strange fear seized her. From under this discreet covering of established security, a creature who might destroy the room could emerge. She sat, willing it to die before it could escape into her ordered room. When she woke, the dream had not lost its power. She continued it in fantasy. She sat in the room, watching the struggle of the imprisoned beast, trying to make herself willing to let it come out. For days she fought the fear that refused the fantasy its continuance. Then one day, in an act of imagination, she willed it to complete itself. She watched the struggling creature and told it to live as it wanted. Whereupon there appeared not a formidable monster but a gay and joyous puppy who rushed to her and overwhelmed her with his gladness at his release, and then dashed about the room barking, jumping, rolling over in ecstasy of joy at his deliverance. As he came to her again, she knew him. He was the spirit of gaiety and joy, stifled by her husband's attitude. The rug was one that he had selected, the first thing that had gone into the furnishing of their home, and in this home she had stifled her innate gaiety. She knew that it should never be buried again under the heavy covering of his disapproval. The joy was hers; perhaps even he would accept it too. But it seemed to him extremely inconsiderate that her unconscious insisted on speaking at this time.

At first the dream seemed absurd. It was irrational and unscientific, but the word "reawakened" haunted him. Had he been more truly awake before he had slept and waked and slept again? He went back into the past, trying to recapture some of the eager desires that he had known in his youth. He had been in love. He looked at this woman who was his wife, and wondered what had happened to those ardent feelings he had once known. Were they mere imaginings? He thought of all the small pleasures that he had sacrificed to the greater demands of his scientific life. Why had the sacrifice brought no living reward? "I have died in my sleep." Could a man be awake and conscious on one side, and on another so unconscious that he dies without ever knowing it? Could ego consciousness itself be a sleep?

Then another dream came to him:

I am *once more* leaving my father's house, for again my father is dead. In the dooryard is an evergreen tree, a Christmas tree, that is also dead. It is a skeleton, a ghost tree, a rootless thing stuck in the ground. Birds are flying about it, but they do not interest me. Then I see in the dead branches a small emerald-green bird. Its wings are barred with lines of black that resemble the twigs of the tree. I stretch out my left hand; the bird lights on my wrist. I leave my father's house carrying my own bird with me. As I journey, the bird becomes white, and fear comes upon me.

"I am *once more* leaving my father's house." He had left the house when he was a very young man, and had gone out to take up his own life in the world. "Again my father is dead." His bodily father had died many years ago. Now he is *again* dead. Jung says:

Among all possible ghosts that haunt man, the spirits of the parents possess the greatest significance. When father and mother become inner factors, they are no longer fantasies of childhood projected upon persons, but parts of the psyche that hinder advance.[10]

We think something that has lived long ago in our conscious life is dead, but frequently it has only sought its rebirth in ghost form. It leads a very active life in the unconscious and has a power of attract-

10 Jung, quoting from his writings, in conversation with the author.

ing the conscious libido into its ghost land, depriving it of its power to function in the world of reality.

In other forms these forces return not as ghosts that haunt, but as spirits that quicken. The mother archetype returns as compassionate mother who nurtures the seeds of new life. The archetypal father returns as inner authority that speaks within the man the truth of his own being. Even ghosts may have rebirth and become spirit.

"Again dead." After his first death this father took up residence in his son's unconscious. From there he still ruled the choices that the son believed he himself made. He was a ghost that had not been cleaned away by God. As ghost he must die. In outer choice of profession the dreamer had rebelled against his father's authority, but inwardly he had taken on his ruling idea: that a conscious, rational attitude was the final and only authority in life. His was the voice of scientific provable truth. It had forbidden any excursions down the bypaths of feeling or irrational experience. "Thou shalt have no other gods before me." This voice of absolutism must die if the ghost is to be cleaned away by God and the spark of creative energy be reborn within him, lighting again the fires of emotion and original desire.

In the dream the tree is also dead. Once in his childhood it had lived as a Christmas tree, a symbol of the divine child; but in his father's house it had become a rootless thing of creed and dogma, stuck into the barren ground of conscious morality. Yet in its bare branches he finds the green bird, symbol of creative life that has a transforming value if he will awake to its meaning. A creed in its dogmatic form is a dead thing, yet it may contain the living symbol that will quicken new life and lead to transformation in the one who discovers its meaning for the future that is dawning in the consciousness of contemporary man. It waits within the old creed even as the green bird waited in the dead branches of the Christmas tree.

"I stretch out my left hand." The left hand is the dreamer. The dream is the gateway to the unconscious. He stretches out his left hand, he chooses the dream, and the bird of intuitive perception that flies between the two worlds lights on his wrist and goes with him.

He had known this green bird in his childhood when the Christmas tree was also green. Then, to his childish imagination, the Christ child was not only a spiritual mystery but a factual historical reality

to be accepted in the literal interpretation of the creed. The eschato-
logical Christ now held no meaning for him; his old beliefs had died;
but the eternal symbol, the divine element, had maintained a hidden
life within him. The green bird, the living spirit of the Christ tree,
now goes with him when he leaves the place where the old life has
died. As he meditated upon the dream, intuitions and feelings that
he had believed to be dead were reawakened; his creative imagination
took on new life; his perception of spiritual mystery returned: the
green bird became white. It filled him with fear and awe, for this
white bird was the dove, the Word that descended from heaven:
"This is my beloved son." Through accepting this Word, Christ
accepted his divine sonship and with it Gethsemane, Calvary, the
cross, and the agony of his human-divine destiny. The white bird
brings the spark of individual life. John the Baptist warned Christ
of this danger. He knew the nature of the baptismal dove and of the
Word, the spark, that it brought. "A spark of fire in the air waits for
thee over the Jordan. If thou followest it and willst be baptized, then
take possession of thyself, wash thyself, for who has the power to
take hold of burning fire with his hands? Thou, who art wholly fire,
have mercy upon me."[11] The baptism by the Holy Ghost and by fire
demands that he who receives it take possession of himself.

The dreamer supposed he had taken possession of himself when in
reality his ego ambitions had taken possession of him. Now he found
a great many quite unexpectedly disturbing things that he had to take
possession of. Realization of them burned like "a spark of fire" into
his consciousness—a fire in which much of the old life had to be
burned away in order that he might possess the new. He saw the
choice before him: to take possession of himself meant to acknowledge the limited and autocratic nature of his ego life. To this—
"awake and conscious"—he must die in order that he might be reborn into the new life of sonship. This involved taking possession of
all that his ego life had despised and rejected. Only through this
could he enter into the kingdom of the whole man who chooses and
is chosen by the spark of individual being—by the Self who is the
spark at both the center and the circumference, which includes the
all of life.

This choice of redemption from the ego life is not the blissful

---

[11] Syrian hymn (Ephrem), quoted in C. G. Jung, *Psychology of the Unconscious*, pp. 547–548, n. 61.

state it is assumed to be, for the Self can be the most difficult and perilous of all possessions, as it was to Jesus. It can lead to crucifixion of all that the ego has held most dear.

Through this chosen death he can, like the child, walk out on the waves of the living waters "and come back and live all over again" in a world that is the same and yet eternally new, because ego and Self have become reconciled through the death that is rebirth.

We speak of the once-born and the twice-born, but in reality life is a process of deaths and rebirths. We must die to become. "God must be brought to birth in the soul again and again." What is not brought to birth in consciousness never exists in the man himself save in the dream world of preknown things. These must be forgotten in order that they may be reborn. For what is preknown is not yet part of the personal consciousness. To be made real, it must be re-discovered through individual experience. This involves a severance from that state of unconsciousness in which the child, the primitive and the unawakened man can dream their life instead of living their dream.

The first death is birth. The womb life of dreamless sleep is over; the umbilical cord through which nourishment has flowed is cut, but not by the infant's choice. Physical earth life has begun; the infant is no longer part of the mother. But there is another cord, a psychic one, through which the child's as yet unborn ego is fed through identification. This too must be severed if the ego is to start on its journey toward consciousness. The child plays his part in the cutting of this psychological cord, through which his every need is nourished without his conscious effort. By severing this cord he finds his own identity.

Back of the personal mother stands the Great Mother, the unconscious. Out of her womb consciousness is born. Yet to this mother there is a strange mysterious return, a continuous process of birth and rebirth. It is this power of return to the Great Mother that gives to the child that odd wisdom of innocence. This wisdom is not yet individually his; it speaks through identification with the unconscious, from which he will ultimately be born into consciousness.

A six-year-old child dreams:

There was a big, big woman and she had all the world inside her stomach, everybody in all the whole world. And she opened the

door in her stomach and told me I could go in too. But there I was inside her stomach, and I could look in and see myself inside her stomach—and then I walked in and there I was.

The child naïvely accepted the fact that she was inside the stomach of the Great Mother and outside in the world at one and the same time. It couldn't be so and yet it *was*, and she knew it because it happened and she was there. The dream said so.

As consciousness grows, boundaries between these worlds become defined. A middle-aged woman dreams:

I am in front of a great bronze door which I know must be hung in balance upon two hinges so that it may swing freely between two rooms; otherwise I would be trapped in one or the other. This would mean imprisonment and death.

She interpreted the rooms as the two worlds, inner and outer. Unless she can move freely between them, she may be caught by outer events that have attained reality, or trapped in a region of beautiful and terrifying ghosts that cannot return to a life of human actuality. If there is no way open between these two rooms, the life of transformation dies.

For the child this door is not yet forged. Only a veil—mist-shifting, image-filled—drifts between the two worlds. Witches, fairies, demons, angels, magic powers of light and darkness come and go and have for him the same reality as persons he meets in his daily outer experiences. As he grows and consciousness takes over, the veil solidifies, becomes the door; the images retreat into the realm of the unconscious. More and more he lives in the outer world of ego-conscious experience. The wisdom often known to the child who is closely connected with unconscious images fades, and in its place comes acquired knowledge. "Knowledge comes, but wisdom lingers." The primary wisdom of the child must meet the test of individual experience before it can become the wisdom of the individual. Then conscious choice opens the door to the inner world of the images.

An initiant asked of a rabbi, "Why does God demand sacrifice of man and not of the angels? The sacrifice of the angels would be purer than that of man could ever be." He answered, "What God desires is not the act, but the preparation. The holy angels can only

do the deed; preparation belongs to man." Conscious choice is an act of man's own preparation through which he learns the true meaning of the sacrifice of that which he has achieved in order that he may receive the new which is coming to birth within him. At each birth into new consciousness, when heart and mind are re-awakened, the images that come to him have new meaning and speak newly to his condition.

In the life of transformation the images themselves are transformed; the childish concept of the angel as innocent, unknowing, becomes the image of the terrible angel—he who, armed with the flaming sword that turns in every direction, now guards the gates of the lost garden of unawakened innocence. At each turn of the spiral of choice an angel, newly beautiful and newly terrible, offers him the gift of a death that is life. If after acceptance he turns back, the angel is indeed terrible, for the sword has become the flame, the fire that will consume his newly won purpose.

As man passes from one life level to another and confirms his own progression by conscious choice, each angel is beautiful in promise, terrible in demand, for he forbids the return to a level of lesser consciousness.

At the apex of the spiral, in a moment of illumination, may be seen that angel of living light whose sword cleaves the darkness of matter and makes the invisible world visible. This image is of a being of superhuman, undivided and complete consciousness. The vision of this ultimate angel is won through loyalty to every choice of consciousness, through inner willingness to become aware of the nature of the one who speaks through the image. For he "maketh his angels spirits; his ministers a flaming fire."[12] By the light of this fire man draws near to another image, the image of the unknown and unknowable God. The image of his God is created by man himself and in this image he lives and moves and has his being[13] until the image recreates the man and new light breaks upon him and a new image stands revealed.

It is at the "turning point" of the spiral that the angel transforms into new visibility, fiery in command, fiery in opportunity, death-dealing and life-bestowing. Only choice that has attained the stature

---

[12] Psalm 104:4.
[13] Acts 17:28. "For in him we live, and move, and have our being."

of decision can endure the moment of visibility when the flame rises into the transforming invisibility of the unseen which is eternal. The tip of the spiral flame, its ultimate attainment, is that instant when the visible and invisible merge into the eternal *now* of life—the fiery transformation of the forever changeless.

CHAPTER 3

Early Choices of Good and Evil

◆§ §◆

Do not think that there is more in destiny than can be packed into childhood.[1]

We will gradually learn to realize that that which we call destiny goes forth from within people, not from without into them. Only because so many have not absorbed their destinies while they were living in them, and transmuted them into themselves, have they not recognized what has gone out of them; it was so strange to them that they, in their bewildered fright, thought it must only just then have entered into them, for they swear never to have found anything like it in themselves before.[2]

IN THE LONG PROCESS of self-transformation through which each man must work out his destiny, it is not only the strangeness of the outer world that he must encounter but also the strangeness of the inner world, where creatures hitherto unknown to him may suddenly emerge and take possession of his choices. A new situation confronts the uncertain ego. Fear, curiosity, fascination, desire, hate, wonder— any of these makers of destiny may spring to life within him. He looks, as he supposes, with the same eyes upon a once-familiar object, but its face has changed, grown hostile or perhaps obsessively to be desired. The inner creature chooses, acts, and actor and object confront each other, each wondering what uncanny power this now alien object has exerted, making the once familiar strange and threatening.

---

[1] Rainer Maria Rilke, *Duino Elegies*, Seventh Elegy. Privately translated.
[2] Rilke, *Letters to a Young Poet*, pp. 65–66.

These inner forces are creators of images that have the power to superimpose themselves upon objects of the outer world. By a magic, black or white, the good or evil image that the actor has himself projected upon the object now seems to assail him from without. Only slowly does he learn to recognize as his own the antagonist or friend who makes decisive choice as his destiny comes to meet him from within himself. Increasingly he must become aware of the nature of these messengers of fate who come from the heights and depths of his inner kingdom.

The child lives in a world of immediacy. Impulse and act are contained in the single moment. Object and subject are often undifferentiated. Yet for the child, as it was for dawn man, the veil of mists that hides the unknown is full of images that come and go between the two worlds, making both worlds new, strange, mysterious. And in the changing, shifting, compelling world of images, the child must learn to choose and to take responsibility for his choices, even those that seem to be made for him by the creatures suddenly called to life by unexpected and unknowable events. Slowly, very slowly, he learns to recognize the inner actor who has chosen and begins to see the relation between the act and its consequences.

From experience and reflection on experience the ego gradually comes to the knowledge of good and evil as forces that move within the self yet are greater than human knowing. This is not the knowledge of the child. Choice prematurely thrust upon him may trap him in a guilt that he cannot understand.

In its first experiments in the world of choice, the small uncertain ego must have a place of security from which to venture forth and to which it may return. Each successful encounter with the outer world adds to his sense of safety; each choice affirmed gives confidence for future adventurous choices. Yet the ego is very small, and both inner and outer worlds very big; the venturesome child, while slowly building a place of confidence within himself, must also find security in a world of outer objects. This first comes to him through instinctive trust in the love of an adult who has himself learned the meaning of choice.

Only the individual who has, through trial and error, learned to take responsibility for that which he has chosen can impart this sense of responsibility to the child. Only a trained disciplined ego that has discovered the life-giving power of the images that arise from the fountainheads of being can help the child to face the creatures that

rise within him and to make friends with them. This power, which the adult has himself attained through willed purpose and loyal fidelity to working out the meaning of inner and outer experience, has its indirect but vitally important influence upon the child. Without this self-training, his intuition and love cannot awaken the positive and life-giving potentials that are "packed into childhood"; nor can he help the child to choose the experience in which his own creativity will develop.

The adult who has not become loving through having, over and over again, chosen love rather than power, cannot draw forth from the child the potentials of love latent in his being. If he has not learned to distinguish between the conventional voice of that "conscience that doth make cowards of us all," and the inexorable inner voice that "speaks to our condition" and commands obedience to our own highest ought, he cannot impart to the child the meaning of the obedience that leads to freedom. Nor can he help to establish the rhythmic undercurrent of wise habit that can take over many secondary activities and set the energy free for individual choices that involve thought, feeling and courage for the new adventure. In giving the child freedom of choice, the adult must himself have a clear sense of relative values. Otherwise he may only burden him with petty detail that loving firmness could dispose of for him. Continuous demand that he choose often produces restlessness or obstinate resistance, fostering will to power and depriving him of a structure that he sorely needs. We might well remember that

> The centipede was happy quite
> Until the toad, for fun,
> Asked, "Pray which leg comes after which?"
> Which wrought her mind to such a pitch
> She lay distracted in a ditch
> Considering how to run.

Are we not sometimes the toad when we ask the child to choose in every small matter that could be taken over by restful routine?[3] Habit may become a bad master, but it is an excellent servant whose value must be acknowledged.

---

[3] No wonder that a small boy who suffered from one experience in an over-progressive school asked, on setting out again, "Is this a school where I have to do what I want all day long?" He had known the burden of "nondirected activity" and "freedom of choice." His small ego was very much perplexed; it was weary for the comfort of a place of security in which to rest between choices.

Imitation also may be a servant helpful in building the structure of personality. It can act as a clever craftsman molding the outer pattern of conduct. As a spontaneous response to a person who stirs the imagination, it is the expression of a desire to become like the admired object and so to be accepted and to "belong." Social qualities that help the child to adapt to his milieu become his through imitation. The wise adult helps the child to use these servants, so that he may automatically choose right responses to custom and established conventions.

Then the energy of the child becomes available for meaningful choice. But here we encounter another danger. Choice may be thrust upon a child too early. He has not the wisdom needed to enable him to choose in critical situations that are too great for his immature understanding. Not until he is able to discover the why of his own act can the burden of choice be thrust upon him. As his attention turns inward, he comes to the recognition of motive, the seed kernel from which choice has sprung. When motive can be brought into the light of consciousness, the child sees, living within himself, the one who chooses and, knowing him as friend or enemy, perceives good and evil as forces that have made choices for him.

While we are helping the child to realize his motive, it may save us many moments of embarrassed self-revelation if we can remember that he is often instinctively aware of our own motivation. While our conscious will is intent upon making him see the reasonableness of our demand, an unconscious desire may be intent upon establishing our authority. The "do-gooder" is often met by unexpected repudiation, because the victim-who-is-being-done-good-to has an intuitive distrust of the force that is being brought to bear on him. He sees will to power hiding behind the cajoling or threatening word. A child does not need to be told to beware the love of one not truly loving. Nor does he need to be warned to keep his inmost thoughts from the professional brain picker who interprets the act without perceiving the inner actor. Theoretical knowledge and statistical thinking label both child and motive, so making him a specimen that will prove a theory. The child, unconsciously perceiving this, withdraws his reality lest it be dissected. But the clever investigator would be greatly astonished could he see the images moving in the heart and brain of this "correctly" and theoretically interpreted child.

The child's world is an interplay of images that shift and change as new situations constellate new reactions. The image of parent or

teacher, or of friend may take on archetypal proportions if the situation rouses sudden overwhelming emotion and brings to life latent predispositions that determine the ego's reaction to the images. This is especially true in the interplay between parent and child where the child may create a highly colored image that would surprise the human creature on whom it is placed. The parent for his part often has an image of the child formed from his own ambition, his blind love or his concept of what is good or evil. He may have an abstract concept of what *a* child, or *the* child, or *his* child should be. He tries to pick and choose potentials that accord with his ideal and to force them into premature development, so attempting to stamp out inner reality. He decides upon the personality of the child long before personality is come into being. Integration of the personality is a lifelong process. From the beginning the self seeks its own reality, and this cannot be determined by any preconception of what a person ought to be. If the parent seizes upon every act that confirms his own preconception, he may even convince himself that he knows what the child thinks and feels. This "understood" child then retreats to his own inner world, leaving the persona to deal with the relationship. This produces a split in the psyche. In the outer world the child may choose in accordance with expectation; in the inner world he lives a life more and more at variance with the expectations put upon him by his admiring parent.

The often invisible god images that rule the inner life of the adult will be the ones that he imparts to the child, for being speaks louder than word or act. The parent who worships the "bitch goddess Success" will impart to the child the values of the high standard of living rather than those of the high standard of loving, no matter how noble his homilies on love. If he worships the god of law, his judgments are harsh and demanding and his concept of obedience does not include freedom of choice. His authority rouses rebellion.

The adult who admits only the literal aspects of the truth and rules out the mystery of the truth contained within the symbol will fear the quickening power of the great myths and withhold them from the child. Then his spirit is undernourished, for "packed into childhood" are seeds of wonder, reverence, awe, and the urge to create—to dream and to make the dream part of his own reality of being. The longing to penetrate the unknown and to participate in its mystery are qualities that differentiate man from brute. These

potentials are seeds of the child's being and can be called forth by one who has deep reverence for the quickening power of the living symbol.

How much of the beautiful morning dawn of wonder man would have missed, had not the myth-making power of the soul helped him to apprehend the gods without the premature burden of attempted identification! Both man and child draw near to the knowledge of good and evil, in their terrible and beautiful god forms, through wonder, which is the gateway to wisdom. Plato said, "Wonder, for this is the very beginning of philosophy." And Socrates: "So the lover of myths, which are a compact of wonders, is by the same token a lover of wisdom." For myth contains the nearest approach to truth that can be embodied in words. It portrays the inner meaning of life.

To the listening child, mythical creatures open the doors of inner magic. He is not at all disturbed by the paradox. "There is not a word of truth in it, and every word is true." He can share in the joy that comes from wonder, from the thrill rising in glad surprise at the eternal mystery of creation, where even God is surprised. In my childhood an old Negro woman told me the story of the creation. "An' the Lord God he sure worked hard, an' it came along evening, an' the Lord God he jest reared back, an' looked at what he done that day, an' it was *good*; an' the Lord God he certainly was pleased with hisself." Creation has its roots in wonder, its fulfillment in joy.

Wonder, joy, awe, terror, creation, re-creation move in the myth where the great images, heroes and gods, monsters and demons, play out their parts in the eternal drama of transformation. As the child listens, he is caught up for a moment in a world of elemental forces. He slips back to the mystery of "a time before there was a time," when these forces arose from dark chaos and good and evil emerged as stark motives that took on form as god or monster. He sees them in their interplay, acting out their parts. Perhaps he re-creates the drama in his own creative play, so participating in the life of hero or god, dragon or demon. For a brief moment he *is* the protagonist whom he portrays. In his re-creation of the myth he awakens within himself intuitions of motive and of reasons *why*. Then he returns to his own little life; yet something of the role lives on within him, not in identification, but in intuitive perceptions. In after years, words of mystery return to him and he perceives new aspects of their truth, for seeds of wonder have been planted in his small garden of new

beginnings. Later they may blossom in numinous experience, which reverence and awe lead him to recognize as his own experience of truth. Then he discovers, hidden within the eternal myth, the personal myth of his own destiny.

When man loses wonder the images of the inner world lose their life-giving energy. Ritual becomes repetition, symbol only a sign of that which is already known. Creed and dogma erect walls against revelation. The god voice, having uttered the final word, is silent and new beginnings bring no thrill of glad surprise.

If man holds wonder in his heart, the eternal child of new beginnings can live within him, even in old age. To this child man returns when his ego has become weary of much knowing.

The text never said, Except ye *remain* as little children, but "Except ye . . . *become* as little children."[4] You must be something else first before you can "become." Having become a man, you can realize that all that adult knowledge can give is nothing to what wisdom can really be. And then you again become a child, full of wonder and beautiful curiosity linked with awe, and simplicity full of pure essence, and you start again into experience with the world new before you. And, choosing wonder and experience, you choose which wonder will be your wonder, for the world is full of new wonders, no matter how many you have already explored.

Let the gods remain upon their mountains where they may be seen by wonder. Let the child live in his own garden where sometimes the gods will come down to enter into his creative play, or to stir his imagination in dream. The great myth is not forgotten. It has an unperceived influence in choice. But if myth is used to superimpose moralistic meaning, the archetype becomes ossified and the ideal concept may act as a snuffer, extinguishing the flame of original impulse and forcing the child into cold dead choices not really his own. He may live in identification or in imitation that has become repetition of prescribed conduct. He may think or feel amazingly well within prescribed confines. But the flame of creative desire and awareness of inner meaning will not illumine his choices. He sees himself in the prescribed role and identifies with it, so shutting the door upon the shadow and light of his own reality.

Identification with an ideal image is ego inflation, whether it occurs in the life of an adult or a small child. Children have a quality

---

4 Matthew 18:3.

of reverence as well as a predisposition for magic that enables them to step in and out of the role of hero or god; but when the heroic or admired is stamped upon a child's small life as an image of what he is intended to be, or worse, already is, he identifies with the image and may see himself the hero while acting the prig. *I am the good child, or the knowing child, or the unselfish child.* Looking only into the mirror of admiring eyes, he perceives this persona as himself, and shadow and motive slip from sight as the persona chooses the act of self-approval.

I remember one of these "good" children. She was as correct in every response as a mechanical doll. Her mother was very proud of her. Why not? It was she who had created this adorable little image reflecting her own glory. One day during the school chapel service an errant thought, unsuitable for a Good Little Girl listening to the Scriptures, entered her head, and she communicated it in a loud whisper. An awful silence walked in. The eyes of the headmistress were fixed upon her, a terrible voice spoke her name, three hundred pairs of accusing eyes were focused upon her.

The child's face changed. A creature who "must just have entered into" her looked through her eyes at the friendly headmistress, now changed into a hostile figure delivering her over to a world of inquisitional eyes that judged and condemned her, that stripped her bare of the enclosing persona garment. At this moment the inner door opened and an archetypal image entered. It transformed the once-friendly headmistress into a black witch with monstrous and malignant power.

The moment passed. Bible reading was resumed. Back in the chapel sat the outraged mother. At her instigation, the child made a charmingly suitable apology; but to me she said, "I have been a good little girl. I have told her I am sorry, and now I can hate her for always as much as I please." Within the shining image of herself, goodness claimed its righteous privilege of hate. Virtue the figurehead at the prow, hate the pilot at the helm: a strange way for a child to start on her voyage of transformation through inward choice!

We talked it over as she sat in my lap. We could talk because we liked each other and liked finding out about things together. But suppose we hated each other? What an absurd idea! But one of us might make a mistake—everybody does sometimes, even headmistresses or good little girls. Then if we hated, we could not find

out the truth because we should not like being together in our finding out.

Our conversation took a meandering way but kept coming back to the central truth. The child was not sorry and she hated. But to say she was not sorry was *bad*, and she was *good*. Mother said so.

Then, quite irrationally, something real—could it have been the Self?—sprang to life and faced hate and fear. This creature said, "I guess I'll have to tell her the truth. I'll go now." (Would I have let her venture alone had I not trusted the integrity of the headmistress and known that underneath austerity lay a living desire for truth?)

The child came running back. "I told her I wasn't sorry and I told her why, and she told me why, and then I was sorry and she was sorry and now *I don't have to hate her ever again*." The image of the headmistress projected by hate had been shattered by a mutual search for truth. So had the child's image of herself as the good little girl. She was now both good and bad; in fact, she had caught a glimpse of her own small *self*.[5]

What had we discovered in our search? Hate as separation, love as belonging, truth as the guide on that dangerous venture of the ego which leads to the unmasking of the image and the discovery of inner reality—all these potentials, "packed into childhood," awaiting the releasing touch of life.

But choice is not once for all, is never once for all. A single choice may be meaningful, important but fragile, a choice that must be confirmed by many experiences, rebuilt by many choices. This was a child's first choice of her self, through a perception of good and evil as inner factors and through an unmasking of the images they created. Many choices would have to strengthen and confirm the child's early choice, so that it might grow into a knowledge of the enemy or the advocate dwelling within the citadel of the self. On such "small" early choices the doors of fate may hinge. Through these doors come those inner images that have power to direct our choice and our decision.

Such choices of the self may be hidden, but they are not as infrequent as we are prone to think. Only to perceptive love can inner choices be revealed. Tread softly, love, when you draw near to mystery.

---

[5] The other children, without knowing why, liked her better. The mother? After all, I had brought that job on myself.

Sometimes a child has so strong a sense of his own reality that he refuses to accept the ideal presented by the loving parent. A child of eight reacted in this healthy way to the ideal of unselfishness. One day she burst out, "I don't see why I should be an unselfish little girl just so Johnny [her spoiled little brother] can be a bigger pig than he is already." Unselfishness—is it a form of ego inflation that focuses attention upon the perfection of one's own ego, or is it based upon a sense of relative values that perceives the meaning of sacrifice and what it is doing to oneself and to the other fellow? Does it feed the shadow (the pig) or a living creative potential?

The child, like the adult, comes to a knowledge of what is happening in himself, in the other person and in the situation not through a generalized and superimposed concept but through facing his own actual qualities and seeing the part they play in his relations to both inner and outer, to persons, to experiences and to his own development.

A nine-year-old boy had a violent temper that could at times sweep him into a frenzy of exultant rage; he had also a quick intuition that perceived the vulnerable spots in the other person and showed how his anger could make cruel use of them.

The world was his potential enemy. Anyone who thwarted him— his mother, his teacher, his playmate—instantly became the adversary to be overcome by violence. At these times he *was* the hate that took possession of him.

He had also another hate, "that old beast Hitler," whom his father, an army officer, was fighting. He indignantly denied suggestions that the intensity of his hatred of Hitler was related to a disturbing intuition that a Hitler who lived in him was getting stronger than he. *He* had no Hitler.

Who was it, then, who took control over him and made him try to bully other children and terrorize his mother by his prolonged storms of violence? It sounded like Hitler; it acted like Hitler.

He refused to discuss the inner Hitler, but his imagination became caught in trying to discover what made the outer Hitler "tick." At moments one could see his intuition turn inward, recognizing similarities between the two Hitlers, the inner and the outer, but his intuition was allowed freedom; no moral was driven home. One day, after talking of how Hitler enjoyed being swept into storms of anger, and working himself up into a frenzy of excitement, he was silent

for some time, and then announced, "I'm not going to have that old Hitler running me any more." That day his battle with Hitler became an inner conflict, and his struggle was no longer primarily with his mother or his teacher or his playmates but with Hitler, the shadow personality within his own psyche.[6]

He began to talk to the inner Hitler. In this way he succeeded in one of the greatest tasks of our present day—that is, *to introvert war*. "For Hitler was the most prodigious personification of all human inferiorities. . . . He represented the shadow, the inferior part of everybody's personality, in an overwhelming degree, and this is another reason why they fell for him."[7]

Watching this inner warfare, the boy could see how the Hitler force rose within him, making him feel strong and powerful when he was really overpowered by Hitler. Seeing Hitler as a power that took possession of him, he could disidentify from him and see a self that could oppose him, a self that could choose between the forces of good and evil in the conflict within the psyche. In interiorizing his own war, he played his small (and great) part in war or peace in the world.

For every war has its beginning in the heart and mind of man. The primary battle is with the inner enemy. Until a man has conquered in himself that which causes war, he contributes, consciously or unconsciously, to warfare in the world. And since there cannot be a self-governing nation unless it is made of self-governing people, this child was preparing himself to be a citizen of a world in which peace is not a static concept but a creative act of inner conquest.[8]

---

[6] We recall the Negro spiritual:

> Not my mother nor my sister, but it's me Oh Lord
> Standin' in the need of prayer.

[7] Jung, *Essays on Contemporary Events*, p. xv.

[8] An amusing incident shows how deeply the boy accepted this warfare of personalities within himself. One day he asked me, "Do you ever say gosh and darn and all those things?" "I say even worse," I answered. "I often say damn." "Then why is it so bad when I say them?" "Do you say them," I asked, "or does Hitler?" "I get you," he said. That evening his mother told him to do something he did not want to do. He stood with clenched fists, fighting with Hitler. After a perceptible time he ran to her, put his hands on her knees, smiled up at her, and said, "Damn you Mummy, won't you please go to hell?" Then he kissed her and did the thing she asked.

He also had conversations with Stomach, who was the coward, the betrayer; for when Stomach was afraid, Stomach threw up the food the boy had eaten.

If the projected image is never accepted as part of the self, its shadow qualities are unperceived and the ego becomes identified with the good.

This happened to a woman who could not sustain any relationship unless she dominated the situation. It was she who knew what was right, not only for herself but for others. Her rather nasty tempers were called righteous indignation. Failures in relationship were always caused by other people's faults. This woman had a dream. She had come to a green place. She was carrying in her arms a child, a little girl dressed in white. She thought, "How wonderful, how lovely this child is." Yet she had so much to do. How could she take on a child? She put the child down on the grass beside her. Suddenly a nameless beast appeared in front of them, but the woman felt no concern. He vanished, and in his place stood Hitler, who raised a gun, took careful aim and shot the child, who disintegrated at her feet. She looked on, interested but unmoved, and she and Hitler were left standing together.

When she awoke, she made no attempt to understand the symbols contained within the dream. She did not see that the green place was one of upspringing life, nor that the child was her own potential of womanhood which even yet could come to her in the green place of new beginnings. She did not question Hitler or the nature of his being or try to discover the meaning of his act in relation to her own life. She did not go back to see how in her childhood she had used her tempers, her "righteous indignation," to dominate situations where she felt her all-knowing ego had been thwarted, nor how this unfaced childhood alliance with the inner Hitler had led to her present indifference when he killed this child of her feminine self.

To name the personalities who appear in dream or fantasy, or whom we detect at work in disastrous experiences, helps both to confirm the reality of these entities and to disidentify from them. Their unlovely acts are real; they are performed by living actors; yet

---

and so of course the boy was too ill to do the thing he feared. He started conversations wih Stomach. They had one greatest fear; it was gymnasium. One day the boy said, "I guess that old Stomach knows where he belongs. I said to him, 'Stomach, today you're going to gymnasium,' and Stomach threw up my breakfast, and I said, 'Stomach, you're going to gymnasium.' And we got to the elevator and Stomach tried to throw up the breakfast he didn't have, and I said, 'Stomach, you pipe down, it won't do you any good, you're going to gymnasium'—and he went."

such an actor is not the protagonist of the drama unless we choose that he be given the hero's part.

As we watch the inner actors play their roles in children, we realize how natural these dramatic experiences really are. They take place spontaneously. The players are imaginary companions, personifications of inner entities. As the child grows and the outer reality claims him they go underground. They reappear in even more significant form in adult life, when man turns back to the way of his own nature in his search for consciousness.

The dramas that a child acts out with his imaginary companions are experiences of active imagination. Often it is his need that creates fellow actors who will speak words he longs to hear, or who will preserve for him the silence lacking in his too-active parent. Then the imaginary companion, like the fairy godmother, or the good-magician father, or the understanding friend, assumes a compensatory role, supplying the quality missing in the child's relationships. He may also use his imaginary companion as scapegoat on whom he can put the blame for his own faults, or as hero who achieves all that the child himself finds too difficult, or perhaps as magician whose power can be evoked to overcome the outer or inner object that makes the too difficult demand.

A little girl, only eight years old, modeled a repulsive clay beast. The body, with long legs ending in claws, was half spider, half crab. The semihuman face was full of cruelty and malevolence. It was, in its crude way, a masterpiece of primitive art, permeated with unconscious power. Of this self-created object she said, "I dreamed him long ago. He is my best friend. Sometimes when I have too hard a job put on me by someone he will sneak up behind and kill that person by magic. Sometimes I talk to him. One day I asked, 'Are you young or old?' and he said, 'I am very, very old, yet you are my mother.' "

Evil, though older than man, may be born anew within a child by almost unconscious choice. Yet it is choice.

The child took this beast home with her. Her description of her relation to him gave a key to acts that had been called "annoying habits." She was never openly defiant but would creep behind people and pad about after them. She frequently visited an aunt who, in overzealous love, wanted to "bring out the best" in the child. At times the aunt would become conscious of a disturbing presence and, turn-

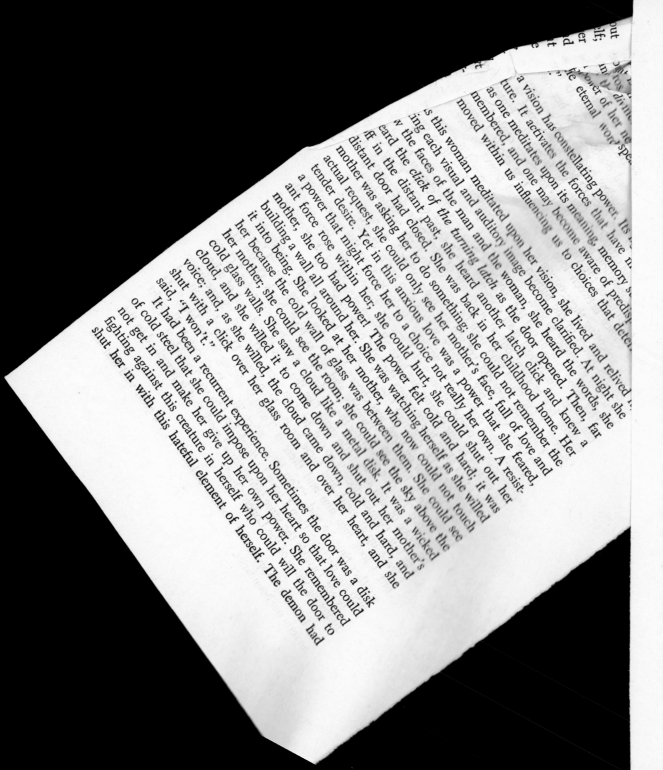

a vision has constellating power. Its
ture. It activates the forces that have
as one meditates upon its meaning, memory
membered, and one may become aware of predisp-
moved within us influencing us to choices that dete-

ing each visual and auditory image become clarified. At night she
s this woman mediated upon her vision, she lived and relived
w the faces of the man and the woman, she heard the words, her
ard the click of the turning latch as the door opened. Then, far
in the distant past, she could not remember the
distant door had closed. She was back in her childhood home. Her
mother was asking her to do something; she could not remember the
actual request, she could only see her mother's face, full of love and
tender desire. Yet in this anxious love was a power that she feared. A resist-
ant force that might force her to a choice not really her own. A resist-
a power that might force her to a choice not really her own. The power felt cold and hard, it was
it into being. She looked at her mother. She was watching herself as she willed
building a wall all around her. She was between them, cold and hard, and she
her because the cold wall of glass was between them. She could see
her mother; she could see the room; she could see the sky above the
cold glass walls. She saw a cloud like a metal disk. It was a wicked
cloud, and as she willed, the cloud came down and over her heart, and she
voice, and as she willed it to come down and shut out her mother's
shut with a click over her glass room and over her heart, and she
said, "I won't."
It had been a recurrent experience. Sometimes the door was a disk
not get in and make her give up her own power. She remembered
of cold steel that she could impose upon her own heart so that love could
fighting against this creature in herself who could will the door to
her in with this hateful element of herself. The demon had

ing quickly, would find the child stealthily creeping behind her. In the street the child would follow catlike, almost touching her. She found her aunt's ideals "too hard a job put on me" and invoked the beast of black magic in order to overcome the person who made the demand.

"I am very, very old, yet you are my mother." The beast was child of her own desire to destroy any force that opposed her will. That desire, old as human life, was reborn through her choice of alliance with its potential in herself. In her nearness to the world of the unconscious she had entered the region of black magic where the ego attempts to invoke the impersonal creative force in its destructive aspects, in order to kill the demands life makes. In conversation with the beast she heard him speak words of wisdom that arose from the depth of the unconscious, "I am very, very old, yet you are my mother."

This realization of good and evil as forces existing before personal life, yet born anew within the individual through an act of choice and acceptance, is shown in the dream of a woman of mature age. For over and over, from birth to death, the element that we refuse to accept as our own destroys values that seek new life within us. The following illustration is given in the exact words of the woman who had the experience.

It was in the darkness of the night. I was in the shadow land that lies between sleeping and waking when I heard a knocking and found myself behind a closed door. I was afraid; also I felt a stubborn resistance, like a negative force acting within me, refusing to hear the knocking, yet I knew another inner presence within me opened the door. Standing before me was a man of ordinary simple bearing, and with him was a woman, earthy and peasantlike, yet with a luminous quality as though an inner light shone through her. The man said, "I am Jesus and this is Mary, my daughter, who is also my mother." And then I was again in the darkness and I was left wondering at the words. Surely, I thought, I must have heard them incorrectly. He must have said, "Mary, my mother" and added "also my daughter"; but I knew this was not so. What could it mean to me that Mary, the daughter, was given first importance? For days the sentence kept coming back. Over and over again I heard that quiet voice of authority telling me of a mystery on which I

needed to ponder. "And Mary kept all these thing[s] [and pon]dered them in her heart." That was all I could [do,] humility words that I could not as yet underst[and.] meaning came to me—at first only small frag[ments] thought—that my heart accepted.

Jesus was his human name, the one gi[ven him in] life. He was also Jesus the Christ, the [...] Son of earth and Son of heaven, re[...] and the divine element. He was th[...] the defining word that speaks with[...] ing and gives structural form a[...] diate reality and the eternal [...] mind a passage that I had [...] things lay in the midst of s[...] from on high, from the [...] it was this secret word[...] the earthy figure of [...] mother. And the next [...] leaped into me, and the [...] meaning, the reality of this [...] Word, the Spirit, the Logos se[...] which had entered the womb of Mary[...] stood too why he had told me first, "Thi[s...] for though this word existed before him, h[e...] human form of Jesus, begotten this Word as [...] feminine principle illuminated by the secret word.[...]

The words had been spoken by the man Jesus to me, [...] If he is the Logos, the word that gives eternal form to the p[...] of individual life, was the meaning of his words that for wom[an] the form of her masculine energy, her Logos, must be born o[f] love and must also give birth to love—that Logos, the meaning-ful structure of reality, must be patterned and directed by Love?

To the early Christian Jesus was not only a person; He was the Christ, the *poimen*, the helper, invisible yet always present. He was also the divine spark, the light that shone within the darkness. As the man Jesus, he was also the Christ existent in the eternal, the divine son who, through his choice to enter human life, became both Logos and Eros.

This, then, was what the dream meant to me, a woman—the acceptance of the masculine element of my own being, Logos,

often been exorcized by the love[that had sur]rounded [her] childhood and by an answer[ing] love spring[ing] up [with]in her[s...] but in reliving the childhood fanta[sy] she perceive[d] that [...] really come to grips with this shad[owy] force withi[n] hers[elf...] never faced its power to act in moments of choice. No[w...] she we[...] back, facing moments of choice betwe[en] love and its refu[sal...] saw how she had opened or closed doors [th]rough her own c[hoi...] how her refusals to face this shadow had shut her out from e[...] ences, and how opening the door to love had opened it to n[...] relationships and opportunities. Only by facing the fantasy th[...] showed the predisposition born of desire for power could she und[er...] stand the meaning of the vision and know that she had again bee[n...] offered a choice between love of power and power to love. On[ly] through accepting these opposites within herself could she see the[m] as eternal forces in the human soul and commit herself to central[...] choice—a surrender to love.

Her vision said, as did the clay beast who was the chosen friend of the child, "Individual man does not create good or evil. They have existed before man; but at moments of choice he determines the nature of the child who shall be brought to birth within him."

"This is Mary, my daughter, who is also my mother."

Such words come from a wisdom far deeper than the personal un-conscious. In conversations with these imaginary companions or with the images of our dreams, we have all been astonished at receiving a reply quite alien to conscious thought or feeling.

Another, a far different friend from the beast or the creature who closed the door on love, was chosen by a very young boy. "I have a friend. He is little as a Twinkle and big as Pitch-Black Dark." He described Twinkle as "a little spark like the ones that fly out of a bon-fire; but Twinkle doesn't go out, he stays there." He said, "Sometimes he spoke of him as a Twinkle than a star, but he really is a star." Once I wake up at night, and there he is—Pitch-Black Dark. I am afraid but I look into him, and there is Twinkle sitting inside him." At another time he said, "You know Pitch-Black Dark can walk right into the daytime; then I have to *think hard* to see Twinkle."

Is not Twinkle the same infinitesimal spark that is perceived in the following vision of the Lonely One?

I looked upon space and I beheld darkness . . . a great void that had no form nor boundaries.

Then from the center of the void rose a single shaft, whether of stone or of a gray and lifeless tree I could not tell. As the shaft rose the creatures fell away till nothing was left but the void with the shaft standing in the midst. Then I saw that on the shaft there hung a human figure that held within itself all the loneliness of the world and of the spaces. Alone, and hoping nothing, the One hung and gazed down into the void. For long the One gazed, drawing all solitude unto itself. Then deep in the fathomless dark was born an infinitesimal spark. *Slowly it rose from the bottomless depth and as it rose it grew until it became a star.* And the star hung in space just opposite the figure, and the white light streamed upon the Lonely One.[9]

This vision is of the same substance as the child's image of his Friend. Here is the void—Pitch-Black Dark—from which the spark is born, a spark "that rose from the bottomless depth and . . . grew until it became a star." He is "littler than a star, yet he really *is* a star." He is the light seed that may grow into the star of individual being. Heraclitus calls the soul "the essential spark of the star"; Meister Eckhart speaks of it as "the *scintilla vitae*," "the spark of life, the soul spark," and again as "that very essence of God, the highest and the purest which is seized upon by the Holy Spirit and carried upward by the flame of love." The child likened it to "a little spark like the ones that fly out of a bonfire," only it "doesn't go out." This world of the spark is the "Vale of Soul-making" where, "as various as the Lives of Men are—so various become their Souls, and thus does God make individual beings, Souls, . . . of the Sparks of his own essence."[10]

But the child, with that wisdom which is beyond knowledge, realizes that Pitch-Black Dark can walk right into the daytime. Fear, ignorance and evil contained in the shadow, the sense of impotence, the terror of the unknown, can overwhelm the daytime light of consciousness; the spark is threatened by the suffocating darkness of unconsciousness, and by the unknown peril that he must encounter in meeting a threatening situation. Yet the dark is also the friend, the angel with whom each must wrestle till he obtains the blessing. Then the courage to *think hard* is needed to hold to the experience; that is, to see Twinkle sitting in the center of daytime darkness and to

---

[9] One of a series of visions seen by a woman. See my book, *The Inner World of Man*, "Visions," p. 245. Also quoted by Jung in *Aion*, p. 220 n.

[10] Keats, Letter to George and Georgiana Keats, Sunday 14 Feb.–Monday 3 May 1819. In *Selected Letters*, p. 258.

hold fast to the light which is "a strength without limit and in-corruptible." For "the spark comes higher to the truth than any human knowledge." To hold to the truth that is higher than human knowledge is the courage to hold to the essence that can behold the light of God even in hell, for it is this essence that lives in the darkness "but that faces straight up to God." It is the essence contained in the opposites, hence it is the element that is beyond good and evil.

The child sees Twinkle *sitting* in the center of Pitch-Black Dark, that is, remaining still, waiting, withdrawn from action, as the Buddha sits within the thousand-petaled lotus, letting the light grow through meditation and contemplation. Twinkle sits in the center of darkness, where the light is at rest.

This child had his times of solitude when he loved to be alone. In such times Twinkle was formed out of his own sitting still, within the darkness where the light also is found. Twinkle was the child's vision of the light seed, the essential germ of the being, the self.

When the sun has set, and the moon has set, and the fire is gone out, and the sound hushed, what is then the light of man?

The Self indeed is his light; for, having the Self alone as his light, man sits, moves about, does his work, and returns.

Who is that Self?

He who is within the heart, surrounded by the senses, the person of light, consisting of knowledge.[11]

---

[11] The Upanishads, in Robert O. Ballou, ed., *Bible of the World*, p. 55.

CHAPTER 4

Enemies of Choice
Part I

◈◈◈

"He takes you and cleans away all your ghosts."

As WE ENTER the country of the enemies of choice, we find ourselves in gray mists where ghosts wander over the waters of unconsciousness. We recall the words of the child's dream: "He takes you and cleans away all your ghosts." How comforting it sounds, this act of grace by which He will do it all for you. How sweet to rest upon this reassurance and to forget the crux of the dream's message, the eternal challenge, the *if* that stands at the gateway of choice. "*If* you die when God tells you.*" It is man's own choice that gives to God the power to clean away the ghosts that haunt his life and keep him back from his own heroic encounter. The act of grace and the act of choice establish a covenant between man and God.

A child dreams of a Tall White Ghost with a magnet in its hands. "It just stood there." But the irresistible power of the magnet drew him nearer, nearer. He woke in terror. The ghost disappeared, but only into invisibility, which gives to a ghost its greatest power. Vanishing into the darkness of the unconscious, it lured his conscious energy away from the tasks of day into a world of daydream where wishes were horses and dream heroes might ride to bloodless victories over imaginary monsters. He was a timid child; also he loved the pleasant land of laziness. It was safer to conquer dream dragons than those that suddenly jumped out of the multiplication table or con-

43

fronted him as energetic playmates. In daydream he could avoid encounter with his own shadow, for his shining little fantasy hero had no substance, hence cast no shadow, no discernible darkness with which the ego would have to come to terms. Shadowless heroes ride into a land peopled by shadowless ghosts who, like witches and sorcerers, cast no shadows but work dark magic, enticing, then compelling, conscious energy down to their shadowless land where all is really in the power of the unseen shadow. The child thought of this land as a place of freedom, but there he was really a prisoner of his own regressive fantasies. Only by killing the dream hero could he liberate his small hero self who could meet his own dragon of timidity and inertia.

When the drifting daydream is followed into the land of nonliving, one finds oneself in that limbo of unconsciousness in which both the world of outer achievement and the world of the creative unconscious lose their reality; the heroic encounter then becomes a battle of phantoms. This land from which they come and to which they return is the floating Lotus Island of somnolent content. Here the crocodile god, Inertia, presides. He invites you to share his sunny log and, as you contentedly bask in the sun, he obligingly swallows the energy that might disturb your sleep.[1] He even guards you against the intrusive memory of the night dream, for the night dream is a vivid living presentation of what is happening in the world of outer reality and of the creative unconscious. It shows the crocodile in his true nature and challenges the ego to fight for the values he has stolen away. It is this crocodile god, Inertia, who gave the magnet to the Tall White Ghost.

Inertia is one of the greatest enemies of conscious choice. Its power is not limited to childhood. A middle-aged woman had lived a pleasantly passive life. Many things—a husband, children, domesticity—had happened to her. Sometimes vague dissatisfactions floated through her or unfocused feelings of guilt disturbed her enjoyment. She had not bothered about them until physical symptoms invaded her territory of somnolent content. She was beginning to have headaches, dizziness; she was always tired; unaccountable discontent became nagging dissatisfaction. What was the use of life anyway? Why

---

[1] We ask to doze away our opportunity to live. In the words of a none-too-efficient cleaning woman as to her somnolent contentment, "When I works I works gentle, when I sits I sits easy, when I worries I sleeps."

did other people seem to get so much out of it? The unconscious answered her indolent query. She had a dream.

Someone gave me a picture of a cow ruminating in a pasture—hoofs tucked under, eyes vacant in contented contemplation of nothing. This "someone" said, "Here is a puzzle for you to solve. From measuring the square of the hypotenuse of the triangular shadow cast by the cow, you must estimate the height, depth and volume of the area of dark attraction."

The dream piqued her by its apparent senselessness. She liked puzzles—when they were not too hard. She also liked cows. Cowlike, she ruminated about the dream. Words came back to her—her sister's voice, "Clumsy as a cow, stupid as a cow, lazy as a cow." She heard her own voice answer from a distant past, "All right, I'll *be* a cow if I want to." Was she really a cow?

Often she envied cows their placid passivity. All they had to do was to lie in the sun and contentedly chew the cud of nonreflection. She was good as a cow, patient as a cow; she gave placidly of the milk of human kindness when it did not involve too much activity on her part. This worked well. She was liked. She was good. Imperceptibly she began to identify with the cow and to live out the cow side of her nature. Even her children were produced by the cow: they occurred in the course of nature; they were easier to create than ideas. But now this placid undisturbed existence bored her. Life drifted by; she was becoming conscious of its emptiness. The biological cow stage was over. She was middle-aged, and inertia had kept her from any development by which she could meet the changing demands of her woman life. She was creating only physical symptoms instead of mature thoughts and feelings. The shadow of the cow had been as pleasant as the shadow of a tree, but now there was chill in its dim protection.

Then another memory confronted her: the day when she had not bothered about the problem of the square of the hypotenuse. Mathematics was all problems; she didn't like problems. She had wished she could drop geometry, and did—by the simple method of flunking. Until that time she had taken it for granted that she would go to college; all her family went. But now her decision was made for her, and she was saved from the hard work that college would have entailed. At her own entreaty she went to an easygoing finishing school

where her education was indeed "finished," and from there she inertly wandered into the cow pasture, the square field of shadowy content.

The dream's misstatement of the mathematical problem that she had evaded piqued her indolent curiosity. As a "puzzle" it amused her. Indolently, she examined the cow and its shadow. This brought to memory her own words, "All right, I'll *be* a cow." It was all her sister's fault. She would never have thought of being a cow if her sister had not kept calling her one. Her sister was a witch whose incantations had transformed her into this placid animal. Behind this projection of her faults her shadow hid. Projections are handy closets where shadows, like family skeletons, may be shut away. But fortunately the door of this closet would not stay shut. The dream jarred her from her somnolent satisfaction with her cow self. A small desire stirred, a desire to be her human self. This desire opened the closet door and the shadow confronted her. As she looked at it, she became intuitively aware of the meaning of the dark area of attraction formed by the shadow of the cow. It was the foursquare field of gray unconsciousness where her shadow had chosen to live—a field free of problems, free of the black and white of differentiated values. It was the refusal of choice that had opened the door to the projected image —had, so to speak, welcomed the cow and led her to pattern her life on an unconscious identification. Could this newborn desire to be her human self companion her on the night journey through the dark area of the cow's shadow?

It was a very small desire. It had to be nurtured as carefully as a blue baby. It had to be guarded from the dreary drafts of futile self-pitying regrets. Vague, undefined, self-pity draws the energy away from the clear-eyed perception of the traitor, the personal shadow that has need of its own darkness to conceal its theft of conscious values whereby it robs the ego of its power of conscious choice.

Such a symbol as the cow is Janus faced. One face turns toward the light, where consciousness reveals its positive aspects. The other faces the shadow and is increasingly fascinated by that which moves in darkness. In examining the symbol in its transpersonal aspects we find its life-giving as well as its death-dealing face.

As mother symbol the cow is the nurturing aspect of the feminine psyche. In the beginning the earth cow licked away the hoarfrost that covered the earth, and a man and a woman sprang to life, and

the cow nurtured them with her milk until they came into their own strength. As the first living creature rising from the primordial flood, the cow is symbol of world-creating motherhood, of fertility and fecundity. In Egypt she appears as Hathor, the cowheaded mother goddess, also as Nut, who "waters the earth with her rain milk and carries the sun god on her back." As Mehurt, she is the goddess of new beginnings, appearing sometimes as a pregnant woman, sometimes with a woman's body and a cow's head. She holds in her right hand a scepter, round which is twined the stem of the great world lotus out of which the sun rose for the first time at the world's creation. As a cow with eighteen stars, she is the night sky. She is also the opener of the way, who holds the key to the gateway of rebirth.

The *I Ching* says:

Care of the Cow brings good fortune. Doubled clarity, clinging to what is right transforms the world and perfects it. . . . Therefore it is said, Care of the cow brings good fortune.[2]

This care brings into clarity the meaning of both the shadow and the positive qualities of the cow as world mother symbol.

The woman had lived only in the shadow of the cow, and all its life-giving qualities had been obscured. Could the cow, as life-giving, energy-endowing symbol, hold for her the keys of rebirth?

In the development of the symbol, the twofold aspect of the mother appeared, both, however, first seen as outside herself. The witch mother, who had turned her into a cow, was still projected on the sister; the good mother, who would give her back her human form, was projected upon the analyst. As part of the needed transference, this projection had to be accepted not in the form the patient desired, which was to find an "always mother" to whom she would be the "always child," but in the form of the creative mother who would help her to find her own freedom of choice.[3] The transference

---

[2] Vol. II, p. 179.

[3] If the analyst identifies with the positive projection, he soon has to deal with its negative aspects. A woman sent by a psychiatrist came for analytical help. After the first few consultations, the psychiatrist reported, "You have done a wonderful thing. She has never trusted anybody. Today she tells me that she trusts you implicitly. In fact, her words were, 'I feel as though she were an incarnation of Christ.' " "How terrible!" I answered. "Wait until a reality rears its ugly head; then she will see me with horns, cloven hoof and tail—complete." The good man protested vehemently. About three weeks later a dream brought in one of those realities. There it sat, stating in the clear, even if veiled, language

acts as a bridge to the discovery of the helper within the self. The dreamer's quest was to find the creative mother within her own psyche who could free her from the shadow of the cow and connect her with the positive life-giving aspects contained within the symbol. She could then, through "doubled clarity," learn to become the good mother to the children of her psyche that had theretofore lived the ghost life in the shadow of the cow. This lifted the mother projection from the analyst.

All these images—cow, witch mother and creative mother, shadowed pasture and sunlit way—she now saw as within herself. This enabled her to realize what the shadow of the cow had done to her inner life and to her life of relatedness.

In each of these dreams, ghost magnet and cow, an outer event, meaningful because of what it constellated in the unconscious, spoke to the dreamer. At a children's party, the boy who dreamed of a ghost with a magnet had watched a game in which a concealed magnet drew tiny iron men about as it moved below a surface where they were scattered. The game did not make the dream: other children who watched did not dream of a ghost; only to this child, who was already in the power of the invisible magnet, did the ghost appear. It revealed the fact that an invisible power, stronger than his ego will, was moving him about like a tiny iron man. He told the dream to a sympathetic adult, and together they talked about magnets that had power to draw one away from one's own life. They studied fairy tale and myth. How did the hero meet his dragons or lions? Not by sitting in his castle and dreaming of his mighty victories over them—that would make him more afraid than ever—but by going out to fight them. Daydream became active imagination. The child named and personified some of the monsters who filled him with fear. Thus he became able to devise ways of fighting them. He even challenged the ghost and robbed it of its magnetic power through his own choice of meeting his daily realities.

The woman's dream also showed that the problem had been con-

---

of the dream, unpleasant truths about her own evasion of responsibility. As the meaning of the dream emerged, her indignation increased. She left snorting. That evening the doctor telephoned me. "You win. I found her waiting in my office. She said, 'I have never been so disillusioned. I trusted that woman to save me, and today she threw everything back at me. She is a devil.' " She was impervious to the fact that the dream itself "threw everything back at her," so offering her a way of salvation.

stellated by a meeting of inner tendency and outer event. It was the hidden desire for a lazy self-indulgent life that had answered, "All right! I'll be a cow." Her acceptance of the role gave her sister's scornful comments magic power that made her welcome the cow as her totem animal.

Using these long-buried memories as signposts along the way, she was able, step by step, to solve the problem which she had evaded so long ago, and to estimate the height, depth and volume of the area of dark attraction through which she had to journey to find her way to the light of consciously-accepted life.

During the analytical journey, the dreamer became aware of the dual action of projection on subject and object. If the object, through a process known as introjection, takes the projected image into his own psyche, it pursues a life of its own that feeds upon the energy of the ego and robs it of the power of choice. She had taken into herself the image of the cow that her sister had projected upon her and had identified with it. The projected image has an uncanny way of discovering the vulnerable spot, the unlocked door, in the psyche of its chosen victim, and through this door it effects its entrance. Her own laziness, her secret desire to avoid effort, was the traitor who unlocked the door and welcomed the image. It is this traitor, this inner enemy, with whom man must deal if he would free himself from the almost magic bond which assigns to each person the part he is to play in the interaction of subject and object. For "we are betrayed by that which lives within."

Projection affects only the one who has created the image unless the object opens the door to the projected image. With its entrance there is a magic interplay in which both subject and object become involved. When we see two people caught in this confusion of unconscious interrelatedness we know that each has left a door unlocked: for if the projection encountered a locked door, it would, like a boomerang, return to the projector.

Nevertheless, there is a legitimate area of interaction, for the person who refuses the projection need not thereby limit his power of sympathetic understanding. Although he may not—and indeed should not—be drawn into a relationship not his, he refrains from speaking the negative word that would increase the shadow element in them both. Whatever small part he plays will be on the side of life.

When a need is not made conscious, desire seeks completion

through an object rather than through self-development. It goes questing for one who will fulfill its own unconscious demand. Often, as though drawn by one of these ghost magnets, the complementary object comes to meet it.

The emotionally undeveloped man who is unconsciously looking for a mother will discover—or will be discovered by—the woman who is seeking a permanent child, one who will not grow up and leave her. He who hates his own life will find an image of hate confronting him in an outer object. He who fears commitment and would shirk responsibility will encounter a tyrant ready to enter in and take over his life.

When two people are caught in this magic bond that is both resented and desired there is often a strange interplay in the unconscious. If either discovers what in himself is creating this bond and has the courage to cut himself free, the other may, through a strange synchronistic happening, find that the bond is mysteriously broken in himself also.

The clue to a case of mutual involvement is found in the words of a "selfless" young widow concerning her relation to her only child, a son. "I cannot live my own life *until he is safe*." She poured her libido into him until he no longer knew which impulses were his own and which were born of her maternal solicitude. The boy was like his father—brilliant, unstable, without self-direction. The father had failed, she felt, because he had been forced into a life not temperamentally his own. She was "between the devil and the deep blue sea." The boy not only must choose for himself but also must be saved from himself. Accordingly she built a nice protective fence about a pasture of well-selected clover where he could safely choose the clover head that was most to his liking. The trouble was he didn't like clover and objected to the fence. He tried to find a way out, but in his inner world he was fenced in by his self-distrust and his fears. At last he leaped both fences. He ran away.

Despair seized upon the mother. Only the thought that he might return and need her kept her from suicide. Nightmares drove her to analysis but, as nightmare changed to dream, she accepted only the associations that dealt with his problem. At last she stopped struggling to let her selflessness interpret the dreams. She let them act upon her, and a consciousness of the meaning of individual life broke upon her.

Summer came; she and the analyst were both leaving town. As the

last analytical hour drew toward a close, a light fell upon her and she said, "I am going to take up my own life and learn to live it even if I never see him again. My sorrow will go with me always, but it will be my own life that I shall live." It was the end of the hour. The clock struck twelve.

Three days later she received a letter. Its date was the day of her decision. It read: "Dear Mother, I am sitting on a hillside three thousand miles away. Just now I heard the clock strike nine and suddenly I felt that a fear that had been with me always was gone. I am coming home."

The striking of twelve had occurred simultaneously with the striking of nine in the faraway village. At the moment of her decision the fear of her enveloping love fell from him. There had existed between them an identification so close that it was not broken by separation or by the thousands of miles between them. Only when, by conscious act of choice, she broke the threads that bound her life to his could he feel released from his fear of her.

Yet no one can accomplish the inner release of another person. Freedom can be offered, but it must also be accepted in order for it to "take." The task of living is an individual one. Her acceptance of responsibility for her own life did not automatically bring about his acceptance of his. Something in his unconscious was also ready.

It is a long journey from projection to clear and conscious relationship. Before this can be accomplished, the magnetic power of the ruling image must be broken by each of the persons involved.

Perhaps the greatest defense against projection is a reverence for life and a respect for the value and the dignity of the human personality.[4]

Another enemy of choice is identification, an unconscious process through which one accepts the thoughts and emotions of another as though they were one's own. The origin of this identification may be undue admiration or blind love that has lost the power of individual perception.

Through this identification one surrenders the creative potential of his personality. Original experiences are no longer possible. One loses the knowledge of one's own identity and of one's unique quality

---

[4] For this and other instances of such power of projection see my article, "Three Illustrations of the Power of the Projected Image," in *Studien zur Analytischen Psychologie*, Vol. I, pp. 247 ff.

which is the essence of one's own being. Then a proxy life lives itself in the psyche. The hypnotic power of a magician is increased if his incantations are inaudible. Since one no longer hears spoken words of authority one therefore assumes that choice, and the desire that dictates choice, are one's own. No conflict disturbs contented acquiescence.

Even the death of the one who carries this image of love and authority does not break the identification. Life may still be lived in terms of the feelings and convictions of the beloved dead. The image, no longer existent in the outer world, still rules from the unconscious. One still follows the established pattern, thinks given thoughts, feels the already prescribed feelings. The image acts; the ego accepts.

Identification may become so strong that it prevents the birth of a new attitude. A middle-aged woman had always preferred the members of her own family to any other persons; especially she admired the women of the family. She rejoiced that her mother's thoughts and feelings were also hers. She considered herself extremely fortunate to have such a family and very wise to have appreciation of them. She pitied people who had family differences. It made life so hard. Then, unaccountably, she was disturbed by the stirring of a personal desire that she secretly knew would not meet with family approval. Life has a way of interrupting contentment. This illegitimate desire constellated a dream.

I am going to have a child. I go home to tell the family about it. They are all in the living room. As I explain, not a word is spoken, but in the silence something is happening. The life process stops within me. The embryo is dissolving. I shall have no child.

Identification had touched the unborn child of her own creative potential with the cold finger of death.

One may oneself choose that the child shall not be brought to birth because it would involve too much trouble. A pleasure-loving man demanded that the woman whom he wished to marry should promise never to have children. He asked flippantly, "Why should I change my life for someone I do not even know?" This is the question many men unconsciously ask of the feminine principle within the self. "Will you promise not to insist that I fulfill my creative possibilities—not to demand your right to nurture and bring to birth po-

tentials for which I shall have to assume responsibility?" In other words, "Will you let my life of creative thought and feeling alone, and not wake me up when I prefer to sleep!" Such a man does not wish to change his life, either to meet the demands of human relationship that love brings to birth, or for the sake of the unknown possibilities that might be born within his psyche and involve him in commitment to a chosen goal. These children would have to be cared for and brought into adult relation to his masculine life.

Yet this is what we are called upon to do: to accept the experience that will bring to birth a latent potential—a child who will dare the leap into the unknown, destroying our contented security; a child who places upon us new responsibility, who may even lead us into the darkness of the unconscious in search of other unborn or lost potentials of the self. This is the child who "is come to seek and to save that which is lost."[5]

The unfulfilled potential, the unlived experience, haunts consciousness, for deep down in every man lives the knowledge that the sin of unfulfillment is a sin against the Holy Ghost, the spirit of life whose breath is the Awakener. In Christ's parable unfulfillment is the sin of the slothful servant who, receiving the one talent from his master, wraps it "in a clean white napkin" and buries it until he is called upon for an accounting. He plays safe and so forfeits that which was originally given. Similarly in life one may hoard a chosen virtue, running no risk of losing it through living experience that may require encountering evil within oneself or risking its loss in the market place of life. Too late, perhaps, we discover that what we have saved through false caution we have most truly lost. We may plead unconsciousness, yet, if we look back with honesty, we know that at a critical moment, an experience, or a dream, or a voice came to arouse a consciousness of new life which we refused. We must accept the unpleasant knowledge that in that moment we chose to remain unconscious, and that "before the bar of nature and fate unconsciousness is never accepted as an excuse; on the contrary, there are very severe penalties for it."[6]

A woman who hoarded her virtue of chastity believed herself to be dedicated to the service of love; but love in her creed was a bodiless spiritual force that took no account of human manifestations. Looked

---

[5] Luke 19:10.
[6] Jung, *Answer to Job*, p. 162.

at through the wrong end of the telescope, the truth of love shrank to a small bright speck called "pure spirit," and as she continued to gaze through this concentrating lens, pure spirit shrank into "purity," purity in turn shrank into "chastity." Focusing upon this revelation of the essence of truth and love, she set out to find relationship. "Seek and ye shall find." What is found depends upon the vision of the seeker and the nature of his desire: sight and discovery are strangely directed by inner choice of that which is to be found.

It is not surprising, therefore, that she found love embodied in a musician whose talent was also dedicated to pure spirit. His music had the high soprano purity of the boy's preadolescent voice, with its haunting suggestion of the spirit world. This quality may be retained far past its time through castration; the voice of the elderly eunuch may still have the beauty of that of the young god. Psychological castration also prolongs this false youth. The man retains the ghost image of the young god within himself and expresses it in that which he creates, but it is held at the expense of maturity and the individual life of transformation. His music is all treble notes, a melody without the harmonies and dissonances of full orchestration. His spirituality does not come from struggle with the realities of life, whether they move as dark passions, desires, conflicts of vocation or as assimilated experiences of the outer world. His unreal involvement with spirit only produces a child cherub with no body below the wings.

In woman he seeks this same type of spirituality. His salvation might have been found through the fascination of a dark earthy woman who would necessitate an encounter with the opposites and a struggle in which he would have to fight for his individual way.

Images of a feather flock together, especially when persons do not want to be disturbed by the conflicts of life. In this case like sought like because of an evasive choice of the same limiting pattern. They both preferred to remain unconscious of the reason for their choice of the love object. We ask for consciousness but resist its coming lest it involve us in a task we do not desire. We are fortunate if a blow of fate thrusts the conflict upon us, for then we are forced to come to grips with the enemy who confronts us, and courage comes through encounter. But failure to meet the challenge delivers us over to the enemy and, if vanquished, we shrink to smaller proportions.

Unconscious of the true nature of their choice, this man and woman, caught in the same limitations, embarked upon a spiritually

inspired love affair. It seemed to the woman divinely directed. She was quite unaware of the fact that a truly masculine man would be scared to death of her, or that she would have looked on such a man with scornful rejection of the problem he would present.

The relationship was moving undisturbed in the way she had chosen when she had a dream:

> I am on my way to the temple of music. I see before me the gleaming white columns and the shining steps that lead to the portal. But just in front of me is a pile of dirt that covers the narrow path from edge to edge. I draw back, looking for a way around it so that my white garment will not be soiled. A voice says, "Why do you draw aside? It is out of this dirt that the stars are made."

She told this as an illustration of the meaninglessness of dreams. She scornfully rejected the suggestion that it might contain a profound truth, a truth perhaps applicable to her life as a woman. At this point she was toying with the idea of analysis. She decided against it and turned to the study of religious cults which she felt would produce inner children of light. Had the dream roused fear of reality, or did she really prefer to be a spiritual whore?

Having turned her back on the task indicated in the dream, she returned to her image of herself, a virgin serving in the temple; but she knew nothing of the real meaning of virginity.

The virgin retains within herself an immaculate essence that will not suffer violation yet is open and receptive. It receives the seed, it bears the fruit of the womb. It is mother, lover, virgin: in it a feminine trinity is brought to life and can function freely in love of life, in compassion and in discrimination. It is the mother-son, mother-daughter, feminine-masculine relatedness, for love is the uniting force, the element that holds the opposites together, the attitude that accepts the word and gives it earth birth. Yet it is inviolate in that it will not suffer dark forces of evil to enter and violate the sanctuary of the heart. Open to truth, it cherishes its wholeness of being. Virginity is, in its essence, sacred not because it is a state of physical inviolateness but because it is a state of openness to God.

Mary is the virginal attitude of receptivity, the opening of matter to spirit, of earth to heaven. "Be it unto me according to thy word."[7]

---

[7] Luke 1:38.

That is, Let me receive that which I have been destined to receive, and let me bring forth that which is intended.

The *I Ching* says, "Perfect indeed is the sublimity of the Receptive, all beings owe their birth to it, because it receives the heavenly with devotion."[8]

The dreamer wore the pure white costume of the virgin, but it was the spinster in her that played the given part and, in a truly spinsterish manner, deprived the man of the warmth and reality of human love in its creative wholeness. Such a woman spins a web of separateness about herself that isolates her from life. Like a spider, she is the center of her own weaving, dangerous to approach, deadly to the masculine principle when caught in her web. Her self-woven fantasy of purity, perfection or of ego power is that of the devouring mother.

The temple to which the dreamer's steps were directed was the temple of music, the language of the heart; but in her pathway was the dirt out of which stars might be made. Love transforms the dirt, the instinctual lust, the possessive emotion, the unredeemed biological element, into the star of conscious love.

The "dirt" was the despised element needed for the creation of the star, the symbol of individuation, of acceptance of one's own life, of wholeness as it comes in our own experience.

In this dream, the inner voice spoke directly to her as woman. It told her where she now stood in relation to the particular experience that life had given to her. She was at a place of choice. She could, perhaps, find a way of avoiding this element which she saw only as dirt, but then the temple would be for her only a place where wholeness is sacrificed. The priest would be the castrated son.

The "dirt" would have saved her. Had she worked to liberate the spark contained in matter, its transformation would in turn have transformed her. Sexuality unredeemed by love is only lust ("dirt"), but transformed by wholeness of relationship it has a magic power to fuse body and spirit together, and the star of love is created. For love liberates the spark from the heart of matter.

Only one who has accepted wholeness as goal of life and has become an individual can love wholly and in freedom. The concept of "pure" love often connotes nothing but a sexless anemic product

---

[8] Vol. II, p. 19.

achieved by one who has separated himself from life. Yet "pure" love may contain all the vibrant passion of sex together with all the deep joy of companionship, all the self-fulfilling wealth of the one who receives and gives fully—who also chooses fully.[9]

The woman made her choice. She refused the gift life offered her. Looking through the wrong end of the telescope, she saw the "dirt" only as dirt, and this it remained to her. It was pushed down into the unconscious and there, in the power of the shadow, it continued to accumulate until she was delivered over to the dark images of the despised elements.

As she grew old, she became more and more merciless in her judgment of those who accepted that which she had rejected. The old who have refused life often become enemies of the young who have accepted it. Her prophesies against the "sinner" remind one of Cassandra who, being loved by the God Apollo, and professing love for

---

[9] A child of four consorts with "such nice witches who do wonderful magics." She is taking her first railway journey. A nun passes the door of the compartment. The child rushes out and, clutching the formidable black garments with both hands, calls to her mother, "Oh, Sallie, come quick. I've caught a witch on the train." Affronted dignity freed itself from small hands. The mother tried to explain the nature of the strange phenomenon, who was not a witch. "And she will never marry?" "No." "And she will never, never have a baby?" "No." Just then the father appeared, and the child exclaimed, "Oh, Peter, I thought I caught a witch on the train but she turned out to be a nothing."

The child did not cease to believe in "witches who do wonderful magics," but she knew that a person who was a "nothing" never could be a witch, especially not a mother witch. Here too an inner intent toward life shows through. One has a suspicion that it was not because the woman was a nun that the child found her repulsive, but because of the unacknowledged motives that had determined her choice of vocation.

There are human beings to whom saintliness comes as a vocation, but before accepting it as the call of the spirit, there must be an inner certainty, especially a certainty of the power of love, within one's own psyche: "Love has shaken my mind as a downrushing wind that falls upon the oak trees." Such love can lead the devotee to the transpersonal power of love.

A nun moved and shaken by the power of love would not have seemed to this child to be a "nothing" even though she could not be a witch who could become a mother. There are saintly methods which are creative energies; but these are always based not on repression but on the leavening power of love. Had this choice been a dedication of the spirit of living love, she would have met the eager onrush of the child with understanding and humor and with some of that gaiety which moves in "the laughter of the saints." Then, even though the small woman self of the child could not understand this strange choice of a destiny, she would have tucked the experience away in the storehouse of to-be-fathomed mysteries; she would not have concluded that a nun must be a "nothing."

him, asked of her lover the gift of prophecy. This he bestowed upon her. When she had received it, she denied the gift his love asked of her, that she should bear him a child. His gift then became her curse, for she prophesied out of her own darkness, which saw only disaster. No man believed her.

The refusal of the task in favor of the saintly identification brought its dark enantiodromia, for in old age the "dirt" became activated in a nontransformed reality of evil. She began to hear voices, to be "tormented by devils." Still clutching her idea of inner purity, she took refuge in a sanitarium. Yet the voices continued their prophecies of evil; the repressed instincts mocked her, calling out obscenities. She died trying to stop her ears to the inaudible voice that shouted down her saintly words. All the evil that her unconscious had projected into the dirt "from which the stars are made" became activated. Then mocking voices assailed her, for if we will not live our dream we may be compelled by fate to enact our nightmares.

The "dirt" to be redeemed is not always the same in each experience. But if the nature of the fulfillment is revealed by the inner voice and by the vision and it is rejected, the rejected element returns as regret or bitterness or sense of the futility of life. Then, as with this woman, the dirt, despised and untransformed, finds voice and shouts down the voice of love.

In refusing the demands of earth, she had also refused the demands of the spirit.

What we deny must be denied in the spirit of love, which is always intent on the greater fulfillment. We deny the body the right to violate, for passing satisfaction, the spirit of love in another human being. We deny the spirit the right to murder in the name of righteousness the instinctual factor that reaches out toward love, even as we deny the instinct the right to hold dominion over the spirit. For body and soul are not two warring substances but two different mediums by which man may become aware of himself and of the life that moves in him. We deny the right to self-destructive repentance that holds the future in the grip of the past, for the purpose of love is fulfillment and transformation.

Thus, guiltlessness may become the greatest guilt, omission the sin against choice, inertia the enemy of creative life.

CHAPTER 5

Enemies of Choice
Part II

❧ ❧ ❧

Restlessness begets meaninglessness, and the lack of meaning in life is a soul-sickness whose full extent and full import our time has not yet comprehended.[1]

Inertia, sloth, identification, projection, nonfulfillment—all are enemies of conscious choice. There is another enemy, twin brother of inertia, whose actions seem completely at variance with those of his slothful twin. This is restlessness, father of undirected activity, of busyness unrelated to purpose, willing worker of the mischief that Satan finds for busy hands to do. Inertia and restlessness both lure man away from the discovery of meaning.

The man who has found the meaning of his life expresses it in countless forms. He is "like a tree planted by the rivers of water, that bringeth forth his fruit in his season."[2] The tree is one tree, its fruit and its season are its own. Its oneness is manifest in multiplicity of branches, twigs, leaves and seed buds that reach up to the unity of the sky above, and in the roots that reach down to the unity of darkness in the earth below. Yet the tree is one; the sap that circulates through all the multiplicity of its form, that moves toward return to oneness in the seed, is the meaning of its individual life. Even so

---

[1] Jung, "The Soul and Death," in *Spring 1945*, p. 415.
[2] Psalm 1:3.

the man who has found the meaning of his life expresses this in many activities; his creativity flows into many forms, yet all are expressions of the oneness of his nature. Such a man "wandereth far yet sitteth still." He speaks, yet he is silent.

The restless man "speaks more than he says." He runs with "criss-cross footprints," and his way is confused. He darts at many goals from which he soon veers off, or "he mounts his horse and rides off furiously in every direction." Sitting still is stagnation; patience and meditation a waste of time. Intent on immediate achievement, he is ruthless in destruction of potentials that might slowly mature in their own form and season. In him wonder never develops beyond childish curiosity quickly diverted by a new interest.

A woman always rushing from activity to activity, enthusiastic today about this, tomorrow about that, dreams of a clucking hen who impatiently leaves her nest and turns to behold her hatching—an egg fully feathered without having bothered to become a chick. The hen glares with indignation at the egg; clearly its fault! Demanding so much time and attention, too! Clucking furiously, she hurries away. One suspects that she intends to lay more worthy eggs in more speedily responsive nests—which, as a matter of fact, is what the dreamer did after an amused glance at the dream.

Restlessness is forever off with the old love and on with the new, in pursuit, not only of petticoats, but also of ideas, purposes or magnificent causes. Or, if busyness becomes an end in itself, it does not relinquish the old but only crowds in the unrelated new. Then it is full of *works*—good works, bad works, indifferent works, but full to repletion.

A woman, very, very full of most estimable works, dreams:

> I am in a great assembly. In the center is a circular enclosure with a little gateway. Here a man is seated writing the names of the people who enter. I see myself walking majestically through the crowd, and as I reach the gate I proudly give my name—"Head of 57 Committees."[3]

The name fitted well in her engagement pad but was oddly out of place in the Book of Life. Her identity had vanished behind her multitudinous works.

---

[3] See my book, *The Inner World of Man*, p. 66. Heinz's advertisement of "57 Varieties" of pickles was much in evidence at that time.

A second dream shows how restlessness had produced meaningless-ness in her life as a woman.

I have come home after a busy day. The nurse tells me that the nursery roof leaks and the rain is coming in on the children. I answer impatiently, "Oh, just stuff it up with French pastry!"

She did not want to interrupt her good works for something as trivial as nursery needs if they intruded upon her important life in the world, even if the nursery housed her own children. In her chosen busyness she had lost the meaning of relationship and love.

In spite of her apparent unconcern, this dream seems to have moved within her, for in the next dream the unconscious shows her a way of new beginning that would never have occurred to her conscious ego.

I have built a new house. It has a relaxing room of which I am very proud; but when I show it to my analyst, I see it is a small dark closet, so small that one can neither stand, lie down or even sit in it. One can only crouch in a strange drawn-up position.

Her conscious would make a grudging concession to the fragment of meaning that she had gleaned from the former dreams. She too could pridefully relax if it did not take up too much room in her life. But what does the unconscious say in its choice of the dream symbol? The dark closet, the womb; crouching, "drawn-up," the posi-tion of the embryo; the relaxing place, stillness, darkness, silence. Could the dark closet be a chrysalis into which she might retreat, awaiting the next stage of development? There is no room for Rest-lessness in this dark closet. There is only quietude in which the life urge for transformation comes to the creature. From the material stored within the Self the psyche spins its own cocoon or chrysalis: a chamber of darkness and silence where transpersonal forces may work out the miracle of the next stage of being. If one chooses refusal of this inner urge, the second half of life is devoted to being a bigger and better caterpillar, or a large dead caterpillar.

This was a crossroads dream. It would not have come had not the potential of such choice been dormant within her. She accepted the small beginning of this "urge for transformation." It was a long journey, but from her acceptance of the dream symbol her analysis and her relationships took on new meaning.

Mr. Restlessbusyness is very popular in our modern world. His voice, over telephone, radio, television, breaks in upon our privacy. At his suggestion, we "time our lives to a production belt whose speed we do not control." He preaches "bigger," "better," "faster," "more." Even the nursery is invaded by his chatter.

A child of seven was losing sleep. Her busy efficient mother felt that "something must be done about it." To an adult who did not even own a television set, the child made her tragically simple explanation. "But I have to wake up at night because I want to *think*. You can't think in the day. There isn't time." The ambitious mother had struggled to give her small daughter every opportunity. She had forgotten that unrelated opportunities become only importunities.

"Man was not made to think the thoughts of others" nor to make of his mind a mirror whose surface, turned to the outer world of jostling hurrying shadows, is again vacant when the shadows have passed.[4] We fear the dark stillness where thoughts arise, images move and words are born out of silence—our immediate silence and the long distant silence out of which the Word was made flesh and feelings emerged in the truth of their own being. Then, through reflection, we make them our own. Jung says: "The richness of the human psyche and its essential character are probably determined by the reflective urge. . . . Reflection is the cultural instinct *par excellence*, and its strength is shown in the power of culture to maintain itself in the face of untamed nature."[5] This urge must maintain itself in the face of "untamed nature" within the psyche. Thinking at midnight is not popular. We shun the living midnight out of which the new day comes. Mr. Restlessbusyness is very, very busy, restlessly urging an immediacy unrelated to the eternal Now that connects us with the inner side of the present experience. Adults who find life meaningless seek to live by the demand feeding that is now offered to our children. They must have thoughts, feelings, sensations served hot off the griddle on momentary demand. Demand is not choice, especially not choice of meaning. We fear aloneness, confusing it

---

[4] This is not the mirror turned inward by the soul, which knows that "our minds are simply God's mirror reflecting the 'here and now' of creation" (Chung Yuan Chang). The reflections that move in this inner mirror are intuitive perceptions of those moments of beauty when the passing event is seen as reflection of the mind of God moving in the process of creation, of "thinking a world into being."

[5] E. D. Adrian *et. al.*, *Factors Determining Human Behavior*, p. 50.

with loneliness, forgetting that "religion is what a man does with his solitariness."[6] The man who fears the companionship of his own thoughts and shuns the silence out of which thoughts come to him and images arise within him is a lonely man. For he does not keep in his mind and heart, in the words of the Irish patriot, "images of magnificence" or "desires that can live in paradise." Such a man welcomes every intrusion of vagrant interest, every outer activity that bids him take without the effort of returning. He uses the radio, the television, the news tabloid to interrupt creative silence. He does not care what he hears so long as he does not have to hear any disturbing inner voices, nor even outer ones that necessitate exchange of ideas.

You cannot carry on a conversation with a radio. The dialectic process, whether with the outer or the inner "other," is a ritual of communication, a reciprocal interchange. Thought challenges thought, feeling reaches out toward the oneness of sympathetic understanding, a spark of intuition meets an answering spark, a concept emerges that without the interchange might never have taken on individual form. Taking-in-whatever-happens-to-come-along and creative receptivity are denizens of widely different worlds. Also—and of this there is no rational proof, only an irrational awareness—it may be that synchronicity, the acausal law by which things related in meaning spring simultaneously into being, works best in creative silence. In a familiar room, and simultaneously in a far-off laboratory, when minds are quiet, new perceptions of truths hovering on the brink of world consciousness flash into life. Can we place ourselves in such communion of silence that we become aware of the new that is moving in the deep stream of the human-divine spirit awaiting its release in man's consciousness?

It is easy to blame the radio or television, forgetting that one may choose one's listening or seeing, even as one may choose one's reading. We remember the words of the old sea captain, "Don't hold with books, readin' rots the mind." Any device used to escape from original thought "rots the mind." Yet books awaken thought if we are willing to think. If an original thought comes to us and we stifle it by reading on, we sin against the creative spirit. Escape into a book to avoid carrying through one's own thoughts or feelings is a kind of proxy living. One may use books, television, radio, to wallow

---

[6] After Alfred North Whitehead, *Religion in the Making*, p. 472.

in feeling that diverts us from the problems confronting us in our life. But this, after all, is our own choice which we cannot project upon the instrument. Completion is the aim of the creative spirit, but whether or not we complete the idea or give the awakened feeling form in experience is ours to decide.

For the workman and the artisan as truly as for the artist there is honor in the completed work: pride of workmanship in each thing well made, whether the object be the sturdily fitted parts of a workbench or the great symbolic carvings in a cathedral portal. There is always the call of the work that wants to be done. Unheeded, it still troubles the spirit of man. Form lies quiescent within the word, image within the formless material. "Hew the wood and I am there, cleave the stone and you shall find me." The release of the image in its indwelling form, whether it becomes manifest in material, in word or in act of love, is the choice of the artist in life, no matter how humble his calling.

A woman traveling in India chanced upon a maker of brass bowls. She picked up one of intricate design and asked its price. "Two annas." She thought of a friend who ran a "gifte shoppe" in America and of the profit she could make. "Ask him," she said to the interpreter, "how much they will be if I take fifty like this." The maker pondered. "Four annas." "But," said the bewildered woman, "tell him if I take so many they must be less, not more." The craftsman answered, "Tell the lady that if I repeat myself so many times I must have much money, for I shall need to go away into solitude so that my spirit can re-create itself."

I once found in a junk shop a Ming temple painting. The spirit of beauty shone through its battered surface. I took it home and sent for an Oriental man who restored such treasures. He stood before it a long time. "Yes, I will fix it. I will take it now." "What will it cost?" "I do not know." "When can you do it?" "I do not know." After several months he brought it back. He had re-created it. I stood reverently before it, then said, "No wonder it took so long." "Not the work," he answered. "That was swift; but the vision. I go into the country. I sit all day under a tree. It does not appear inside me. I am too far away. I may go again and again. One day I see it. Then I work quickly."

"And the price?" "Fifteen dollars." "For this!" "A man came yesterday bringing a terrible untrue object—such dreadful shape, such

angry color—I charged him four hundred dollars, so now I charge you fifteen. It likes this room."

The sand painter knows that not one grain of sand must fall except in accordance with the ancient pattern. He knows, too, that his work will be wiped out at the setting of the sun, but in the ritual act he re-energizes (re-creates) spirit in himself and in his tribe. Tranformation, which is the purpose of the creative spirit, moves in original concept, in re-animation of the image, or in reverent ritualistic repetition. For the eternal images contain a spiritual energy that transcends the limits of time and awakens new life in the one that serves them. They move from wholeness and re-create wholeness.

The machine age has in many cases denied the working man the wholeness of his creation. He has become "just the machine's contrivance for producing another machine." He feeds something into the maw. It is spewed out for another man to feed into another maw. Somewhere a finished product emerges, but it is not his, hence he no longer looks for the meaning of what he does but thinks only of how to get it over with. As the machine age moves into the age of automation, more and more the functions of men are usurped by the machine that now thinks, calculates, regulates, that can do everything but choose. Creative choice remains a human attribute if individual man is open to the vision and the voice.

The machine has thrust leisure upon modern man. Will he fill these hours with object worship and lust for possessions? Will he have surcease from toil which is rest, or escape from toil which is boredom? Undirected energy, released by boredom, drifts into inertia or runs restlessly in search of excitement. Man tries to compensate for his inner emptiness by an increasingly complicated outer life. Meagerness of spirit can live in abundance of leisure hours and of material things.

Leisure and the individual choices that it involves have been thrust upon mass man before he has attained the maturity to use them in ways that have individual meaning. The problem is how to re-energize the leisure, how to return man to the state of individual creativity which he used to experience in doing an entire job.

Even the word "creative" has come into bad odor from its popular misuse. We have creative advertising that produces demand for goods in a sheep-minded public; we have creative salesmanship that per-

suades the consumer to purchase unneeded goods; we have creative packaging that distracts attention from the quality of the contents; creative writing that fits the empty mind as a peg fits a hole; creative thinkers who turn out clichés, pep talks and slogans (often pious) that provide mass man with packaged thinking. In all this urgency for the ready-made, the urge to transformation, the true end of the creative process, is lost to a lock-step conformity strangely misnamed freedom of choice.

But does man want this choice? The bait that the totalitarian state holds out is that he will be relieved of the burden, the responsibility and the sacrifice that choice entails. It asks the question the Grand Inquisitor asked of a Christ who had returned to a modern earth. "Didst Thou forget that man prefers peace, and even death, to freedom of choice in the knowledge of good and evil?"[7] The totalitarian state relieves man of the burden of choice, and even of the burden of sin, provided his special brand of sin does not interfere with collective patterns.

The welfare state, so necessary in every period of change, has a similar danger, for the temporary necessity may become the habitual pattern. Social security can be substituted for inner security and man may drift into dole-mindedness claiming the rights of a dependent child. "Father must provide for me" or "Mother will take care of me" becomes "Society owes me a living whether or not I earn it." If one lacks the maturity of inner direction, willed purpose and a sense of chosen goal, the "right means in the wrong hands" produces only dependency.

Society, for its own sake, should make possible an individual creation that enriches our culture. But man can also become grant-minded, seeking permanent support for an embryonic talent or for a personal idiosyncrasy that he does not wish to have estimated at its real value. Then the talent assumes gigantic fantasy proportions and its demands become inordinate.

A young man felt that his family or the world or Providence owed him the support that his unproved talent demanded. He had the following dream:

A two-story house has been built exclusively for the use of the fabulous young man. He permeates it, oozing in some insub-

---

[7] Fyodor Dostoyevsky, *The Brothers Karamazov*, Book V, Ch. V, p. 302.

stantial manner into every part of it. He must be completely protected: no chill wind must blow upon him, no harsh sound must disturb him. Men are putting up storm windows, but they must step on tiptoe and use no nails; ladders must be put in place without a sound.

In fact, this fabulous young man must be hermetically sealed from all intrusion of reality. His precious essence must be kept like a wax flower in a glass case. And the fabulous young man succeeded in producing a sonnet which, like the wax flower, was perfect in form but static and lifeless.[8]

Whenever restless ambition or inertia directs the energy, the connection with the unconscious is lost and no pampering of embryonic talent can infuse the product with inner meaning.

When unearned privilege is denied, the frustrated ego seeks to avenge itself upon society for the "injustice" inflicted. It calls upon the Three Sisters of Fury: Restlessness, Jealousy, Vengeance. Restlessness leads; Jealousy, born of a secret knowledge that one has not fulfilled one's own potential, tries to tear down the one who has fulfilled the meaning of his individual life; Vengeance whispers the heroism of acts of violence. It exalts the shadow, the hero of the melodrama of destruction. The urge toward the heroic encounter, a deep urge in man, can be taken over by the shadow. Then the renegade becomes the hero.

Faced by demands of the reality that he has evaded, the alcoholic reaches for the bottle and pours himself the releasing drink. The renegade reaches for the bottled-up fear, emotional "fire water," intoxicating fantasy, and dispels the demand for conscious choice. Predisposition determines which drink is chosen, but the effect is the same: one cannot act, one should not be asked to act; the situation is wrong or the time element is wrong or the parents were wrong. Therefore the renegade is relieved of individual responsibility. At all events, there is nothing to do about it now. Better wait for another situation, one better suited to one's true potential, or for another dream, better suited to one's secret wish. For the renegade is a conscientious objector to reality.

The renegade may find false vitality in ego inflation, a minor but dangerous form of insanity that permits him to reject human claims.

---

[8] See my article, "The Creative Process," p. 36 *passim*.

One of its symptoms is a sense of god-almightiness that lifts him above choices and commitments demanded of the ordinary man. "Can one," he asks, "question the right of a god to a divine inhuman choice? Can one ask an eagle to scratch worms for barnyard fowl?" He makes secret fantasy a refuge from demanding reality. Here energy can be expended without conscious effort. The danger is that this energy becomes sealed off from the rest of the personality and is unavailable to consciousness.

Reality intrudes, fantasy breaks; then, seized by sudden fear, he magnifies his helplessness until he sees himself in a histrionic role. Or he may embrace disaster, exulting in the storm, riding with the winds, shouting with the waves and challenging others to ride with him to his magnificent tempest-wrought doom.

Or he may enter the realm of black magic where he listens to the crafty insinuations and rationalizations of his own peculiar devil. When the devil becomes the friend he worms his way into the confidence of the victim, bidding him stand choice-free lest, entrapped by commitment and fidelity, he may lose a new opportunity. Friend Devil counsels free love in the sense of love free from love's responsibilities, free choice as choice that can shift at any moment. The renegade, caught in any situation that demands commitment and permanence, prides himself on the cleverness by which he has wriggled out of the trap. A man who fancied himself in the role of Don Juan found himself unaccountably engaged to be married. He dreamed:

I see my fiancée sitting on the bank of a stream, fishing. She has hooked a great prize. Her line plays out, the rod bends, she draws in her struggling catch—a fat squirrel. It drops upon the bank, shakes itself free, makes for the woods and, just at the edge, turns and exclaims, "Jesus Christ, what a narrow escape!"

Such escape is the renegade's victory—escape from loyalty in all its forms.

He is the incarnation of compromise, hence his perpetual dodging behind the sudden excuse. To him religion becomes not a process of self-transformation and self-transcendence but part of this same "hedging." He seizes upon the convenient promises of salvation and soars into religious ecstasy only to backslide gloriously down the

devil's shaft when the demand comes to make good on his enthusiasms.

Perhaps as he reaches the bottom and seeks another escape he envisions himself the heretic who has broken from blind adherence to conventional religion. But heresy in its old definition meant individual choice. The heretic chose truth as it revealed itself to him and followed it even to martyrdom. Through this choice he left the spark of truth that he had made his own as a heritage to coming generations. The renegade refuses to examine truth, his own or the traditional heritage. He defies it to bend him to any choice. Nothing connects with the central self, neither virtue nor vice, neither love nor cruelty; nothing is worked out in loyalty to life experience. And yet it is he who boasts most loudly of the importance of his "self."

What is this self of which he boasts? It is best described by Peer Gynt, who is himself the apotheosis of the renegade desire:

> The Gyntish self, it is the sea
> Of fancies, exigencies, claims;
> All that, in short, makes my breast heave,
> And whereby I, as I, exist. . . .
>
> That "once for all" I can't abide . . .
>
> I must be myself *en bloc*
> Must be the Gynt of all the planet.[9]

But this "myself" that he proclaims "the Gynt of all the planet" is in reality only the infantile, demanding, unintegrated ego that defies the self and its commands. Through these ego choices the self becomes the enemy. Form, willed purpose, discovery of meaning, that make the Word incarnate in the life of man, are lost; for the renegade is only a trickster, a shadow form of Logos.

A shadow form of Eros is mood which, unpredictable as an ocean fog, rises from the unconscious in moments of choice and obliterates clear values on which conscious feeling depends. It can take possession of the ego at decisive moments and precipitate disaster. Unconscious man may suddenly become the victim of his mood. Jung tells of an African chief who returned from an unsuccessful hunting trip in a mood of white hot anger against the fortune that had betrayed

---

[9] Henrik Ibsen, *Peer Gynt*, Act IV, Scene I.

him. His little son ran to meet him, obstructing his path. He seized the child, wrung his neck and threw him into the bushes. Afterward he was overcome by an excess of grief and despair.

The I Ching says:

If a man remains at the mercy of moods of hope or fear aroused by the outer world, he loses his inner consistency of character. . . . Humiliations often come from an unforeseen quarter. Such experiences are not merely effects produced by the external world but logical consequences evoked by his own nature.[10]

If "the essential, the continuing cause" is sought in the outer world, the seeker is like "a man who persists in stalking game in a place where there is none"; he "may wait forever," for "what is not sought in the right way is not found."[11]

"The right way" is not repression. Even a child knows that if you stop up the spout of a boiling kettle the lid will blow off. Repressed or unused energy may boil deep down in the unconscious and blow the lid off a situation that has appeared to be as friendly as a purring tea kettle. Nor is excess virtue the answer, for it operates in the drawing room of lofty ideals or conventional pattern while in the kitchen below the shadow is boiling up resentments, righteous indignation and hurt feelings. It is better to let off a little steam before the overheated emotions blow up a relationship. And it is wiser to seek "the continuing cause" in one's own unconscious.

A neglected shadow is always busy cooking up moods. A fit of rage releases so much pent-up energy that an infantile person is carried out of himself into an intoxicating illusion of the ego's power. Emotion is a fiery force, a dynamism that, when possessed by the ego, can energize and illuminate every act; but when it is only unconscious mood, it possesses the ego: *it* acts, *it* destroys, *it* creates fear. Then the fire burns itself out, the mood has done its work and the ego feels no responsibility for the devastation it has caused. The wounds inflicted by the unconscious upon the unconscious of others may not show, yet often they do not heal. A potential of relationship may be destroyed by a psychic storm. When the storm has passed and the sun is out, the ego is in another mood and wonders what all the fuss is about, since it is quite ready to be amiably related. At other times,

10 Vol. I, p. 137.
11 Ibid.

the ego is fully conscious of the hurt and enjoys what mood has accomplished for him.

Since the ego of the person who has been emotionally possessed takes no lasting responsibility for what the mood has done and, moreover, does not reflect upon the nature of inner events that have caused the catastrophe, there is often a resulting bewilderment at finding the desired relationship has been shattered. The ego feels itself unjustly repudiated and rejected. It then takes refuge in that dreary self-deception of being the injured party. In a new burst of emotion, it claims the unearned privilege of equal and adult relationship.

When this is refused, indignation may turn to self-pity into which the ego creeps to lick imaginary wounds and brood on the injustice of life and the lack of human sympathy.

Mood is subject to oscillations of hope and despair that invade the unconscious personality. A sudden gaiety may arise from an unknown source. The world is beautiful, God is all-good. The mood-possessed ego is bursting with promises—promises to itself, promises to others, promises to life, generous outpourings of a lavish stream. Intuition traffics with magic, and possibilities are boundless. Then reality intrudes with a dull demand of duty, or with the equally dull demand of a person who wants a prosaic factual fulfillment of a poetic promise. The mood vanishes. Promises? What are promises? Life has taken back its promises, has snatched away the momentary glory.

Unrestrained mood falls into the power of dark, undifferentiated emotion, a chaotic condition where meaning and choice are swept away. When this happens, the extrovert succumbs to waves of mob psychology, the introvert to waves of hope and fear. In either case, all power of individual choice is lost to a suprapersonal force against which the disintegrated ego cannot stand. It is not until we listen to all the voices speaking in mood that we can know the creatures who may usurp our conscious choice at the crossroads of decision.

The immature woman and the man unrelated to his feelings are at the mercy of mood, for mood may have all the dynamism of emotion, but it never connects with the stable quality of conscious feeling. It never becomes rooted in love.

This is what one woman says of her encounter with the unconscious force which so often possessed her.

I had fought the mood so many times. I had escaped down any corridor of arrogant thought and willed words, of self-assurance of my own superiority, or of excuse because of my utter inability. Always I found waiting at the end of the corridor the mood—despair, self-hate, guilt, and defiance of guilt. I remained impotent and defeated. The mood could spring upon me at the moment when I felt most free. I remembered words read somewhere: "One must live with one's moods and be them, before one can escape from them." I was afraid. If I should once let myself *be* the mood, could I ever be myself again? Who was "myself" if not this creature so possessed? But I said to my despair, "The mood is reality because it exists. It is my reality because it has happened to me. Until I accept it as real because I am as I am, I can do nothing about it. I cannot talk with it. I cannot even hear what it is saying."

I knew I must be still and let the mood talk to me. At first my thoughts went rushing on like a shrill wind that shut out all sounds but its own shrieking. It stopped my ears from listening. Then I let the wind pass over me. I ceased struggling. Something deep within me acquiesced in acceptance of this force that was sweeping over me. The tense muscles of my soul became unstrung, relaxed; the compulsion of thought stopped and I heard the many voices of the mood and knew that all these many voices were my own. There were my denials of life, my lack of truth and honesty about myself; my mistakes, my refusals, my meannesses, my arrogant assumptions spoke from within myself, and I accepted them as my own. Then came quiet, and with quiet a light began to move in the darkness, and I said, "All these are my own; the good, the evil; the fortune, the misfortune; the light, the shadow; all are life, my life. I accept my life, I accept myself."

It was here that the miracle occurred, for I became myself.

Becoming myself, I was no longer imprisoned within myself. Myself was no longer my enemy, but my friend and companion, one who could forgive. And I saw—or felt—how acceptance means forgiveness and forgiveness means love. Then one comes to the center and finds not the storm but the quiet at the heart of the storm; not chaos of fear but quietude of love, a love that accepts and forgives all these creatures within the circle of being.

This happened many months ago. Moods still beat upon me like waves of darkness, but the rock is still there, at the center. Consciousness of the meaning of love and the experience of

myself as one who could experience love stood as a rock when the waves of the unconscious rose about me. I perceived this was not merely love of this or that, but love as a central energy, a power beyond yet within the self. It is to this experience that I must give loyalty. Through this I can learn to accept the mood and become aware of my own responsibility for dealing with it. I suppose this is what one means by accepting the shadow.

If these two shadows, renegade and mood, meet, unaccepted by consciousness, it is indeed a marriage made in hell in which only the twin children, restlessness and inertia, are produced. It is hard to realize that inertia, with its blood-sucking swamp progeny, and restlessness with its darting, purposeless midge children, can be named as twins. It is not until we see that their goal is the same that we realize they are brothers traveling toward the dead city of unfulfillment, which is set in the land of nonliving. Their motivation also is the same—the destruction of the potential whose development would involve them in commitment to creative living.

A man dreams:

I am walking on the shore of the ocean. My wife is there a little ahead of me. She calls out, "William, come quick! I have found the egg of Osiris." I answer, "For God's sake, let it alone. We have troubles enough without hatching that!"

In interpreting the egg of Osiris, we must examine the dreamer's condition of being. He was a brilliant intuitive. In youth things had come to him easily. With a minimum of effort he had outdistanced the plodders, but when the choice of a vocation confronted him, he fled to new interests. Intuitions of new possibilities rose, flitted into consciousness, intrigued him momentarily, were gone. What challenge did the egg of Osiris offer to this man?

In the Osiris myth we find "a new psychic constellation in which the son has a positive relation to the father."[12] ("I and the father are one.") That is, the son knows himself as the son of a king and accepts kingship by taking upon himself the authority and responsibilities of a king. The egg of Osiris contains the troublesome germ of individual kingship, which fills this man with dismay. What will "hatching" mean? His wife was also quickened by creative intuitions,

---

[12] Erich Neumann, *The Origins and History of Consciousness*, p. 245.

but she was purposeful in giving form to the perceptions that came to her. She received with devotion that which was given her and worked upon it, making it part of her own life purpose. It is she who in the dream appears as the image of creative purpose. It is she who discovers and offers him the egg. "For God's sake let it alone," he cries out. In his life he made the same choice. He refused the egg. Restlessness again produced meaninglessness. The potential of his kingship remained unborn.

What of that other brother, inertia, with its blood-sucking offspring? What is its purpose concerning the egg? A woman whose life seemed drained of meaning woke one morning in the old familiar cloud of despair. An inaudible cry for help rose in her. As if in answer there appeared in the air above her a shining egg. It was motionless, as though held by invisible hands. In imagination she reached out. The egg was beyond her grasp, but it was there. A feeling of awe came upon her. She lay wondering and amazed. The image itself faded, but the reality of the experience as the manifestation of an unknown power remained. Then she knew—this egg was *hers*. She must recapture it through her own effort. A command was upon her. Obeying an inaudible voice, she rose and, as daylight crept in the window, began to paint the luminous egg surrounded by the gray of the unknown. As she painted, a creature emerged on the canvas. He was holding the egg. Not until she finished the portrait did she recognize him—a sloth whose small eyes gleamed with the only triumph a sloth can know, the theft of the potential of creative energy. So this was her problem. It was not that she had no talent or ability but that she had allowed sloth, the slow parasitical creature of unconsciousness, to steal from her the egg from which her own creative spirit might emerge.

It was not easy to get this egg away from the sloth, to hatch it in reflective attentiveness to inner happenings and to give form to her own potential as it emerged. She persisted. She fought her inertia, her despondence, her self-distrust. She believed in the human-divine potential. She chose to make real the thing that had been revealed. Through long devotion to the meaning of the vision, she released her energy from the sloth. The "egg" gave birth to a transformed self.

From such an experience comes the knowledge that choice acts in every moment, not a choice of doing this or that, but of living or nonliving. The thought or feeling that is repudiated, the occur-

rence unregarded, is a choice of nonliving. This same moment can, through choice of awareness, be made a turning to instead of a turning from life.

A luminous egg appears in the air. Will it be dismissed as a momentary illusion or taken as a message of hope given by an unknown love answering the heart's cry of despair? The woman's inner ear heard the mysterious command to hold it in consciousness and to work out its meaning in her own life, a command as authoritative as "Arise, take up thy bed and walk." Her own act of obedience was the first step on the new way of turning toward instead of turning from life. This choice has the power to change the direction of the life journey. At every turn of the way we meet two figures, the Helper and the Shadow. If the Helper is chosen, a new way opens from the place where one is.

We think we must climb to a certain height of goodness before we can reach God. But He says not, "At the end of the way you may find me"; He says, "I am the Way; I am the road under your feet, the road that begins just as low down as you happen to be." If we are in a hole the Way begins in the hole. The moment we set our face in the same direction as His, we are walking with God.[13]

These two dreams show very clearly the attitude by which the ego approaches the Self as friend or enemy. The man saw the egg that held his potential kingship only as a "hell of a lot of trouble," and he could not be bothered with it. The woman saw it as a revelation of her own potential, still existent in spite of long neglect and denial, a symbol vouchsafed in need, and she followed the intuitions it awakened within her till she found meaning in her own life. By her act of choice, by doing the little that she could, step by step, she came to the realization of the Self as the friend who would help her as long as she did her part. Again the act of choice and the act of grace meet in the process of transformation.

Whether we see the Self as friend or enemy depends upon whether we are willing to accept the challenge the Self presents at every crossroads.

---

[13] Helen Wodehouse, "Inner Light," as quoted in Dorothy B. Phillips (ed.), *The Choice Is Always Ours*, p. 41.

CHAPTER 6

Childhood and the Friend of Choice

୶ ୧ ଛ

In the heart of the creature is contained the self . . . smaller than
small, greater than great. . . . Though he sitteth still he wandereth far.[1]

The self lies hidden in the shadow; he is "the keeper of the gate"; the
guardian of the threshold. The way to the self lies through him; behind
the dark aspect that he represents there stands the aspect of wholeness,
and only by making friends with the shadow do we gain the friendship of
the self.[2]

W E HAVE BEEN MOVING in a world of shadows that, unacknowledged
and projected, are indeed enemies of choice. Let us turn back to the
vision of the child who saw both the darkness and the light as contained within the image of the friend. "I have a friend. He is little
as Twinkle and big as Pitch-Black Dark."

The statement is made with childlike faith and certainty. It has
happened, therefore it is true. The child did not invent, nor even
imagine, the friend; he experienced and so found him—as the true
mystic discovers God—not as an object of thought but as a numinous
experience. A transpersonal and timeless image confronted his small
personal ego, and his ego accepted it and let it act upon him without
questioning its truth or its authority.

It was an image of wholeness that appeared, not in the undifferentiated unity of preconscious beginning of life within the womb of the

---

[1] Katha Upanishad, I, ii, 20 in Macnicol (ed.), *Hindu Scriptures.*
[2] Erich Neumann, *The Origins and History of Consciousness*, p. 353.

Great Mother, the unconscious, but as the one that has become the two through the emergence of consciousness with its powers of differentiation. With the birth of the conscious ego, separation is made between the known and the unknown, between darkness and light. This duality now confronts the child in the image of the friend— minute known and vast unknown, "smaller than small, greater than great," all contained within the image of the friend, all existing together "in the heart of the creature"—a small human child. The union of darkness and light in the image of the one is a statement of the eternal paradox, "It is impossible, therefore it is true." With that strange wisdom that comes before knowledge, the child accepted the paradoxical nature of the friend and did not question the truth of the experience. The image was a gift of the creative Self. The child's own act of creation and choice was his affirmation of the reality of the experience.

The boy did not try to explain the image. He let it act upon him. In this way his ego became the co-operating object of a subject greater than itself. He was awed, frightened, fascinated: he was afraid and not afraid. In the image of the friend, fear and not-fear appeared as darkness and light existing together. They both confronted him in the immediate moment. The eternal paradox, the union of the opposites, existed within the image and within himself. A mysterious indwelling *someone* greater than his ego had to direct his choice. This greater one chose the not-afraid—that is, chose the urge to go forward into the experience in spite of his fear of the unknown. Fear, which gives to the object monstrous proportions, is as terrible in childhood as in any adult experience, for it evokes the archetype and so brings the ego face to face with illimitable powers of darkness contained within the unknown experience. To face one's greatest fear is the heroic encounter; and the act of accepting the fear gives birth to the small spark of courage that enables the ego to go forward.

In the meeting with Pitch-Black Dark, Twinkle, the light spark, is also there. He is dawning awareness. He penetrates the dark revealing perhaps dimly visible shadow forms that lie hidden within the unknown. By giving them form he makes possible the encounter. One cannot challenge formlessness and invisibility. Twinkle shows potentials not only of danger but also of values hidden within the dark. In this way he reveals Pitch-Black Dark as friend for he is the shadow, the "keeper of the gate," that leads to the self-knowledge

contained within the threatening experience. Through this gate even a child must pass.

Pitch-Black Dark is also guardian of the threshold moment of choice when the ego must decide to step across the threshold into the perils of the unknown that lead to greater self-knowledge or to retreat into the safety of the known. Pitch-Black Dark appears as the perilous aspect of the heroic encounter which for the small child may be contained even in the apparently trivial yet frightening problem of the next step in growing up.

We cannot explain why these images appear at transitional moments when the next step in the development of consciousness is indicated or why, even though they may disappear from consciousness, they have power to reappear in the same or in new symbolic form at some future hour of need. But we do know that, unless they are confirmed by the ego, they may vanish into their original formlessness. Even in a child the transforming process can be arrested by the nonacceptance of inner experience. Then the image returns to the unconscious and nothing happens in conscious development. These images seem to arise spontaneously and act with arbitrary authority, yet if we study the immediate situation we feel that the transpersonal image has been mysteriously evoked by a personal—perhaps unconscious—appeal. The co-operation of the ego is an essential element in giving them form. We might say that a timeless, spaceless, numinous image takes on temporal and defined meaning through encounter with the spark of consciousness that, even in a child, acts as a light that defines the forms within the shadow. Something hitherto unconscious enters consciousness. A fragment of the transpersonal Self becomes integrated in the personal ego.

It is extraordinary that this boy should perceive in his chosen friend the union of, and also the differentiation between, the opposites. He speaks of both the Darkness and the Light as components of the friend, the Other, who is both helper and adversary. This friend is one to be loved but also to be feared. (We must love God but we must also fear him.[3]) This god image is of an omniscient power which can be very good or very evil, for all is contained in him. This image is one with which each man must reckon, for he is an indwelling god who demands both consciousness of, and choice be-

---

[3] "Ye that fear the Lord, trust in the Lord." Psalm 115:11.

tween, the opposites. He is not only darkness and light but also the central spark of individual consciousness by which they may both be perceived. Through this light both known and vast unknown may be seen as friend.

The child could not reach any knowledge of this friend through a process of conscious thought or feeling. All he knew was that the friend was there and he must trust him. Through this he made a childlike acceptance of the Thou and I, which is the relation of Self and ego.

The intuitive insights of the child are prefigurations, intimations, stages in the process of becoming conscious. The deeper meanings contained within the image are not consciously known to this child. Such knowledge is hidden in the wisdom of the beginning. All that the boy consciously knew was that Twinkle was there and would go with him in his encounters with Pitch-Black Dark. He did not identify with Twinkle nor did he identify with Pitch-Black Dark. Identification with the image of the Self is an inflation that can take place even in childhood if the ego feels that it has created the inner image. But this boy, with an intuitive perception of the true meaning, accepted the indwelling of the friend, and acknowledged his power.

As he developed his relation to his friend, he took sides with Twinkle. Yet he continued to see Pitch-Black Dark as the angel with whom he must wrestle till he received the blessing of new courage and new consciousness. Pitch-Black Dark is fear; he is also the peril that arouses the fear. He is the unknown adversary that can walk right into the daytime of inner consciousness or of outer experience.

This boy was not a "problem child" but a child faced with all the inevitable problems of growing up. He was an introvert. Outer perils activated inner images that had more power than outer objects. Faced by a new situation in the outer world which aroused fear of the unknown, he asked the natural questions: What am I going to find? What is the new world about? What can I do about it? The unconscious gave answer in the image of an inner friend who was already there. For this strange creature who was one in spite of being two came to meet him from within himself.

I do not know when the friend first appeared, for he was already there when the boy said to me, "I have a friend." This was not until a relation of confidence had been established. Another child who

told me of her image of fear said, "I can tell you about it because you know it too." The child tells about inner experiences to one who he intuitively feels already knows them, one who he feels assured will neither pry nor offer clumsy interpretations that seek to make the image a laboratory specimen. The seeker after statistical data would attempt to vivisect even an angel visitant. We do not know how often these images come to children because we are not near enough to enter the realm of their inmost realities. All the events of his daily life, even his small personal angers, enthusiasms, friendships and encounters, he will share with a kindly, reality-minded and familiar adult, but the things of the spirit are different. They are deeply one's own. If we have lost our own connection with the living symbols, our comments would be like dry desert wind that withers the flower it touches.

What are the steps by which this boy affirmed the reality of his experience and accepted the friend? Since they are deduced from his own words and reactions, let us review these words. "I have a friend." This acceptance of the experience as his own creates his inner relation to the reality which has come to him. "He is littler than a star, but he really is a star," "a little spark" that "doesn't go out." It is his assurance that Twinkle will not go out that is the source of his faith and courage. When Pitch-Black Dark, very big and very black, walks "right into the daytime," he says, "I have to think hard to see Twinkle." "Thinking hard" is not an intellectual process but an act of concentration and willed purpose by which he holds to the total reality of the image. In psychological terms, he chooses, at the moment of encircling darkness, to affirm the light. Through this affirmation, he himself chooses that Twinkle shall not go out but shall continue to live within him.

He affirms Twinkle; he also affirms Pitch-Black Dark. Intuitive perception "knows" that this contradiction is not only caused by the outer object but exists within himself. He looks his fear full in the face. He acknowledges the shadow and its negative power. It is the *unacknowledged* shadow that stands between the ego and the self. When the shadow is not perceived, the ego relies on its own knowingness and does not seek the wisdom contained within the unknown. In times of fear, ignorance and confusion, the light of consciousness is still there though the outer eye can see only the shadow. Twinkle, the inward eye, is the light that will not go out.

True consciousness is not an intellectual achievement but an emotional realization which involves a complete commitment to all that is perceived as true, thus letting it live within the psyche. Twinkle is "like a spark that goes up from a bonfire." The eternal fire of creative transforming energy is the world of the individual spark that "doesn't go out." It is warmth as well as light, emotion as well as intuitive thought. The ego's response is the will to continue to see clearly what awareness has revealed. It is the response of a central reality that is present even in a child. This loyalty to the vision is the child's way of "thinking hard." It is an act of faith beyond fear. It does not require much courage to take risks when you have no sense of danger. Fear is not a coward quality. The courage to go forward into one's greatest fear, sensing both the danger and one's own limitations, makes of the threatening moment the saving moment from which the small spark of courage and new consciousness is mysteriously born. Holding to this small spark of courage is the child's way of "thinking hard."

"Thinking hard" hurts. It turns the sharp point of truth back upon the thinker. It pricks the bubble of ego complacency blown up by thinking easy. Its sharp wound forbids the forgetfulness which is the goal of evasive thinking. If one can forget the inner experience and its challenge can be evaded, the ego can remain comfortably unborn in the womb of the already known. Then the numinous experience becomes a momentary illusion. Nothing has happened. The ego is undisturbed by any sense of guilt or of responsibility, for evil is all outside—and so is God.

"Thinking hard" makes of projection a boomerang that turns back upon the thrower, wounding his infantile feeling and deflating his ego satisfaction. "Thinking hard" shows the ego's acquiescence at the moment when the shadow acted as enemy, stealing the values that should be won by the heroic encounter with the perils of the way. It says, "This is your own shadow and this is what he is doing in your own life." "Thinking hard" hurts!

Even to a child it says, "Follow your fear to find your destiny." We are instinctively afraid of our weak vulnerable elements, of the reaction of the inferior function, the one we have pushed down into darkness. It is this that Pitch-Black Dark has in his keeping. But it is this very inferiority that we must raise to the light of consciousness. It is then that the boy affirms Twinkle. This affirmation gives him cour-

age to face Pitch-Black Dark, now grown to gigantic visibility, and within the darkness he still sees Twinkle. By "thinking hard" the values held in unconsciousness by the shadow become visible to the ego. They are fought for and redeemed to consciousness, and the next step in development is taken.

The image fades; the unconscious wisdom of the child gives way to the necessity and the joy of acquiring knowledge. Interest, curiosity, wonder, achievement sweep him into the exciting life of the world that is so wonderfully new. New thoughts, new impulses, new intuitions arise from the inner world and explore the immediate possibilities that the outer world opens to him. There is so much to discover and to know. Yet when knowledge becomes the goal, it leads only to an ego life, which is separated from the transforming life of the self. Then knowledge is like miser's gold: it purchases no inner values. Underneath knowingness lie things beyond knowing. Knowledge must again return to wisdom; the sage must again become the child; and the child must find continuance of transforming life within the sage. Then that which has been acknowledged as true reappears, bringing profound wisdom to the meaning of life in the new stage of being. That is what happened in this instance. Years later the image returned and the child, still alive within the man, recognized his childhood friend: the often invisible guide who had been there all the time as the reconciler of the ego and the non-ego, the Other who is also the Self. Was it because the child "thought hard" that Twinkle did not "go out" but attained the power of return and transformation?

Connection with these images does not draw a child away from outer activities; rather it connects him with outer experience in a new and inner way. Whatever he formulates when he talks about his dream or fantasies or inner experiences to one who understands makes them part of a world of personal relationships. He sees that his problem is not a strange personal one but part of life which is known to other people. The familiar and trusted outer friend knows through experience the nature of the inner friend. This confirms its reality in a way no explanation could and brings inner and outer worlds together so that the image companions him in new experience.

In another instance the dream of a small girl and her acceptance of its meaning show the nature of the integrity that can choose what is true for the real self.

I was on a beach with my nurse, only she wasn't there. A big wave came in and I ran away. When I came back, there were lots and lots of things on the beach and lots and lots of starfish, but one starfish was a *blue* starfish and he had an eye right in the middle of him, and he looked at me and he knew me—me-myself, I mean, and he was my starfish because he knew me-myself. So I took him home. And then I woke up.

This, too, is a "great" dream. Its images have transpersonal meaning and belong to anyone to whom the dream speaks and who also accepts them within his heart as a gift of life.

The "big wave" is symbol of the power of the unconscious to sweep the ego from its moorings in consciousness. In the dream the small dreamer runs away from the big wave to the safety of the land beyond its reach. Otherwise she might have been carried out to sea and become one of those "lots and lots of things" cast about by the waves. The great ocean of the unconscious from which such images arise has, like the receding wave, a deadly undertow which can draw the presumptuous little ego down to the depths from which there is no return to the solid ground of consciousness. Then the ego cannot "come back" to find among the "lots and lots of things" the treasure, the eye of self-knowledge.

We know these waves also as irresistible impulse, overpowering emotion, rage, assertions of power, fantasies of greatness or the fascination of the unconscious, all drawing the ego away from work on that which has been given and from its powers of change and transformation.

The next image of the dream is abundance. From the vast waters of the unconscious the "big wave" washes up "lots and lots of things . . . and lots and lots of starfish." There they lie in undifferentiated profusion, the flotsam and the jetsam, the shell and the treasure, the "lots and lots of things" from which the child may choose. The unconscious is always moving, always casting up new creative possibilities contained in immediate moments of experience when the ego may or may not perceive the essential value. These moments of choice often pass unperceived and another wave sweeps the potentials of creative consciousness back into the ocean from whence they came. The moment between the waves is the moment of choice—of promiscuous grabbing or of instinctive recognition of the treasure. The child sees the blue starfish with the eye "in the mid-

dle of him." There is a flash of mutual recognition. In that moment she both chooses and is chosen. "And he looked at me and he knew me—me-myself, I mean, and he was my starfish because he knew me-myself." Both child and starfish affirm the reality of the self at the moment of illumination. Meister Eckhart says, "The eye with which I see God is the same eye with which God sees me." This is also the child's affirmation; for the eye of me-myself is also the eye of the starfish who sees her. She distinguishes between the "me-myself" and the "I" of ego assertion. "Me-myself" is her reality including the good and the bad, the shadow and the light. In accepting the eye that sees the truth about her self, she becomes oblivious of the eye that sees only the outer appearance, "my nurse, only she wasn't there." The nurse (Mrs. Grundy?) can guard the child only in the outer world of conduct. She is guardian of the persona. She cannot perceive the inner experience: she just "isn't there." The child chooses the eye that can see into the workshop of her own small soul. "Thou, God, seest me."[4]

All the details of the dream bear out the central meaning of the image and its integrating power. The fish is a starfish: the star is a symbol of individuation. He is *blue*, the color of the heavens and of spiritual discernment. His eye is "in the middle of him," that is, at the center, the dwelling place of the Self. The child did not know the symbolism of the wave, the treasure or the central eye as the all-seeing eye of the Self, but she chose to live the dream's meaning, which was the acceptance of her own reality by some inner power greater than the ego. In her own words, "I took him home. And then I woke up." That is, she took him back to her daily life.

---

[4] The all-seeing eye is not always the chosen friend. A small child was caught in a lie. When her "sin" was discovered and punishment administered she was told, "God sees everything you do; he knows everything you think." She was sent upstairs to meditate on this threatening truth. Her indignation turned upon her cat who followed her. "Pussy, you go back. It's bad enough to have God snooping into everything I do without having you tag along too." It is the unacknowledged shadow that resents the "snooping" eye of God. But the child does not understand the shadow any more than he understands the self. The reasons for shadow acts are vague. The lie is "a very present help in time of trouble." The child has little real knowledge of the meaning of these acts. The awful judgments of elders are quite rightly resented. Children do not know the morality which rules the adult world. Judgment cannot be pronounced without knowledge of motive. Naturally the child would hate the all-seeing eye that saw only in order to judge and to punish.

It is what the dreamer does when he wakes that gives power to the dream. Anyone can have a dream, but not everyone can live out its meaning. The child's innate love of truth, her almost uncanny perception of motives, not only her own but those of other people, her candor about herself, her willingness to understand the meaning of the act, gave to the image a continuing reality through which she lived out the dream—not only in her attitude of honesty about herself but also in her openness to the thoughts and feelings that occurred to her. Was it her own need of finding out what was really true that evoked the dream? At least one may be sure that if she had not been willing to have her reality known, this moment of mutual recognition would not have become part of her waking life.

The openness to truth through which the relation of the ego to the Self is maintained is not a problem of thought but of integrity and of self-acceptance. One of my valued relationships was with a retarded child who, though surrounded by sympathetic love and guarded from undue strain, was intellectually never able to go beyond the capacity of a child of eight. But her feeling perceptions outran her thinking powers. Often she anticipated others' needs or, intuiting warring elements, spoke the word of peace—in fact, she learned to think with her heart. When she reached adolescence, the question arose of a new school where she could go as a special student and, through handicraft, riding, woodcraft, have the companionship of shared activities. "Who will talk to the headmistress?" she queried, "you or Mother?" "Whom would you choose?" I asked. "You. You and Mother both love me but Mother still thinks I am brighter than I really am. If you talked to the headmistress, I would know if she really wanted *me*." This child could not grasp the fundamentals of mathematics but she could grasp the fundamentals of relationship. She could also accept her own limitations and through this accept herself. Later the headmistress said, "She has a genius for understanding feeling situations." In accepting her own limitations and developing that which was given, she too accepted the eye that sees the "me-myself" and was not dismayed by the truth it revealed. Trust in a person who saw her limitations but accepted *her* was the bridge over to her own self-acceptance.

One does not feel inferior if one is being oneself and functioning in accordance with one's true nature. The feeling of inferiority comes from an intuitive perception that one is not fulfilling the possibilities

contained within one's *own* potentials. Acceptance of innate limitations is part of this fulfillment. The "inferiority complex" cannot be dispelled by false reassurance that one can achieve nonexisting values beyond one's true capabilities. This only adds a burden of guilt when one fails to live up to outer expectations; but overemphasis upon limitations makes the ego feel foreordained to failure and tempts it to sink back into an effortless acceptance of outer judgment. In either case an amorphous sense of guilt separates the ego from the life of the self.

"Even a slug is a star if it is willing to be its slimy and hornèd self."

A third childhood dream, also that of a little girl, deals with the image of the Self and tells of the heroic adventure by which the essential value may be made one's own.

I had a golden baby with a silver star on his forehead. One day I was standing by a river and the awful thing happened. My baby fell into the river. Then I asked the dragon where she was and he said, "I am going to keep her." Then I stood on a triangle island with trees 'round about; I had a friend with me. Then some black children came and held hands surrounding the island. Then I said to my friend, "Let's push through the black children." There was a gap between a few of the black children. We slipped through. Then I went to the river, I dived down and got my baby.[5]

In this dream we again find the star. It is now upon the forehead of the golden baby, the "radiant child," who is the Self and herald of the Self. Gold is a symbol of the essential value. We speak of an act of "pure gold," that is, free of the alloy of base motive. Gold is the sun color, symbol of the light of consciousness and of masculine strength as a creative life-giving force. The "baby" is of gold. On its forehead is a silver star. Silver is the moon color. Moonlight penetrates the unconscious, the night world. Silver moonlight is symbolic of feminine intuitive feeling. The star, symbol of individuation, is on the forehead, which is the place of the "third eye" of spiritual insight. The golden baby of the dream represents the highest value existent

---

[5] This dream was told in a lecture given by Dr. Michael Fordham and is used with his permission. Dr. Fordham did not elaborate upon the child's own use of the dream, but he told me that she kept it in remembrance and it worked out its meaning within her. The symbolic interpretation comes from the dream itself.

in the psyche. Its substance is formed from sun, moon and star. It is the symbol of the inborn potential of individual life, a value which the child's self already has, but which the ego must win through many encounters on the spiral way of its own heroic adventure. This dreamer is a girl, and the star that must guide her is the silver star of feminine perceptions. Yet we note the language of the dream—"a star on *his* forehead"; "I asked the dragon where *she* was." Here the hermaphroditic aspect of the Self is expressed in the apparently naïve statement of the dream. The hermaphrodite is an image of the self-fertilizing oneness. It is at the beginning; it is also at the end. It is both masculine and feminine—the symbol of the self-creating self.

In the dream the "awful thing" happens: the baby falls into the river, that is, into the stream of the unconscious where the dragon is. This dragon is an ancient mythological creature who guards the treasure of new consciousness that the hero must rescue. It personifies the regressive pull of the unconscious that would keep the child from growing up and taking over her own problems, especially the lifelong problem of being herself and so creating her own personality. The overpossessive or overloving mother is often the "dragon" who decides what is right or suitable in each new experience and protects the child from the danger of choosing to be herself. Yet in the dream the dragon is "he," for it is the masculine principle (the maternal animus) in the form of will to power that the mother may use to keep the golden baby, the germ of her own separate personality, from the child. In the dream the child naïvely asks the dragon to tell her where her own values are and how she is to find them. But the dragon says, "I am going to keep her." The unconscious gives warning of its own black magic. Something in the child's self warns her that she cannot ask the dragon to tell her how to find herself; that discovery is her own life adventure. If she leaves the direction to the dragon— that is, clings to her secretly desired dependence on what she is told to do or think or be—the golden baby, her unique value, will remain in the waters of the unconscious and in the power of the dragon. She will let the unconscious steal away her opportunity of self-choice. She must, so to speak, grow herself up, bring up her own values. This she cannot do when the dragon keeps the golden baby at the bottom of the river, that is, in a condition of unconsciousness.

The dream changes; she is on an island. The island is a symbol of ego consciousness. Consciousness rises in fragmentary "islands" from

the waters of the unconscious; by psychic gravity these fragments of consciousness, elements of the personality, come together to form the island of ego integration. The ego of this child seems to have attained sufficient integration for her to stand on it and see what is happening. The dream says, "stand on your own feet and see what you can do for yourself." She is not alone on this island. She sees that it is encircled by black children"—difficulties, inner and outer, that she must "push through" if she is going to rescue her baby. She has a "friend." Is this perhaps the shadow who, like Pitch-Black Dark, can help her see the dangers and also the values to be won? But this adventure is hers; not even a friend can see it through for her. She dives into the river: she goes down into the unconscious to rediscover and rescue for herself the unique value of her own personality. When she acts upon her own decision, the dragon of the dream seems to vanish as though it had been called into being by her own regressive wish and had vanished when she pushed through the black children (the obstacles), defied the dragon, and accepted the challenge of the encounter.

Such dreams frequently occur at crucial points of development. Their meaning cannot be fulfilled in childhood nor can their symbolic and archetypal aspects be explained. They seem to bring their own reassurance and release from immediate anxiety. But the situation contained within the dream will recur many times. The encounter with the dragon, the rescue of the potential, is enacted and re-enacted on many different levels. There are so many dragons. There are so many "awful" happenings!

It is easy to let the "awful" things happen, to let the individual treasure slip away by forgetting the meaning of one's own experience. The "awful thing" is not to realize the awfulness. Without this realization one begins to think *easy*. Then Twinkle, the starfish, the golden baby demand too much "thinking hard," too much consciousness of what one really is, of what and why one does as one does. To hold the experiences that have been vouchsafed means concentration, separation of motive and integration of ego consciousness. The deep understanding of this process of change and transformation is an adult task, yet the immediate response of the child to the image has a vitality that the adult reaction often lacks. The child receives its visitants, its experiences, is nourished by them, appears to forget them.

We speak of such images as forgotten. It would be more truthful to say they are, temporarily perhaps, forgotten by the ego but remembered by the Self. Insofar as these experiences have been lived by the ego, they have become part of the structure of the developing personality and so enter into every future choice. The Self remembers in ways beyond the ego's knowing. Yet the ego reacts to these hidden memories, for past choice acts in every future choice.

There is a creative type of "forgetting," a merciful quality contained within the Self. The image arises, plays its part, and withdraws into the grayness of unconsciousness, yet it is endowed with power to return to conscious memory when the ego can accept the deeper meaning without being overpowered.

The power of return is inherent in Twinkle, the blue starfish and the golden baby; also in Pitch-Black Dark, the threatening wave and the dragon. There are dark moments when we encounter shadow forces on a new level of the spiral. Fear and doubt again assail us. But these dark moments also bring opportunities for choice of greater consciousness.

There are also golden moments never forgotten by the ego. A small boy is walking on a country road. He is coming home from a neighborhood party. It is early evening, cold, moonless, starlit. The North Star is bright with clear radiance. It is the star that never changes its ordered place in the heavens. Sailors steer their ships by its light. A few nights before he had dreamed of a star. He stands still, looking, wondering. Yes, this is the star of his dream. It is remote, lonely, alive with its own light, unchanging in its steadfastness. It is beautiful; it creates beauty. It is his star. It is telling him something. He must listen. It is about light, about beauty. It is about something that he must do. Is it to make remote beauty real and near? He is alone—alone with the star. To it he makes his wordless promise, and a premonition of his destiny comes to him. Long afterward he put it into words: to find and to release the essential meaning of the moment of daily life so that through its portrayal it will reveal the beauty of the transpersonal life—the life of the gods; not just to make beautiful things, but to follow the spirit which is beauty and so awakens beauty in the beholder. All this is phrased as nearly as possible as he told it to me years later. He did not know then in what medium his promise might be fulfilled. Was it music? color? form? relationship? All he knows was that he must keep the spark of his own

being connected with the remote star of his dream and vision. Long afterward he found his own way and always, even in moments of despair, he saw

> . . . this brave o'erhanging firmament,
> This majestical roof fretted with golden fire,

and there, central, unchanging, was his own star of purpose. Then he knew that he must keep his childhood promise, whatever difficulty or danger it entailed.

Hildegarde von Bingen says:

From my infancy up to the present time, I being now more than seventy years of age, I have always seen this light in my spirit and not with external eyes, nor with any thoughts of my heart nor with help from the senses. But my outward eyes remain open and the other corporeal senses retain their activity. . . .

But sometimes I behold within this light another light which I name "the Living Light itself." . . . And when I look upon it every sadness and pain vanishes from my memory, so that I am again as a simple maid and not as an old woman.[6]

Laurens van der Post writes:

One of the most moving aspects of life is how long the deepest memories stay with us. It is as if individual memory is enclosed in a greater which even in the night of our forgetfulness stands like an angel with folded wings ready, at the moment of acknowledged need, to guide us back to the lost spoor [footprints] of our meanings.[7]

There are also moments when childhood is touched by the finger of fate. Like dark passion flowers they have their centers of light. A child is going down a village street, carefully hopping over every crack. A shadow falls across her path. She looks up. There is the woman in black who always walks alone, silent. Jumbled memories, overheard whispers, crowd up in the child. Someone—not this woman, but someone near to her—did something terrible, unmentionable. In a mysterious way it has condemned the woman to be alone, never to be spoken to. The child bursts out in vehement denial of this incomprehensible situation: "But *you* did nothing wicked. Why do you act as though you did it yourself?" For a moment child

---

[6] From Migne Collection 18, quoted in Charles Singer, *From Magic to Science*, p. 233.

[7] *The Lost World of the Kalahari*, p. 61.

and woman are together, enclosed in the same impenetrable shadow, imprisoned in the solitary confinement of rejection. This moment has nothing to do with time. Nevertheless, the words of the child are a pact with herself. Her small ego will forget them, but the Self will remember and will repeat these words to her in a future hour of choice, in a moment when, in spite of circumstance and relatedness, she must refuse identification with an act which is not her own. All this the child did not know; nor had she any concept of how our lives are interwoven and how subtly our shadows touch the shadows of those who are near to us; nor how the nonunderstanding or even the unspoken word may have its influence in the choice of one whose life has become closely related to our own. In another's guilt we have a share that we must acknowledge as a mutual burden, yet the central choice is always the actor's own. If we identify—and this is true of guilt or of achievement—we deny our own truth, we become separated from our central Self, rejected by our innermost reality.

In this instance, the childhood words came back to the woman exactly as they had been spoken, but now they had to be fulfilled in a way that childhood could not know. This could not be accomplished by any form of escape from the situation now confronting her nor by denial of involvement and of responsibility. Yet the words of the child were a promise of the ego to the Self. Unless the promise made by the child is kept by the woman, she will be caught in the darkness of self-rejection. They were spoken by the child; they must be confirmed by the woman in ways of mature understanding. Such understanding means bringing to bear on the situation all that life has revealed. It means listening to the inner voice, accepting the interpretations that arise from the Self, remaining alone yet involved, related but not identified.

If we ourselves look deep into our own past, memories dormant perhaps for decades return with all the sharp poignancy of immediacy, and something that, as we tell it to our adult ego, might well appear as trivial is again freighted with the original emotion. We feel that in this moment an inner possibility came alive or was killed, something whose importance and meaning have only just now, in this moment of memory, been realized, something that must be redeemed if we are to become that which we were intended to be. Let us be careful how we use the word "forgotten" in connection with a childhood experience.

Can we not all of us recall some childhood confrontation with a

situation that roused a sense of being "called by a voice," and recall, in this sudden moment, having heard an inner voice say, "This thing I will do some day," making in these words a contract with our destiny? These moments are not so rare as we would like to believe. Caught in the habitual and the ordinary, they flash back into memory and we shut them out lest they confront us with our early promise to ourselves. Or, if we are fortunate, we may find that, in spite of the demands of necessity which seemed to make our pathway lead us far from the chosen goal, the greater memory which lives within us has kept the meaning of the promise alive, and the spark of meaning has guided us in strange and devious ways to the place of its fulfillment. Then in surprise we say, "This is what I meant to do all along, but I did not know that was the way I should do it."

This arrival at the goal of the early commitment has come because, in all the experiences, when the imperative voice of life called to us to take up a responsibility that seemed to necessitate a sacrifice of the goal that the personal self had chosen, the Self kept alive an intuition of the essential element contained within the early promise, and so found in various situations a way to confirm the original intention of the voice of our calling.

In every life that retains its creative energy, there is a vital connection between the ego and the Self. This Neumann has called the ego-Self axis. It is a line which, though invisible, is like an electric wire over which the dynamism of the Self can be conducted to the ego as it moves into the world of conscious experience. When this axis is broken, the ego lives on only one level of being, the conscious rational world of outer reality. There is no guarantee that in the second part of life the man who has lived out his ego ambitions and has enclosed himself in rigidity will return to the vital connections with the creative images of the self. Disaster, depression, psychotic invasion may make him seek self-renewal; or he may, when ego achievements are no longer possible, descend into trivialities or seek to reinforce his ego with the tyranny of absolute belief and dogmatic authority.

Let us remember this and seek to keep open the child's connection with the images of the Great Memory. We must always remember that the child lives on two levels—on the level of the immediate interest, and on the level of unforgotten things. He is caught up in the immediate. Poignant delights or sorrows with their power of

transformation appear forgotten; yet if they are still alive under all the "normal" active life, they will reappear. We have spoken of the Self, as it manifests itself in childhood, as *friend*, but often these images that reappear are far from friendly. The small limited ego cannot control or really forget the force of emotion that lived in these "forgotten" experiences, nor can the adult teach him to control them by repression. The unconscious is a dynamic world of instinct, impulse and dream. Its energy has an independent life of its own which is always present under the surface of the daylight world of normal casual ego existence. Psychic wounds that are ignored fester in the unconscious. No conscious bravery, no diverting daylight activity in which the child's interest flows into the immediate, will divert or control this tremendous electrically charged force of the unconscious. Nightmares, uncontrollable fears, sudden distrust, or "unwarranted" emotional outbursts are all symptoms of the disregarded unconscious. In these irrational outbursts, we see the results of the pitiful attempts of the adult to divert the attention by interesting occupations—unreal because formalized—"creative activities" of "self-expression." If the resulting product be ugly or distorted, it is passed over in well-bred silence, or a most disastrous attempt is made to substitute reasonable factual explanations for unexplainable mysteries. The explanations will not help the child meet the inner powers of darkness. Things forgotten in the daytime remember themselves at night, or reappear suddenly in a sunlit room when an odor, a footfall, a shadow, a careless word awakens memory, and the image is there with all its magic powers. The adult who feels superior to manifestations of the unconscious is the one who most effectively isolates the child in a world of irrational fears or drives him into an ego-created world where he builds walls against the intrusion of Self-created images.

When the small uncertain ego is faced by a new experience for which it needs to fortify itself and to assure itself of its own identity, its own ability to meet the experience, it may draw circles that represent the unbroken enclosure, the place of safety where the ego prepares itself for the encounter. Sometimes these circles are the home of a beneficent power, the good magic, the fairy, the helpful spirit, that is really an image of the self who is the friend. Even a very young child may express this need of security in mandala form. Jung tells of a three-year-old child who could not go to sleep unless these circles

were pinned on the wall over his bed. Another child in hours of play whisked in and out of identifications in which she *was* a horse or a pussy cat or a great big giant. One night when she was being tucked into bed her mother said, "Good night, Bunny Rabbit." She responded, "When I go to sleep I am *not* a bunny rabbit. I am me—myself—Susie Robinson." It was her own self-identity that would preserve her from the extinction of her conscious ego by the powers of darkness.

There are circles of security, images of wholeness, that are also pre-figurations of the self as friend, foreknowledge of the way as "my way," that may appear at any time. These too may come to a child. They are like reassuring presences or images of future harmonious relation between the ego and the Self. A little girl dreamed of a blue flower, a perfect circle, whose every petal spreading out from its golden center seemed to create its own beauty. It was her flower. It had come to her. The outer circumstances of her childhood were of confusion and disturbance. She loved things of beauty that did not make sense to her common sense parents. She also dreamed dreams that she instinctively guarded because they too would make no sense. Often when she was disturbed she saw the blue flower, and it comforted her. It was her flower. At times it seemed to represent a talent or gift that she must cultivate with care, that she must never neglect. As she grew older, it became more than this. It became a symbol of the flowering of life where each petal of experience unfolded in its own true place from the golden center which was its source. The child had never heard of the fairy tale of Hans and the blue flower of healing, or of the Golden Flower of Chinese philosophy whose attainment is the harmony of the self where "the Light circulates according to its own law, if one does not give up one's accustomed calling,"[8] but this blue flower had to her the same wordless meaning. It was a circle of being whose center was also the living light. In times of perplexity or defeat she saw this flower, and it compensated for ugliness and frustration. But it was more than that: it was an image of the goal, the harmony of the Self.

Such a commanding image as that of the Self, coming when the doors between the conscious and the unconscious are not yet forged, must of necessity recede as the child takes over his task of integration

---

[8] *The Secret of the Golden Flower*, p. 90.

of the ego. Through facing his own limitations and uncertainties, he knows that he does not know and so becomes willing to find out. The will must be strengthened, knowledge acquired, emotion "civilized." The child must discover his own abilities and use them purposefully and with concentrated willed effort if he is to gain self-reliance. He must learn how much there always is and always will be for him to learn, and that learning is not always easy; that without will to conquer outer difficulties he will have little power over the inner enemy, and without knowledge of the inner shadow the outer obstacle will appear too formidable or—even more disastrous—not worth the attack. He must learn the knowledge and wisdom of the elders before he can understand the wisdom of the Self and become able to distinguish between the many voices, whether they be of good or of evil. So the image-filled mist gives way to the daytime light of consciousness, the images retreat behind what we have called the "ego-forged door" that separates inner and outer. Yet the door must never be locked or the ego will find itself enclosed in a world of conscious knowledge that shuts out the creative images of self-transformation.

From the original formless unity of unconsciousness the ego must emerge. Man within himself is many; so too is the child. The entities stand forth in their separateness, are differentiated, are chosen and reintegrated through slowly emerging consciousness. The ego must find form before the One who is neither ego nor shadow nor well-brought-up persona, but the Self, can speak with authority and the choices of the Self and the ego become one. This is a long journey, one never completed. The child glimpses and lives, so far as he is able, the truth the man perceives.

Twinkle, the starfish, the golden baby were accepted as friends. Their meaning was affirmed in experience. These children testified in their childhood way to the truth that was in them. They were in their vision and their vision was in them. The lode star, the blue flower, coming as immediate perceptions of the eternally abiding image of the self as helper and guide to the already existing goal, had a continuing reality because the covenant of grace was fulfilled through many acts of choice in childhood ways that led to mature understanding of the mystery of wholeness, the god image of the Self.

These children did not know that it was a god image that came to them, touched them with light fingers of awakening awareness. God, if they thought of Him, might be a remote creature who lived in a

"Sunday house," or, as in the imagination of many modern children, a name in a story recalled from a remote past. Nor had they any concept of the Self. It was their willingness to be aware, to enter into the unknown as into a greater reality, that gave to the image a power to live itself within them for a moment of time. This is to know eternal life. Though this moment may be forgotten by the ego, it is remembered by the Self.

CHAPTER 7

Return of the Image

❧

"And he looked at me and he knew me, me-myself I mean. So I took him home. And then I woke up."

Wʜᴀᴛ ɪs "home" to which the child returns when she awakens from the world of dream? It is a world of openness both to the images which come to her from the unconscious and to the images that are derived from the interaction of her own unique qualities with the personalities of all the various people who make up the world of family and of relatedness.

In both worlds "we live in images." No matter how objectively we attempt to see another person, the unconscious enters into the formation of the image that determines the inner relation. Children of the same family describe mother, father, brother or sister, and the images evoked are so various that we wonder where the truth lies. These portraits must surely represent different personalities; yet they bear the same name and fill the same position of authority or love in the same family group. Then the person walks in, and the image that we perceive is not any one of the varying pictures already described. Since our own reaction tinges the portrait even in the first encounter, how much more does the personal reaction enter into that close relationship of daily family life where the emerging self of the child, his innate predisposition, and the often unconscious reaction of the parent constellate an image which is more real to the child than words or conscious acts? In childhood every experience is personal and transpersonal, every relation unique and archetypal; also it is immediate.

97

The child or unconscious adult reacts with the totality of the affect to the totality of the image which has been evoked. The parent too may react to his or her own image of the child, which may be constellated by the response of this parent's unrecognized shadow, ego pride or possessive desire. These images of parent and child act and interact in far-reaching ways. It may be only long years later that we find that the image, not the actual personality of mother or father, has dominated the scene and acted in choices of relatedness or distrust, of dependence or self-development. Only slowly, by understanding what is roused in our own unconscious and what we rouse in the unconscious of another, do we come to the perception of the person behind the image and of his essential quality. There are moments when the individual drops the garment of the image and stands revealed. We then know whether or not we can trust this central quality even though the form of relationship may change.

A family of refugees was looking for an abiding place. A sympathetic adult said to one of the small boys, "It must be very hard not to have a home." The retort was immediate. "We *have* a home. We just have to find a place to put it in." If a man and woman were looking for recommendation as parents, they would need no testimonial beyond that! Only love and a courage that defies disaster could have made a home that was so secure in an insecure and changing world. These were not what Jung calls "accidental parents," that is, two people who, in following their own instinctual urge, happened to give birth to a child, but ones to whom the experiences of love and parenthood had brought a deep sense of joy and responsibility. Instinctively one knows that this family must have become inwardly secure through experiences of love and trust which no outer insecurity could destroy. It is often in times of outer insecurity that enlightenment comes which makes us know the inner security rooted in the meaning of one's own life and in its relationship to others.

The family offers a natural opportunity for relationship but does not insure it. Relationship is a creative act to which the individual must bring understanding, loyalty and devotion. Differences, oppositions, mutual interests, acceptance of individual abilities and of faults and frailties—all lead to tolerance, admiration and sharing, which are of the essence of love. And the greater images of love and authority, evoked by the central attitude of the personal parent, mold the child and penetrate his unconscious. Without this understanding the

family may be a breeding place of ambition, jealousy and distrust. It may be a place where relationship flourishes in an atmosphere of goodwill or only a place where "strangers live together." The orientation of the child, his attitude of trust or hostility, of affirmation or negation, as he meets the outer world, is founded upon the early experiences within the family. Here one may learn to love people, not because they are wonderful and unusual, but because they are part of one's life and mirror problems that are intensely personal yet also impersonal. Or the family circle may be a false circle of security, a place of limitations, if family beliefs, attitudes and customs are held to be unquestionably best and even truth is identified with family tenets, or if family prestige becomes the estimate of individual values. When a nurse asked a disobedient six-year-old, "What will people say if you are such a naughty little girl?" She answered, "Oh, they'll just say, 'Her father is a millionaire and her grandfather was a bishop.'" Does this family relationship breed security?

Home is not the house where one lives but the relatedness in which one lives.

The love of the mother is the infant's first experience of security.

Mother, you made him small, it was you that began him;
he was new to you, you arched over those new eyes
the friendly world, averting the one that was strange.
Where, oh where, are the years when you simply displaced
for him, with your slender figure, the surging abyss?
You hid so much from him then; made the nightly-suspected room
harmless, and out of your heart full of refuge
mingled more human space with that of his nights.
Not in the darkness, no, but within your far nearer presence
you placed the light, and it shone as though out of friendship.
Nowhere a creak you could not explain with a smile,
as though you had long known *when* the floor would behave itself thus . . .
And he listened to you and was soothed. So much it availed,
gently, your coming; his tall cloaked destiny stepped
behind the chest of drawers, and his restless future,
that easily got out of place, conformed to the folds of the curtain.[1]

If, as the child grows, the mother's discerning love sees the reality, the "me-myself" of the child, she helps it to grow to an independent

---

[1] Rilke, *Duino Elegies*, Third Elegy, p. 37.

consciousness of itself. It is the primary relatedness to and gradual separation from the mother that gives the child the first sense of I and Thou, both in the outer world and within the psyche.

If this image has its proper influence upon the awakening consciousness, the emerging ego experiences the security of love in the small circle which is adapted to its own early need. The ego is then ready for the unfolding of the next image, that of the father, who represents authority, willed purpose and adventure in the outer world. It is he who leads the developing ego into the wider circle of world experience. This is a natural process of growth from the world of family life to ideas and emotional reactions to the life of the group and of the community. Both the father and the mother help the child to preserve the openness to life and to the images of authority and of love.

But if the maternal eye is one of possessiveness, the child must too early draw its own magic circle as security against invasion. This can destroy the openness to experience both of the outer world and of the inner image. Possessiveness may show itself as all-enveloping solicitude in which the child finds itself enclosed in a warm incubator from which it has no desire to emerge. Or, if the unconscious of the child senses the danger of encirclement or suffocation, fear and distrust produce inner resistance. Irrational rebellion may then grow into an attitude of distrust toward manifestations of that most precious of all gifts—love.

A six-year-old child, who was the adored object of a possessively anxious and oversolicitous mother, dreams:

> I was very sick and my mother came into the room and she said, "I'll put these blankets over you and you'll feel better." I thought, "She doesn't want me to feel better, she is going to pull them over me so I'll die." She came nearer and nearer and tried to pull the blankets up and I screamed and woke up.

When she told the dream, she said, "I felt the blankets up over my face. Wasn't that funny?"

Even more insidiously possessive is the mother's dominant image of the good and desirable destiny toward which she tries to direct this child who, to her, is "my child."

Love, the possessive, encircles
the child for ever betrayed in secret;
and pledges it to a future that's not its own . . .

. . . .

Oh, how far it's from this
watched-over creature to everything that one day
will be its marvel or else its destruction.[2]

The ideals secretly injected into the arteries of the psychic blood stream, the taken-for-granted assumptions that are sprayed into the atmosphere to be breathed in as though they were life-giving oxygen —these may, through the dominance of unacknowledged possessiveness, infuse the child with ambitions alien to his given nature and impel him toward a "future that's not its own."

I knew a mother who, with a look of holy consecration, said, "My son will be a clergyman. When I first looked at him and knew he was *mine*, I gave him to God and pledged him to the church." Skillfully, "lovingly," she directed his steps, carefully she circled him about with prayerfully selected influences. She imbued his father with the sense of the child's sacred mission, and the boy's ego accepted the honor "God" had conferred upon him. But his Self and his given nature did not accept it. Before the time came for him to enter the church college of his mother's choosing, the unconscious broke through the circle of holy security and took possession of his ego. He projected the images of evil, of the devil and his unholy crew who spoke with deceitful tongues upon the people surrounding him. At other times his ego, in identification with the hallucinatory images, became the avenging angel, God, or in a form of negative inflation, the triumphant devil. He saw himself omniscient in good or in evil.

It was not until some time after the psychotic episode had passed that I knew him. He had been released from the institution and was living away from home under careful supervision when the strange voices again began to speak. This time he feared them and sought help for himself. In a long analysis he relived the experiences that had overwhelmed him, and the images that had possessed him took on new symbolic form. With dawning awareness of the relation of his small ego to the suprapersonal forces, the same images that had overwhelmed him became agents of release. In his analysis dreams re-

---

[2] Rilke, *Correspondence in Verse with Erica Mitterer*, p. 35.

hearsed the inner drama of archetypal interplay, but now his ego was as a worshipper in a vast cathedral, touched, transformed, but not identified. In this way he became an initiate in the mysteries, and the images that had brought destruction became agents of healing and transformation. He passed through many fantasies which in the psychotic phase had appeared as hallucinations, but now he found in them symbols of healing and new life. So he came back into his own life. It had an outer form far simpler than the one to which his mother's "love" had dedicated him; but it was his own. It embodied interests repressed in his childhood by his acceptance of a future to which his mother's "love" had pledged him. In his analysis, another image of mother love was constellated; but it was the Great Mother, the unconscious, who really freed him. The healing power lives within the sufferer, and the experience of the suffering god and the meaning of rebirth are to be found within the man himself. It is only through his own choice of the new images that arise within him that he can become free of bondage to a future not his own. The release from the power of the mother's possessive "love" made possible a return to the original childhood openness to the images of his own destiny. With rebirth of "the watched-over creature," everything which had led to destruction became the "marvel" that guided him to the choice of his intended life. But to the mother his acceptance of a future that was his own remained a subject for anxious prayer. Nor could she understand the mystery of betrayal that had snatched back to "the life of the world" the soul of *her* child whom she had "given to God." To the day of her death she struggled to regain her pious possession of *her* son.

The spirit of possessiveness is an insidious and persuasive power of the shadow, which can often confuse parental judgment. As the child grows in ego assertion and demands for independence—which may be only the "infantile lust for freedom" and greed for irresponsible license to do what one wants when one wants—the most loving mother may be dismayed. She finds herself insecurely balanced upon the narrow bridge of too much or too little freedom. On the one side is the chaos of license, on the other is death of original experience. On this razor edge bridge that stretches from infantile dependence to freedom of choice, the parent has only the slender shaft, the juggler's balancing rod, of inner motive to help her on this precarious way. Lacking the balancing rod of ego-free motive, they both may fall into

the gulf of mother-child involvement where freedom to be oneself is drowned in the waters of unconsciousness.[3]

Maternal possessiveness is an insidious component in the unconscious of the human creature. Woman can learn much from the animal: the robin knows when the reluctant fledgling must be pecked out of the nest, the cat cuffs away the grown kitten who still desires the maternal nipple. Instincts, unconfused by ego purposes, have a knowledge of reality superior to that of the ego which, intent on its goal, does not see the movement of opposing forces in the unconscious either of the self or of the object. Mother-mindedness is not always a question of sex. It may inhabit the bodies of trousered males who, as teachers, preachers or oversolicitous mother-minded fathers, seek to direct and limit the freedom of their spiritual sons or daughters. Possessed by their own creative idea, they become Jehovah's Witnesses for the chosen way. Even the most creative teacher may fall victim to this blinding enthusiasm and seek to direct and set boundaries. One of the most inspiring teachers whom I have ever known was greatly astonished when this dream intruded into her quiet sleep.

A huge six-foot white rabbit is sitting in the center of my bedroom. Solemnly she unzips herself down the front, and a frisky young rabbit hops out. As he hops about the room, she regards him with complacent rabbity pride. His hops grow higher, his circle wider. As he comes near her she picks him up by the ears, tucks him back neatly and zips herself up again.

As she told the dream, I saw a long procession of rabbity mothers whom I had encountered over the many years and remembered the consternation that had ensued when the child refused to be tucked back, zipped in and so saved from the perilous choice of making his own mistakes and widening his own circle of experience.

Fortunately the dreamer possessed not only a sense of responsibility but a sense of humor. She did not identify with this maternal monstrosity which had invaded her quiet bedroom but tried to see

---

[3] Sometimes, confronted by a perplexed parent, one remembers the sign nailed over the melodeon in a church in a crude mining town. "Please do not shoot the organist. He is doing the best he can."

how it had managed to get in and what she could do to exorcise it. Another dream gave the clue:

> I am on top of a high ladder facing a wall that stretches out before me like an empty canvas. I have a vision of a great circle of light in which figures of light move in great arcs—beings of light that create light. This I must paint upon my wall. A voice says, "You will never paint that picture until you get that rabbit out of your bedroom."

She is on a high ladder, a place so far above the maternal monstrosity that she can forget its existence. Yet it is a precarious place if she is unmindful of the distance between her creative aspirations and the floor of reality beneath her where the rabbit sits waiting. The ever-creative Mother, the unconscious, has given her a vision to which she longs to give form. But there with her on the ladder is her ego that will subtly direct and manipulate her own creative product unless she first gets the rabbit—the thus-far-and-no-farther of ego dictation—out of her bedroom. Her ego will seek to possess as its own the spirit of creative life that seeks to possess her and, through her hand, to manifest itself. If her ego is overintent upon its own goal of achievement, she will not let the free creative spirit move in her and direct her hand. In her own life the rabbit will try to set bounds to the creative efforts of the children of her psyche and she in her turn will seek to direct and limit the original creative efforts of her students.

Rabbity-mindedness may be so small an element of the personality that it appears to have no importance. A cinder is a very small particle, yet if it happens to get into one's eye at a critical moment, it raises hob with clear vision. If the rabbity mother had no right to be in her bedroom—the place where the elements slumbering in the unconscious become manifest—it would not have appeared in her dream.

Fulfillment of one's own vision produces an atmosphere in which the child is inspired to make his own creative experiment. This sense of mutual inner freedom does not create rebellion against form but rather establishes a trust in the long and arduous task of self-discipline through which the adult has himself learned to give form to the creative image. To the teacher the dream says, "Trust the creative power to manifest itself through your own devotion to it. If your way is the child's own, he will follow; if not, he will seek out his own form of creativity, and what you have given him will go with him."

To the rabbity mother it says: "Work out your own salvation and so give your child a chance to work out his. In this way your unpossessive love can still remain the guiding principle in the perilous moment of choice."

If the mother's eye is the eye of cruelty, power or isolation, the child may be so caught in fear or need that he cannot develop a necessary independence of thought or an inner power to love. Choice is paralyzed. It is here that the archetype acts with dark, magic, life-forbidding power. Though it has been constellated by a negative trait of the personal mother, it is imbued with all the negative fate-compelling aspects of the suprapersonal image. When the image returns in later life, we realize it is the archetype, not the personal mother with which we have to deal. The victim does not know the meaning of his powerlessness, but the unconscious knows and may create or bring to memory a dream that clothes the image in visibility, so showing the power that has dominated early choices. The childhood dream that follows was not told for many years. Its imagery was too terrible for a child to face; but the archetype portrayed continued to dominate the life of the dreamer though she did not consciously acknowledge its existence.

She was forty-five when she came to analysis because her fears, suspicions and negative intuitions had transformed the people who surrounded her into potential enemies. For many years she had held a position as secretary to an executive in a large office. She said she never had anything to do with the other employees. She was "there to do a job, not to get mixed up with other people." In a crowded office she "kept herself to herself." In her small apartment she lived alone. Yet now she was "followed on the street, looked at strangely by the people in the apartment house, spied upon by everybody in the office." One man, whom she tried to avoid, kept "making overtures." He had even wanted her to go out to dinner with him. Was he trying to find out things to tell the boss? Was he trying to get her fired? It later developed that he was a kindly, rather simple soul who was fascinated by her remoteness. Isolation and secrecy can impart a sense of mystery. They may conceal profound secrets or only emptiness but they rouse curiosity. This quite natural desire to find out made him appear to her a spy and traitor. Did he also stir something in her unconscious that might betray her into emotions that would weaken her walls of isolation? One can hate and fear that which one secretly desires. If he entered her wasteland of isolation, what would happen to

her carefully built-up strength—her well-trained intelligence that made her able to function like a competent machine? Heretofore, she had been able to earn her living through this mechanized adaptation. Now fear had taken over. She was very near insanity, for the phantoms of fear had taken human form and assailed her from every side. She had become uncertain in her work. She made mistakes. The boss looked at her strangely. Were his orders only traps?

One day she came in a state of blind terror. She had put up her shades very early that morning and had seen the woman across the courtyard already at the window staring at her. Everywhere she looked were staring eyes. Suddenly a recurrent dream that had haunted her childhood broke through the wall of repression. Words poured forth in a torrent.

> Blind animals are coming up the back stairs trying to reach the door at the top. They are all blind, blind, blind,—except the octopus who has a terrible eye on every tentacle.
>
> They used to come up night after night, and one night I knew why they were blind; the octopus had snatched out all their eyes. I was so frightened that I screamed. There was my mother standing in the doorway looking at me like the octopus. She told me to stop that noise at once.

After this hysterical outpouring, she became rigid, frozen. The image of the octopus was again constellated. It was there in the room. Its presence was felt by both analyst and dreamer. The analyst's hands reached out to the groping hands of the dreamer. "You poor child, no wonder you are afraid." The touch penetrated the barriers of isolation. The woman burst into floods of tears. For a moment they washed away the blindness and made her able to see in a human being another aspect of the archetype—the compassionate and understanding mother. There was a bond of a shared experience. Participation is part of the magic of the unconscious which can break down barriers of distrust. The moment is there, a part of life. It must be participation, not identification. Nor will this sudden single experience wipe out the traumatic experience of long years of living under the power of the negative archetype. It only opens the way to the discovery of the transforming image.

With this opening of the way came a flood of memories: the long period of childhood isolation, overheard words of scorn, the mysteri-

ous disappearance of the father and her own fantasies of fear. Could her mother make people disappear if they made her angry? Later she learned he had fled to a more accessible woman. Had he ever given thought to her? That she never knew, for he vanished out of her life while she was almost unconscious of his existence. Shut out from love, she tried to find ways of getting in, and the only way she discovered that would open the door a crack was good marks at school. Playing with other children was a waste of time; emotion was lack of control; safety lay in distrust and avoidance. Yet she still looked for love even in the most desolate place—the place of the negative mother. The only way to find mother love seemed the way of the intellect. She continued the search, even taking over her mother's support, until death released her from the personal mother—but not from the archetypal image.

Through the transference a new image slowly came into being. This was of an understanding mother who cared for the neglected children of her psyche, who could open the door of relatedness, and so release her from the old isolation. This image gained sufficient reality to help her meet the disaster which happened shortly afterward in the outside world: her dismissal from her job. Yet perhaps it was not so much disaster as opportunity. She could not both have carried the heavy load of released emotion and kept the intellectual precision demanded by the job. Fear returned, but there was enough experience of the meaning of the positive archetype to make her feel that love and understanding existed and that the whole world was not against her. This made it possible for her to accept a much humbler position as assistant in a home in a simple country environment. She was not cut off from the analyst, though the contact could not be continued with the old regularity. She had no sense of being abandoned; her spirit was not again wounded. In the new environment, her repressed instincts could slowly awaken and she could dare to express emotion. She made friends with flowers and animals and gradually came to accept the friendship of the older woman in whose home she had found shelter.

I wish I could say that the transference magically released her instincts and her emotions from their blindness and returned her to life fully healed of her wound. The way was long, the new vision weak and uncertain. The octopus never quite lost its destructive power over her own choices. She could not fully trust either herself or

another person in a relation of love, nor could she freely venture back into the world.

Such experiences sustained in childhood can cripple the psyche even as infantile paralysis can cripple the body. This may impose permanent limitations. But within these limitations a new way of functioning can be found. In simple form the individual finds self-acceptance. Life may again spring up from the roots. And that is all we can ask; for who of us knows what is great or small in terms of individual life?

Another woman who had known only the forbidding life-destroying aspect of the mother found the long way back to herself through an analysis that awakened the image of the creative and life-giving mother.

The first impression that she gave was of a creature not only shy and reserved but strangely isolated. She had come to see me, she said, in order to discuss certain theoretical questions that had been raised in her professional life. They were other people's problems. Slowly she was drawn into a feeling of relatedness, but this new feeling was so excluded from consciousness that she had no awareness of it. One day she expounded her creed of life. "The only safety is to build a wall around yourself so nobody can get near you, and never to trust anybody with your real thoughts or feelings." "But you have trusted me with your thoughts. I am a person." She looked at me as though bewildered by the strange idea. "No, you are *not* a person. You are a *tree*. You can trust trees. Birds trust them. Trees won't cage them. You are a tree. That is how I always see you when I am here and in my dreams." "Look at me very carefully. Am I really a tree?" The woman began to tremble. "No," she said, "you are a person." "Look again. Are you afraid I will try to cage your birds?" "You are a person," she answered with amazed conviction, "and I am not afraid of you."

The walls of the false circle of security which was only a prison cell of self-isolation crumbled when she chose to walk through them into a world where relatedness to another person became an accepted reality. She now talked of herself, her dreams, her fantasies of trees and of birds. Her childhood had been spent in an isolated frontier settlement. Her mother rejected the land, rejected the man who had brought her there, rejected, except in ways of duty, the child that he

had begotten. Her early years held no memory of angry words but of silences bereft of words. Her father was shut into his dreams, her mother into the solitude of unexpressed bitterness. Often the child wandered across the stretch of plain to the nearby forest, and the trees accepted her. Her childhood fantasies were of adventures in the forest and of learning secrets of the birds.

After this admission of a person into her inner world of fantasy, dreams began; they were often of birds, especially of her own bird. Strangely this bird was always caged, nor could she, except with consciously directed effort of imagination, open the cage door. Yet in hours of analysis this bird of her spirit dared take small flights into freedom of thought and expression.

She dreamed only occasionally of trees, but her fantasies dealt with them. We talked of them as symbols of wholeness, rooted in earth, reaching toward heaven, of the tree of life, of death and of rebirth. Her sense of trust was growing. Yet often doubts took possession of her. Over and over again she seemed to have to try out this new concept of the mother to see if she would again be rejected. One day she dreamed her bird was dead and in her desolation a gray bird came to comfort her. But it could not bring her own bird back. The transference had not yet brought her to a trust in life or in herself—only to the limited trust in a single individual. The bird of her spirit was still caged. It did not dare freedom. But the small seeds of trust, understanding and acceptance were pushing their way up into the light, and she ventured, somewhat tentatively, into relations of friendliness.

When summer came, she had so far broken the circle of isolation that she could embark on a desired trip with a woman who, long a distant acquaintance, was now becoming a friend. It was then that the "big" dream came to her. She wrote of this in a letter.

> I was in a lovely outdoor place. I had been there a long time. I remembered that my bird was at home and that I had not asked anyone to take care of it. But I put the thought away. Then it came back to me more insistently, and I realized that the bird would be dead if I did not do something now. Suddenly I began to run in order to get back to the bird. An auto overtook me but I refused to ride; running seemed quicker; then I knew I needed help and got into the auto. When I reached home (which was not any spot that I have ever seen before) I knew the bird could

not be alive. It was a terrible feeling—remorse for not having taken care of it, a sense of tragic loss. Weeping, I went to look for it, and when I found it alive the shock was almost too great. It was a feeble little thing but *alive*. In the next room, full of light, sat a mother person. I knew it was she who had kept the bird alive. I went in to thank her. As we sat together, I first realized that the door to the cage was open, as was the great arched window back of the cage. It opened on a garden with sunshine and spring-green trees. All at once my bird began to sing the most indescribably lovely song. And I woke up weeping with great joy and thankfulness. I wanted to come straight to you and tell you of my happiness and of my feeling that I had come home.

Do you remember that last year I dreamed my bird was dead and a gray bird came to comfort me, and I felt you were that bird? This mother person was in gray. She was the bird who was the comforter; she was the you and the not-you—and the house was the home to which I had always been journeying even though I had never seen it before.

The image of the barren, isolated, life-forbidding mother, evoked in childhood, was displaced by the image of the mother as comforter and as love that not only fed the bird of her spirit but opened both the cage door and the window that looked out into a world of living light. The golden thread of the transference had, in her wanderings through the forest, brought her to the home of this other mother (the "not-you"), the feminine aspect of her self that set her bird free to sing its own song.

When the personal mother lives out the image of love, the daughter may be quite unconscious of the archetypal aspect of the image. She lives the experience and her feminine self is nourished.

The acceptance of the positive mother relation is a vital step in woman's self-acceptance since she herself is woman. Only by understanding the feminine, matriarchal aspects of her psyche can she become related to the central needs and demands of her personality and to the human relationships that are hers to live. She must win her freedom from its overprotective or demanding and possessive aspects. She must overcome her regressive longing to remain a child or her fear of claiming the right to her own choices as life offers her opportunities; but her essential way is different from that of the son.

When the mother-daughter bond develops into a loving but free and conscious relationship between two adult women, it is of inestimable value in connecting the daughter with the feminine aspects of her own psyche. It also helps her to incarnate within herself the meaning of the mother archetype through which she becomes related to herself as woman.

For man, the "freedom from the mother" has a different meaning. As infant he needs the experience of protective nurturing love as much as the feminine creature does. But far earlier than she, he feels the necessity of establishing his relation to the father image, through which he finds his own masculinity.[4] The mother-son pattern, whether positive or negative, must be broken if he is to enter the world of men. The mother image, so powerful in childhood, may continue to rule over his choices and decisions until it has been raised to consciousness and he has won his freedom from its power. Then the unconscious again becomes the maternal source of his creativity.

A man wakes in the clutches of nameless fear. In his sleep he has been running, running across an endless desolate plain. In sharp memory he is back in the room where he slept until he was five years old. He is also back in a recurrent childhood dream that first made darkness a region of terror and dread.

My mother is the moon; she is a huge funnel. She is chasing me across a great empty space to suck me in; I run and run, faster, faster, but always she is just behind me. I come to the edge of

---

[4] Five-year-old Elliot was "mothered" by his seven-year-old sister. One day he asked for a large sheet of paper, some paints and to be "let alone." When he emerged with his painting he said, "This is a family." In the upper right-hand corner was the mother, to the left the father, in the center a large green "E" enclosed in a red circle, and toward the bottom of the sheet was the sister. "But what," his father asked, "are those gray lines over her face?" "The sister is now in a cage," was the grim reply.

Then he set up a retreat in the corner of the room and said to the sister, "Don't ever disturb me here. I have man's work to do." Some time afterward he announced that he had a friend—a Hard Thinker Dragon. He said, "The Hard Thinker Dragon lives in a cave down in your tummy and when you get mixed up and don't know the answer, if you go down inside yourself and ask the Hard Thinker Dragon, you will be surprised at what he tells you. But you had better do what he says." In China the dragon is symbol of masculine strength and creativity. Did the Hard Thinker Dragon come to birth through Elliot's caging the sister-mother and finding his man's work to do?

the world and jump off. I am falling down, down into darkness. While I am falling, I wake in terror.

This mother *is* the moon, ruler of night with its luminous magic and its dark withdrawals. The moon in its negative aspect is the land of dead souls. This moon mother *is* the funnel whose insucking breath tries to draw the child back into death in the darkness of her womb of night. Breath in its outgoing form is a symbol of the creative spirit. God, when he had fashioned the first man, "breathed into his nostrils the breath of life; and man became a living soul."[5] This is the spirit-bestowing breath of the creative father, far different from the insucking devouring breath of the moon-funnel-mother. In this dream the wind, the spirit, is the greedy devouring hungry breath described in "Khandogya" in *The Upanishads.*

The wind is in truth the All-Devourer, for when the fire dies out it goes into the wind, when the sun sets, it goes into the wind, when the moon sets, it goes into the wind, when the waters dry up, they go into the wind, for the wind consumes them all. Thus it is with respect to the divinity. And now with respect to the self. The breath is in truth the All-Devourer, for when a man sleeps, speech goes into breath, the eye goes into breath, the ear too, and the manas [the word], for the breath consumes them all. These then are the two All-Devourers; wind among the gods, and breath among living men.[6]

The moon-mother *is* the funnel, the instrument of breath as devourer. It may be interpreted as the phallus of the uroboric mother, a negative form of the "sun tube" through which "ministering winds descend." Jung comments on a vision in the Mithraic liturgy:

"And likewise the sun tube, the origin of the ministering wind. For you will see hanging down from the disc of the sun something that looks like a tube." . . . The phallic significance of this attribute is not apparent at

---

[5] Genesis 2:7.

[6] *Khandogya Upanishad,* tr. by F. Max Müller, as quoted in Emma Jung, *Animus and Anima,* tr. by Cary F. Baynes, p. 30.

In contrast to this devouring breath is the fantasy of a child of five who had already been told "the facts" of life. "I came out of my mother's mouth. I guess she breathed me in when my father kissed her. Then she breathed me out again." (Needless to say, this was a girl child). In the kiss the breath of man and woman meet in love and a child is born from the creative breath of life itself.

Mere facts do not satisfy the soul of the child who returns to the fantasy that contains the greater truth and is alive with creative meaning.

first sight but we must remember that the wind, just as much as the sun, is a fructifier and creator. There is a painting by an early German artist which depicts the fructification of Mary in the following manner: a sort of tube or hosepipe comes down from heaven and passes under the robe of the Virgin, and we can see the Holy Ghost flying down it in the form of a dove to fecundate the Mother of God.[7]

The energy descending through the sun tube impregnates with the seeds of life, but the phallic tube of the moon-mother draws the seed which has been bestowed upon the child back into the womb of death. In this threefold form (mother, moon, funnel) she is negative, undifferentiated male and female energy, the uroboric mother terrible because she destroys the individuality of the child.

As the man looked at this dream, he realized that all his life an essential part of himself had been running, running from this moon-funnel-mother. Unable to rescue this child self, his ego had abandoned it and had tried to build for itself a masculine security into which it could escape. His personal mother found sadistic satisfaction in making her son feel small and powerless. She was herself at the mercy of her own violent passions and was possessed by contradictory qualities over which she had no control. Love, anger, cruelty, impulsive generosity swept through her. She undermined his choices; she distrusted his word; she ridiculed his adolescent emotions; she betrayed his confidences—even at the times when she poured out protestations of affection and demanded his love. Such a mother seems to possess all the undifferentiated qualities of the mother archetype. There is no central personality whose reactions the child can trust. In the quick changes from "love" to hate to will to power and cruelty, the negative mother breeds in the child distrust of the dependability of any manifestation of feeling. Love may at any moment change into its opposite. The moon-funnel-mother constellated in the son the fears that such an image can arouse in the dependent child. They still moved in the man in distrust of manifestations of love because love might so quickly change into hate or cruelty, even as the mother's "love" had changed.

In the present dream he is running across the same desolate plain of the recurrent childhood nightmare. Had all the intervening years been only a futile attempt to escape from the insucking breath of

---

[7] Jung, *Symbols of Transformation*, pp. 100–101.

this mother? Who was the child who had come to the edge of the world and had jumped into the void of dark nothingness? Had his ego made any attempt to save this child, or had it instead run in the opposite direction in its endeavor to make its escape even over the edge of the world? In answer another dream arose. But it did not deal with the hero task of overcoming the mother as might, in classic analytic procedure, be expected; it spoke directly to his ego and challenged his image of masculine authority.

The Old King, whose cruelty is completely irrational, must be killed with his own sword, a bent and rusty blade. When this is done, a flame springs up from the lifeless body. As the Old King is consumed to ashes, a gleaming sword appears in the center of the flame.

His first association was with Excalibur, the sword of kingship drawn from the rock by the youthful Arthur, the sword that reappears rising from the waters of the unconscious as symbol of Arthur's return in reborn kingship. The sword of this man's dream arises like the phoenix from the flame. He did not feel like a phoenix but like a frightened child with his back to the wall. But he let the dream speak to him and questioned the images.

Who is the Old King and what is the bent and rusty blade? What masculine authority had ruled over his life? The sword is symbol of masculine libido. We speak of the sword of the spirit, sword of truth, keen blade of discriminating thought and willed purpose that cuts its way through doubt and confusion. The sword of the Old King is rusty and bent. The king is symbol of masculine authority. His will governs the life of those within his kingdom. The son enters into his kingship as man when he can control with understanding the insubordinate elements of his personality, choose with discrimination his advisors and direct them wisely so that all that live within the kingdom have freedom. Or the king may be only a tyrant oppressing and imprisoning all who oppose his ego will. This man's ego had tried by every effort of conscious will to repress the emotions, the impulses, the desires that he believed had, in his childhood, delivered him over to the mother. He had made his ego the king who, with "irrational cruelty," had tried to kill his childhood self. The ego must now use its own sword of willed purpose to destroy its own authority, the Old King.

The sword is rusty. Rust gathers on neglected metal. The rust of inertia, the dullness of depression, had settled upon the once-sharp blade of his conscious will. His intellect, his intuitive awareness, once so keen, had become blunted by a strange indifference over which he had no control. He had tried by an effort of will to concentrate on the values that his ego had achieved in his chosen field, but will was now only the effort of the ego to pull itself up by its own bootstraps. Ego will turned back upon itself and defeated itself. Discouragement over each failure to work out the predetermined solution added the rust of inert depression to the blade.

The sword is bent. "As the twig is bent" came to mind, suggesting that this bending, this twisting out of the intended shape, was begun long ago when he was a sensitive child. He examined his early choices and the motives that had impelled them. They had not sprung from original impulse, nor had they been affirmation of the potentials which had lived in his brief periods of release from fear. They were negative choices—not only against the mother but also against the father, a gentle unaggressive man who, unable to face the problems of his marriage, had shut himself away into nonproductive introversion and simple country pleasures that aroused no spirit of antagonism in the woman whom he feared. Since he was himself in retreat from the mother, he could not help the boy in his battle for independence. Instead he roused in his son antagonistic reactions against all the traits that they had in common—love of beauty, simplicity of feeling and introverted interests. They even cut him off from potentials of his own that opened up to him the world of poetry, music and intuitive thought. All these he felt might spring from the same weakness and lack of will that had destroyed his father.

Fear of the mother cut the boy off from his early openness to the intuitions and images that had once come to him from the all-creative Mother, the unconscious. Scorn of the father's weakness had made him antagonistic to the potentials that were mutually theirs. With "irrational cruelty" he tried to kill those same innate masculine values which his father had let go to waste in his own life. In this way he repudiated not only the personal father but also the father as inner image of individual masculine authority.

Orphaned of parental images, he tried to build up an ego-created world ruled by rational intellectual concepts—a world in which the ego became the king.

Reasons of the intellect become instruments of irrational cruelty

when they seek to destroy the reasons of the soul. Reason itself became the irrational cruelty of the Old King who tried to kill the rebellious impulses that arose from the Self. Ego will may fight against the greater will of the Self with all the courage and discipline it can summon to its aid but, when the ego chooses a way which is contrary to the creative transformation demanded by the Self, its action becomes mere acrobatics of the will. Personality cannot develop without conscious moral choice and willed courage to follow through one's decision; but only if the decision is in keeping with a man's own given nature will it lead to the development of individuality and the rescue of the lost creative elements of the self.

This is a prophetic dream. Its fulfillment depends upon the man's asking the question, "What am I to do?" This question transforms the dream of "divination" into the dream of "wisdom."

The answer to the question is clear. The Old King must be killed by his own bent and rusty blade. That is, no matter how twisted by false purpose, how rusted by inertia and depression the masculine libido has become, it must now be used in the ritualistic murder of the Old King, the ego authority.

Even as transformed life springs from the sacrificial death of the despotic ego, so the flame springs from the dead body of the murdered king. Reborn energy, the flame of emotion, of life and of spirit, can reappear in transforming power after the voluntary death of the old.

Fire is a symbol of dynamic energy; it is the flame of emotion, desire and the glowing, burning idea. Without this flame life is a "cold war" producing no new values. He who is reborn must endure the fire.

Memories can burn like fire. This fire was the searing burning realization of what ego-chosen authority had done to his life as a man. In this fire habits, doubts, ego certainties, inertia and ego will must be burned away. This suffering the man must endure. Only by entering the fire, by sacrificing his ego will, can he draw out the sword of the Self forged by the flame.

In myth and in actual life this sword is the weapon of the hero. With it he can slay the terrible mother and rescue the child who has escaped over "the edge of the world" of his own manhood.

A knowledge of the moment of choice can come without a dream which gives form and visibility to the image. An intuitive perception

"happens" to enter consciousness. If it is received by the ego, a new way opens. The following experience was related to me by a man in his sixtieth year. I give it as nearly as memory permits, in his own words.

Funny how things happen that change your whole life. I remember the first time I ever felt fear, sudden terror without conscious reason. I was eleven years old. We were in the kitchen. My father came in. He said, "Well, Mother . . ."—the rest I can't remember, because a blind fear came over me. *I was afraid of my mother.* I loved my mother. She was the one we all relied on. My father always spoke of her good judgment. "A wonderful woman, your mother. Take her advice and you won't go wrong." That was what we all did. She made the decisions for all the family and they always seemed right. We often talked of her plans for my future. They seemed right too. I *couldn't* be afraid of her, but I *was.* Why? Everything in me was rigid, on guard, watching . . . asking, Why? Our old dog stood there wagging his tail—like my father, tame. My mother asked my father to do something. He went out again. I looked at her. I *hated* her. I knew I had to get away from her. How? An answer rushed up in me. "Disobey her—right now." That was what I feared—defying her: that was what I had to do. After a little, she told me to do something. I have no idea now what it was; it might have been something I wanted to do; but I *had* to disobey. I remember the feeling, as though I were pulling everything inside myself into a tight ball; and "something" inside myself said, "This is it." I refused obedience. She commanded; again I refused. I wouldn't answer any question. I hung onto my refusal. If I argued, I might get weak; she might win. Then she threatened; I refused. And then she cried. I had never seen her cry before. I felt the ball unwinding. I mustn't. I went out of the kitchen into the sunlight that had lost all its brightness. I sat down in the shelter of the woodpile back of the barn. I can still remember how strangely unfamiliar the sticks of wood looked. This was a world I had never seen before. I felt absolutely and completely alone, faced with the terrible responsibility of myself and of what I had chosen. I could never go back. Then, after what seemed an eternity of time, my mother called and I went in to supper. Everything was the same, yet everything was different. Neither my mother nor I spoke of what had happened. But it had happened. I felt alone—and often I was afraid. I didn't know enough to choose, but I knew

I had made an irrevocable choice which meant I had to decide for myself—even when I was uncertain. I had to find out by myself, for myself.

"This is it." The words seemed to be spoken by an inner authority whose knowledge was beyond that of the ego. Obeying it, there came to him a sudden lightning flash of awareness which brought into visibility things hitherto invisible in the darkness of unconsciousness. His father and the old obedient dog both waiting on his mother's word, both obedent to her superior wisdom, both "tamed" by affectionate, instinctual desire to follow her choice. "This is it." Fear, the red light, flashed its warning. Stop! Look! Listen! Be aware, know your own peril, act upon it. Defend your own right of independent choice.

The "drawing together into a tight ball" was the boy's first reaction to the fear that is the beginning of wisdom. Fear met, acknowledged and faced, can lead to a strengthening of the ego so that it can resist the invading forces, whether they come from the unconscious or from the world of outer experience. This is the hero choice of fear, very different from the coward choice of retreat or propitiation. This boy accepted the challenge; he accepted fear itself; he looked into it, trying to see the invisible enemy. Hatred—the opposite of all that he had consciously felt—sprang into life. He loved his mother, but also he *hated* her. The opposites were alive in him. This was impossible, yet it was true; by accepting it, he could find a way beyond it, the way of individual choice which was based neither on love nor hate but his own realization of values.

He had yet another peril to face—the emotion stirred by his mother's tears. This might weaken the tight ball of his willed purpose.

His mother, bewildered by having failed to exact obedience through demand or threat, tried to seduce him through one of the ancient tricks, often called by woman "an appeal to man's better nature." This is really a device of will to power that puts on the mask of feminine need and helplessness. It almost unmanned the boy. "Forbidden compassion," usually considered a feminine temptation, is not unknown to the male. As a manifestation of undifferentiated emotion, it can undermine man's willed purpose. It is a form of compassion that helps weakness remain weak at the expense of the essential value to be won. Tears can be among the sliest cruelest weapons that

woman has in her quiver of poisoned darts. They have a black-magic power of penetrating the vulnerable spot. They can make a man feel a brute because he persists in following the way that he inwardly knows is right for him, and which he often unconsciously knows is right for the relationship.

Demanding tears are not the healing tears that wash away bitterness, that release feeling, that bring reconciliation. They are crocodile tears used to make the victim feel guilty if he holds to his chosen purpose and refuses the demand of the poor hungry crocodile who *needs* to swallow him. Compassion is forbidden when it would destroy a value greater than the one it would create.

The boy did what many a hero has done before him. He ran away from the temptress. He refused the projection of guilt that she tried to put upon him. Her own emotions were hers to face, his way was his. The boy did not consciously think this out; he again accepted a knowledge beyond his knowing. He went out of the now strange kitchen into the well-known barnyard, only to find it also had become strange, part of an outlived world that he no longer knew. Here the sunlight, the familiar sticks of wood, all were different, for his own way of seeing had become different. When he went back, the supper table was the same—yet never again the same. The world had another aspect, another meaning in this twilight dawn of a new day in a new world. This was the moment of enlightenment which can come whenever awareness makes the leap forward into new consciousness. The dark moment when hate, fear and forbidden compassion had almost overwhelmed him and made him turn back was the midnight of his childhood day drawn to darkness. In the darkest hour his self had chosen for him and he had accepted the choice. If at that moment the ego turns back because of fear, if it dwells in hate, if it refuses decision because of weakness, the dark hour is not the "living midnight" but a dead midnight out of which dead day comes. The "new" day has died in the womb of night.

A boy of eleven is not, our sensible normal judgment would say, ready to make so decisive a choice. But no one can say to life, "Wait till I am ready." The spirit "bloweth where it listeth" and *when* it listeth. Something within the boy was ready, or it would not have responded to the lightning flash of awareness. In that moment he dared to accept aloneness in which he must integrate this decision so it would become part of his ego consciousness. But he did not choose

the ego inflation of self-imposed isolation. He went back into the family life and as he himself said, later he learned to understand his mother and to love her as a friend and they advised together. He saw also that though much was unconscious in his parents' relationship, it had a basis in love that had grown with the years and he learned to respect their relationship of interdependence even though he knew that his father's way could never be his.

He went back to discover meaning. He accepted his own ignorance and knew he had much to learn from the fear that suddenly came upon him. But though the frightened ego heard the warning voice of the self, it did not identify with this "other" who had spoken or he would have felt that his small undeveloped ego was capable of knowing the truth without having to find out by experience, counsel and reflection. He would have been an insupportable little monster of ego assertion rebelling for rebellion's sake. The voice of the Self can be very dangerous unless the ego has learned humility. The saving grace was that he tried to find the meaning of this irrational act; he also kept the sense of wonder alive and even in old age acknowledged the presence of mystery.

Transformation of consciousness moves through a process of many rebirths. Many new days are born and reborn from living midnights. "Day unto day uttereth speech, and night unto night showeth knowledge."[8] The new day is born out of the midnight knowledge of what the speech of the old day has prophesied. The dead day is the day when choice is refused, the experience denied, knowledge of the midnight is not sought. The midnight of this day is the death of the power of individual creative choice. The libido turns back to a past from which it no longer tries to free itself.

In *The Dead Day*, Ernst Barlach describes this problem in mythological symbols. A boy conceived by a sun god is born to an earth mother. To this mother the boy is consigned so that she and her blind husband, Old Kule, may teach him the meaning of human experience. The sun god will return to see how well the trust has been fulfilled. He leaves the sun horse, symbol of heroic libido, so that when the earth parents have taught the boy earth knowledge and control of ego will, he will be able to ride out to his own heroic encounter. The sun god knows this must be the boy's own decision, for

---

[8] Psalm 19:2.

not even a god can compel his son to the heroic choice of his divinely conceived destiny.

The existence of the sun horse and hidden knowledge of its connection with the boy's future relation to the divine father fills the earth mother with fear lest her child should come to manhood and leave her. She tries to hide from him all knowledge of his divine heritage. Not so Old Kule, whose eyes, blind to the immediacy of the outer world, are open to a world of vision and of dream.

"When I lay o' nights, and the pillows of darkness weighed me down, at times there presses about me a light that resounds, visible to mine eyes and audible to mine ears; and there about my bed stand the lovely forms of a better future. Stiff are they yet, but of radiant beauty, still sleeping— *but he who shall awaken them would make for the world a fairer face. A hero would he be who could do it.* . . . What would those hearts be like which then might beat! Quite other hearts, thrilling so differently from these that beat today. . . . They [the lovely images] stand not in the sun and nowhere are they lit by the sun. *But they shall and must [come] once out of the night.* That would be the masterwork, to bring them up into the Sun; there would they live."[9]

Old Kule tells the mother of these "lovely forms" and says that this boy, entrusted to their care, might be the one who would awaken them. This might be the heroic task of the boy's future. She only answers, "Son's future is mother's past. . . . I want no hero son. World's good is mother's death."

Old Kule seeks the aid of his wife's familiar spirit, hoping that he can rouse the boy to knowledge of his divine heritage. But this familiar spirit belongs to the mother. He is a form of intuitive thought which can be used by the negative mother to state truth so it will undermine rather than strengthen the will of the child. This "familiar spirit" taunts the boy, making him conscious only of his weakness. "Your mother has a grown-up baby in her house. Men come from men."

Old Kule tries to tell his foster son of the vision whose fulfillment might be his destiny. The boy catches a glimpse of this world of radiant images and longingly says, "Perhaps the life we live is also the life of the gods." As the boy becomes dimly aware of the meaning of his paternal heritage, the mother, fearing that he will escape her,

---

[9] Quoted in Jung, *Psychological Types*, p. 321.

pleads with him. Not her plea so much as his own down-drawing desire for the comfortable answer, his own reluctance to take the dangerous ride into the future, makes him hesitate. He sleeps. The moment of choice passes. Before he wakes, the mother kills the sun horse on which he might have ridden to the meeting with the divine father and to his initiation into the life of the gods.

He sleeps—but Old Kule's words have stirred dormant images within him. Dreams come to him. He sees his father whose head is the sun. He sees himself mounted on the sun horse, riding out to claim his sonship. He asks the meaning of these images. His mother tells him that he "cannot live on bread baked in dreams," and the familiar spirit scornfully says, "A man has no need of a bodily father." The inner conflict mounts. The boy "hears the sun roaring above the mists and the great heart of the earth hammering below." Both voices call him—but he has lost the power to follow the voice that calls from within the self. Instead, he appeals—once, twice, three times—to the father to save him from the bondage of his own infantility. The mother hears and, remembering the prophecy of the return of the sun god through which the boy may break from her, curses the boy and destroys herself with the same knife that she used to kill the sun horse.

Now he is free of her forever if he wills to be free. The death urge of the mother, the life urge of the sun god father are both clear to him. It is the midnight hour of choice. He cries out, "This would not be Father's way"; he chooses the knife of self-destruction—"Mother's way is easiest."

In each of these three histories—where the terrible mother appears in dream, sudden perception and myth—the earth father was himself under her dominance; therefore he could not constellate within the son the image of masculine authority and self-direction which would help the boy in his struggle for freedom. Yet Old Kule, despite his blindness, or perhaps because of it, saw further into the realm of fatherhood than either of those fathers whose bodily eyes were open to the world of ordinary events. He could perceive the sleeping forms "of radiant beauty" that stood about his bed and knew that if the boy could accept his sonship to the divine element—the father as spirit and light—only then could he play his heroic part in awakening "the lovely forms of a better future" that "shall and must [come] once out of the night."

Jung quotes a significant passage in Spitteler's *Prometheus and Epimetheus* and says:

"Those images return again to every man, whose rainbow tinted, dream-like fabric once painted for his childhood's future." This is clearly a statement that childhood's phantasies tend to go to fulfillment, *i.e.* that these images are not lost, but come again in ripe manhood and should be fulfilled.[10]

The hero may be the ordinary man fighting his ordinary battle with his given life, or the great man who, as world hero, brings to birth a new cultural symbol. He is always born of two fathers, human and divine, even as he is born of two mothers, mother of the body and mother of the spirit of love, of connection with the irrational world of the images. The earth father instructs him in the old cultural values; the divine father frees his spirit from the outworn pattern of old convention and brings him knowledge of future possibilities.

Every experience is collective and personal: childhood and *my* childhood, youth and *my* youth. When the personal experience is in harmony with the stage of life development, transformation is a process of the unfolding of both personal and archetypal images.

Youth is a testing ground where experience becomes *my* experience, relationship *my* relationship, truth *my* truth. Yet the more it becomes individual the more it is sensed as archetypal and transpersonal, and truth and love are experienced as wellsprings from which all may drink if the thirst for life is upon them. The old must be reappraised; the saving grace of doubt stirs, questioning the old to see if it belongs to a static past or to the old tree of life from which new growth springs. Without the saving grace of doubt man never arrives at the faith which is his own.

A young woman had been lovingly reared in a home where doubt and question had no place, for the word of revelation had long since been spoken by God. Man, under His direct guidance, had formulated it in doctrine and creed. Her father, chosen friend of her childhood, embodied to her the meaning of faith and trustful obedience to the ways of God. But a restless spirit moved in her. It was neither trustful nor obedient. It stirred in desire, in eagerness for life. It brought intuitions of pathways that opened upon unexplored realms of truth. The thousand "thou-shalt-nots" of the old creed stifled her.

---

[10] Quoted in *Psychological Types*, p. 321.

Conscience told her this new voice must be stilled. Nevertheless, doubting thoughts stirred, quick desires rose unbidden. A dream, also unbidden, came to her.

My father and I were buried in shoe boxes under the old apple tree. He lay comfortably curled in his box but mine was too small for me—I couldn't grow. It stifled me—I could not breathe. I felt myself move, push toward the light. Then I was out and the apple tree was in bloom. I might never have seen it.

The shoe box, receptacle for the shoes that one puts on one's feet before going forth into life, had a special significance in this young woman's relation to her father. Stages of growth were marked by new larger shoes. It was her father who took her to buy them. He was careful that they should not be too small and cramp her feet, and also that they should fit the form her own feet were taking. Carrying the larger shoe box home meant that she was growing up. She had believed that her shoe box could never be as big as her father's. Yet now the dream said that the box, which did not cramp him, was to her only a suffocating coffin. All the doubts that had assailed her childhood faith rushed upon her. Was the unquestioning faith of her father only a coffin to her? Would her loving unquestioning obedience to the old faith end in a contented sleep of death?

She decided to follow the dream. The immediate reaction was as dramatic as the breaking of ice in a great river in spring. She wanted to break from all restrictions; she felt an uprushing energy that was ruthless in demand. She wanted to be free. But what was this newly released daimon defying the old way? Was it self-will, childish rebellion? Was it of the devil? It was hers—it was alive within her. She must risk the danger of understanding it as her own. She knew she must trust it and let it live. Then the symbol of the dream came to her; she saw the old apple tree newly alive with spring. It had burst into blossoming in obedience to its own nature, not denying its roots in the earth or its desires that reached toward the new spring skies. For her the blossoming could come only through a concept of more abundant living which her father had denied. She could not return to a rigid creed that forbade individual revelation and transformation, nor could she choose the license of chaotic emotion and unbridled impulse—for rigidity and chaos are both enemies of creative choice.

If she broke from the coffin of unquestioning obedience to the old, it must be through conscious choice of obedience to the laws of the self that demanded new flowering. The "bursting point" is the moment when all that has been preparing in secret breaks into the light of consciousness; it is the moment of visibility when the ego sees what has been invisibly moving in the unconscious. In the stillness of winter, before the snow had melted, the apple tree had begun, with the secret slow movement of sap rising from its roots, to prepare for the "sudden" response to spring. This then must be her choice: not to deny her roots, not to stifle the desire rising like sap within her veins, but to understand the awakening of new life, so that spring could come to her as it had to the apple tree. The words with which she woke returned with new meaning, "I might never have seen it."

What had she seen when the vision of the apple tree burst upon her? Her spirit had beheld transformation as a living process moving through the whole structure of being. It had awakened a new image of the creative father who implants the seed that is to become the child of individual being. Must she then leave the personal father whom she still loved? In a moment of gratitude to life she saw her relation to him as part of the inner process of the root and the flowering. In her childhood it was he who had taught her the eternal story of love, sacrifice, rebirth and transformation, he had also taught her reverence for the ancient law and "fear of the Lord which is the beginning of wisdom." Though his mind had accepted the limitations of factual historic interpretation, of unchangeable once-revealed truth, though his faith was still credulity, his concept static, yet his heart did not really believe what his mind accepted. The spirit of love had permeated his doctrine of the letter of the law. He had given her the framework of the eternal story. Now touched by the symbol, it quickened to new life within her. Having seen the apple tree in spring's resurrection she could not return to his restrictive creed or his childlike credulity, but in this eternal story, first learned from him, she could find the life-redeeming symbols of sacrifice, rebirth and creative transformation and so come to self-transformation and new understanding of the Father as image of eternally transforming power.

Many modern parents, who have discarded creed and ritual because symbolic mysteries that they contain do not conform to historic form and factual truth, give to their children only an ersatz diet of rationally provable facts. They "throw out the baby with the bath," the

living spirit with the outworn pattern. Since they have not experienced the numinous behind the words of ancient wisdom, they do not realize that they contain the living seed that can come to new flowering when their symbolic meaning is perceived. Symbols are seeds of understanding of the mysteries that move both in self-transformation and in the many creeds and rituals that unite mankind in a universal search for the meaning of life. Symbols have their roots in the earth of spiritual reality. If these roots are severed, the tree may be barren and come to no new blossoming.

Even when the actual father still stands in opposition to the new way, the inner image of authority which contains both the old and the new can set the ego free through acknowledgment of the unity of both the roots and the flowering of the god image. This is the blossoming of the tree of life in the heart of man.

To see with the eye of vision the apple tree in new flowering is to perceive life as a process of transformation that lives itself invisibly within us. When its movement toward renewal bursts into visibility, choice is again offered—choice to affirm or to deny the revelation that has come uniquely to man in his experience of the numinous. The moment of visibility is the moment of decisive choice. It is the moment when the unseen things which are the makers of reality become manifest and the goal is revealed. It shows the nature of the force that moves man toward his heretofore hidden goal.

A man had lived in the father-son safety of given authority. Ego discipline and fear of original experience had closed off for him childhood openness to life and had shut out the haunting world of inner images. The strangely winding way of choice had been forsaken for the straight and narrow way where only conscious virtue, uncompanioned by tempting images, might walk in safety.

But what was happening in the closed-off world of inner images? How safe was this safety? A dream broke through its confines.

I am coming home across the village green. At my gateway is the familiar tree. Children are gathering its fruit. As I come nearer, I see that the fruits they are gathering are tiny skulls; as leaf and fruit these hang from every branch.

What is this home whose gateway was guarded by the tree of death? As the man's inward eye looked at it, images of his present

home and the home of his childhood moved like shifting shadows, merging, separating, recombining, till it seemed that he saw before each gateway this same tree of death. What had "coming home" meant to his childhood? What did it mean now? The dream image was of the house he now called home. He must look first at the present meaning of the daily return. Each evening when he crossed the familiar threshold he schooled himself to follow a pattern that had long since lost the quality of transforming desire. Now he gave lip service to words youthfully spoken—words that had long since lost any quickening power, words never inwardly accepted. Only increasing rigidity of purpose held him to the role he imposed upon himself. That which he had once chosen he now endured. He schooled his intellect to produce that which the situation demanded. Returning home meant concealment, self-discipline, endurance. But

What locks itself in endurance grows rigid; sheltered
in unassuming grayness, does it feel safe?
Wait, from the distance hardness is menaced by something still harder.
Alas—: a remote hammer is poised to strike.[11]

He did not need to know these words in order to discover their meaning, for he had lived in terror of the hammer and in endurance of the pain it inflicted. Memories crowded up reanimating the empty house that his childhood had called home. The remote hammer was no longer remote. The sound of its blows re-echoed from his past and menaced his future.

Once more he was a child convalescing from a painful illness, fearfully conscious that it had come upon him as punishment for an act of sexual experimentation that had been branded as sin. The relation of sin and punishment had been driven in with a hard hammer. Sickness, pain, limitation, disaster came as swift retribution for transgression of the mysterious thou-shalt-nots decreed by a jealous father who would have no other gods before him. He had brought this illness upon himself. He must now accept its justice and endure its pain. When fear and an amorphous sense of guilt become attached to the dangers of original experience and exploration of the unknown, the world of the transforming images is closed off and childhood openness

---

[11] Rilke, *Sonnets of Orpheus*, XII, tr. by Ruth Spiers, quoted in Neumann, *Art and the Creative Unconscious*, p. 197.

to life is lost; endurance becomes safer than experimentation and discovery; a process of unnatural selection and cautious avoidance sets in. This process may be completely irrational, and the origin of the guilt feeling, if examined, appears absurd to the adult intellect; yet, like a drop of poison, it has entered the blood stream of the psyche and is slowly causing paralysis of creative choice. The creative force which seeks to manifest itself in individual rather than collectively acceptable forms is walled off by increasing rigidity which seeks only safety, for exploration of the unknown always includes highly dangerous possibilities. The ego polices creative desire lest it lead to outer disaster.

When the ego assumes that it is sovereign of the psyche, "everything is shifted to the conscious plane and the inner light darkens."[12] Then unassuming grayness shrouds the movement of the images and of their action as makers of destiny. More and more dependence is placed upon ego will and conscious concept. The gulf between conscious and unconscious widens. Where interplay of conscious and the unconscious is excluded, opposition rules. Increasing rigidity of ego consciousness produces an increase of emotional chaos in the unconscious. Rigidity then seeks to build walls of intellectual concepts behind which it can entrench itself, safe from the onslaught of waves of chaotic emotion. In this walled-off region, intellect may roam in search of corroborative aspects of truth and, ostrichlike, bury its head in the sands of unawareness and become oblivious to the approach of emotional disaster.

But only in the rejected opposite can redemption be found, and this can come only through original experience which, with its lightning shaft of perception, "stabs the dead heart wide awake" and brings knowledge of all that the grayness has concealed. The courage to face chaos—a courage so different from endurance or even fortitude —may thus be born within the sufferer, and he may find the ascent to God through descent into the chaos of the self.

Original sin and original goodness, equally feared by the sclerotic ego, may then be perceived in their opposition and their interplay not as forces to be outwardly contemplated but as energies existing within the Self, realities of one's own being. To the ego enclosed in a restrictive ideal of perfection, sin may come as the moment of enlightenment. Meister Eckhart comments on the strangeness of the fact

---

[12] *I Ching*, Vol. II, p. 187.

that so often those who come to God enter through the gateway of sin. Early imposed and misdirected feelings of guilt can drive the ego to seek safety in a narrowing form of virtuous conduct that shuts out understanding, compassion and tolerance toward sinners and toward the "sinful" elements of the self. Or, more disastrous, it may put on the blinders of conscious virtue so that the ego cannot see what the shadow is doing.

To him who has shut out knowledge of evil, seeking within the confines of the self only good—to him must sin come with its revealing power. To him who has closed his heart to knowledge of the good in order to attain the energy locked in the dark forces of evil—to him must come the revelation of the good. Only so can a man come to the wisdom of the God who is beyond the evil in whose light all that lives in the spirit of man stands revealed. Only then does transformation act upon the whole man, penetrating both consciousness and the unconscious. Only then is he capable of understanding the meaning of being chosen, which is the humble yet transcendent act of choice, where ego will submits to the will of the Self. Only then can he accept himself as part of the human stream in which sickness and pain and suffering may become part of the transforming process through compassion and acceptance of his humanity. Then can come the choice that touches the living sources in the unconscious and, in liberating the imprisoned powers, produces a transformation of the whole personality, not just a transformation of the conscious ego.

With this transformation, humiliation becomes humility and the amorphous sense of guilt is replaced by a responsible attitude toward one's own ignorance. The saving grace of doubt enters and the certainty of one's own rightness gives way to a perception of human vulnerability. There is nothing quite so terrifying as the man who feels certain beyond the shadow of a doubt that he is wholly on the side of righteousness. He not only terrifies others; he also terrifies himself. Rigidity builds windowless walls which shut out perception of chaos or creativity and may remain unaware of the sound of the hard hammer whose blow is death of the soul.

In both these dreams—of the tree of life and the tree of death— the unconscious shows the nature of the force deeply at work within and makes visible the goal toward which it is moving. If the man perceives the meaning of the tree of death, his *spirit* can turn from the gateway that it guards. Even though his body re-enters this house,

he will not re-enter its demands for endurance and rigidity. He will meet the old situation with a new attitude. New understanding, a new attitude toward relatedness, will arrest the death process and find a new way of life even in old circumstances. It will be a way of suffering and self-knowledge, even a way of crucifixion of the ego that has found safety in rigid obedience to the father as lawgiver. But in the end this new way will discover a new and different authority image arising as divine father of the spirit within the self. God as a creative force demands of each individual that he fulfill his own given powers as creator.

The moment of illumination may come through a human experience which reveals "the inexhaustible wellspring of the divine in man's nature."

A young doctor in his first year of internship consulted me because he found himself possessed by irrational impulses which made him destroy that which he most desired. In medical school, he had become interested in a special line of research, and had followed the reports and findings of a doctor whose work stirred his ego ambition. His goal became an internship in the hospital where this doctor was the leading authority. He obtained the desired post, but now, to his dismay, he found sudden blind compulsions forcing him to disregard this man's orders, or even to act in defiance of them. He was in danger of losing the position he had worked so hard to gain. There seemed no plausible reason or any excuse for his negative acts, so we sought an implausible way to deal with this irrational situation. This was that he would expose himself to every suggestive opportunity where, being outside the situation, he could keep his mind quiet and feel instinctively what was happening inside himself. When the doctor was making the rounds with another intern or giving general directions, he would listen to the sound of his footsteps, of his voice; he would observe, without consciously seeing, his gestures, his various movements, his expression. In short, he would let the doctor himself become the creator of images that would reveal themselves in the mirror of his quiescent consciousness.

In about a week he returned.

I heard his voice giving a quick direction. Instinctively I hated him. I wanted to spring at him and strangle him—and in that moment I *knew*. The tones of his voice were those of a young

teacher whom I once adored and who had betrayed me. My
father, for some reason that I never fathomed, distrusted and dis-
liked me. I never remember a time when I was near to him. I
was sent to boarding school before I found security in a father
relationship at home. I became passionately devoted to a young
teacher who was kind to me and uncritical of my areas of ignorance. He became a kind of father-god to me. He slept in the
cubicle next to mine and often I had an almost infantile awareness of his nearness. One day I was called to the principal's office and told that I had been seen climbing into my window at
two-thirty that morning and that such conduct meant immediate
expulsion. I knew what had happened. I had heard a sound the
night before and looked out; I had seen the young teacher climbing through his window. He was there in the office now, listening
to the accusation and to my denial. I waited for him to tell the
truth but he upheld the judgment of the headmaster. I was expelled and went back to face the cold hostility of my father
which was now apparently justified. When I listened yesterday,
the voice of the doctor was to me the very voice of the teacher
who had betrayed me. Everything that I had thought forgotten
was boiling up in me. I was again betrayed. I hated. I wanted to
kill. I would again be expelled.

"But this man has not betrayed you. Why don't you go to him
and tell him the story?"

In spite of doubt which was almost certainty of the futility of such
a request, he asked for an interview. On the doctor's desk lay the
young man's record. The older man listened quietly; then he took up
the record, tore it into fragments and dropped it into the waste
basket. "We start from here," he said.

The simplicity of the act and the words of trust and acceptance
were to the younger man the moment of enlightenment. No discussion, no words of compassion or of forgiveness, could have revealed
more clearly the essential being of the older man than did his immediate perception of the inner meaning of the young man's failure.

The new image of the father released by the doctor's reaction was a
revelation of the divine that lives within the human. Yet this could
not have been perceived by the younger man had he not prepared
himself for the vision through choice. He chose to expose himself to
the dangers of the father-authority; he chose to risk the act that might
lead to another expulsion; he chose to accept the numinous moment

when, through transformation of the image, he himself might be transformed. Even God cannot free a man from his past until he is willing to leave it. This young man could not have been freed from existing compulsions, nor could he have been inwardly ready to confirm the words, "We start from here," if he had secretly clung to resentment, bitterness and hatred as his right and as his excuse for future failures. His *record* would have gone into the scrap basket, but his *past* would have remained active within himself. We cannot say, "Because I did not have this, I shall never have that." If we do, we shut the door on transformation.

Nothing is irretrievably lost unless we continue to refuse the return of the image when it comes with transformed meaning.

In that numinous experience when the lightning flash of perception revealed the divine moving within the human and made manifest in immediate reaction, the father image returned not as judge but as redeemer, and the young man accepted freedom from the past and his own responsibility toward his future. Thus he was released from the old fear of the father as lawgiver and from the bitterness and distrust which had unconsciously held him in bondage to the ancient image. It was now not the father's knowledge that stirred his ego ambition but the father's wisdom that spoke to his newly awakened self and aroused the creative spirit within him. The line of research which he now followed through to his successful term of internship opened up new horizons. The road branched out and he chose the path that led him into a new region of discovery which he felt to be essentially his. He did not continue the same line of research, but the creative spirit of research moved in him and led him into a realm of discovery that was uniquely his.

When man is awakened to new awareness of the creative powers of the unconscious and to an understanding of the movement of the archetype in human life, mother and father become inner images that move as creative love and creative word, and the man, whether great or small in outer life, becomes aware that "the life we live is also the life of the gods."

CHAPTER 8

The X in the Calculation

୶ఢౕౖ

The x in the calculation is predisposition.[1]

IN THE MOMENT of illumination the essence, the reality that lies behind the images, breaks through to visibility. We no longer "see
through a glass darkly but . . . face to face"—face to face with the
essential meaning of the archetype, face to face with the essential
reality of the individual, and, if we look within ourselves, face to face
with the hitherto unacknowledged element, the x, the predisposition
that has so colored or distorted our perception of the images that we
have not known the nature of our reaction to them or how they have
compelled us to choices we thought were our own. This moment of
illumination comes as a light arising out of the darkness, or as the
word that pierces the ego's armor of self-satisfaction. It is the word
become the wound. It reawakens the heart to its own livingness.

Here choice confronts the ego. Will the heart admit that it is self-
wounded? Will the hearer descend into darkness to find the one who
has spoken?

Now comes the command.

> Be still, and let the dark come upon you
> Which shall be the darkness of God[2]

To relinquish conscious endeavor may also be the hero way. The
wu wei, the letting things happen, slowly restores sight to the eyes

---

[1] Quoted by Jung in *Two Essays on Analytical Psychology*, p. 12.
[2] T. S. Eliot, "East Coker," III, in *Four Quartets*.

that were blind, courage to the heart so that the eyes can look upon the dark where one waits for what is before thought and beyond thought.[3] Thought would try to form, to limit and circumscribe. Awareness awaits the images arising from "the darkness of God."

> Wait without thought, for you are not ready
>   for thought.
> So shall the darkness become the light and the
>   stillness the dancing.[4]

As the inner eye becomes accustomed to the darkness, it perceives a dance coming out of the stillness, a strange macabre dance. As we watch these dancers, they come into recognition as the manifestations of our own shadow elements, which interweave with figures of light. We see these shadow forces choose the pattern. As the drama of the dance unfolds, we become aware that it is this dominating shadow that directs the steps and changes the pattern at decisive moments. We had thought it was the outer event that had happened to us, but now, watching this director's movement, we see that it is we who have happened to ourselves. Here where the Other, the non-ego, has lifted the curtain, we see these dancers of the night as we could not see them in the bright noonday of consciousness. To hold one's will steadfast in the stillness which is both wound and healing of the wound, to let darkness become visible as an inner reality, brings the admission: "This dance is mine, these dancers are also myself." Then comes, from deep within the darkness, the challenge of the light. Shadows are not all.

Looking into the depth, we perceive the spiral way where choice has confronted us on different levels of being. Here, as the spiral turns, stands this shadow figure. We look at him, and strangely he changes from darkness to light and again to darkness. Seeking his name and meaning we move downward on the spiral. We are back in a land which is known, yet unknown. Have we been here before, or was it some other self who lived long ago? We are enclosed in a childhood past which is also a mythological past still alive within the

---

[3] It was following the *wu wei*, emptying his mind of intellectual concept, waiting "without thought," that made the young intern able to receive the image of long-past experience as it rose from the world of buried memories and seized upon his emotions, reanimating his past, illuminating his present irrational conflict.

[4] Eliot, *op. cit.*

present. We perceive new meanings; we hear faint whispers of long-ago prophecy, perhaps already fulfilled within us; we may even perceive the nature of the creature of light and shadow who from his stronghold of invisibility directed distant choices. Holding the past in consciousness, we discover why its memory has returned at this time. We have again come to a place of choice where once more we are in danger of following the old pattern. Predisposition in shadow form may again choose for us.

This recognition of the shadow aspect of predisposition may come through a series of many dreams that slowly bring this factor into the light of consciousness. This happened to a woman who was almost forty years old. A much desired relationship was threatened with disaster because the object of her love could not endure her excessive demands. The libido which she had invested in the object turned back upon herself and she became the victim of her own devouring emotions. She protested that she had been ready to offer up all—even her uttermost self—upon the altar of love. Why was her gift refused, her sacrifice denied? She raged against an unjust fate that she insisted had pursued her all her life. As she recounted the story of her many frustrations, a recurrent childhood dream repossessed her with its portent of doom.

Two great giants are rolling dice. The noise is like thunder but sharper, more alarming. I wake in the darkness knowing that something terrible is going to happen to me.

The dream came first when she was about three. Her terror became a question, "What are they going to do to me?" As the dream repeated itself, always with the same content but with increasing affect, a strange certainty grew. "They are playing for *me!*" And as her fear increased the question became, "What will they do *with* me?" A child knows neither the nature of the creature within the self who asks the question nor why the question changes in form, but the words "*with* me" gave to her terror an undercurrent of fascination, as of being drawn into a mysterious situation over which she had no control.

She did not remember just when she first became conscious of angry voices in the room next to hers, but the sound aroused the same fear as the rolling of the giants' dice. Actuality and dream wove

themselves together and the images became one—the earth giants quarreling and the dream giants rolling their dice in a game in which she was the prize and also the victim. The same fear that she felt in the dream was now part of her feeling toward her parents. This was not surprising for indeed it was the hidden violence in their natures that constellated the archetype of the giants that had appeared in the dream. The unconscious is aware of situations of which the conscious ego knows nothing. The dream is a picture not only of the inner meaning of the objective situation but also of the subjective reaction of the dreamer—often of the x that responds and questions. Fear asked the first question, "What are they going to do *to* me?" The aroused x asked, "What will they do *with* me?" This word "with" reveals not only the dread, the sense of impotence aroused by the archetype, but also the increasing fascination of the image and the child's undercurrent of desire to be possessed.

The dream, with its foreshadowing of doom, came before the child had heard the angry voices, before her ego was aware, even intuitively, of the situation that existed between her parents, before she knew that in reality she was the stake for which they played. Their marriage had been based on an unconscious attraction that had never developed into love. Instead it had turned into a battle of hostile forces. They were now held together more by compulsive desire for power over each other and for conventional recognition by the world in which they lived than by any lingering affection. Possession of the child's love, ambitious direction of her life, became a symbol of victory of the one over the other.

And the child dreaming the dream, waking in the lonely dark, hearing the voices, caught in the sinister magic of the parents' will to power, felt the upsurge of a deep buried desire to give herself over to this power. A vague remembrance of this stirred in her now and, sharpened into the recollection of a night when she had said, "There is nothing I can do about it. They will do whatever they please *with* me," she recalled the relief that swept over her. If the struggle was theirs, it set her free from responsibility. If she gave up, she would belong to the winning giant; she would be wholly possessed and wholly accepted.

Yet this acquiesence was only one element of her being. She was a child with a rebellious will, a creative imagination, an intensity of feeling, and a talent not at all in keeping with the parents' conven-

tional, worldly ambitions. She kept the talent apart, nurturing it secretly. It was her refuge; it created for her a circle of security which the earth giants could not invade. It was also a place where pent-up rebellion could avenge itself and rejoice in secret defiance. In the drama played by the conflicting elements of her personality, rebellion and conformity had their roles—one in inner, the other in outer life. So well did they play their parts that she was unconscious of the hidden battle between them that kept her ego from any real security. When rebellion broke through in outer defiance, she was caught in storms of emotional demand; when defiance made her venture into an independence that she could not maintain, the end was disaster. Each disaster, she told herself, was the fault of the earth giants (the parents) or the dream giants (fate). She never tried to examine the part her own inner action played. Nevertheless, each failure returned her to the old situation, even more closely bound by her need for acceptance at any price. The giants had again won; again she was the victim. At other times she tried to play one against the other, not realizing that by so doing she became increasingly valuable as the prize in this game of each against the other.

One of the subtly dangerous traps was that "someone" within this daughter's unconscious perceived the falseness of the claims that her parents made upon her. This "someone" felt justified in rebellion and resistance. Even worse, while she longed almost compulsively for their love, this same curious inner creature refused to love them. Was she in truth what they asserted—a rebellious and ungrateful daughter? In such a situation there is no one who can explain the words of the Self, "He that loveth father or mother more than me is not worthy of me,"[5] nor is there anyone to help the confused ego to see that the "accidental parents" are only parents of the body and that the spirit must find its relation to the divine mother and father who are the sources of its true being if it is also to find itself. The dream and the reality combined to show her no saving presence back of the parental image but only the archetypal figures of the giants in their bigness and power. She could not know that weakness uses will to power as a substitute for inner strength, nor could she know how vulnerable the earth giants might really become. For they not only possessed the energy of shadow forces but also the support of outer circumstance

---

[5] Matthew 10:37.

which, regardless of fitness or unfitness, gives the parent authority over the child. "Everybody" knows that a child "must" love its parents and be grateful to them. This was rubbed in as a self-evident law of life.

She felt at one with herself only in a secret place where, by giving more and more skillfully contrived form to her compulsive thoughts, fantasies, fears and conflicting desires, she temporarily separated herself from them—even achieved a sense of power over them. She possessed an extraordinary ability to do this because, in spite of all the turbulence of her emotional life, she was conscious of a talent that lived within her and insisted upon its own life. Her realization of this gift gave a sense of purpose to those secret hours in which she felt dedicated to the fulfillment of its demand. This talent she would not surrender. She was not aware of the true meaning of the creative force that at such times possessed her, yet she cherished the talent. It was her own. It made her a separate person. It even made her feel that she belonged to herself. Jung says, "The chief aim of the individual is to create out of himself the most significant product of which he is capable."[6] Though she did try to create from the talent the most significant product of which she was at that time capable, she was not yet an individual; her ego seized upon it and identified with it. Its nurture became her justification for rebellion and her excuse to herself for her failure in other departments of life.

She returned from these excursions into inner reality to face her failures in outer life for which her parents saw no justification or excuse. Again they withheld love: she did not deserve love. Whether she deserved it or not, she craved it. She was not ready for the aloneness that the creative daemon imposes upon the one it possessed and made the creator. As she grew older and the archetypal world retreated, she tried to project her often too-personal feelings into her work. She did not reckon with the power of emotion to break through all barriers of purpose and demand its own fulfillment. You cannot teach the instincts to play the piano or paint a picture or write a poem even though the libido, when possessed by the creative energy, may pour into these channels, stilling the demands of the blood. The emotions are there, awaiting release, and if they are too long denied they break through, insatiable in their hunger and need. When this happened to her, wild tempestuous moods possessed her.

---

[6] Jung, quoting from his writings in conversation with the author.

Quite early she learned that storms of emotion frightened her parents and made them try to propitiate her. She used her moods against them even while the moods used and possessed her. Then they passed, and she faced inner emptiness and outer "righteous indignation." Again she was defeated; again she longed to be accepted; again the victim element took over the leading role. She *wanted* to be the prize for which they played.

By the time she reached adolescence the dream of the giants had long since ceased to haunt her nights, for the conflict had become a daytime battle.[7] Yet she still reacted to her personal parents and to others on whom the parental image was projected as though they were gigantic forces that could do with her as they willed. Often dreams blew past her like storm clouds, but she was too engrossed in the battle that she was waging with circumstance to register their portent or even note their passing. Nor did she understand the inner storm. Though the dream of the giants did not return, its archetypal power lived and irrationally gave to human beings, or even to situations, the aspect of gigantic forces of doom concentrated upon her small person. The dream image retreated to the unconscious but was not transformed. Therefore her own transformations of consciousness were uprooted and subject to sudden changes: emotions, impulses, desires, elations and depressions swept through her. Her own inordinate need made her project a savior image upon a human being, and when that human being failed to meet the projection, her first reaction was to pour herself out in a limitless form of giving which was repudiated because undesired. Again, repudiation aroused her childhood feeling of being victimized.

In late adolescence another theme enters her dream world—that of the journey. Sometimes it is the well-known one of starting to catch a train or a boat, forgetting her money or ticket, turning back, losing her way or being lost in a fog. Sometimes she is looking for a house that she knows is her home or searching for a treasure she has lost. Always at the important moment a terrifying "someone" or an invincible "something" bars her way. She gives up. She turns back and, at the moment of her turning, she wakes to the old feeling of frustration.

---

[7] Many times when the child who has had recurrent nightmares talks of his repressed emotions, temper tantrums break out in the day and the nightmare gallops out of the window of the night.

Then circumstances brought her face to face with a decisive choice that she had evaded, either by playing one parent against the other or by living her secret life while she outwardly conformed to the demanded pattern. An opportunity came which she felt would give scope to her talent. Both parents refused their consent. She was faced by an unpleasant reality. She could not choose her own way in defiance of her parents' commands and expect to be supported by them. She was told this in no uncertain terms. She must either conform to their idea of what a good daughter should be or find a way to pay for her own rebellious choice. Self-pity and rage swept through her. She stormed against her parents, against the situation, against the injustice of life. All the fantasies of her self as victim of a cruel fate arose. Her martyr role took on histrionic proportions. Such histrionic roles often cover human reactions that more truly, but less dramatically, might be worded, "There's nothing I can do about it. What's the sense of trying? Nevertheless, I mean to have my own way."

The talent and the victim were the contesting heroes of the drama. The talent won the immediate battle. She left home. But this new outer freedom was not sustained by an inner freedom. She had forgotten that wherever we go we take ourselves with us. She still clung to her resentment, her fear and compulsive emotions. She had made a step forward in conscious choice but she had not yet faced the enemies of choice in her own unconscious, nor had she separated herself from the infantile attitude that support was her due whatever use she might make of it. Much happened that was good. She threw herself into the new situation. She worked with enthusiasm. Her talent developed and opened new worlds.

She felt the days of the giants were long past. But the mythological past exists in the present moment. The age of the giants was alive within this modern woman. It had never been raised to consciousness, and therefore, as indwelling myth, it might overpower her conscious adaptation.

Now after many years, a frustrating experience, which again denied her demand for love, wiped out all the intervening years and she was once more a child hearing the sharp thunder, the roll of the dream giants' dice, and the quarrelling voices of the earth giants. The journey seemed to have come to an end in the same dark beginning.

But the return is never quite the same. The choice that confronts us is on a higher or lower level of the spiral. Her relation to the un-

conscious had changed through her devotion to her work and her willingness to listen to the inner voices that spoke to her as she tried to give form to her concepts. Even when they told her unpleasant truths about herself, against which her ego rebelled, she listened. Again she started on the long, long road, but a change in her attitude made it a new beginning. She tried to accept the shadow that had held her potential of love bound in negative form—the inner witch power that can transform even a princess into an animal. At this point of new beginning there came a return of the dreams that had haunted her adolescence when she had first broken from home. In her sleeping hours she is on the old quest, the search for her as yet unknown goal. She is searching, in a dangerous and unknown region, for a place of buried treasure or for a way to a new country. The setting of the dream changes but the purport of the quest is always the same. Sometimes she is in a strange city going through dangerous dark alleys to find her lighted house; sometimes the journey is into dark mountainous regions where rocks forbid entrance to the path she feels leads to her goal; or she may be in a boat trying to steer through seething waters. In every dream she comes to the place of peril. She hesitates, and, at the moment when she turns back, she wakes with the old sense of impotence and defeat. Again she feels that she is the victim of circumstance.

This time she faced the dream and asked, "What is it in me that forces me to turn back without accepting the challenge and attempting the encounter?" She had become willing to ask the question. Willingness to ask is a decisive step toward consciousness, but finding and accepting the answer is not easy. There was no moment of sudden enlightenment. The road was long and difficult. The old rebellions rose and fought for their life. The old excuses put on alluring garments and tried to tempt her into old paths. The old voice spoke the familiar words, "There is nothing I can do about it. They will do whatever they want *with* me." Yet this time she tried to struggle with these forces, not as outer impositions but as inner enemies. It was this attempt that moved in the unconscious and produced an answer, though in prophetic form. Another dream came.

I am driving with my mother. I leave her and drive straight through houses where women are playing cards or gossiping in little clacking groups. I come out on a rocky coast. I am standing alone. The way is through the waters. The waters separate sud-

denly, and as suddenly come together again. At the instant before their parting there is an increase of the churning of the waters. If I dare plunge at the instant of greatest peril it might be the instant of salvation. Now a little boy is beside me. I lift him on my back and tell him to hold tight. I feel his arms about my neck. His legs encircle my waist. Chaos comes upon the waters. I dive. The waves gnash together behind me. I am through. I hear a voice say, "The light was never before so radiant upon the shining bridge."

"I am driving with my mother." The road in the dream is one that she had often taken in reality. It is a famous road of great beauty. The houses along the way are imposing palaces of the very rich. "I leave her [the mother] and drive straight through these houses." She drives through them as though they were built of straw—as indeed they are, for the "women are playing cards or gossiping in little clacking groups." It is the old life of outer riches and inner poverty. She drives "straight through the houses"—straight through the old life that had so often entrapped her with its false lure of safety. "I come out on a rocky coast. I am . . . alone." She is alone, as everyone must be when he comes to the moment of greatest peril, which is also the moment of decisive choice. Before her are the dangerous waters. If she is not to turn back, her way must be through them. She sees the parting of the waters, their ferocious return, the churning of the waters of chaos that comes just before the parting of the waves. With a flash of inner conviction she knows that if she dares "the instant of the greatest peril [the churning of the waters], it might be the instant of salvation." At that moment when she sees and accepts the challenge a little boy appears beside her. She lifts him upon her back—she dives—she is through—the shining bridge is before her.

The gnashing waves are symbol of the active door, the jaws of the monster, the gates of Hell. In the myth of the "transitus" the hero leaps in his given second of time, leaving his own past bitten off by the snapping jaws. He is through—his past, his old ego life, has been "bitten off"; his future, his destiny, is before him. He has carried his essential value through "the active door" and faces—what?

The children of Israel, after their passage through the divided waters, faced the desert. Yet they brought through the perilous passage a saving element: *faith.* It has been told that when the Israelites

came to the Red Sea, the waters did not open until one man, trusting in the promise, plunged in. Then of themselves the waters parted and the children of Israel passed over on dry land. The Egyptians—their past in the historic aspect of their slavery—were swallowed by the closing waters. The children of Israel were free—*yet the desert was before them.* She felt free, but she forgot both the long stretch of water (the waters of the unconscious) that she must go through before she reached the shining bridge and also forgot the desert aspects of the conscious life to which she must return.

The desert was before her. Is the name of the child Faith? What was her faith? Consciously it was still a faith in her talent as her essential value; but this talent was still too much bound to the ego and to its infantile demands for outer support to be an expression of the creative life of the self. It was not the treasure for which all else is given. That treasure she had still to find before her faith could become faith in the transforming power of the Self.

She now expected a new and glorious freedom. But there was that damn desert! We may remember that the children of Israel did not always behave very well in the desert. Neither did she. Also there, whispering in her ear, was the same old familiar shadow, Self-Pity: "They shouldn't put this desert right in my way now." But the desert, after the manner of deserts, stayed just where it was—a reality to be faced.

A desert born of past choices is an unpleasant reality. Even though we have made a decisive choice and do not inwardly regress to the past, the old choices, the old mistakes, have made desolate the immediate way. It is then that the willing, choosing, suffering ego must carry the child of the future through the wilderness that leads to the city of the Self. It is then we must face our own dark ignorance. It is then that the prideful ego must accept its limitations and, with humility, patience and courage, learn the meaning of the new way, learn also to trust the guidance of the vision that comes as "a pillar of cloud by day and a pillar of fire by night."

After a long journey through the desert, a journey factually long in time, in struggle, in defeat, in despair and sometimes in conquest, she had another dream.

Before me is a wall of molten stones that glow with a sullen orange light. Four giants, born of this same molten stone, tower

up from the center of the wall where the stone reddens into a gateway of wicked sullen flame. As I look at the giants, a voice says, "Challenge them!" I shout aloud. At the sound of my voice, the wall, and the four giants who are the towers and pillars of the wall, fall as ash that dissolves into air.

In the dream the giants dissolve, the wall falls even as the walls of Jericho fell before the children of Israel. We note the miracle; we forget the way that led to it—the dismal years of mistaken or redemptive choice, the slow years of growth of decision, the sevenfold circling of the walls and *then* the sound of the trumpet.

The challenge is given, the walls fall: all this has happened in the dream. What will happen within the dreamer when she wakes from the dream? Whose voice will she choose as hers? Will the old predisposition, the victim element, again ask, "What will they do *with* me?" or will the newly awakened potential challenge them with the word like a small, a clear stone of truth that can prevail over giants?

She was awake now. The wall was still there. The giants still confronted her. She faced them waiting for the challenging word to rise within herself. Instead, from the dark cave of remembrance, came the voice of one of the earth giants—"What are these four fears everyone is talking about?"

Four freedoms! Four fears! A slip of the tongue. Had the tongue slipped, or had it spoken the negative word that the earth giant had chosen as its own?

She named the giants with their self-chosen names: Fear of speech, Fear of worship, Fear of want, Fear of fear. These were the fears of the earth giant who had uttered these words. They did not belong to her. Yet in the dream she knew the four giants were the guardians of the gateway of the city to which her journey had brought her. Again she rebelled against discovery of meaning. Why should she be called upon to challenge giants that were not hers? Or had she made them hers? In the dream she was face to face with them, and the dream was her own. What were these giant fears? She named each with his own name.

Fear of speech, of self-revelation through the word. Words were made to cover up, not to reveal essential inner meanings. Truth was dangerous. It could betray you to a watchful enemy. It could betray

you to yourself. By a strange twisting pathway she found herself caught in the very fear that she repudiated. Even while she was repeating the name of the giant, she was searching for evasive words that would prove her guiltless of evasion. Her clever brain was twisting and turning among self-justifying words like a hare before hounds. She was afraid, not of many ego-chosen words but of the self-revealing word of truth which would bring her face to face with herself. Was it to the unknown self that she spoke the Judas word, thus betraying the truth of the self through fear of what the revealing word might do to her ego security? What was the Word (the speech) she feared? "I am the Word."

As she questioned herself, the next giant fear, took over: Fear to worship openly the god image that had been, in a strange moment of illumination, revealed to her. The living god is very dangerous. "Whoever is near to me is near to the fire."[8] Even while denying her fear, she trembled to think what this living god would do if she acknowledged him. He would burn away her defenses of conformity, convention and respectability that kept her safe with all the giants of inner and outer world. Propitiatory words, platitudes, repetitions of their creed had paid lip service to their god and saved her from the fire. Who had spoken these words? Was it the x, the one who secretly longed to become the sacrifice to this giant fear? She wanted—she desperately wanted—freedom to worship, but the price made her afraid of her own desperate wanting.

The third fear, Fear of want, took on giant form. She had always been afraid of hungry wanting—hunger of the spirit, she had called it. She had wanted love, assurance of being completely loved, of being secure in the life for which she hungered, secure in circumstance so that her talent could grow without fear of outer responsibility, without fear of what *they* would do. She had a right to her own hungry wanting, a right to have her hunger fed. It *must* be fed or she would die. Once more she was in the clutches of the giant, Fear of want. All the hungers of her childhood rose in demand. She must—she *must*—be given love, understanding, abundant compassion. No one had ever given her what her starved child self must have. She could not at this point see that people are not going about the world seeking to adopt starving children who claim all the privileges of neg-

---

[8] *The Gospel According to Thomas*, p. 45.

lected childhood and at the same time their right to adult relationship. Waves of self-pity engulfed her and her ego cried out, "I must
have what I want when I want it—else I shall starve." Suppose "they"
withheld it? Panic took over and she was afraid to face her own fear
lest it show her the nature of her peril. She must not fear; that would
give strength to the giants.

The fourth giant, Fear of fear, possessed her, and her ego fled
from her own city of freedom and tried like a hunted animal to find
a place to hide. This was what they had done *with* her. Her pent-up
emotions flared up, so seeking to divert her from her fear and prevent
her from discovering its meaning. She raged against her parents,
against the niggardliness of life, against an unjust God. Again she
heard the giants rolling their dice and the sound of angry voices
behind closed doors. She remembered her parents' sullen silences
when she had been conscious of the buried hatred that burned under
their outwardly controlled acts. It was the earth giants' hate that had
engendered the smouldering fire that had formed the giants of fear
who now kept her from her city of freedom—giants molten, glowing,
but without power to create, with power only to keep her, the dis-
coverer, from entering the city. It was this sullen fire that had consumed her own life. She had been its victim. Self-pity rushed through
her like a wind fanning the flames. She embraced her self-inflicted
role. She glowed in the suffering of her martyrdom. Then came
another dream—humorous, blasphemous, unmistakably clear.

I have come into a room where God, the Holy Ghost and Jesus
are having a pleasant conversation. I am horrified and cry out,
"But have you forgotten the crucifixion? I must tell the world
about the crucifixion." Jesus gives me a dime and says, "Well,
if you feel you *must*, there is a long-distance telephone over
there." I rush to the booth but over the telephone is hung the
word, "Sorry."

She told the dream in these words but she afterward remembered
that in the dream itself the meaning was conveyed through silence.
It was the expression on the faces, the silent gesture, that spoke the
words she had later phrased. The expression on the face of Jesus as
he handed her the dime was humorous, tolerant—a look with which
one might regard the pretensions of an ignorant and willful child.
As in a moment of illumination, she saw the use her ego had made

of the symbol of crucifixion and how this perversion of the symbol gave its negative form power over her life. The sacrificial element which might have been used in love and creative power had been manifest only in its self-victimizing form; it had exalted meaningless suffering to a place of value that demanded recognition and support. She had not distinguished between neurotic suffering, untransforming because it feeds upon self-pity, and the suffering that leads to transformation because it brings to birth pity and compassion. Neurotic suffering is the ego's proclamation of crucifixion, its desire that it be "lifted up" and worshiped as a value in itself. This is the suffering that passes and leaves no trace, that returns and feeds upon itself. It is self-inflicted death, leading to no resurrection. It destroys the victim, to no purpose. Its message is, in short, hardly worth a dime, even if it could find a channel of communication.

No advice, no imposed interpretation of the action of her own victim desire, could have brought this meaning home to her as did this picture painted by her own unconscious.

She tried to find the meaning of sacrifice and crucifixion. In its shadow form, it had destroyed her power to see the needs of others in relationship; it had exalted her ego. What was its transformed power? She tried to follow the symbol back into the mist where the ancient images move in eternal transformation.

Far back in the dawn of consciousness, the victim and the unknown god were linked together by the power of a mysterious preconscious bond, whose meaning lay in the cloud of unknowing between man and God. In the dark of fear, the unwilling and impotent victim was slain to feed the savage blood lust of the gods and to win their favor. The Great Mother (the earth), on whom the victim's blood was poured out, bestowed her gift of fertility. The Father, whose wrath was appeased by the offering up of the human sacrifice, bestowed his favor of power upon the tribe. Cruel rites, dark mysteries distorted man's concept of the god image and of the relation of man and god. As the god image was transformed in the heart of man, the role of victim changed. It moved from primeval fear, through the dark of magic, into the awe of mystery, into ritual in which man and god met. Through participation in the symbol, the energy of the god became alive in man as an inner force unknown, never fully known, but more and more revealed as a transforming process. Man slowly became conscious, and God found human form.

In this emergence, the victim played his self-imposed or doom-imposed part. As the god-image was transformed in the heart of man, the image of the victim changed and the values involved in sacrifice dawned upon the human consciousness. The victim, through his willingness to encounter death for the life of the tribe, became the hero who, through the experience of the transitus, would bring a new concept of truth, a new relation between God and man. Desire for death as a coward substitute for the battle of life is the suicidal victim-motive. The willingness to face death if that is the price of rebirth is the hero way of sacrifice. "God first became man, and underwent a most miserable fate in order to become God,"[9] also to bring the image of God alive in man. The god-image that lives in man took on new life and meaning through Christ's willingness to accept sacrificial death rather than deny the truth that was in him. He affirmed his truth, even unto death, so making it his. He possessed it and so could bequeath it to humanity. Through this bequest, a new god-image might be born in the human heart—if the heart would accept the innermost meaning of sacrifice.

The woman faintly glimpsed this meaning of the sacrifice of ego demands to the higher demands of the Self. This Jesus who had looked at her in her dream knew crucifixion as the way over to new life, the triumph of the one who endured the torment of death so that truth might triumph over ignorance, and the cross become the tree of new life. She had a sudden realization of her own pretentiousness, and a revelation of the meaning of sacrifice. The victim who is nailed to his own dead past is crucified on the tree of death, which will never flower into a tree of new life, and the victim is a useless sacrifice to an ancient unchanging image of an untransformed and untransforming god, who has lost the power of creation and re-creation.

This was the message that had come to her out of silence. She had feared silence. The silence of the earth giants was more terrible than their words. It shut her out. She dared not approach them. It was sullen silence fed by smoldering fires of resentment, even of hate. She remembered silence as one of the most terrible things of her childhood. In the dream, words came out of it. They convicted her of her own arrogant egoism; yet they also forgave her even while they showed her the truth about herself.

[9] Jung, quoting from his writings in conversation with the author.

All the sullen silences of her childhood seemed to be about her. Again she saw the giants of fear and heard the voice, "Challenge them!" As she stood alone, awaiting the coming of the word, her dream of the transitus returned, and the child stood beside her. She relived the dream. She took him on her back and faced the churning water. The child was a weight on her back, a burden, but her arms and legs were free. Feeling that burden, a myth of the transitus came back to her as she had read it in childhood. She recalled Saint Christopher striding into the river, the burden of the child growing heavier and heavier on his shoulders. He reaches the other side and as he puts the child down, he asks his question:

"Child who art thou?" and the child answers, "I am the new day about to be born."

These words were also known to her. When, in adolescence, she had read *Jean Christophe*, these words had leaped at her from the printed page, registering an apprehension of something as yet unknown.

Again she saw the face of Jesus as it was in her dream, the humorously loving, infinitely expressive look as he gave her the dime; again she went over the words into which she had translated that look— "Well, if you feel you *must*." She felt the sudden stab, the recognition of her own ego assumptions and her own smallness. *Must* she continue to cling to that self-pitying, ego-demanding past, or could she, through acceptance of this new symbol, set herself free from the old compulsion to exalt the victim above the god? *Must* she remain under the domination of the shadow form of sacrifice, or could she, by an act of choice, set herself free? Was this the message of the child who answered, "I am the new day about to be born"?

In many dreams the child appears as the *puer aeternus*, the child of new beginnings, the new attitude that can set the ego free of its own past and so bring to birth that inner day when the sun of new consciousness shall arise within the psyche. This is the child of the Self whose life must be fulfilled even when it leads to crucifixion of the ego. It is also the child of inner vision who sees both the reality of the personal self and the greater reality of the inner world of the eternal images.

She had supposed that her vision was turned to this inner world, for the play of images that moved behind her eyelids, the thoughts that rose of themselves, had been, she assumed, the sources of her

creative thought—as indeed they were. But too often her ego had seized upon them and trivialized the images, using them as means of expressing her own personal sufferings. Her ego considered these products to be self-expression, when often they were only ego expression.

The new image that informs us of the symbol that is coming into being cannot be expressed by an ego that is unconnected with the archetypal images. Such an attempt trivializes the product and robs it of any numinous quality, for it does not arise from deep original experience. Beauty of technique may arouse admiration, but the strange compelling power of the word that comes out of silence touches the spirit, awakening awareness of the unknown that is coming into consciousness.

One's own personal problem may be eloquently expressed in word, in painting or in hewn form, but if it is divorced from archetypal meaning it carries no message to the heart, no premonition of that which is now to be born. Only the revelation of the eternal symbol in its new form can give to the product its power to awaken the image slumbering in the unconscious of the beholder.

She perceived that the child was not her talent but the child born of the transformation of the sacrificial element within herself, which might become love that knows the meaning of sacrifices of the ego to the greater demands of the self and of love's high values. As inner vision, this child could help her see how the unfaced predisposition had produced the outer catastrophe, in which she assumed her own inner warfare to be a fight against alien circumstances and personalities. The self could face the inner conflict now and so bring to birth a new attitude.

Then in fantasy she asked the question which brings the dream into the realm of creative choice, "What can I do about it?" The child answered, "Go down into yourself. There you will find the fire that has bred these giants of fear. If you will endure the fire so that you can understand its devouring nature and its power to destroy, you will also find its power to transform. At the fire's center you will find that which has remained unconsumed. It is the stone which is also the word. With it you can challenge the giants."

She now realized that it was the unredeemed element, the x within herself, which had given power to the giants of fear. The twin of freedom is responsibility. In freedom you accept the responsibility of

your own life. This is the drama whose tragedy, whose triumph, is brought about by your own choice; the doer is yourself, the betrayer is yourself, the hero is yourself, the opportunity, the avoidance, the choice is yours. Fear has a twin, Self-Pity. It says, "This should not happen to *me*. This hunger should not be my hunger, this disaster should not be my disaster." He hides from life, refusing to accept the truth that living is being oneself *in life* and knowing oneself vulnerable to all that it contains.

She began to see a further meaning of the sacrifice: the sacrifice of the personal life to the greater life of the truth that lives itself within us. The sacrifice of the ego that makes possible the release of the word, challenging the giants, transforming fear into freedom.

A fantasy may drift away, its meaning may be lost; or it may be lived in self-examination leading to a knowledge of the inner factor, the one who has made decisive choices. The fantasy that is lived in true introversion becomes the most real of realities. Going through the fire meant to this woman facing the smoldering resentments, the flaming angers, the consuming self-pity, the desire to be victimized, so that her ego could claim the martyr crown. All were her own. None of these could be externalized or put into acceptable form and so exorcised. They had to be endured—and so given actual life as agents of her destiny—during a long period of many difficult experiences and many dreams.

When the inner giants of fear were faced as her own, her vision turned outward: she saw the earth giants not as powerful forces that had been given dominion over her life but as pathetic human creatures caught in the smallness of their own resentments and hatreds, never able to go beyond the petty and the trivial. She saw that they were themselves prisoners of their own choices against life. It was her own choices against life that had kept her chained to them. Now the chain was broken. Resentment could give way to pity, and pity could become compassion. Yet she still had a relationship to fulfill, a new part to play in her attitude toward them, even though she could never accept their way.

Looking outward, she saw not the desert but a world in which the slumbering images, those held captive by fear, had awakened. She was part of life. She could say, "All these are in me and I am in them. I am myself."

Such an experience makes one part of the human stream, vul-

nerable to any human experience of joy or of sorrow. One can no longer say, "This should not come to me," but one asks, "What can I do about it so that, through the experience of all that may come from the whole range of living, I can find the meaning of relatedness and of love?"

Jung has said, "Redeemed love is the extraverted aspect of individuation." This for her was the redemption of the x—the victim become the redeemer.

What had she brought to love? Fierce desire and willingness to sacrifice her own truth if she could possess and be possessed by the beloved object; if denied, she identified with the crucified victim, demanding that her suffering be accepted as a divine sacrifice which must compel love in the beholder. What was the meaning of the cross—a meaning that reached back into a remote past not yet touched by the Christian symbol and on into a future whose meaning was beyond human prophecy? Where did she stand now—what was this place? She was through; behind her the waves had gnashed together.

Once more she returned to the dream of the transitus. She had driven through the houses, taken the child on her back, crossed the white water. What was ahead? She lifted her face and saw the bridge shining.

The bridge is a symbol built between the known and the unknown, between the everyday event and the timeless. This is the joining together between past and future. "In folk lore as well as in myths the bridge is always accounted an exceptional and special place, under the protection of the divinity."[10] Its priestly significance comes down to us in the title of the Pope, Pontifex Maximus, for "in ancient Rome the priest was entitled *pontifex* (bridge builder)."[11] This is the crossing whose center is at the deepest point of the abyss beneath. At this center the ring was thrown to the river god.

The bridge is built between the earthly and the heavenly worlds; the Rainbow Bridge, quivering in color, swaying as the souls pass over, stretches from earth to Valhalla; the Milky Way makes the long bridge from earth to the outer universe. Bridge and abyss form a cross at the point of deepest intersection; this is the cross of the

---

[10] Aniela Jaffé, "The Person and the Experience," *Spring* 1959, p. 25, n. 4.
[11] *Ibid.*

transitus where, through acceptance of the cross, one passes over from the old life to the new.

The words emerged from the end of the dream, "The light was never before so radiant upon the shining bridge." She looked far down into the split within herself: love and hate, night and day, darkness and light, all the opposites that faced each other across the seemingly bottomless abyss. She knew that the bridge was her own desire to accept the split, and that with true desire she might cross over to the place of reconciliation of the opposites.

Do we desire this reconciliation? It means facing the night and day within ourselves; it means building our own bridge which is the cross, the death, the transitus. For the cross that each must bear is hewn out by the mysterious indwelling Self that brings man face to face with his own conflict, his own experience and his own choice of the way he will live out his destiny. It is through acceptance of this cross that the tree of death becomes the tree of life.

When four roads come together, here too the cross is made, of east and west and north and south; and at the center where the opposites meet, choice of the way is made, a choice of death or of rebirth and transformation of the personality. At this center the traveler is faced with the necessity of decision. Will he choose the difficult way over the shining bridge that spans the abyss between the old life of ego demand and the new life of self-knowledge? If he dares the crossing his feet are set upon the pathway that leads to the city of wholeness toward which the soul journeys. "Therefore know yourselves, for you are the city and the city is the kingdom."[12]

In such an inner-journey dream, fantasy and vision bring their moments of enlightenment when both the former choices against the self and the transforming power of the symbol are revealed. The fiery moment of illumination passes. The ego must again face the perils of the way—the return to the old situation, the old temptations, the old encounter with the x in its shadow form. Has the ego been an observer or a reverent participant in the mystery? Unless there has been a true participation in which, with utmost integrity, the experience has been accepted, it cannot act in transformation of the whole personality. For in a transformation of the whole per-

---

[12] After the Oxyrhynchus papyri Sayings of Jesus in *The Apocryphal New Testament*, pp. 25 ff.

sonality, not only the conscious concept but also the inner image of the archetype is transformed, thus creating a new relation between ego and non-ego. "Unless changes in consciousness go hand in hand with changes in the unconscious components of the personality, they do not amount to much."[13] Such changes in the unconscious components must be confirmed by humble and reverent loyalty to that which has happened and by endurance of the pain of self-knowledge that it has made possible.

Step by step the journey must be taken, and only by keeping an openness which permits the flow of energy between the unconscious and consciousness can the redeeming symbol continue its creative act of transformation. The truly religious attitude toward life and toward one's individual revelation of inner and outer reality integrates the experience into the structure of the personality so that the new attitude becomes part of the unconscious reaction to events. The mystery may be refused, the temporary worshiper may shut the door upon the inner sanctuary and step back into the market place where the ego and the x again take up the old life. This is the peril and the opportunity made possible by the gift of choice.

The way of the Creative works through change and transformation, so that each thing receives its true nature and destiny and comes into permanent accord with the Great Harmony.[14]

The I Ching, from which this quotation comes, is called The Book of Changes. It was also known as the book of divination:

When it happened for the first time in China that someone, on being told the auguries for the future, did not let the matter rest there but asked, "What am I to do?" the book of divination had to become a book of wisdom.[15]

In like manner when man, confronted by difference, opposition and change, asks of the Thou within the Self, "What am I to do?" he steps beyond the conflict into the way of eternal transformation which is the Divine Harmony.

---

[13] Erich Neumann, *Art and the Creative Unconscious*, p. 151.
[14] Vol. II, p. 4.
[15] Introduction, Vol. I, p. xxxiii.

CHAPTER 9

Opposition and Interplay

❧ ❧

May the paradoxical harmony of antagonistic principles forming one whole, balancing each other in the same vision, fill your being. . . . This paradoxical union of conflicting forces and attitudes . . . forms the essential enigma of reality.[1]

Until these dreams with their changing, moving, unfolding symbols, had set their stamp upon her being, this woman had been quite unaware of the dualities contained within her concept of love, or of how opposites warred within her psyche. Generosity, possessiveness; submission, domination; freedom, fear; redemption, destruction; these held her in the sway of primordial instincts. Personified in the dreams, these polarities were shown in their antithetical forms. Perceiving them also in their transpersonal power as they were manifest in archetypal images, she could accept them as life forces moving in the unconscious of all mankind, forces with which each human being must reckon. The numinous experience of the images gave form to their opposing qualities; she could see their action in her own life. Through accepting their meaning and enduring their affect in her own personal struggle, she could accept herself, not only as part of a human stream but also as a unique individual who had a definite role to play through her own choices. Until these dreams brought home to her the use she had made of the symbols of suffering and sacrifice, she had been unaware of the neurotic element that made her suffering

---

[1] Jung, quoting from his writings in conversation with the author.

futile and dragged down the energy which the ordering and under-standing principle of her conscious mind and heart might have used in the choice of which quality should become operative in her life as woman. The victim complex had gained an autonomous power since it existed in a realm beyond the ego's conscious control. Origi-nating in the childhood image of the parental giants as fate, nurtured by her own innate predisposition, it had charged every experience with an emotionality that distorted the reality of each personal en-counter. The nature of this power could not be recognized until the dream personages made conscious their action in her life and she ex-perienced, emotionally understood and assimilated the role the victim had played in her own life drama.

The complex consists of a nuclear element and of emotional factors whose meaning is beyond the confines of the ego's will. It is uncon-scious, therefore uncontrollable. It develops through a ramification of associations which stem from the nuclear element. These associations are derived in part from innate predispositions and in part from per-sonal and environmental experiences. The affect that they arouse colors and distorts all future reactions in the field which they have made their own. When actually constellated in the psyche, the com-plex can act "as an animated foreign body in the sphere of conscious-ness," defying the ego and making choices and decisions over which the conscious has no control. Neither a knowledge of the existence of the complex nor intellectual or even psychological understanding of its nature—its why and wherefore—will dissolve it.

Jung says,

A complex can only be really overcome when it has been drained to the last depths by life. In other words, . . . we have to draw to us and drink down to the very dregs what, because of complexes, we have held at a distance.[2]

This "drinking to the dregs"—emotionally experiencing—had been the real suffering through which the neurotic victim element had been redeemed, and the energy had been freed for conscious choice and willed purpose. The emotionally charged concepts, drained of their neurotic element, no longer held negative dominion over her psyche. She could face the inner chasm and perceive the meaning of the bridge as a symbol of the transition.

---

[2] "The Psychological Aspects of the Mother Archetype," *Spring 1943*, p. 24.

Neurosis is an inner cleavage—the state of being at war within oneself.
. . . What drives people to war with themselves is the intuition or the
knowledge that they consist of two persons in opposition to one another.
[Man wants] to learn how he is to reconcile himself with his own nature
—how he is to love the enemy in his own heart and call the wolf his
brother.[3]

This desire had lived below the conflict and was released in meaningful form when the complex had been drained of its affective power.

The reconciliation of man with his own nature involves that most
terrifying experience of descent into the self where he is brought face
to face with all that stands in opposition to his cherished image of
what he really is. He not only perceives the hate underlying his acknowledged love, the self-seeking that destroys the values produced
by his good intentions, but he must face the downdrawing power of
the hidden motive, of the complex that stands between his ego and
its acceptance of the truth about himself. "All that we have held at a
distance" he now perceives to be those despised and rejected elements of which he would fain remain unconscious. Such reconciliation of man with the opposing elements within the self reveals a way
of reconciliation with others and with the world. It brings about a
new attitude that constellates a new image in the unconscious.
Though the archetype is timeless and remains unfathomable in its
original unity containing all the opposites in undifferentiated form,
the individual relation to the archetype changes as the ego perceives
its many-faceted meaning and is able to see its positive and creative
aspects. Without this differentiation, in the critical moments of decisive choice, the elemental emotional forces—whether appearing in
a numinous experience of possession by the archetype or acting
through the magnetic, downdrawing power of the complex—can destroy all that the partial transformations have accomplished.

These partial transformations produced by the development of
consciousness and the ego's assimilation of new thought forms, new
experiences, are, however, of great significance. The heightening of
perceptive powers as the child develops into the man, the cultural
steps that lead from primitive to highly developed consciousness, are
steps in the integration of the ego which make it better able to meet
the onslaughts of life. Yet, unless the relation to the unconscious is

---

[3] Jung, *Modern Man in Search of a Soul*, pp. 273–274.

maintained, a onesidedness develops which stands in direct opposition to the creative transformation of the personality.

The archetype still holds all these opposing factors; that is what gives it its unconscious power of fascination and frightfulness. Yet the image in which it may appear, the form in which it dominates ego choices through creation of fear, ecstasy, love or hate, may suffer change and transformation as the relation of the ego to the non-ego changes.

This new attitude does not set one free from confrontation by the opposites, for "that's what destiny means—being opposite."[4] From the first stirrings of consciousness the ego develops—not only through experiencing similarities and relatedness, but through confrontation of differences and through the opposition or the interplay of dynamic polarities: introversion and extraversion, good and evil, shadow and light, reason and passion, factual reality and imagination, nature and culture, conscious and unconscious, male and female. All these many dualities that seek warfare or reconciliation must be encountered on the pathway toward selfhood.

Life, being an energic process, needs the opposites, for without opposition there is, as we know, no energy.

Conscious and unconscious do not make a whole when one of them is suppressed and injured by the other. If they must contend, let it at least be a fair fight with equal rights on both sides. Both are aspects of life. Consciousness should defend its reason and protect itself, and the chaotic life of the unconscious should be given the chance of having its way too— as much of it as we can stand. This means open conflict and open collaboration at once. That, evidently, is the way human life should be. It is the old game of hammer and anvil: between them the patient iron is forged into an indestructible whole, an "individual."[5]

The unconscious has a curious way of not agreeing with our conscious appraisals, especially our appraisals of ourselves. We walk upon the solidly constructed floor of our conscious life and are surprised to find a controversial crack. Peering down, we discover a world quite foreign to our world of well-constructed conscious actuality, and an intrusive voice says, "Look down and see the reality of the world in which you felt you had no part." How disconcerting this is to the man

---

4 Rilke, *Duino Elegies*, Eighth Elegy, p. 69.
5 Jung, *The Archetypes and the Collective Unconscious*, p. 288.

who has his feet so securely planted on this dependable ego-constructed floor. All sorts of alien creatures, even dragons and serpents or angels and heavenly creatures, can slip through this widening crack. How many have already invaded his territory? He has an uncomfortable realization that after all his careful work he is perhaps not master in his own house.

Modern man, with his sharp separation of the realities of inner and outer, conscious and unconscious, ego and non-ego, with his cherished neurosis, his fear of total creative transformation, faces a crisis in which, if he clings to the perilous safety of ego-acquired knowledge, the forgotten god may assail him from the below which is also the above, and—even as in the present moment—he and all that he has created may be faced with destruction. Science, with its lure of dominion over the heavens, its disregard of earth relatedness, its underestimation of human life and of feeling values, may prove to be only another Icarian flight to the sun: a flight that, now attempted by power and the hybris of intellectual knowledge, may bring disaster upon the human race. Knowledge must seek council of wisdom; but "where is wisdom to be found" if not in that source from which consciousness is born—the unconscious where all the dualities exist both as opposites and as dynamic polarities through whose interaction new forms of creation may come into being? The co-operation of a disciplined ego that is capable not only of definiteness and direction but also of sacrificing its direction to an active receptivity is needed if the wisdom of the unconscious is to be available for conscious choice. The ego must become willing to submit, to observe, to participate and *to feel with emotional intensity* the experience which the non-ego presents. Sometimes the opposition arises through an alien thought, an undesired memory that awakens an awareness of a long-buried guilt or of an unfulfilled opportunity. Ghosts of the past can spring to vital life. Consciousness may be strong enough to exorcise them, but it may be that they have come with a quickening message which the ego refuses. The power of consciousness to triumph over all that it chooses to disregard is often its tragedy. Repression may act on either level, depending on the central attitude of the ego. Victorian respectability and the zealousness of the Puritan conscience once sought to repress all that conventional social morality and righteousness preferred to ignore. In this present phase it would seem that often the ideals, the hopes, the aspirations, the stirring of divine

imagination are repressed in favor of violence, license, the deadbeat attitude and unrestrained sexuality shorn of the dignity of love, or even of the godlike fire of elemental passion. But morality repressed also produces conflict. "Morality was not brought down on tables of stone. . . . Rather is morality a function of the human mind, as old as humanity itself."[6] Consciousness, with its selectivity, its exclusive pursuit of a single aim, its carefully nurtured adaptability, may temporarily make the ego of more use to society. But this usefulness can be destroyed by the enantiodromea—the law by which the extreme goes over into its opposite. At the moment of highest achievement a sense of futility, depression or violence may seize upon the personality and the power of choice and decision be snatched away—even the power to act as a good machine.

Or the opposites may be constellated in the warfare of human and divine: on the one side untamed instinct, on the other the highest spiritual aspirations. Triumph over nature is dearly paid for; so is triumph over the spirit. Nature and spirit are not at war in the depths of the unconscious but are mutually sustaining; it is the time of differentiation that is the moment of peril and also of redemptive choice. Good turns to evil, light to darkness, love to hate, even as in another transition light comes out of darkness, consciousness returns to the wisdom of the unconscious, order again comes out of chaos; and the man may discover that only by remaining conscious of the existence of the opposites within himself can he accept the conflict involved in change and transformation as part of the divine harmony, or what Whitehead has called "the creative advance into novelty." For the divine harmony is dependent upon confrontation by the opposites, rhythmic change, interplay.

The power of differentiation in relation to the images that subtly govern choice is not an act of mere consciousness but involves an actual transformation of unconscious content. The fear or temptation or ordeal may be met by the trained, disciplined ego through repressing the instinctual, unacceptable elements, but unless the unconscious, nonpersonal factors have also suffered transformation, these unredeemed elements may erupt in sudden possession or, in a moment of decisive choice, they may act in complete opposition to all that the ego wills or determines. Only a transformation of the entire

---

[6] Jung, *Two Essays on Analytical Psychology*, Dodd, Mead edition (1928), p. 25.

personality can effect a change in the spontaneous reaction to experience. For this the opposites must be faced consciously and the meaning and potential value of each made clear before one can reach the position where spontaneous choice and willed choice are one.

This choice is man's necessity if he is to become an individual, for the archetypes as innate reactions to age-old situations are inborn in the psyche of every man. The dominant images of mother and father as undifferentiated archetypal forces indeed possess the power of gods and as such determine man's often unconscious but decisive choices, so bringing about those fatal disasters or creative achievements that determine his destiny. When they appear as embodiments of the masculine and feminine principles, man's creative life is dependent upon their opposition or interplay.

A five-year-old boy painted a picture of a green man. He dictated the following caption to his mother: "This is the Green Man. He lives on 97th Street. He lives alone." He asked her to take the picture to me saying, "She will know what I mean." The next time he came to see me he asked, "Did you know what I meant? Do you know the Green Man?" "Yes," I answered, "I think I know him as the 'someone' who makes new green things come up in the spring, who touches the buds so they wake and dress the trees in greenness. I think he is the same 'someone' who makes new thoughts and feelings, new pictures and stories, come alive in us when we are alone. I have an old, old picture of him that I look at very often."

On my bedroom wall hangs a Tibetan painting of the Green God, the god of newborn, growing things, the god of new beginnings. This the boy had never seen. He stood before the Green One looking intently into his face. "Yes," he said, "that is the one I mean." Then, backing slowly across the room, never taking his eyes from the god's face, he said, "When you are close he is a man, but a little way off he is a woman too—he would have to be."

The same perception of the duality of the creative god came to Edward Maitland when, in an attempt to penetrate "inner and central consciousness" while retaining his hold on "outer and circumferential consciousness," the experience came to him which he felt to be a vision of the essential nature of God. He says:

I found myself . . . mounting a vast ladder stretching from the circumference towards the center of a system, which was at once my own system, the solar system, and the universal system . . . confronted with a glory

of unspeakable whiteness and brightness. . . . [I looked into it] with a great effort . . . and the glance revealed to me that which I felt must be there. . . . It was the dual form of the Son . . . the unmanifest made manifest, the unformulate formulate, the unindividuate individuate, God as the Lord, proving *through his duality* that God is Substance as well as Force, Love as well as Will, *Feminine as well as Masculine, Mother as well as Father*.[7]

Here in the words of both child and man is the statement of an already apprehended reality, the dual nature of the creative God.

"He is a woman too—he would have to be."

"That which I felt must [already] be there . . . Love as well as Will, Feminine as well as Masculine."[8]

Both child and man found that God, like man, is two in one.

Should we not also say of woman in whom the seed of creativity is from the beginning implanted, "She is a man too—she would have to be"?

In both man and woman this duality of the masculine and feminine principles is inborn, and every act of creation is dependent upon their interplay. Their polarity makes possible the flow of dynamic energy, the lightning leap between the positive and negative poles of being. Both separation and reunion are necessary steps in the life process of individuation. For without separation and discrimination unity is only unconsciousness, and without interplay and reunion there is only opposition and warfare, or the dull content, or discontent, of a half life where the mind ignores the heart or the heart is unconscious of meaning, even the meaning of love itself.

---

[7] Edward Maitland, in *Anna Kingsford, Her Life, Letters, Diary and Work*, quoted in *The Secret of the Golden Flower*, pp. 102–103. My italics.

[8] He perceived that the union of masculine and feminine principles in the divine being of the Lord took on form, that is, became manifest in the person of the Son whom he saw as the Christ within, the "other," the non-ego, which we call the Self.

CHAPTER 10

The Masculine Principle

❧ ❧

Masculinity means to know one's goal and to do what is necessary to achieve it.[1]

He carries through his own life not as a continuation but as a beginning. Continuity is a business already provided for in the animal, but to initiate is the province of man.[2]

As a cosmic force active in both the macrocosm and the microcosm, the *I Ching* calls the masculine principle "the Creative, . . . light-giving, active, strong and of the spirit. . . . Its essence is power or energy. Its image is heaven. . . ." It is designated as father, ruler. It possesses "the power of duration" and perceives that "the beginning of all things lies still in the beyond in the form of ideas that have yet to become real. The Creative furthermore has power to lend form to these archetypes of ideas. . . . It remains in touch with the time that is dawning . . . making actual what is potential."[3] In all this the masculine urge toward consciousness moves on the plane of creative dynamic energy. It is the upward thrust of consciousness that brings a new cultural form, a new idea to life.

The discovery of meaning through creative understanding is designated by Jung as the basic characteristic of the masculine principle

---

[1] Jung, *Contributions to Analytical Psychology*, pp. 179–180.
[2] *Ibid.*, pp. 184–185.
[3] These definitions are taken from the first two hexagrams of the *I Ching*, Vol. I. They are quoted freely and not in the exact order given.

that finds its expression in logos, the defining and separating word that moves toward the creation of consciousness.

There is no consciousness without discrimination between the opposites. This is the paternal principle, the logos.[4] " 'Masculine' and 'feminine' are symbolic magnitudes, not to be identified with the 'man' or the 'woman' as carriers of specific sexual characteristics."[5] So too matriarchal and patriarchal do not refer to sociological systems but to inner psychic forces.

As "the word made flesh," logos entered into man in many forms: as power to will, to act, to clothe the idea in word itself and as spirit that searches out meaning.

Without will power nothing can be given form either in the realm of deed or in the realm of thought.

The definiteness and directness of the conscious mind is an extremely important function which humanity has acquired at a very heavy sacrifice, and which in turn has rendered humanity the highest service. Without it neither science nor society could exist, for they both presuppose a reliable continuity of the psychic process.[6]

For this willed effort, power of duration, concentration, discipline are necessary. The masculine principle is continually shaping, forming, observing, inquiring and directing energy toward a chosen goal, a new structure.

The goal of the individual is an indivisible, even if minute, part of the goal of the cultural structure in which he develops. It is this man's contribution, for good or evil, to the life stream of which he is a part and in which he has his being. This contribution may bring to consciousness something that stands in opposition to collective mores but awakens new consciousness.

On the physical plane man may dominate by mere brute force or by the beauty of his physical fitness. He may become the hero of the boxing ring or the baseball or football field, or, on more meaningful levels, the organizer of new enterprises, the warrior or adventurer into new lands. Or he may be the man of skills who can give objective form to a concept whether the concept to be rendered actual be a table or a boat, a cathedral or sculptured form. It is the sense of pur-

---

[4] Jung, "Psychological Aspects of the Mother Archetype," *Spring 1943*, p. 21.
[5] Erich Neumann, "On the Moon and Matriarchal Consciousness," *Spring 1954*, pp. 83–84.
[6] Jung, *The Transcendent Function*, p. 6.

pose and of giving form that connects him with the masculine principle.

Logos moves in thought where, through clear separation, it gives independent logical existence to the idea. Its symbol is the double-edged sword which cuts away all that does not belong to the defined and often isolated concept. In extraversion thought takes form in deed; in introversion the meditation upon the deed appears as the paramount value. The deed demanded by life often appears as a sacrifice rather than a fulfillment.

As logos moves in a world of spirit, finding subjective living meaning which relates man to life as a whole and also to the wholeness of his own experience of life, it finds its expression through the teacher, priest, sage or seer. Its habitation is the valley of vision where spirit is engendered which enables man, says the *I Ching*, to "dare relinquish his foothold on earth and soar to realms of uncharted space and utter solitude." When this spirit takes possession of man, he fears the feminine principle which would call him back to earth, to the realities of relatedness, to those situations that seek to invade solitude. He then may see the feminine principle not as a complement but as enemy opposite. Yet spirit also enables man to see the spark contained in the earthly material and to release spirit contained in material or instinctual form.

The goal and achievement of Western man has been his development of consciousness and its separation from the unconscious forces that would overpower and possess his individual choice. "Let there be light" was the first command when God created form out of chaos. Light is the prerequisite of conscious life. It enables man to discern the nature of the opposing forces that war within him. It is this light of consciousness that enables the ego to say, "I am I" and "thou art thou." It is also this light that gives memory its meaning. Memory is not mere factual recall; it has an aura of emotion that gives it dynamic power. Nor is it confined to the personal sphere, but it is related also to the transpersonal memories of things once known in childhood when factual memory and fantasy are intermingled and an inner experience has the same impact of reality as the events of the outer world. Inner and outer are inexorably intertwined, and deeply penetrating fantasies may later become apparently indisputable memories of outer events. These memories may return in later life with all their original emotional impact, for they are really the experiences that have made us what we are. Here one must be able to

separate subjective and objective memories, for inner experiences are also real and may be recalled even more vividly than actual objective experiences. Without this distinction between inner and outer one may still project early fantasy images upon outer events or persons. When differentiated and understood, both inner and outer memories enable us to say, "I am this, I am not that" and to accept both our limitations and our potentials. It is here that the light of consciousness must be called upon in order to perceive the *meaning* of that which is remembered and to give it form in the world of idea. When memory arises in images, symbols and numinous experiences, man must find his own relation to the transpersonal life; otherwise the ego is overpowered and drawn back into undifferentiated unconsciousness, or is caught on a treadmill of unresolved memories.

"What heaven confers on man may be called his nature, and acting according to this nature may be called Tao."[7] Though he must be true to his inborn and essential nature, he finds wholeness through facing the opposition of the demands of life and by submitting to their necessary interplay. What he conceives in solitude he manifests in idea or in deed; what he experiences in outer life he integrates within himself.

On whatever course masculine energy moves, the introverted or the extraverted, it is directed by willed choice and the sense of purpose which brings about a new concept of the world in both its inner and outer aspects. The *I Ching* says:

A twofold possibility is presented to the great man: he can soar to the heights and play an important part in the world, or he can withdraw into solitude and develop himself. He can go the way of the hero or that of the holy sage who seeks seclusion. There is no general law to say which of the two is the right way. Each one in this situation must make a free choice according to the inner law of his being. If the individual acts consistently and is true to himself, he will find the way that is appropriate for him. This way is right for him and without blame.[8]

Remembering that "perhaps the life we live is also the life of the gods," let us turn back to see how this daily life and the life of the gods meet in the development of the small masculine creature on his journey from infancy to manhood. In infancy he needs the security of enveloping mother love, even as does the feminine child, but

---

[7] Opening sentence of *Chin-Yang*.
[8] Vol. I, pp. 7–8.

far earlier he needs to find the reinforcement of his own masculine nature in his growing relation with the father.

The image of the father may be formed in the unconscious even in the first year of the child's life, long before there is a conscious ego to register its meaning. It manifests itself in instinctual reactions of trust and reliance, or in distrust which makes him reach back to the security he finds in the mother. Also in his first year the masculine desire to take apart, to reassemble, to investigate and to see how things work appears, and if the father shares with humorous understanding the importance of the discovery of how to make wheels move, disks spin or a toy dog bark, a comradeship is established between them.

As the boy develops, the father opens for his son the world of order and fair play, the world of knowledge and ego achievement. He helps the growing boy to interpret the daily experiences that he must meet in his transitions from infancy to childhood and from childhood to youth. This is not so much by precept—anyone can voice abstract ideals—but through daily living and by the way he enters into the small event that has formative power in establishing a sense of fair play. The father's attitude toward defeat, his tolerance in situations that arouse hidden emotions and, not the least of these, his sense of humor and ability to laugh at his own predicament and absurdities —all these enter into the child's picture of the way a man behaves. Humor, far different from ridicule, is the ability to laugh with another or with oneself—even at oneself; ridicule laughs at another and separates by arousing a sense of inferiority. Ridicule attacks self-respect; humor restores a sense of relative values.

If the father has, in his human, imperfect way, fulfilled his own early dreams and youthful aspirations, he will help the boy to understand his own childhood visions of the future and to see how a man meets the difficulties he must encounter in order to make his dreams real. Yet he will not overemphasize these early aspirations for he knows that, though childhood visions return demanding their fulfillment in later life, they may return in new form and with a different message. If he has a sympathetic attitude toward the creative urges and youthful ambitions as they come and go in the life of the child, accepting them as tentative experimentations of the creative spirit to which the child must give form however crudely, he helps to establish in the boy a masculine attitude toward perseverance, endurance and concentration, and to bring the joy of giving form and expression to the concepts that are his. Instability and the ability to accept the new

when the old has fulfilled its purpose are worlds apart. To complete the small task and turn to a new and different one is freedom, not lack of purpose.

Intolerance of the questing spirit or even indifference may drive the boy into a shell of protective secrecy or, worse, make him distrust his own growing masculine powers. To understand when to help and when to let the boy alone to struggle with his own small problem and so know the joy of achievement is also part of this understanding relationship.

Without a relation to the father as the image of what it means to be a man, the boy may distrust masculinity, even his own. He needs respect for the father's own dedication to his chosen work. This is quite apart from the nature of the work, which be it that of a bricklayer or a professor, must never be shirked. Very early he accepts the fact that a man's work must be done and whatever form it takes, he is proud of his father's achievement. Nevertheless it is the father's acceptance of the child's own potential manhood that reinforces the boy's growing sense of his masculinity even more than the image of achievement that the father represents, for the father may, if he excludes himself from interest in the boy's world, only reinforce the child's feeling of his own inability.

The small boy who put the sister-mother in a cage because he had "man's work to do" had already an established relation with his father. They went on adventures together; they shared small jobs; they discussed his day-to-day childhood problems from a man's point of view. Without this father relation, the boy would not have been able to cage the mother-sister image; that is, the regressive desire to remain in comforting dependence would have been a hero task too great for his small ego.

When the youth has no firmly established relation with the father, even separation from the mother may mean only surrender to the anima and identification with the feminine principle within himself. Witch ridden by the anima, he may follow his fantasies and irrational intuitions into more or less creative realms. Under her compulsion, he may bring to birth creative images which were his to bring forth, yet in his personal life as a man, he is too insecure and unrelated to enter into a heterosexual relation which would require his assertion of his own masculinity. In a homosexual relation, he may play a feminine role which makes him act the woman, seeking in this outer way to

connect with the masculinity that he lacks. Or the urge to bring to consciousness his as yet unborn masculinity may make him assume the masculine role in the homosexual interplay, becoming father-lover to another man. In this way he tries to live out within his psyche an image that should have been met by the personal father who failed him.

Since his masculinity has never been established through realization of his human sonship, even breaking the mother-son involvement may not free him from dominance by the feminine principle. The anima may become "she who must be obeyed." This can make him an artist or only a womanish creature incapable of asserting himself. In either case, there is lacking the opposition or interplay of antagonistic principles or the paradoxical union of conflicting forces through which his energy as a man is generated.

The negative father as spirit of absolutism may play a disastrous part in holding the son from his own advance into new cultural values, in which he can play his own creative role. This negative father (the devouring father, the old king who must be slain with his bent and rusty sword[9]) stands between the youth and his own original experience, his adventure into the future. The father may be entrenched in an outmoded pattern or he may represent within the man's own psyche the inflexible quality of ego will, a negative decisiveness that sees change not as transformation, but as an enemy to steadfast purpose. When the connection between conscious and unconscious is broken, the ego falls into the power of its own willed purpose and refuses to allow creative desire to fertilize and enrich the being and to bring forth new concepts. Instead the man struggles to maintain his masculinity by sheer effort of will—pulling himself up by his own bootstraps—or by clinging to ambitions not truly in keeping with his own nature.

A man dreams:

My father is talking, talking incessantly. We drive past a poor farm. Two dead children are lying by the roadside. Other neglected ones are dejectedly sitting on the ground near them. Still my father talks on, expounding the way a man should live up to his ideals. I feel a passing impulse to stop and see what I can do

---

[9] See Chapter 7, "The Return of the Image."

for the neglected children, but I am caught up in his stream of eloquence and drive on with him.

In his life this dreamer was devoted to the ideal concepts embodied in the Christian tradition. He sermonized about them, he wrote intellectual articles in defense of fundamental faith, but he was quite unmindful of their meaning in his personal life. Under the inflexible dominance of his father's will, he had chosen the father's way before he knew the needs of his own nature. Once chosen, his will kept him chained to early choice, and he was as ruthless to his own vagrant desires as his father had been toward his boyhood deviations. In manhood he was still being driven by this incessantly talking father who had become in himself the driving force of consciously accepted purpose. The leash of ego will can restrain the wandering mind, but the reason for the impelling urge that tempted its wandering remains unknown, and all the possibilities that vagrant desire would bring to life are repressed and become dead or neglected children.

As the boy moves into the world the authority image is carried by the teacher, the boss, the law; and his reaction of trust and respect or of rebellion and defiance depends upon the inner image of authority that he has conceived through the early father-son relationship. He may then be caught in confusion between liberty and license, courage and aggressiveness (courage, the redeemed instinctual drive; aggression, the still unconscious often negative impulse toward mastery), respect and subservience, chaos and form, rigidity and transformation.

A knowledge of the past and present cultural values is a prerequisite for evaluating the new and for choice of its incorporation into the present cultural pattern or transmutation into new form. For this man needs patriarchal consciousness, a knowledge of existing laws and established mores. For this youth must seek the wisdom of the old men of the tribe or nation. He must try to understand the symbolic meaning which has kept these patterns alive. He must also prove that he can meet the hardships that they have met, that he can endure the trials of strength and can keep his mind and spirit awake when his power of endurance is tested by a prolonged demand upon his strength and fortitude. Through tests of these qualities in the rites of initiation, he earns the right to a place in the council of the men of the tribe. Such individually attained wisdom leads to discovery of spirit. All these processes are necessary for the forging of masculine will.

Among many peoples initiation into manhood is on both an individual and a communal level. Before the youth can be accepted into the council of the elders, he must discover the suprapersonal principle to which in his personal life he must give allegiance. For this he must go into the solitude of forest or desert and await the messenger of fate who may come in dream or vision as bird, water, cloud, beast, man, or spirit but who is always indicative of the nature of the spiritual force that the youth must manifest in his life. It is from this visitant who comes to him in isolation that he receives his manhood name. He tells the experience to the old men of the tribe and they judge the power of the vision and the reality of the youth's own commitment to that which has been vouchsafed to him. If the revelation is adjudged as coming from the Great Spirit and the boy recognizes its origin, it is confirmed by the rites of initiation into the tribe. It may be a dream or vision that indicates a form of personal prowess, or a great vision that indicates the course the whole tribe should follow. Of such a great vision, which came to him when he was only nine years old, Black Elk says,

The man who has the vision is not able to use the power until he has performed the vision on earth for men to see. . . . Now I see it all as from a lonely hilltop. I know it was the story of a mighty vision given to a man too weak to use it; of a holy tree that should have flourished in a people's heart. . . . But if the vision was true and mighty as I know, it is true and mighty yet and it is in the darkness of their eyes that man gets lost.[10]

Even for the personal vision of the meaning of one's own life it may be "in the darkness of their eyes that men get lost."

In tribal initiation the wisdom of the old men is reaffirmed by the tribute of the young. In Taos when the gold of the year is on the slopes of the mountains the young men go out to gather golden aspen boughs. They carry them to the south kiva. At sunset the watcher on the housetop calls out from the roof of the pueblo each man's name, and as his name is called he goes down into the north or the south kiva according to his youth or his age. Then, just before the sun sinks below the edge of the world, the drums vibrate beneath the earth and the young men come from the south carrying the aspen branches which, as the changing light falls upon them, move like a sea of gold across the bridge that divides the south of summer from the north of

---

[10] John G. Neihardt, *Black Elk Speaks*, p. 2.

winter. The young men move in dance rhythm uttering the cries of birds and of animals. The old men come up from the kiva at the north to greet the dancing of the young and to receive their gift of gold. Then, as they carry it down to the sacred place so that it may be added to the harvest of all the years, darkness falls. Each year the young men bring their gift from the present that it may be added to the harvest of the past, and in so doing they acknowledge the authority of the old men who are guardians of the continuing, yet changing, wisdom of the years.

The wise old man, image of masculine inner authority, is a spiritual guide and bringer of healing. He it is who combines the wisdom of the old and the urge of the newly conceived purpose. He is frequently companioned by the child who symbolizes the essential meaning of the old which will in the future be embodied in new symbolic form.

His image may appear even to a young boy when faced by a choice that he instinctively knows will have deep meaning for his future life. A boy of eleven had, in spite of physical handicap and consequent lack of preparation, been admitted to a school that challenged his courage and aroused his enthusiastic loyalty. A letter came from the headmaster to his parents stating that he could return if they felt it wise for him, but advising that the difficulties would be too great for his strength and that they should withdraw him in favor of a less demanding school. That night the boy dreamed:

> I am in a large hall with arches of gray stone like a cave. There is a light streaming through a crack in the ceiling. At a table sits an old man with a long beard and wise clear eyes. On the table is a dice box. Over his head is a clock whose hands point to two minutes before twelve. I know that I must throw these dice before the hour of midnight. I hold the box in my hand and look straight into the old man's eyes. I feel the moment has come and that the old man will in some way help me, but it is I who must make the throw.

In the morning he said, "I have to decide this alone, for myself." He went into a solitary place where he could see the nature of his problem and seek the answer from a source beyond his ego's knowing —that is, he must prepare himself to throw the dice in that before-midnight moment when choice may determine the nature of the new day. He saw the risk of failure and defeat, but he saw the greater risk of playing safe and avoiding the conflict. He must play the game and

take his chances whichever way the dice fell. Throwing the dice meant to him taking the risks involved in acceptance of the challenge, which might lead to failure. In those hours of solitude was it the wise old man, the sage within the child, with whom he communed before he threw the dice? He had never heard of the *I Ching* or of waiting to throw the coins or yarrow sticks until one feels within oneself that the moment has come to consult the oracle. Yet he enacted the ancient ritual in the way he consulted the inner oracle, the wise old man within himself, before he threw the dice. Then he could ask the question, "What can I do about it?" He wrote his own letter of acceptance. He went back and proved by this choice his ability to play the game in failure or success.

When in later life the ego, strengthened by success, has taken over choice and decision, there is danger that it will be satisfied by its own achievement and shut out possibilities that would interfere with its consciously chosen goal. Yet even here at a crossroad of decision the vision and the voice may break through in a dream and the image of the mana personality bring the unlooked-for answer. A man dreams:

> I am coming home from a meeting where I have been the speaker and the authority. I am very sure of my way. A sudden darkness descends upon me. A wolf, a wildcat and other animals spring upon me. I feel the torment of their tearing teeth. Then there is a sudden light and before me is a fire that rises to a peak of white flame. By the fire stands an old man. I call out to him. At his approach the animals seem to melt away. He wraps me in a gray garment and carries me to the fire that now seems to be a fire within a fire and the outer fire encircles us. I hear the words, "The fire consumes, the fire heals." I know myself to be the sacrifice and leap into the inner flame. I feel the torment. I am consumed. The fire mounts to heaven and is gone. I—another I —stand before the wise old man. He grows gigantically tall; I kneel before him, and I am baptized in his semen. Creative life flows through me.

In the hour of the ego's greatest certainty darkness falls and the man is delivered over to the tearing teeth of the untamed thoughts and passions, doubts and despairs that he had repressed and that now rose from the unconscious with all the force of untamed instinct. In his moment of extremity a sudden light breaks upon him and the

saving figure, the wise old man, stands beside the flame. He calls out; that is, in his extremity he calls upon the helper who comes to meet him, and, as the old man approaches, the animals fall away. Through his own recognition of a power greater than his vaunted conscious strength, the instinctual forces of chaos are stilled. He then submits to the direction of the non-ego. Wrapped in the gray garment (the encircling unconscious) he lets himself be carried into the circle of flame and perceives the inmost fire—the burning inner flame of spirit. The voice of the wise old man warns of the risk but reveals the healing. "The fire consumes, the fire heals." Will the fire that consumes the old life of conscious achievement leave nothing of himself unconsumed or will it act in healing by releasing the ego to the greater life of the non-ego? He dares the leap into the heart of the fiery moment and, as he is consumed, he is healed; another I, a reborn creature, receives the symbolic baptism of the stream of masculine creative energy.

To both boy and man the meeting with the wise old man was initiation into the meaning of the next step demanded by life in his advance into his own manhood.

In the search for meaning man discovers the relativity of time. Time is eternal and time is of the immediate present. There are timeless meanings whose truths become apparent only through increasing awareness of pre-existing knowledge, the *a priori* knowledge of the unconscious, from which consciousness is born. There are moments when new concepts hover on the brink of consciousness when man must watch for the dawning of new thought forms that will be a "means of making actual that which is potential" in relation to the culture and achievement of the era in which his life is set, for each man must find his own relation to time as it exists in his present life. There are moments of the intersection of timelessness with time when an outworn concept, meaningful in another era, returns seeking rebirth in new symbolic form. Thus, pregnant with new meaning, it re-enters the present and goes on into the future.

The permeability of the ego to the messages of the unconscious enables man to perceive and to play his part in these moments. One winter Jung's dreams were strangely concerned with the thirteenth century. Night after night he found himself in a medieval town searching for he knew not what. Responding to the message of the unconscious, he began a research into the archives of this period. He

studied medieval texts and searched through old manuscripts trying to discover why the unconscious directed his steps back to this century. He came upon the archives of the alchemists and perceived the hidden meaning of their search and saw the subjective goal of their work. At the same time he began to note these alchemistic symbols in the dreams of modern patients. Wandering down the dark passageways of the mind, he saw how these timeless symbols entered in a living way into immediate time in the inner journey of these dreamers. That the alchemist confused the symbolic with the material quest did not alter the living energic power of the symbol. Through this he opened a new field of research, a new pathway to the understanding of psychic processes and the search of the soul for the gold of the spirit. Of such search he says, "Long experience has taught me not to know anything in advance and not to know better."[11]

Through his experiences of the interweaving of time with timelessness, man learns also to understand the interplay of continuity and change and recognizes that

> . . . Change' is the nursery
> Of musicke, joy, life and eternity.[12]

Even in the changes of light to darkness, man comes to know change as an essential factor of experience without which energy would cease to flow into new forms: either its opposite, the enemy stagnation, would take over or man would fall prey to the obstinacy of his own will, and his very strength of purpose, so necessary for his masculine development, would keep him from knowing that there is also a reality constant within change which makes it not an opposing factor, but a complementary force in which his life purpose may find expression. Through this one is not borne along by the stream of time with its winding courses, but achieves a relation to time so it can become a meaningful reality. One can then experience the opposites contained within the immediate and, through loyalty to one's own inner attitude, come into harmony with both the immediacy of the moment and with the eternal aspect of transition into new form —the changelessness of change. For "eternity is time in divine harmonious change."

---

[11] Jung, *The Archetypes and the Collective Unconscious*, p. 293.
[12] Donne, Elegie III.

Knowing this aspect of continuity through change, man decides, but holds the decisions of his reason and of his will open to the changes that may come through the command of the Greater Will, so realizing in his own life the interplay of stability and change. Jung exemplified this truth. No one exerted greater will in carrying through his purposes, or was more whole in his decision, yet he held choice and decision open to change if the word came from the Other, the non-ego.

A young Jewish woman came to him. She had been to many analysts but nothing had touched her because her central reality was barricaded, it seemed, by trivialities. She dressed smartly; she was rouged, powdered, manicured and marcelled; she carried a perfect handbag and a small folded umbrella always in its case; her very persona was marcelled and manicured. For several months Jung labored to get through to some reality. Then he decided that the whole venture was a failure; the woman was essentially trivial and unanalyzable; in her next appointment he would tell her that he would not see her again. He felt assured of the rightness of his decision. Yet that night he had a dream in which he went into the appointment holding the folded umbrella and, as he reached the place where she was standing, he went down on his knees and offered her the enfolded object. He did not question the command; he told her the dream and asked, "What is it that you have kept folded away, something that I would go on my knees to, and would reverence as I did in the dream?" She burst into tears and told him. "I come of a line of mystics and seers. My grandfather and those before him had visions and heard words of revelation. I too hear the voice and see the vision, but when I tried to tell of them, people laughed and thought me queer. So I became ashamed and have hidden them away." Then began a brief but vivid analysis and the woman went on her way healed and bearing her treasure by whose light she could live. He had reconnected her with the living symbols, the timeless energy-creating truth that she had known before she was born into a world of conscious knowledge, a world into which she must now return.[13]

---

[13] By Dr. Jung's permission I told this in a brief speech at a meeting in London in honor of his eightieth birthday. He also gave permission to use it in this book which he suggested I write from the seminars on choice that I was giving in Zurich.

Respect for the command of the greater will when it speaks through another may also bring about change of decision which is still continuity of purpose. Another far-different woman came to Jung. In her personal life she felt dismembered by the demands of conflicting relationships which drew her into such *participation mystique* that she hardly knew whose life she was living; when she tried to find quietude in her inner life, she was often overwhelmed by the terrible or beautiful experiences of the unseen and unknowable. Jung decided that in her case analysis was too dangerous an experiment. She came for her last hour before he was to go on his spring vacation. He told her that he would not see her again. She felt shattered and could hardly emerge from the inner chaos to tell him her dream of the night before.

I am an atom whirling through space. After what seems an endless time, I see a majestic cloud far, far off. I watch it because of its quietude, wishing, oh! if I could be such a cloud floating quietly and at peace! It approaches nearer and nearer, its vastness shrinking. It is not a cloud, but the smoke from Dr. Jung's pipe.

"He [Jung] listened in silence, rose and began to pace the floor like a lion, then stood quite still before me and said, 'I have changed my mind. I will see you after the holidays.' Chaos—and then the light penetrating—a mystery. I could not fathom, nor could I see any reason for his change of purpose."[14] Only long afterward did she understand the working of that divinely human intuition that penetrated the utmost meaning of the dream and, anticipating the transformation that analysis was to bring, reversed his decision and accepted the dream's message: that the cloud of quietude might become both earth and spirit to a soul in its last extremity of dismemberment. His decision was changed and, for this whirling atom, the quietude of the cloud became earthly and spiritual reality.

In greatness to know humility, in decision to know the meaning of change, in the finite to glimpse the infinite, in immanence to perceive the transcendent—that is to decide with God. It is the quality of openness to the messages of the unconscious that brings understanding of the truth. "Continuity in change: this is the eternity of the universe."

---

[14] Used by permission of both Dr. Jung and the dreamer.

In these changes, these creative advances into new consciousness, it is the timeless symbolic image re-entering into time that sustains and enriches the continuity of the individual life. Masculinity finds its highest expression in the eternal meaning of the symbolic image of sonship—the search of the soul for the unknown which was known before the ego's birth into conscious knowledge, and the awakening through which a man journeys back to the kingdom which was his inborn heritage, the kingdom known before the birth of consciousness.

There is a continuity of purpose and a dedication to eternal meaning in the life of one who knows himself to be son of a king. The natural and normal development of the father-son relationship on the human plane is a carrier of the symbolic meaning of divine sonship. The spark of inborn knowledge can be obscured but not extinguished by the lack of the human relationship. The man who has never known the creative power of the human pact is not shut out from the pre-existent knowledge of what it means to inherit the kingdom. There are numinous moments when a man, deprived of his human heritage, leaps the barrier between the world of nature and the world of spirit and claims his heritage as son of the king. In that moment he chooses his father, the god image originally implanted in his own nature. This corresponds to the divine spark of his own being, which no man can take from him. It is the mystery beyond choice, yet it is chosen.

Reaching back into the ages of the awakening of consciousness, the symbol of sonship has held unknown meanings that unfolded as man reached new levels of consciousness. This symbol contains the central meaning of our Christian heritage.

It was the symbol of divine sonship that led Jesus the Christ to the understanding and fulfillment of his destiny as Son of Man and Son of God. We trace this thread of purpose throughout his life. "Wist ye not that I must be about my father's business?" As Son of Man, he returned to his human parents, obedient to them—that is, to the demands of daily relatedness—yet remaining conscious of the purpose of his other sonship. He accepted this sonship in baptism when the words, "This is my beloved son," lighted the spark of passionate fiery purpose within him. An old manuscript records, "The whole Jordan blazed with fire when the Lord stepped into the water," so, as Son, accepting the baptism of spirit and fire, he himself becoming

afire with acceptance of divine sonship. Then came the temptation to renounce the voice of his calling or to accept it and misuse it in ways of rebellion to the truth that was in him—his sense of vocation and his knowledge that "for this came I into the world." He acclaimed his heritage in the triumphant statement of his return to the kingdom that he had known before he had been born into earthly life. "I return to my father and your father." The final agony, the doubt of his accepted sonship, was voiced in the cry, "My God, my God, why hast thou forsaken me?" and the triumphant certainty of the meaning of his sonship in the words, "Father, into thy hands I commend my spirit." Through these steps of sonship, he realized—and so revealed—the power of each man to become a son of God.

Was the deepest meaning of the crucifixion this knowledge of the inborn sonship of every man through the indwelling spark of sonship that, even at the end of life, may in a moment of recognition set fire to the spirit and leap the barrier between God and man? This spark flamed in the crucified thief when he recognized a kindred self in Christ and, rising above sin and dishonor into the simplicity of the mystery, said unto Jesus, "Lord, remember me when thou comest into thy kingdom." The answer, "Today thou shalt be with me in Paradise," is the supreme utterance of one who, in his last agony, perceived the living spark that lighted the self of the thief and accepted the kinship that could make of each man a son of God. And in this moment both thief and the divine son who was also Son of Man chose the same father.

Masculinity as well as femininity demands complete surrender in order that it may be able to say, "For this came I into the world." This is divine sonship—that man shall attain to the certainty of his own vocation through which the essential purpose of his life is made manifest.

CHAPTER 11

The Woman in Man

❦

Every man carries within himself an eternal image of woman, not the image of this or that definite woman but rather a definite feminine image. This image is fundamentally an unconscious hereditary factor of primordial origin and is engraved on the living system of man.[1]

MAN'S NATURE is attuned to woman. He presupposes her existence in his life as mother, sister, early love, wife, inspiration—and also as problem.

Inborn in his nature is another woman—the feminine side of his own psyche—who, from the beginning, brings him intuitions of things beyond masculine ken. She too moves in him in intuitive perceptions of feeling situations, in mood and in creative inspiration. "Woman means soul to man." She is the anima, the breath, that which animates. She "is by nature luminous and living, mortal by reason of the body, immortal by reason of the eternal substance of light."

Being that has soul is living being. Soul is the *living* in man, that which lives of itself and causes life. . . . God breathed into Adam a living breath so that he should live. With cunning and playful deception the soul lures into life the inertia of matter that does not want to live. It creates belief in incredible things. . . . It is full of snares and traps in order that man should fall, should reach the earth, entangle himself there, and stay caught, in order that life should live. Were it not for the motion

---

[1] Jung, *Contributions to Analytical Psychology*, p. 199.

and the colour-play of the soul, man would suffocate and rot away in his greatest passion, idleness.[2]

Eve, formed from Adam's own substance, acted as soul when, through subtle suggestion, she enticed him into the choice by which he became entangled in his earthly life. Hardly had she come into being when, consulting the serpent (her own serpent wisdom?), she injected the first doubting thought into the childlike mind of Adam, namely, if he ate of this forbidden tree, the tree of the knowledge of good and evil, would he surely die, or had Jehovah a hidden motive in keeping the fruit of this tree to Himself? By this suggestion she implied that Adam should find out for himself and that the risk was worth taking. Thus she lured him into that act of choice that closed to him forever the garden of childlike innocence and unconsciousness. Through this choice of disobedience, this first step toward consciousness, he became entangled in his earthly life where all that did not want to live might, through this fall, reach the earth and stay caught until, faced by the eternal opposition of good and evil and buffeted by fate, he should come to a knowledge of choice and its relation to his own destiny. We must also remember that the woman's serpent eyes saw the forbidden tree as "a tree to make one wise" and, with an as yet unborn wisdom, foresaw that, if one takes the fearful risk of choosing one's own earthly life, "at the last comes wisdom by the awful grace of God."

It is the soul as intuitive spirit who brings premonitions and perceptions of the verities that may come to consciousness in individual man, so linking him with immortality. As soul this inner woman reminds him, "Life is a pure flame and we live by an invisible sun within us."[3]

But we must also remember Lilith who seems to have borned herself out of some daemonic power of darkness and who, as the dark perils of the soul, also became an active agent who might entice an unwitting Adam down into the underworld (the world of Kali and Hecate and the other wrathful devouring goddesses) where the dreadful secrets of his own soul would confront him as psychic entities. Here too is the isle of Circe, the enchantress, whose magic

---

[2] Jung, *The Integration of the Personality*, p. 75.
[3] Sir Thomas Browne, "Hydriotaphia or Urn-Burial," *Works*, IV, 3, p. 49.

can return him to the status of the beast that lives concealed within him.

This uncanny world of the sorceress is a horror to the man whose impeccable persona looks outward on a world where such creatures exist only in alien people, the man who has never gone slumming in the dark alley of his inner city nor known the terrors of the interior jungle. To him, as to the intellectual realist, the world of the anima is a land never to be visited even when, in her bright form of spirit, she would reveal to him the creative images. For such an excursion is to him not only dangerous but absurd. When a rational-minded man finds himself possessed by an irrational idea or image he is as dismayed as a moralist who finds himself in bed with a prostitute.

On the other hand, man may become identified with this wayward irrational creature, who then lures him from his masculine goal. Through this identification with the undeveloped but emotionally charged side of his feminine nature, he lives a soft oversentimental life which is womanish but far from womanly. Many a man, whose hard persona shell protects him in his battles with the world, has a soft underbelly of undeveloped feeling which makes him vulnerable to every thrust of life. It may be outer criticism (real or imagined) which touches upon his zone of carefully concealed sensitivity, or perhaps he is caught up in the snare of flattery and delivered over to a woman on whom he projects the soul image. Often such a man is unable to escape from his unacknowledged dependence upon the woman on whom he has placed this image. For, having failed to find wholeness through his relation to the inner woman, he is forced to lean heavily upon the outer woman to fulfill that need.

When there is a secret mother-son bond, the anima image remains tied to the mother and in her honor the man may become a homosexual, his early imposed loyalty demanding that no other image be enthroned in her place.

Or the identification with the anima may carry him into a world of unreality where he dreams his creative life but fails to give form to the dream or to see the connection of these creative images with his life as a man.

The attitude of society that demands that he achieve something materially substantial in the masculine world may also give him a feeling that a developing relation with this wayward irrational creature is not manly, but makes him a sissy and a softy. He may become

ashamed of his feeling in both its extraverted and its introverted manifestations, and especially of the secret aspirations and longings, the fleeting glimpses into a world of wonder and poetic beauty that the inner woman brings to him in the moments snatched from masculine endeavor. Therefore, he banishes the anima to the unconscious whence she came and, in maturer years, lives out only the inferior qualities of the feminine component of his psyche, never knowing that his weakness might become his strength, his secret shame be transformed into his glory if, as conscious man, he would acknowledge the eternal feminine element which disregarded exerts a power that often defeats his ego choices, making them denials of the very decisions that would reinforce his masculine nature if he could let the anima become a friend of choice.

The anima is not only the unknown woman in man; she is also the unknown element existent in all women. This makes of every woman a fascinating mystery and a potential danger, for she possesses the illusive feminine qualities that lurk in his own unconscious. In dealing with her he might have to deal with himself.

As personification of the unknown she may appear as the midnight woman. Midnight is the hour of the greatest darkness, the hour in which the kindling spark of the new day is born. The midnight woman leads man into the deepest darkness of his own soul where the potentials of the new day are coming into being and where he can discern the nature of that which he himself is bringing forth, either of darkness or of light. In that midnight when the "pillows of darkness weigh him down" the woman also shows him "the lovely forms of a future" that must be awakened within his soul if the journey into midnight is to bring to life a living day. For midnight is the hour of choice and "the stresses of choice are man's opportunity to be blessed." Here in the hour when the stresses of choice are thrust upon him man may discover that "the radiance of paradise alternates with deep dreadful night."

Sometimes this unknown woman companions man from the beginning and so keeps him related to people, to situations, to emotional undercurrents, and to creative images of the unconscious. "The Green Man who lives alone" continued his dual existence as "woman too" in the life of the boy who often chose to be alone by himself.[4]

---

[4] See Chapter 9, "Opposition and Interplay," p. 161.

This aloneness was never loneliness because the hours were filled with explorations, discoveries, experimentations and adventures of the imagination. Two years after the picture was painted, he wrote a story of a green world where the green man lived with his little green wife and there they discovered "new green things." As the boy became more and more immersed in the masculine world of school and sports, the green world apparently sank into the realm of forgotten things. Yet, though the little green wife was never mentioned, her invisible presence could be perceived in his reactions to feeling situations and in his intuitions which often showed a feminine perception of emotional undercurrents. The same feminine quality appeared in his continued openness to images of the unconscious. A number of years afterwards he casually referred to "the street of the green man." As he talked it became apparent that the seemingly forgotten world was still existent and the little green wife had continued an active, though invisible, life within his psyche.

William Sharp, who was known to the world as an essayist and critic, also had a "green wife" whom he named Fiona Macleod. She opened to him a world of nature, myth and faerie. Under her guidance he wrote imaginative stories and living interpretations of myth, folklore and fairy magic. These tales were published under her name. He also wrote letters to her and carried on long conversations with her.[5] It was Fiona Macleod, becoming more and more a living reality within the personality of William Sharp, "often married in mind and one in nature," but "often absolutely distinct" who really wrote the stories that he published under her name. She never interfered with his relation to his wife nor did she usurp his masculine existence. Through his inner marriage to this soul image he could, as a completed personality, live his man's life more fully.[6]

Connecting him with the nature world, interpreting for him the world of the unconscious, this inner woman wants of man the invisible rising within of the springs of creativity and demands his obedience to the urgent command of transformation.

---

[5] *William Sharp* (Fiona Macleod), a Memoir Compiled by His Wife.

[6] This technique of inner dialogue with an autonomous factor of the personality is not a modern invention though Jung, in developing the technique of active imagination, has made it available to modern man. An Egyptian papyrus records the conversation of a World Weary Man with his Ba (soul), and in the thirteenth century Hugo de St. Victor argues with his soul to win her allegiance to God.

She knows that woman means not only soul but earth, relatedness to the personal and human aspects of life and to the problems of feeling and love. Swedenborg said, "Man represents the love of truth and woman the truth of love." Man learns the meaning of love not only from his relation to the anima but also from every experience of love in its human aspects. For "the first man Adam became a living soul. The last man Adam became a life-giving spirit. Howbeit that which is first is not spiritual but that which is natural; then that which is spiritual. The first man is of the earth, earthy. The second man is of heaven."[7] That is, he no longer is merely that which was created. He has become he who creates. This the soul knows and in her transformed and transforming power leads man on the pathway of his earthly life until he is ready for the transformation by which he may become a "life-giving spirit," a creator of new life. In this way the anima moves in every creative man revealing to him not only the meaning of his masculine will to create but also the meaning of love, which is often the stronger motive power in a truly masculine man. Through this revelation, the feminine element of his being achieves her full stature and her receptive qualities give him perception. Through this union with the feminine, he knows, as woman does, the rhythm and tides of the vast ocean of the unconscious. He awaits the receptive hours of solitude and of the emptiness out of which fullness is born as well as the hours in which he gives form to that which has welled up in the hours of fullness. So he makes his relation to the soul as that which animates.

Nevertheless, in his daily life man must never forget the dual nature of this invisible woman who can so mysteriously alter the face of his world by her sudden possession of his feeling and intuition. He does well to inquire into the form this creature will take in an unexpected situation and whether her commands will lead to good or evil, to transformation or destruction.

A man, whose life work was the study of sociology and who was "devoted" to an intellectual study of meaningful forms of human relations and to the formulation of the laws by which they should be governed, evolved excellent theories of relatedness. But the reality demands of actual relationships continually got in his way. Even his

---

[7] First Corinthians 15:45–47. This is a translation from a German edition of the Bible. It was given in this form in the Memorial Address at the funeral service for Dr. Jung, June 9, 1961. The address was translated by Hildegard Nagel.

wife did not always realize the importance of his dedication and of his need to be protected from intrusive demands of human relatedness.

At times the woman irritated him unwarrantably. Feeling was her function. He expected her to train it so it could serve him better. He was in one of the periods when all his problems and interrupting moods were projected upon other people when he dreamed the following dream:

> I am standing at the window of our living room looking across the courtyard. In the window opposite I see a dark sinister figure. He raises his hand. I feel an unaccountable terror but I reassure myself. He is across the deep courtyard. Then I am aware that the hand is in my room. It is invisible. I see Patchey, our friendly cat, picked up by this invisible hand. Her throat contracts as if by strangulation. Her eyes start from the sockets; human sweat pours from her. Her paws reach out frantically towards me. I stand watching with horrid fascination.

On waking he re-enacted the role that he had played in the dream —he stood watching. As an onlooker he was interested in the drama. He could see that the villain, the shadow aspect of his masculine ego, had uncanny power to strangle his instinctive feeling; his mind perceived this meaning but he did not let the dream penetrate his heart. He did not admit the action of the shadow in his daily life, hence it seemed to him safely removed, in some other man's apartment; nor did he ask of this destructive creature, "Who gave you this power? Who let you into this room?" He did not question the mood that rose like a dark cloud within him. If he had, he might have perceived behind the sinister shadow figure, seemingly so safely distant, another creature who had not only made possible the shadow's entrance but had also rendered him invisible while he strangled the instinctual feeling that might have acted in the human situation. All this man's carefully worked-out theories had proved relationship to be a woman's job, one she must attend to while man dealt with matters of intellect and spirit. Unfortunately these theories had quite neglected the role of the inner woman who in the unseen world had acquired a strange dark power over the shadow and so could use him to carry out her stormy purposes. For behind the shadow stands the anima and, as long as the shadow is not faced as one's own and its dark purposes

brought into the light of consciousness, the actions of the anima are obscured. Then in critical moments she arises in dark and stormy mood and, using the shadow's hand, destroys the instinctual feeling that might act in moments of choice.

At a much later date a situation arose in which his feeling was involved. But every act, whether performed by him or by the other person, whose feeling was also involved, had to be carried out according to his carefully worked-out theories of how such a relationship should, and therefore must, be conducted; for the laws that he had laid down permitted no exceptions to rule, no waywardness of impulse, no intuitive perception of the changing and irrational demands that a human situation may contain. When in this special situation he met with unexpected resistance, he did not examine either his own feeling or the feeling of the one who opposed his demand but, swept by a mood of violence, he reacted with such animosity that the possibility of re-establishing any relationship was shattered. Once more, in a moment of critical choice, he let the anima open the door to the shadow and the end was catastrophe. He suffered; but his suffering did not lead him to an examination of the part his anima had played or of how much of the calamity might have been prevented had he possessed the mood instead of letting the mood possess him. Instead he maintained that it was the other person's violation of the theory, not his own violation of relationship, that had produced the disaster. His verdict was, "I was right." In fact, the feminine side of his nature behaved like an animus-ridden woman in its assumptions of possessing the absolute truth applicable to all the varying elements that might be involved in any human relationship. But a human situation is always unique. It happens in this moment of time. It never returns in exactly the same form, and only the anima in her fluid, changing and creative form can come to man's rescue in an unexpected situation that demands perceptive feeling.

This way of disposing of the anima by projecting all her evil power upon the outer woman and so feeling justified in getting rid of her is a very ancient device of the masculine psyche. One wonders how often the banished anima's voice spoke through our Puritan forefathers and whether, if they had accepted the embarrassing reality of their own emotions and gone to bed in pleasant sin with one of the young witches, more women might have escaped the stake or the

ducking pond. Nor would Susanna, surprised by the elders in her woodland bath, have seemed so much a device of the devil had those interpreters of the law been a little more cognizant of the emotions she aroused in their own righteous loins. Who knows how much the discarded anima has altered the records of history?[8]

Another way of disposing of the problem of the inner woman is to remove her to the world of pseudospirituality where, from a safe distance, her image may be worshiped. An egocentric man who was deeply involved in intellectual explorations of medieval mysticism and its relation to the soul as spirit, but who was singularly blind to the movement of the spirit as it affected his own life, found himself isolated because his disregard of the rights of others had alienated the very people who had tried to help him. Since their withdrawal was quite inconvenient, he felt very sorry for himself. At that moment, as often happens in times of self-pity, he discovered a gentle, feminine young woman who was quite ready to join him in this sorrow. She was also interested in his ideas, mainly because they were his. She could not make head or tail of them, but she listened beautifully with flattering attention and little appreciative interjections. He found her comforting, and at times her very emptiness of intellectual ideas and her receptivity stimulated his thinking as well as charmed his vanity. But he expected to treat her as he did his car, to park her wherever he might choose and always to find her passively awaiting his return. He began to be annoyed when she was not always just where he had left her or just as he desired her. She astonished him by her lack of understanding of his need to explore the spiritual heights and by her reminders that she too existed.

One night he dreamed that they were sitting together on a sofa. As she drew toward him, he felt himself to be retreating. The scene changed; he was seated upon the moon looking at her through a powerful telescope. She seemed to go farther and farther away until she became a mere speck in the distance. Then he discovered that he was looking at her through *the wrong end of the telescope*. Yet this

---

[8] The process of projection of the contrasexual element is not limited to the masculine sphere. We remember Mary Baker Eddy who recognized no evil as existent in its own reality, nor any animal instinct as present within her completely spiritual being. Her animus identification with the wholly good Spiritual Father did not save her from terror of "pernicious animal magnetism." In fact she had to have a guard of spiritually minded disciples about her bed lest carnal emanations from men who were steeped in error attack her while she slept.

did not seem to matter—in fact he felt a sense of relief when even the small pinpoint of her visibility disappeared. On waking he made no effort to turn the telescope the other way but shortly afterward broke off the quasi-relationship and again absorbed himself in his own imperious needs.

He was, at this time, greatly interested in taking notes for an article on the place the Virgin occupied in the writings of the early Church Fathers. Into his speculations this dream intruded:

> I am standing in the clerestory of Chartres Cathedral. I watch the light streaming through the rose window. I feel myself to be high above those empty seats which soon will be filled by credulous worshippers, tourists and unimaginative peasants droning over their rosaries. Then I am aware that below me waters are rising in undulating waves in which a shark, monstrous as a whale, is swimming. Slowly the waters mount till they engulf the lower half of the rose window and flood into the clerestory even as they rise about me. I stand fascinated, hypnotized by the slow rising of the undulating waves as they creep higher and higher and by the rhythmic movement of the great fish as the waves carry it nearer and nearer.

Drawn more by fascination than by realization of his peril, he brought the dream to an analyst, and in its discussion he recalled the former dream where, safely seated on the moon, he looked down upon the anima. The connection between these two dreams was not apparent to him: that he was also regarding the image of the Virgin through the wrong end of the telescope which made her also safely removed from his human life in the remote realm of spiritual speculation. So far as emotional reaction was concerned he might as well be on the moon as in the clerestory. In this unreal world of pseudospirituality he had lost all contact with human reality. As his contemplation of this image—*rosa mundi, rosa mystica*—became more and more theoretical, the image of the anima as the mother took on dual form. High above him she appeared as pure, though unrelated, spirit while below him, in the rising waters of the unconscious, she appeared as shark-whale, symbol of the uroboric mother, who has power to separate and dismember as well as to swallow and possess, so combining in undifferentiated form the destructive masculine and feminine attributes. In this dark image she was carried

nearer and nearer until the waters rose about him. And still he stood fascinated, untouched by terror.

Nor did the discussion of the dream arouse a sense of his peril. Both worlds, inner and outer, had lost their reality. Into this world of shifting shadows came a dream so startling, so different, that it awakened something long dormant within him:

> I am on a great plateau that sweeps with magnificent curve about huge snow-capped mountains. My spirit is uplifted by the vast distances, the superb sunrise colors. An old man, an impressive patriarchal figure, is pushing a plow; each furrow follows the curve of the plateau. He is accompanied by a shadow that moves rhythmically with him. As I go up to him, he speaks to me in a chanting voice of archaic King James English. The wisdom of the earth speaks through him, a wisdom that he has absorbed through the reality of his daily task, tilling the soil in this high place of beauty, preparing the earth to receive the seed, to bring forth the harvest.

He woke feeling that the chanting archaic words revealed a wisdom that he had once known, in another life perhaps; a wisdom that he must now, in his present life, rediscover. How or why such awakenings come is beyond our ken, but as he pondered the figure of the wise old man he had a sense of communion with him that was almost a feeling of sonship, and for the first time he entered into the mystery of an accepted experience of the inner world.

Awed, humbled, he painted a picture of what he had seen in the dream, and put it on his wall. The figure of the old man seemed permeated with life and in active imagination he communed with him. This dialectic process continued to awaken masculine potentials within him and with their awakening came a desire to know the wisdom of the earth that should lead him to the discovery of the meaning of his humanity. This, then, was a first step toward the discovery of what he had known before he was born into ego consciousness, and this awakened the image of the anima as soul and revealer of the mysteries. So exploring the heights on which the old man dwelt, he came to a knowledge of the earth.

I wish I could say that this first experience of the union of the opposites—spirit and nature, earth and heaven—as complementary rather than opposing forces created a miracle in his life; but the

downdrawing lure of the anima was still too strong. Again the reality of his masculine life faded. Intellectual concepts took over. He was once more drifting in an undersea world when another dream intervened:

I am unwrapping my picture to show it to the analyst. It is wet and soggy as though it had been under water. The colors are running into puddles. The old man is gone, the magnificent curve of the furrows obliterated. At the corners of the canvas are sodden army tents.

He woke in the grip of chaotic emotions. This time his terror was real. He looked for the picture. There it was upon the wall. A sense of relief flooded him. He felt as though fate had given him another chance. As he looked, his eye rested on the shadow that moved in rhythmic harmony with the old man's every act, and he remembered words that he had once heard. It seemed now as though the old man uttered them: "It is always dangerous to attempt to reach the height or depth of the unconscious unless the shadow is with you." He had tried once more to escape into a world where unreal spirits cast no shadow because they had no accepted reality in the life of the soul— the soul who would show him the meaning of his earth life, thus revealing the secrets of the spirit. The way was long, and often he was lost in a realm where spirit mocked him. Yet the vision had not been obliterated. It returned with quickening power long afterwards, and he discovered that the high things of the spirit are found only when one keeps contact with the reality of earth.

Intuition and perception of hidden wisdom are gifts that the anima brings, yet a man may make himself believe that these things beyond his ken have been thought up by his clever intellect. Then he is like the rabbi of whom it was said, "the spark was in him but it was caught in the snare of his own pride."

Such was the condition of a young minister who at times seemed to "speak with the tongues of men and of angels." His congregation increased rapidly, though many of the humbler members felt themselves strangers in the church.

One night in a dream he found himself in the pulpit addressing a large congregation of ministers. He was filled with pride at the importance of the occasion. His voice rang out, "My text will be found

in Second Corinthians, Chapter Six, Verse Six." He opened his Bible, but where the verse should have been, a blank space stared up at him, and he found himself preaching a sermon about a hen who had laid a too-enormous egg.

He woke and the missing verse flashed up in his memory: "By pureness, by knowledge, by long-suffering, by kindness, by the Holy Ghost, by love unfeigned." Against these words stood this dream image of his soul—a hen who had laid a too-enormous egg.

His first impulse was to regard the dream humorously and so de-potentiate and dismiss it. But this, fortunately, he was not able to do, for the dream had behind it the authority of the unconscious force, the will that moves toward transformation. It evoked memories that drove its meaning home. All day and through the next night he fought against the memories that his pride had put from him. He recalled his high school graduation when as class orator he had been carried away by his own eloquence, by the congratulations of his teachers and by the words of an older man, "You have the gift of oratory, my boy. You could be a great politician or a great preacher." In imagination he saw himself making his first speech in the Senate. His vocation was clear. But the World War was approaching and he had no heart for fighting. The ministry was noble; it was also safe. He enrolled in a sectarian college, making clear to the president the strength of his call to the ministry. When after two years the draft became an actuality, he had almost succeeded in persuading himself that it was nobility, not cowardice, that had made the decision. Did not his success confirm his choice? His major function was intuition easily fired by suggestive words, able to play upon thoughts that rose of themselves. So he could become a mind afire, and be temporarily possessed by the words that filled him. Now the words of this text which he had often used glibly but which had been blotted out of his personal Bible turned upon him like tongues of flame, for it was the first time these words had been turned inward.

"By pureness." Often when he left the pulpit, he stepped into the greediness of his own body, his homosexual fantasies, his nagging, instinctual cravings, his secret life where, pursued by illicit desires, he found himself driving at night into places where he could, at least by proxy, live out these fantasies, which he would neither acknowledge to himself nor accept as part of his own connection with the dark element of the unconscious. His purity had become a persona

attribute, which he maintained by elevating himself above the congregation and concealing the impurities even from his image of himself. "By knowledge." It was this concealment of his inner life that barred the way to self-knowledge which is the first step to the knowledge of the inner god. "By long suffering." Irrationally—for he knew the text well—these words assumed a different meaning. The word "suffering" leaped out at him, revealing his greatest fear. This was what he had run from, the suffering that he might meet if he did not escape into the hypocritical safety of the noble ideal. "By kindness." He had evaded human relatedness and the kindness which brings man close to his fellow men, for he saw safety only in standing above and apart, lest, by stepping down—or up—to an acknowledged humanity he betray the split within himself. "By the Holy Ghost." The wind of the spirit had blown through him as through a hollow reed, and when it had passed had left him empty or had filled him with unrelated, unreal, spiritual exaltation. "By love unfeigned." The pretense, the feigned love of the spirit on which his life was founded, confronted him. "Though I speak with the tongues of men and of angels, and have not charity, [caritas, love] I am become as sounding brass, or a tinkling cymbal." He had written beautiful sermons on love, but had he ever loved?

He tried to escape the dream but he found he could not blot it from his memory. The inner voice pursued him; the images appeared before him whatever way he twisted and turned. The old dark avenues of escape were closed by the pursuing images. He was compelled to seek help. At first he desired only the release of the confessional and an unearned absolution for which he would not even pay a penance. But pardon can come only from within the self and the price is humility and self-knowledge. This knowledge first came from examination of the dream.

What was the image of the soul to whom he had assigned the task of spiritual revelation? A hen who had laid an egg so enormous that no brooding could hatch it into life. He despised hens and hen-minded women—women of "one idea and many perplexities" who ran in confused squawking when they felt themselves in peril. Was this hen the image of his soul, his anima? Had she, from her invisibility in the unconscious, so ruled his ego that he had "run squawking" from threatened danger and had tried to clothe his squawking in borrowed language of the spirit? He had run from death, so escap-

ing life and rebirth; and the image of his soul had taken on the form of a hen!

And the too-enormous egg! How had it come into being? A fleeting picture rose unbidden: an agitated hen consorting with a self-important rooster. Had this creature of one idea become impregnated by red-combed pride and from this union produced the enormous egg of ego inflation? The fantasy gripped him, the enormous vacant shell closed about him. He was imprisoned in the empty idea that he had imagined would offer him escape from the reality of the soul's demand. Who would now deliver him from the power of this death?

At this point he was seized by a poignant desire for the human experiences that he had feared and scorned. But where would he find them? Could he confess his poverty to the congregation that had been enriched by his eloquence? Again he wanted to escape, for now every service brought home to him his inner conflict and called up the humiliating image of his soul. In his extremity he sought the advice of an elder who had, he felt, both spiritual understanding and deep sympathy. Was he still, he asked, an asset to the church? The answer he received is similar to one given by an Indian guru to a former disciple. The disciple, after plunging into a western world of extraversion, was unable to face the temptations and responsibilities of the life that he had chosen, and had returned to the guru asking him to give him back the peace that he had lost. The guru answered, "Where you have lost your soul there you must return to find it." The elder's advice was the same, though his words were different. "Through you, even in spite of yourself, the congregation has been enriched. Go back to find love where you have betrayed it. Perhaps your people have something to give to you. Wait and see what grace will do." This was what his ego had never been able to do—to await the word of grace; for until now this was the word he feared.

This time he accepted the word and followed the way indicated and went down among his people, receiving with humility their gifts of trust and love. He continued his analysis, though distance made long periods of interruption necessary. The dreams changed as he followed his anima who became guide in the unconscious and also a ministering spirit in that daily relatedness without which no real integration can take place.

The dream of the hen and the enormous egg was a crossroads dream. It startled him into consciousness where his ego assumptions

were confronted with the reality of his own evil. Even so his ego could have turned from it and the image of the anima would never have revealed itself as soul, breath and quickening spirit, the one who brings knowledge of the mysteries of love and who opens the door to the world of transforming images that arise from the limitless realm of the non-ego.

In writing such a history years are compressed into a paragraph, but on this journey the image of the anima was reborn. And on his heart she inscribed in letters of fire the verse that had theretofore been left out of his personal Bible.

A fantasy journey in which the nature of the anima as soul reveals herself may be long and arduous. It may be broken by many dreams that connect the personal situation with the eternal archetype, by outer experiences in which the conflicts of the opposites must be endured, by memories of former choices, by the penetrations of those fiery intuitions that illuminate the pathway of the as yet unknown future, by archetypal visions that bring to consciousness the interplay of the divine and human within the soul. The following fragments are taken from the log book of such a journey into the unconscious, a journey that lasted for over two years.

As introduction to this log book are these quotations: "Let us honor Prometheus, the Titan, for he brought to light the fiery symbols that were heretofore wrapped in darkness." And these words from Plotinus: "For the soul, a divine thing, a fragment, as it were, of the Primal Being, makes beautiful, according to their capacity, all things whatsoever it grasps and moulds."

I am standing at a crossroad that is almost buried in mist; I am uncertain of my way. An unknown woman comes out of the obscurity and puts in my hand a ball of red wool. It glows like fire. At her unspoken, mysteriously conveyed direction I throw it to the left, to the east. As it unwinds, a pathway opens before me. I follow the thread. The mists close about me; in front the way drops steeply down into an unknown abyss. The ball disappears over the rim of the chasm. I follow the thread. The mists lift as I go down. The light that penetrates them is like moonlight yet no moon appears. At the foot of the descent is a wasteland with nothing visible but a cross made of a substance like moonstone. Does the light come from this? I am seized with fierce desire to

possess it. I descend to the valley. I seize the cross and pull it from the rock on which it is placed. As I hold it a strange transformation takes place. I am a beast covered with coarse hair; a beast soul is raging inside me. I bite the cross with my fanglike teeth; I tear it into fragments; I throw the pieces from me. One of the fragments becomes a misty pool. A wind blows over it and lifts the mists. The pool is now clear like a mirror. I look into it and see my beast face. I remember words I read long ago: "The moon has a faculty of generating and augmenting the body." I remember Circe and her power of transforming the man into the particular beast form that has lived concealed within his bodily form. Rage turns to horror. I look into the face of the beast and know he is my brother—myself. Again rage possesses me. I would tear and destroy the beast as I have destroyed the cross. I am powerless. I acknowledge this. I submit to my beast nature. I am dumb before the mystery of transformation. I kneel. I look deep into the eyes of the beast. It too is dumb and suffers from its own dumbness. The moon rises. In its light the cross reassembles itself upon the face of the water. I look upon it. I, the beast, worship it. At the foot of the cross I see my beast face. As I look into it a shaft of moonlight penetrates the water and I see, far beneath the beast face, another face, a spirit face. Slowly they are drawn together by the magnetic power of the shaft of moonlight. They lie together—devil and angel. They pour into each other; they mingle; they separate; they reunite; they fuse into a face that I cannot make visible. It disappears. Memories crowd about me. I remember scenes of my childhood—ugly brutal scenes— animals butchered—blood—useless sacrifice—indifference to pain —masculinity, crude, strong, sensual, violent—daydreams of myself as a child artist, a creature too ethereal for this world of men in which I found myself. I remember nights when the secret fascination of the dark cruel aspects of this masculine power thrilled me with delicious fear and I sat up in bed huddled in my blankets reading horror tales or looking at Doré's pictures of a masculinely conceived Hell until I would fall into frenzied dreams. Strangely, these often were not of men but of women with cruel vulturelike eyes, or fat bearded faces like gluttonous men. I remember my own great-aunt Tildy who lived with us, a mountainous gluttonous creature with a power of saying the poisonous devouring word that ate into one's consciousness or devoured one's fantasies. She had a way of ferreting out my greatest fears and playing upon my timidities. She intruded into my terror dreams and actualized them in outer life.

Morning. The outer world of the so-called real. The escape into the unreal, but more than real, world of beauty. The two worlds—must they separate, or can they merge, flow into each other, fuse into a new world of heaven and earth?

I look again into the pool. I see the red thread. It makes a wavering pathway through the water. The red ball lies at the center of the floor of the pool below the meeting place of the arms of the cross. I plunge into the pool. The cross upholds me. I am stretched out upon it. I am impaled upon it. It glows with inner light that reddens into fire. The flames lick about me. I struggle, I suffer, I submit. The center of the cross burns away. I fall through waters of fire; petals of flame close about me. Are they blood or fire or burning petals of some strange flower of life? I descend through them into still green water where the red ball lies. I seize the ball. I throw it upward. It falls back swiftly, it pierces through the earth at the bottom of the pool. The earth below the waters opens and, as I go down, closes after me. I descend on the red thread. Here is another world below the world of my first descent. I go down through darkness. I see stars gleaming below me. I fall through this deeper firmament onto the central point of crossroads of steel intersecting at right angles. The ball lies motionless. Does it now await my will? I hear from the far distance a child's voice singing,

> Star of the East
> Thou light of my soul.

It was the song the child Emily sang at the Christmas celebration when I too was a child. I adored her. She was my first image of virginal love and spiritual light. Later she grew sordid, ugly. I tried to escape from even speaking to her. I feared her. This fear has never left me. I see her image in all women who try to exert power over me. They too may change, grow dark and evil. Now her voice comes from the far land of unsullied past that holds promise of another clearer future. I turn to the east. The ball is already moving before me. I follow it down a long corridor. On my left is a curtain of blue threads blown by an imperceptible wind. Back of the curtain I see three women. One is robed in gray, one in red, one in green. I try to part the blue threads. They become an impenetrable veil—Maya? The veil becomes a wall that shuts them from me. I hear their voices that now float to me from a region that lies far ahead. I cannot distinguish their words but their voices are like the plucked strings

of a harp, clear, distinct, vibrating in harmony, fading into a single clear chord.

I go on. I come to a black cliff that bars my pathway. At the top stands a tree with three branches on either side. It is growing from a white skull buried deep in the rock. The words come to me, "first cometh death before life." At the foot of the tree a beautiful dark-haired girl lies sleeping. She is guarded by a six-armed medusalike monster with an old wrinkled face and evil eyes. I break a branch from the tree. It becomes a sword. I attack the monster. Its arms close about me in an attempt to strangle me. I hack them off. I hack off the monster's head. I awaken the woman. She yields to me. She slips from my arms. She vanishes into darkness of a dense cloud. I hear her voice, "Not yet, not yet." I shall find her again in another awakening. I enter the darkness of the cloud—the "Cloud of Unknowing" that stands between man and the light.

I come through the cloud into a gray dawn. Before me is a mountain of black basalt, sheer as glass. I see a small triangular door just to the left of the pathway. I try to push it open but it is locked. I seize the red ball. It burns into my flesh yet I hold it firmly. I knock upon the door with the red ball. It opens. I see a long passageway that opens into a circular garden flooded by moonlight. In its center, borne high on a shaftlike stem of clear aquamarine green, is a great crimson rose. At its center lies the moonstone cross—*Rosa Mundi–Rosa Mystica*.

The rose is, first of all, the supreme symbol of woman, of love, of the life of the heart. Blake's poem rises unbidden, stirring strange fears.

> O Rose, thou art sick!
> The invisible worm
> That flies in the night,
> In the howling storm,
>
> Has found out thy bed
> Of crimson joy,
> And his dark secret love
> Does thy life destroy.[9]

I hear a voice, "It is being destroyed from within! Look to it!" I think of Laura, a woman who exerts an uncanny possessive power over me. Her dark beauty entices me from my creative

---

9 William Blake, "The Sick Rose," *Poetry and Prose*, p. 71.

work that she scorns. Is she the witch worm who "flies in the storm" and invades my heart destroying love in the dark of lust?

I hear again the words, "destroyed from within."

I feel the stirring of the beast within me. I see the figure of A, an actor—peasant born, heavy, slow, instinctive, uneducated, dogged, weak. Yet he could, on the stage, give a sense of reality. When I discovered that his sexuality was promiscuous and without shame, I was obsessed by him. His image haunted me. What did I want of him? What value did he seem to withhold from me that I had to possess? Was it the dynamic energy that could sweep away all barriers of conventionality or even of moral law? His power I believe sprang from the fact that he was a symbol of maleness, a form of dynamic primitive maleness that I lacked within myself. My obsessive need of him was as though my own repressed sexual man self rose against me and devoured me. Now I see beyond him a forest; something moves. It is a young antelope, white, delicate, ethereal, crowned with pale moonlight. It dissolves into the moonlight.[10] I see the two faces, beast and spirit, deep in the shadows of the forest. The whole picture dissolves. Only A [the actor] remains. I look again at him. He is no longer a terrifying figure. Is this because in the hours of my analytical journey my own life has become clearer, stronger, and I am no longer so afraid of life, of love? I am no longer so afraid of my own sexuality or the dark erotic woman who can evoke it. Now as I look at him a strength wells up in me, the dynamic strength of instinctual life. I see the beautiful dark-haired girl whom I freed from the medusalike monster when the dynamic power of the male—the hero—entered into me. Has this brute self a strength that could be mine if I could accept it? Could I make it serve the greater will that sometimes moves through me? Words once heard return. "The animal is often the pre-stage of the god." God and animal, beast and spirit, again mingle and come together forming a face that I cannot yet see. Is it the face of the as yet unknown self? I look again. Now it is the beast who stands before me. I open the door of my inmost self. I feel him enter into me. At that same moment I see the Rose—the Alchemical Rose, the consummation of mystical vision. I remember the words of Yeats: "There are moments . . . when the indefinite world which has but half lost its mas-

---

[10] In the Kundalini Chakra of the Serpent Power, the first vision of the Self is a young antelope appearing at the edge of the forest. Cf. Avalon, *The Serpent Power*.

tery over my heart and my intellect seems about to claim a perfect mastery."[11]

Here is the danger and the beauty of introversion—to lose oneself in the unfulfilled dream or to give form to the dream whose meaning always remains beyond form, to the vision whose mystery defies definition; to awaken in oneself and perhaps in another the sense of the wonder of life.

Again I see the Rose and hear the words:

> Far off, most secret, and inviolate Rose,
> Enfold me in thine hour of hours. . . .
>
> .   .   .   .
>
> . . . I too await
> The hour of thy great wind. . . .
>
> .   .   .   .
>
> Surely thine hour has come, thy great wind blows,
> Far off, most secret, and inviolate Rose![12]

Once more the mountain of black basalt rises before me. The triangular door is open but the passageway is dark and narrow. I crawl through it—utter darkness, weakness, struggle. I emerge. I stand before the Rose.

"Thine hour has come, thy great wind blows"—a commandment, a promise.

Is it the same promise that I made in childhood when, long, long years ago, I stood alone on that solitary, wintry road, alone with the north star—my star—and felt within me the call of destiny? As I stand before the Rose, I look into the heavens and see this star above me. Has it always been there in spite of my blindness? Has it sustained me when my own weakness would have delivered me over to the terrible mother whose presence always menaced me in the dark of the night?[13] Even in this strange journey I have been conscious of a purpose, a direction. Star and Rose, symbols of innermost beauty—of steadfast purpose and of love.

Now I kneel before the Rose and the star shines above me. I do not know how long I kneel bathed in the fragrance of ineffable love. The fragrance becomes a strong wind. I breathe it

---

[11] William Butler Yeats, "Rosa Alchemica," *Early Poems and Stories*, p. 497.

[12] *Ibid.*, "The Secret Rose," p. 319. Copied here as the lines were in the dreamer's notebook.

[13] Once more we find a childhood vision returning to demand its fulfillment in the life of the man. This man was the child who walked upon the solitary road where he first knew the star of his destiny. See Chapter 6, "Childhood and the Friend of Choice."

in. I stand with arms outstretched before the Rose. The star glows with radiant white light. It penetrates the heart of the Rose—star and Rose, purpose and love, are one—a commandment, a promise—a commandment to create out of this moment, a promise to fulfill in love the early command of the star. Only so can I create and be created; for the command of heart and the command of mind are one command and the promise is one promise.

I feel strength enter into me. I see the red ball at my feet. It glows with inner fire—fire of the rose, fire of the star. The ball begins to move. My journey is not at an end. This love that draws me, this voice that calls me, challenge me to the never-ending journey of transformation and to the discovery of new meanings.

"Star and Rose, purpose and love, are one." With this recognition of the union of the opposites, the dualistic struggle within the man was at rest. He opened his heart and mind to the meaning of the vision and so became filled with the strength that entered into him from the reservoir of infinite potentials.

Again the road drops downward and I see below a green and leafy valley where small houses are set. The dark maiden of my vision comes out of one of the small houses. She gathers flowers —roses. She is herself—no more, no less. How marvelous! My telephone rings. The outer world makes its demand. Today it does not seem an intrusion.

Through acceptance of the meaning of this inner journey, the opposition between the demands of the inner and outer worlds could be seen in their interplay. He could return to the demands of daily life without losing the deep connection with the vision. Meaning flowed through both and united them. He had opened his heart to the fragrance of the rose and to the light of the star—to the great wind of spirit and of love—and he was swept by it into an experience of that divine love which touches the deepest depth of cosmic life and which, by its very being, must manifest itself in human relatedness. Through this, his earthly world has attained a new reality and he can move from one world to the other without a sense of violation. The inner voice of the anima now calls him to translate these newly apprehended meanings into his individual life.

For the anima builds a bridge for the images of the unconscious to

enter consciousness and become active agents in the world of consciously directed choice. Only that which is lived attains reality. Logos must be given form through acceptance of vocation; eros must be lived in human relatedness. Only so can the conflicts of the opposites be endured and a way that transcends the conflict be discovered. With this discovery man finds that he is woman too and, accepting this union of love and spirit, enters upon the journey toward wholeness.

CHAPTER 12

The Feminine Principle

 و§ ई৯

The sea in a chasm, struggling to be
free and unable to be
in its surrendering
finds its continuing.[1]

Love has earth to which she clings.[2]

As inner woman the anima lives out the feminine principle active
in creative man. Through his relation to her as soul as well as earth,
he finds a way of reconciliation between the opposites existing within
himself. In woman the feminine principle is her natural center—the
home of her spirit. Relatedness is her world, eros the god of her being,
a god whom she must learn to serve with clear-eyed devotion.

"The essential character of eros is the divine creative force that
reaches out from the seclusion of the subject to reach the object."[3]
Its source is the dynamis of the emotions; it draws its vitality from
living experience both of the outer world and of those instinctive and
numinous experiences that arise spontaneously from within the
psyche.

The feminine principle is the earth force, "the dark, earth-born
feminine principle with its emotionality as instinctiveness reaching
back into the depth of time and into the roots of psychological con-

---

[1] Marianne Moore, "What Are Years?" *Collected Poems*, p. 99.
[2] Robert Frost, "Bond and Free," *Complete Poems*, p. 151.
[3] H. G. Baynes, *Mythology of the Soul*, p. 612.

tinuity."[4] Through these roots it is connected with the primordial wisdom of the instincts, with the reality of immediate event and its need, with the patience of nature and its changing aspects of life, death and renewal. It is also connected with the waters deep under the earth, springs that may be tapped by the divining rod of eros. Acted upon by the hidden waters, this divining rod bends down to indicate the place where work must be done to release the hidden springs of creativity. From these creative springs arise visions of mysterious beauty or portents of terror and disaster, thoughts and impulses that spring to life from the "nowhere" which is far below the region of conscious knowledge. The unconscious is the wellspring of the feminine being.

> The earth is still. It does not act of itself. . . . It does not strive . . . to achieve everything of its own strength but quietly keeps . . . receptive to the impulses flowing from the creative.[5]

These creative forces rise in emotion, mood, desire, wish, intuition and perception of the irrational. They may erupt in sudden impulse—fierce courage that springs up in defense of the child or the beloved, generosity, love, rage—all directed toward the object that has aroused feeling. Or the force of the emotion may be directed toward the images of the unconscious and the hidden subjective problems of inner relatedness. The unconscious then acts with its magnetic "downdrawing" power which induces meditation, dreaming, wishing, waiting and awaiting the time when the meaning of that which is happening is perceived and the wisdom of the unconscious is accepted, so letting the experience speak for itself as it unfolds within the psyche. This process in which the whole person unfolds is directed toward self-revelation. It is an inner knowing manifest only through a change in personality which shows itself in indefinable ways.

Feminine emotions instinctively flow into personal channels, busy with perceptions of what can come alive and grow between people. A down-to-earth quality[6] senses the immediate need, and a practical earthly wisdom moves to meet it. Thought, sometimes to the astonishment or bewilderment of the actor, comes later as afterthought,

---

[4] Jung, quoting from his writings in conversation with the author.
[5] After *I Ching*, Vol. II, p. 22.
[6] Sensation, which the French term *la function de realité*.

which scrutinizes the act and assesses its values. Yet the sense of the reality of the immediate situation is not accepted as an exclusive standpoint, for the feminine psyche is always concerned with bringing things together. Woman's statements are not this or that, they are, rather, also. The also admits intuition, whose voice says, "Look below the surface; question; peer into the depth. See not only what is, but also what may evolve." For feminine intuition is intrigued by the possibilities that the special human situation offers in the opportunity to create, to bring forth, to stir—even if what is created is only a dramatic moment or a "scene." The act springs from a desire for relatedness rather than from any code of ethics or humanistic theory. Jung says of woman, "She can do everything for love of a man. But those women who can achieve something important for the love of a thing are most exceptional, because this does not really agree with their nature."[7] Yet this "everything" is ruled by instinctual perception, for woman must learn to measure and not to measure, to withhold and to pour forth without stint. She cannot say, "A little here and a little there" to a child, lover, friend or the stranger who comes to her door. For who can measure need, or know when the pouring forth will bring the rose to blossom in the desert? Yet she must be alert to perceive the moment when giving can impoverish the spirit of both giver and recipient so that even her withholding may serve life.[8]

---

[7] Contributions to Analytical Psychology, p. 169.

[8] A woman, anxious to help a youth in a difficult position, learned that he had been offered an opportunity which he felt would enable him to enter his chosen field. To accept this he would have had to give up the uninteresting job on which he depended for his self-support. She thought that, by practicing self-denials she would be able to furnish him with the needed money. She felt quite sure the opportunity was one in which he could develop his talent, and her sacrifice seemed meritorious. She decided, therefore, upon the "unselfish" course. But a strange dream intruded:

She was standing in a large bare room. At her feet was a gleaming two-edged sword. In front of her stood the youth, naked, and as she looked at him a voice said, "You can cut off his testicles if you want to."

She woke with a shock—the dream seemed remote and barbarous, yet it was too vivid to dismiss. Was this then what her "unselfishness" might do—take from him his virility, his ability to become a man? Had her generous outpouring any hidden motive of power? She recalled small instances of his too-easy acceptance of help, of his reluctance to face reality, of his concentration upon the importance of his talent rather than upon facing the difficulties of the task. In

Turned inward, intuition becomes prophecy, perception of unconscious forces moving toward change or transformation, or it becomes brooding, meditating. It gazes, lingers, ponders and searches out the wisdom of the heart. Or it may busy itself with spinning dreams and wishes into fantasy fabrics. Intuition says,

> I dwell in Possibility,
> A fairer House than Prose.[9]

Possibility may become actuality if woman works to bring intuitive perceptions into line with reality, whereas unchecked intuition plays with a possibility, assuming that it is inevitable destiny. This gives to the wish a magic power over her spirit.

When the narcissistic infantile element rules, the ego calls upon a kind of primitive magic that seeks to compel life to conform to its wish. Then both subject and object may fall under its compulsive power, for it moves in the unconscious and is felt by both. Jung speaks of "that quiet, obstinate wish that works, as we all know, magically, like the fixed eye of a snake."[10]

This snake eye may exert its magic in the present age of enlightenment as subtly as in what we are pleased to call the far-distant past of primitive superstition, for it is connected with the black and white of the matriarchal image. In one of her temples Ishtar is depicted by two images, like in form and feature but one black, one white, portraying the duality of her nature. If in her phase of darkness her wish went forth, it was beyond power of recall, for once released it caused itself to be inevitably fulfilled. When the dark phase had passed, Ishtar, appearing in her white form, lamented the destruction and again turned her creative face upon the world, rescuing the remnant

---

considering his abilities, she had repressed her intuitions of his need for struggle and independence as a man. She also had repressed desires within herself that made her wish to hold him, through ties of gratitude. These desires she had disposed of by permitting the image of selflessness to swallow them up. Now, looking upon her proposed act in relation to his reality, she reversed her decision and realized that what might seem ruthless selfishness would serve life better than any apparent selflessness. She saw how a false image of herself had destroyed not only her sense of reality but her intuitive perception of what was coming to pass in both herself and the object of her solicitude. This excerpt, in condensed form, is from my book, *The Inner World of Man*, p. 12.

[9] Emily Dickinson, Poem 657 in *Poems*, p. 506.

[10] "Woman in Europe," *Contributions to Analytical Psychology*, Harcourt, Brace edition, p. 174.

of her people, causing floods to subside and the earth again to bring forth. Yet this did not restore that which her evil wish had destroyed.

When the ego becomes inflated with a sense of its own daemonic power, it finds an equal elation in destruction or creativity, for, if woman becomes identified with this magic, she sees people as pawns to be moved about or removed from the game of life according to her wish.

The snake eye works in silence. A woman of keen intuitions and violent passions, capable of loyalty and intense hatred, fell under the power of her own wish. In a room full of people she could surround herself with a silence that permeated the atmosphere, electrically charging it with its own energy so that things appeared to happen of themselves. Her image of herself was of a creative person whose wish could communicate itself through channels of the unconscious and produce new life in others, making them create in ways she "knew" to be valuable. But when she met with an "obstinate" counter wish, her energy was, in a flash, redirected from creation to destruction. She was keenly aware of this power and exulted in it. What she was not aware of was that the wish acted as a boomerang, destroying her own power to love. Nor was she aware of her identification with the all-powerful goddess or with the black and white aspects of her own nature. Finding herself defeated in one of these attempts and piqued by the discovery of her human limitations, she was considering analysis as a way of tapping the infinite sources of the unconscious when an unwelcome dream broke through.

It is early morning. Below my window are rows of young fruit trees that were set out yesterday under my direction. The gardener said this was not the place for them. The soil and drainage were wrong. I told him it was my wish that they should be there and he was there to follow my orders. I have a sense of satisfaction on seeing them and go down to revel in what I have done, but as I pass through, all the trees wither and die. I look back upon a dead and sterile orchard.

The dream startled her, for it revealed her ruthless disregard of the innate nature of other people. Their living values must grow where she wished them to and where they would enhance her own domain, whether or not the soil was suitable for them. So intent was she on this that her very presence, her "passing through" could blight the

living potentials that she had tried to manipulate in accordance with her wish. Her own interpretation of the dream was, "This is what all these petty people, all these demands and restrictions of my present life are doing to me. They are destroying my power to make things happen as I know they should. I must break from these tiresome responsibilities and explore the sources of my magic power so that I can make trees grow where I know they should grow." She came to the analyst as to a super witch, offering tribute money for initiation into the dark world of necromancy. Dreams revealed the primitive savage qualities that underlay the many layers of her cultural life. Her superior function, intuition, refused to listen to reality whose voice pronounced this judgment: "Until power yields to love your unconscious motive may, at any encounter, activate your wish so that you will serve Thanatos the destroyer, rather than Eros the quickener." This picture of herself did not please her, for the wish had created a highly colored image of herself. She left analysis and went back to magic.

The wish shapes dreams, forms images, draws patterns upon the clouds. It can carry the ego away from willed purpose, or it can become the keen desire that generates energy and vitalizes thought and feeling. As star of creative imagination, it becomes the lode star by which the helmsman steers his course, for "the wish turns the wheel of the mind." It often directs instinctual choice. From secret wish springs the inopportune word or gesture, or the sympathetic response that releases feeling.

Feeling, not law, is the basis of feminine judgment. Feeling is a rational function whose pronouncements are founded on a sense of subjective values and on basic laws of relationship. Negative feeling must also be accepted as having its rightful place in determining relationship. To like everybody and everything is to smother all distinctions in a meaningless ooze of pleasantness and conformity. Sentimentality is often confused with feeling but it is without the power of discrimination and judgment. It can spread "like molasses on hot gingerbread," and be quite as cloying to the object enmeshed in its sweetness. Undisciplined emotion may also pour itself out in sweetness, or it may erupt in violence and, like a stream of molten lava, bury the living potentials of a relationship. Conscious feeling, with its sense of relative values, must come to her rescue if woman is to discern which relationships really agree with her nature.

The love of a woman is not sentiment—that is only man's way—but a life-will that at times is terrifyingly unsentimental, and can even force her to self-sacrifice. A man who is loved in this way cannot escape his inferior side, for he can only answer this reality with his own.[11]

Though feeling is a rational, judging function, feminine feeling retains an irrational element which is concerned with inner causality and with the emotional aura—the hidden why and wherefore—that surrounds factual truth. It is directed toward the exception rather than the rule, and each encounter is exceptional and statistically and factually unprovable. The feminine attitude toward factual truth is often, "There are lies, damn lies and statistics."

When oriented by love, feeling is nearer to mercy than to justice. It knows its own purpose in this realm where it is the administrator. In its negative aspects it can be cruel as a "hanging judge," and cold as burnt-out ashes. Its true source is the fire, the warmth, the creative flame of emotion which forces it to enter into the conflicts and challenges of life.

Conflict lights the fire of affects and emotions and has two aspects like every fire: namely combustion and the production of light. On the one side the emotion is the alchemistic fire whose warmth makes everything manifest and whose heart burns away all superfluities and, on the other, the emotion is the moment when steel strikes stone and a spark is produced. For emotion is the chief source of becoming conscious. There is no transformation from dark to light or from inertia to movement without emotion.[12]

Conflict is the source of dynamic energy. We *are* the conflicts. They are all contained within us. Without this flame kindled by conflict, feeling would never be transformed into love nor would it engender fierce hate.

Primitive emotions are always ready to spring into action whenever the personal and individual way is sacrificed to the upsurge of the collective. A crowd is swayed by the essentially weak inferior one who, as protest against his own inferiority, calls upon kindred inferiorities inciting them to icononclastic violence. There are mobs in every personal psyche—savage emotions, inferior and despised potentials—that can be either roused to violence or, when accepted and

---

11 Jung, *Contributions to Analytical Psychology*, p. 174.
12 Jung, "Psychological Aspects of the Mother Archetype," *Spring 1943*, p. 22.

consciously acknowledged, redeemed by newly awakened consciousness. They are elements that can be restrained but not eliminated,
for shadow and light are eternal elements of human wholeness.

Woman's sense of wholeness is not based on an ideal of perfection.
In fact, as Jung says,

Perfection . . . does not agree with women and may even be dangerous
for them. If a woman strives for perfection, she forgets the complementary role of completeness, which, though imperfect by itself, forms the
necessary counterpart. For, just as completeness is always imperfect, so
perfection is always incomplete and therefore represents a final state
which is hopelessly sterile.[13]

Woman's acceptance of the interplay of opposites is based on an
awareness of good and evil as continuing forces both in the world
and within her own psyche. She knows she is both good and bad, and
she knows that as long as she lives she is going to be both good and
bad. She knows that the same forces are existent in every human
being whom she encounters. Her business is to find out how relationship—inner or outer—can grow through conscious acceptance of this
reality and through growing perception of what individual, not stand-
ardized, goodness means in its relation to each developing situation.
Through the urge to understand the effect of her own compulsive acts
of violence or ruthlessness, she learns balance and restraint, so that
evil will not take possession of her in moments of unconsciousness
and destroy the meaning of love. Here instinct and intuition enter,
for, paradoxically, at the very moment when she is struggling to solve
the conflict on a rational level she will be beset by a wholly irrational
concept which her heart knows contains the solution. It takes a great
sense of balance to live a paradox, but this is life's demand of the
feminine being. This she discovers not through a study of ethics or a
logical process of thought but through seeing the effect of her shadow
upon persons and situations and through learning to see the underground working of her motives and how they may emerge in acts that
destroy both herself and others. For woman's interest flows into life
itself, not into concepts and philosophies about life.

"The earth in its devotion carries all things, . . . it tolerates all
creatures. . . . This is its greatness."[14] On the human level this may

---

13 Jung, Answer to Job, p. 52.
14 After I Ching, Vol. I, pp. 12–13.

also be its weakness for, like nature, it is undiscriminating and unconscious. We have spoken before of "forbidden compassion," the compassion that destroys the foundation of feeling. All things good and evil flourish in the unconscious even as they do in the jungle. Discrimination and separation must enter into feminine choice if compassion is to follow the ways of love. This does not mean separation from the instinctual irrational side of feminine wisdom, for often this subtle wisdom is a mediumlike power that enables woman to penetrate the veil of appearances and see contained within the evil the potential of good, embryonic within its darkness; or it warns her of the evil that is coming to birth in the seemingly good. Through this perception, her compassion may be directed upon the wheat, not the strangling tare. Jung speaks of that "understanding at all costs" which is so bent on sympathetic interpretation of the other person's experience that it can become a state of "uncritical passivity coupled with the most complete subjectivity and lack of social responsibility."[15] Indiscriminate tolerance may serve evil as effectively as it serves good. Yet here again is the paradox. Shadow and light must both have their place in every feeling situation if it is to portray the three-dimensional reality of life, its solid fact illumined by the aura of inner perception.

Confronted by an apparently insuperable task demanding discrimination and perception of the nature of the seeds of many demands, woman can rely only on the urge of love to fulfill its purpose. Only the searcher of hearts can sift the tares from the wheat. In this task, a wisdom deeply buried in the roots of her own being can come to her aid. Far below consciousness, a logos force—invisible, unthought yet purposive—directs her actions.

Early in his investigations into the nature of the psyche, Jung observed this purposive, directive agent working toward consciousness, an urge of the self to become realized. This can be spoken of as the logos active in the unconscious. It is "the unconscious point of view developing itself in its own way." The ego must "let the unconscious speak for itself and unfold its own immanent creative and curative possibilities."[16]

It is this logos that directs woman in her encounter with the dragon of unconscious eroticism, whose fiery breath consumes consciousness,

15 Jung, *The Undiscovered Self*, p. 51.
16 Gerhard Adler, "The Logos of the Unconscious."

or with the sloth of inertia that seeks to paralyze discriminating love. If she fails in this encounter, she enters the "dark paradise" of undemanding or ecstatic submission to a god whose nature is unknown to her.

Here in this darkness the shadow may reinforce the logos urge toward consciousness. Distrusts and jealous demands inflame her desire to discover the nature of the god who has enslaved her. It was this urge toward consciousness that moved Elsa to ask the fatal question that drove Lohengrin from her. It was this urge that led Psyche to wound both Eros and herself and forced her to undertake the heroic labors that led her to conscious love.[17]

Psyche's first task was to sort and separate a mass of seeds so that the nature of each would be discernible. The friendly ants, little creatures who came up out of the earth, instincts directed by the logos of the unconscious, performed this seemingly impossible task of love. The seeds in their chaotic mingling represent undifferentiated fertility. Separation and differentiation save woman from promiscuity, not only in her sexual life but in her life of mind and spirit, and make her both willing and more able to face the increasingly difficult tasks and sacrifices necessary if she is to win a relationship of love made conscious.

The instincts contain also an unconscious spiritual principle that warns woman against yielding to blind primeval forces that would overpower and destroy her sense of values, so rendering her unaware of the nature of the force that sweeps through her. Heedless of this warning, she can be swept away into the dark whirlpool of unconsciousness and sucked down into its vortex. Then she may snatch at anything—even the soul of another—to save her from the flood and hurricane forces that have been loosed within her psyche.

When two human beings are caught in this force, they may cling to each other for support, but when the flood subsides and they are cast up on the shore, one or the other may again take up the egotistic motives, the desire for power, the small tricks of god identification and use them as he creeps into the comfort of the old accepted routine of daily life. But if in the experience of "inloveness" the flame of love has been lighted, its transforming fire will burn away the shoddy

---

[17] For a masterly description of this journey, see Erich Neumann, *Amor and Psyche.*

motives and leave the lover with an understanding of the mystery of love.

"Inloveness"—possession by the magic of the unconscious—is not love, nor is feeling that accepts only rational judgment and conscious commitment a love imbued with human and divine energy. Only when the interplay exists—consciousness yielding to, yet controlling passion and emotion lest they betray the purposes of love, passion and emotion soaring above consciousness in the ecstatic moment when spirit and instinct are fused together—only then can love come to its own fulfillment. Love, *caritas*, *agape*: love in its meeting with the whole person of the beloved object; *caritas*, with its almost unbearable moments of perception reaching out in good will to all mankind; *agape*, the soul afire with love of the divine, which is all-inclusive and knows the creative joy and the eternal suffering of the human-divine spirit as uniting man and God—how far is this ultimate attainment from the ordinary life! Yet in her heart the feminine being knows this is love's truth and journeys toward it.

The flood and the ebb—in all the many forces of love this rhythm is true. Woman learns this in accepting the alternation of prosaic daily routine with moments of creative vision, moments of disillusionment with moments of illumination, moments of ecstatic faith with periods of unillumined duty—always the sorting on new levels, for love is the reaper, winnowing the heart, leaving only the kernel that nourishes.

"Earth waits on heaven"[18]—eros receives from logos the power of discrimination directed toward understanding of motives and judgment of values in relation to the object, and logos receives the kindling fire that sets the heart aflame. In this interplay, logos does not separate woman from love but helps her to discover its meaning. This voice of spirit acts as the masculine principle of apprehension and perception which balances and regulates feminine receptivity. It strengthens the ego so that, no longer swept away by archetypal forces, it can make the fateful decisions of human love.

In this experience woman relinquishes her dependence upon the fascination of her own unconscious feminine magnetic power and enters upon the human life of encounter with another, which involves separation, submission, oneness, suffering, trial and continuously re-

---

18 After *I Ching*, Vol. II, p. 2.

born consciousness. Through this encounter her feminine self becomes able to meet the masculine on higher levels. And yet again the paradox: unless she yields to forces deeper than consciousness, the encounter is a surface play never touching the greater realities. Yet even here choice moves, for all the former choices of the truth of her own feminine nature enter into this unconscious choice of yielding to the moment of love's supreme demand. It is her own reality that determines the nature of the relationship which can grow out of the magic moments of love.

Woman is never woman until she has experienced the domination, the mastery, the rape by the divine aspect of the masculine force that impregnates her with its own seed of light. It is the experience of the numinous, the mysterium, the interplay of the eternal polarities. It can be destruction; but if the woman is centered in her own feminine self, the surrender is the victory: the ultimate choice of letting herself be chosen.

The essential character of Eros is the divine (i.e. the creative) shaft which leaps across the unguarded frontier of the subject in order to reach the object. The creative shaft is the impregnating phallus, the impressive fertilizing image, the creative word, the idea which gets home, the divine leap by which the individual subject is able to transcend his own subjectivity and take an effective part in the work of creation. This is Eros, the god who brings the twain together in the interest of life,[19]

through

> The awful daring of a moment's surrender
> Which an age of prudence never can retract
> By this, and this only, we have existed.[20]

Woman cannot dare this surrender unless she has accepted herself as woman. Her first image of womanhood comes through her relation to the personal mother. Here the mother's man-hating shadow, a potential present in the feminine psyche, may separate the growing child from love and trust in the father who is the first image of man. A loving and joyous acceptance of the mother's life as woman centers the girl in her own femininity. This relation to the personal mother constellates the maternal archetype in its negative or positive form.

---

[19] H. G. Baynes, *Mythology of the Soul*, p. 132.
[20] T. S. Eliot, "The Waste Land," *Collected Poems*, p. 89.

Woman cannot and should not separate herself from the Mother, as man must; her freedom lies in her increasing consciousness of how this image lives itself within her own psyche. She must perceive not only its duality but also its archetypal unity if she is to see the wholeness of herself. The relation to the image of Earth Mother is the fundamental determinant of the feminine principle. The image takes on various aspects as woman penetrates its meaning and sees it in its manifestations as instinct, as conscious love, and as spirit that penetrates into the heart of love itself. The spirit form of the Earth Mother is the "Wise Woman," who knows the secrets of the heart. And for woman, the innermost secret is the mystery of love. This the Wise Woman knows. Without security in her relation to the Earth Mother and Wise Woman, she cannot make a positive relation to man or to the masculine principle within herself, because this principle is to her an opposing force that threatens her own security.

A woman who had lacked this elemental experience found the problem of relatedness as full of difficulties as a hedgehog is of quills. She worked in one of those charitable organizations that was more organized than charitable. The most human creature in the building was a friendly but quite independent cat who went where it pleased and liked whom it pleased. It often came into her office, and its purr seemed an expression of contented relatedness. One night she dreamed:

> The cat leaves my office and goes out of the building disappearing in traffic. I see her threading her way through the crowded streets. I feel an imperative need to follow her. I push aside the unfinished papers on my desk and take the direction she has taken. I can no longer see her, but an inner sense seems to guide me and I weave my way through a maze of traffic and around bewildering turns. Then I am in the room of the analyst and there, purring in soft content, is my cat curled up at the feet of the Kwan Yin. Seated to the left of the Kwan Yin is a woman who is the analyst yet not the analyst; she is the Kwan Yin yet not the Kwan Yin; she wears the blue cloak of the Virgin yet she is not the Virgin. Then I find myself, a child, sitting on a footstool at her feet. I feel that I have come home.

She woke; darkness and silence were about her. The room in the dream had been filled with a silence more penetrating, more healing

than any word. She sank back into silence, letting it drain her of thought so that she could again be filled by the sense of compassionate acceptance that she had felt in that room.

After an immeasurable time she heard the soft purring of the cat, running under the silence, accentuating, not breaking it. Its rhythm became a song.

> Out of yesterday song comes.
> It goes into tomorrow,
> Sing your own song.[21]

Yesterday had been demand, pressure of work, with an undertone of irritation and frustration. What song could come out of such a yesterday? Then the dream came back. She sat looking into the eyes of the woman who was the analyst yet not the analyst, who wore the cloak of the Virgin yet was not the Virgin. She saw the cat curled at the feet of the Kwan Yin—the protector of little children, the one whose compassion, descending into hell itself, had clothed itself in demon garments so that the lost souls would not fear its approach. The figures seemed to merge, and a spark of recognition lighted her inner darkness. She too was a woman. A sense of kinship and of her own womanhood filled her heart. This was the gift of the dream.

What did it mean to be a woman? Again she was as a child facing —yesterday? tomorrow? Her thoughts went back to yesterday where there had been no song. Then, like a note of music, a memory flashed. She saw the face of a lonely child who had failed in a test that she was giving in accordance with the routine of the office—a dull child of course, and yet something had stirred in her as he looked back on leaving—a perception of some inner potential that the test had failed to reveal. It had been a fleeting recognition, buried quickly under a pile of "results" to be classified and added to the growing evidence of statistics. What constituted the average normal child? There was so-called mass normality; but the mass, unless possessed by a slogan or an incendiary emotion, is made up of human creatures all of whom differ from each other. Could you determine the strength of underground emotion, the reaction to the unknown situation, the downdrawing of depressions by scaling them to the average? Jung says that if you weigh a thousand pebbles and take the average weight, you still do not know the weight of a single pebble. Do statistics dis-

---

[21] Catherine Cate Coblentz, *The Blue Cat of Castle Town*, p. 16, a book familiar to the dreamer.

cover the potential value of a human soul? Was there an element of wonder hidden away under the surface of the day's demand? Was there something also hidden in people under the mask of the habitual? She found herself interested in tomorrow.

Nevertheless, when tomorrow came it buzzed with the old routine. But there was the cat linking together the dream and the office. "If you can purr here," she said, "I guess I can."

And there was the next analytical hour when she entered the room almost fearful of facing its actuality. But out of the silences that interspersed the words of communication came deep affirmation of the transpersonal message of the dream and the acceptance of the relation of woman to woman.

Slowly, very slowly, the transforming power of the dream entered her life. She held long conversations with the (present or absent) cat and was frequently surprised at the answers she received. She talked with the changing images that appeared in her dreams, asking whence they came and why their appearance altered. She became aware of hidden human reactions unconsciously revealed, accepted or suddenly withdrawn. Her very awareness of these subliminal happenings roused latent potentials of feeling in herself and in others. She learned to listen to what her impulses told her, and to question, not distrust, their messages. In the office where yesterday she had felt imprisoned in an overrationalized structure, she began to see human undercurrents that could be freed, to perceive that each relation was an exception that proved the law not of reason but of love. Thus out of yesterday came tomorrow, and tomorrow, as it became today, opened into a new world of communication and relatedness. This was her song.

All this happened less smoothly than it is recorded here, for, as in the dream, the way led through "a maze of traffic"—the confusion of the collective life that surrounded her and threatened her new way. "Bewildering turns" seemed at times to double back upon themselves, yet the thread of purpose guided her as in the dream, for she had given herself to the new adventure and, as happens when woman journeys toward a new goal, she may "keep the crooked straightness," proceeding in "an absolutely abandoned zigzag that goes straight to the point."[22]

---

[22] From a letter from Robert Frost to Elizabeth Shepley Sergeant, in her *Robert Frost, The Trial by Existence,* p. 20.

The memory of the room remained, and the journey was always toward "home," that is, toward the place where, through her relation to the Earth Mother and to the Wise Woman, she was initiated into womanhood, which is the home of the feminine principle, a home that not every woman finds. And always there was night with its darkness, its dream, its silence and its power of renewal.

It is when night brings withdrawal from conscious activity that the creative draws near to the receptive. It is then that the moon spirit descends, dream and vision enter and perceptions of transpersonal meaning arise. These night thoughts must be held clear in their inner reality when the pitiless light of day would dispel them. "When the word of Sinn [the moon god] descends to the earth, the green comes forth."[23] The moon spirit is the quickener of the earth womb, the bestower of fertility. He is manifest in the green of Siva's sprout, in the green wheat of Osiris; he appears as Childer who can become manifest in a grass blade. He symbolizes not only the verdure of physical renewal but the growth and development of spirit and soul.

It is Sinn who impregnates the feminine with the seed of the creative word. He appears in a threefold aspect: the young crescent whose waxing brings awakening of possibilities and potentialities that have remained latent in the hours of darkness; the full round when energy is at its height and the earth, impregnated by the descent of the word, conceives and brings forth; the old silver sickle whose waning is a portent of diminishing power and oncoming darkness. Then comes the time of complete withdrawal, when energy is at its lowest ebb and the powers of doubt and self-distrust assail the soul. In ancient days no new enterprises were undertaken or new seeds planted at the dark of the moon. It is a time of sleep before awakening when the seed lies dormant awaiting the green sprout.

All these rhythmic phases of lunar energy repeat themselves in the creative life of the feminine psyche; not only in the moon time of the menstrual cycle, but creatively and spiritually. From accepting the waxing and waning of the light of psychic energy, its emergence into consciousness or its withdrawal into unconsciousness, woman learns to go with her own instinctual energy. Her consciousness is dependent upon the emergence of inspiration, the possessive emotion that arises

---

[23] Cuneiform inscription quoted by Erich Neumann in "On the Moon and Matriarchal Consciousness," *Spring 1954*, p. 92.

in its own mysterious way and its own given time. At its full, this emerging spirit may seize upon the whole personality, taking possession of it, bending it to the greater will of the non-ego, forcing upon the passive recipient its prophetic, poetic or ecstatic demand. Feminine creativity is dependent upon receptivity to these moments. The ego's part is to come into harmony with that which has been conceived within the psyche, so becoming an instrument of the creative will. That which has entered feminine consciousness must be carried through the dark night of the soul. It must be brought forth, nurtured and given form so that it may go from her and yet abide with her. Yet, throughout the process, moon time, with its unhurried rhythm, rules. In periods of silence and withdrawal, comprehension grows and ripens like sown seed, and when the time is fulfilled, there comes the moment of illumination when the inmost meaning is perceived. The whole self responds to this miraculous moment when that which has been conceived attains its own fulfillment.

In the time of fullness the conscious and unconscious are in harmony, and the time is favorable for that which was conceived to take on form in a human relationship or in an artistic creation.

Rhythm and music activate the unconscious, re-create themselves and are given new form by the creative devotion bestowed upon them by the woman who receives them. The dance as expression of pure emotion is a natural form through which these emanations flow. In ritual or dance drama creative energy emerges from the fiery depth of esthetic possession or from the thunder of a silence that lies deeper than words. It apprehends the unknowable mysteries of myth, religion and prophecy. It is attuned to the incomprehensible movement of the forces of nature.

Or the music and rhythm of the word, touched by intuitions of nature and spirit at play in the human situation, may seek form in poetry, drama or narrative. The tale, woven out of the intricate web of human relationships—the complex within the simple, the simple within the complex—portrays the interplay of human and daemonic forces upon the vaster stage of life.

All those art forms which deal with human emotions and human destiny exert a magic influence upon the feminine psyche. We therefore find women, or men in whom the feminine spirit moves preeminently, achieving prominence as dancers, actors, novelists, poets. For feminine intuition perceives the inner meaning of the human

play and its relation to the cosmic drama that is eternally played out upon the vaster stage of the archetype. It accepts the eternal paradox of nature and spirit, of life, death and the triumph over death, of freedom and fate. It is the wisdom of instinct and of earth-born spirit. It remembers that "love has earth to which she clings."

The moon rules the rhythm of the tides. From the vast ocean of the unconscious it draws up the great waves that bring in the treasure or the wreckage of the sea. The feminine unconscious responds to this rhythmic movement. At the flood, desires, yearnings, dreams, instinctive and intuitive perceptions are borne in by the great waves, the tides of the psychic being. Woman cannot command these tides, nor can she decide what will be borne in from the deep waters, but she can choose that which is meaningful and appropriate to the inner and the outer situation; she can learn to take home to her heart that which is truly hers. She learns the moment of the tide's turning and the time of the return of the waters. She learns the rhythm of pain and gladness that beat like waves upon her heart. She learns that love is joy and sorrow, fulfillment and renunciation, and that at the last, love becomes what she herself has made of it.

She learns not only the need to protect herself from the fatal undertow which would draw her from her earthly life, but also to submit to the inevitable happenings beyond human control—"acts of God," i.e., operations of uncontrollable natural forces, tidal waves sweeping up from the deeps of the ocean of human events that may bring disaster, even death.

Before the onslaught of a tidal wave, the waters retreat to lowest ebb, while deep below the surface, far out from land, the same waters are gathering in oncoming strength.

In times of the water's retreat portents of disaster may haunt the spirit, or a dream like the following may break through into consciousness:

> The tide is out. I am walking on a seemingly endless strip of white sand, carrying in my hand a chalice? a casket? On one side is the withdrawing ocean, on the other an unscalable cliff. I see far out across the waters a great wave gathering in towering menacing force. It approaches with incredible swiftness. I throw myself upon the sand just as it is about to break over me. It encloses me in a cave of clear jade. Then there is utter unfathom-

able darkness. How long it lasts I do not know before the wave recedes, leaving me spent and treasureless. After a timeless interval I open my eyes. The waters are quiet, but there is a narrow opening in the cliff where the wave has broken through. Beyond this rocky passage is a meadow full of flowers. In its center is a green and leafy tree. Birds are flying in its branches.

This dream was incomprehensible to the dreamer until disaster struck and, like the tidal wave, carried away her treasure, the relationship without which she believed she could not live. The inner wave of despair threatened to sweep her from human realities into the vast uncharted sea. Its passing left her spent of all feeling. Yet some instinct, stronger than reason, stronger than faith, bade her cling close to the barren strip of earth that was left to her. She chose to follow the dream, even though its promise meant nothing in the first months of overwhelming darkness. Her life moved mechanically, almost lovelessly, in its round of duties, for love had been swept away and her heart was empty. Habitual acts of service had no inward regenerating power, for she had buried love in a sealed tomb. One night, in a dream, she found herself walking on a desolate road that stretched into a bleak land bereft of life, and a cry rose in her, "I must go back to life—I must go back!" She awoke. Almost unconsciously she said aloud, "I will accept and love whatever comes to me. I will honor love by loving." At that moment she made a choice between death and life.

A few days later she was awakened by the cry of a hurt animal. On her door step was a half-starved cat with blood dripping from its paw. As she cared for its wounds, compassion renewed itself within her heart. Strange that love should return in such a humble way, but she accepted it and, in the slow-moving months that followed, perceptions of the kinship of suffering brought her into new relatedness, even the contrasting relatedness of human joy.

Her earlier dream returned, and in active imagination she went through the narrow opening in the cliff and was in the meadow. Before her was the leafy tree like a green fountain rising from dark subsoil, rooted in earth, reaching toward heaven, a world of renewed life, where a bird, "like a green thought in a green shade," could find safe harbor. She thought of all that the tree meant: tree of life, tree of knowledge, tree of death, tree of renewal and transformation. She thought of its patience, its acceptance, its endurance of sun and

storm, of summer and winter. In that moment of perception, the rhythm of the earth and the rhythm of the sea were felt as one, and she knew the tide had turned and the waters were flowing back. Then, for an instant she *was* the tree. She felt the sap rising from root to farthest leaf bud. She accepted spring's renewal and life's return. Out of the bleak winter had come another, different spring. It was an irrational happening. So many things not logically belonging together were simultaneously alive and at one within her: the cry of the hurt animal and the universal cry of the human heart, the wound and the healing of the wound, the loss and the finding, the swift passing and the eternal continuity, the death of the personal and its renewal in a transpersonal form in which all the personal still lived and had new being. In that moment she knew that joy and sorrow can live together in the heart. Neither dies, but spirit unites them in a deep realization that love is dishonored when it is shut into the grave. It is honored when one gives back to life all that the experience of love has taught the inmost soul. The moment when she had been one with the tree she had known this continuity and renewal.

The tree rooted in the earth of human events, growing toward heaven, the world of spirit and transpersonal reality, is a symbol of the way of life, and of those balancing principles, above-below, ascent-descent, of harmonious communication between root and branch, which bring a sense of continuity and wholeness of being.

All these archetypal symbols flow into each other; woman is tree and earth, ebb and flow, light and darkness, within herself a balance of opposites, a continuity within change.

Woman is earth, and as earth she responds to the changes and transformations which, like the process of birth and rebirth, are not only symbols of the stages of life—the springtime of youth, the summer of maturity, the autumn of old age and the winter of death—but are seasonal returns of emergence, fulfillment, renunciation, waiting—of many rebirths within the same being. Each cycle adds to the strength of her being just as each year adds a new ring to the pattern growing within the concealment of the tree's bark.

The rhythm of time is also known to woman—the eternal cycles of cosmic time, the individual beat of mind time and heart time. Through the understanding of heart time, woman senses the moment when a relationship can come into being and "knows"—that is, inwardly experiences—the immediacy so that this moment, swifter in creation, longer in duration than years of ordinary time, does not pass

without bringing to birth the intended "child" who will fulfill the moment's purpose, a purpose that may go beyond her personal existence and find its fulfillment in other lives. Woman can learn to open her heart to these moments and to let them bring forth their purpose within her.

Heart time and mind time throb to a different beat, and the clock by which woman times her life ticks off minutes measured by the heartbeats of the emotions. She moves swiftly or waits patiently for the striking of the hour on this clock of heart time. Then she acts in accordance with the new that has come into being, even when it seems to contradict the old. Though this may seem to involve a change of purpose or direction, it is not evidence of instability or caprice but a response to a new note, a new motif which must be woven into the music of her life and thereafter have its place.

The duality of the feminine principle is deeply connected with time in its rhythm of darkness and of light and with its aspects of death or of healing. The time of darkening of the light of consciousness may be one of increasing power. Woman must know that both healing and destruction are contained within darkness as well as within light, for these dualities are the very essence of her being. She must learn when the light of consciousness will scorch and destroy or when it will quicken to life, and when the dark of the unconscious may lead toward death or toward transformation and renewal.

To be in harmony with the movement of life, woman must respect the intrusion of the immediate, however much it alters her predetermined plan or intrudes on the hour she has set apart for herself. Harmony and discord depend upon the ability to meet the changes of tempo that come as interruption and return. If she is vitally connected with the purpose of her life, detail may interrupt but does not distract, and when she has met the immediate demand she swiftly returns just where she was.

It is hard for woman to see the threads of immediacy as important when they require place in what she feels to be a larger pattern. The household tasks—dishes to be washed, clothes to be mended, errands to be run—seem to bind her to a treadmill of daily routine. Sometimes their importunity stirs only irritation, and she feels shut in by trivialities. If she uses them as an excuse for evading thought and becomes intent upon "getting things done," she falls prey to that most insidious disease, "detailitis," whose virus develops rapidly in the soil of frustration and barrenness. Details pile up around her,

shutting her into a smaller and smaller space. But when they are seen as part of the pattern that relates her life to others, the light of love made conscious—and only this—can rescue her from the darkness of shrinking walls.[24] The soul has windows from which it can look out on cosmic spaces, even when the hands are busy with daily tasks. Thoughts come and set the mind at peace. One can entertain the spirit even while washing dishes. Each meal can be a ritual of love, a place of communion and interchange of ideas, and can contribute to creative life by building strong bodies to sustain the energy of mind and heart. When woman's hands perform these seemingly endless tasks and her spirit is set free by love, she learns that "to labor is to pray," for prayer is openness to the creative spirit. This openness is itself a gift of grace which must be cultivated with devotion. Patience, tolerance, forbearance, forgiveness and an almost divine willingness to forget private wants when real need calls to her are attributes of the feminine principle, though often they are hard come by.

There are other importunities. A child's need must be met *now*, in this immediate moment. A child's question, seemingly irrelevant, must be answered by the understanding word that will enable hidden fear to come into the open and will entice an answer—just hovering on the brink of consciousness—to frame itself within the child. To meet such needs, not only must the hands pause but the thoughts must suffer interruption, and awareness spring to meet the child's shy emergence into a world of growing perception.

Perhaps the woman is caught in the details of a job or a career. As tired businesswoman she may be quite as much at the mercy of detail as is the household drudge. Yet she too must learn that her problem as woman is not only the task but the central purpose with which the task is imbued. If the "invisible sun" reveals the hidden motive, she may be delivered from ego ambition and petty intrigue and may release her feminine feeling so it can function in appreciation and generous co-operation. For the "invisible sun" can throw light upon

---

[24] The impelling motive is the guiding spirit and also the generator of energy. I remember spending a few days with an old friend whose husband, always generous, had become wealthy. One evening she said, "I cannot understand why I am always tired these days. Last winter when the two children had typhoid fever and it was impossible to get enough nurses, I had endless energy for day and night duty. Now at the end of the day I am always tired." I answered, "You have been very busy with innumerable details all day. Perhaps you saved a dollar and a half which no one wants you to save. I can imagine life energy welling up to save the life of a child, but not to save a dollar and a half."

all the frustrating interruptions, the innumerable demands, transforming them to fragments to be set into the mosaic of her daily life. She must also keep herself from being drained by demands that violate her and make her accept drudgery that is not rightfully hers. She must conserve her energy so it can function in her life as woman, both within and outside the hours demanded by her career.

In both office and home feminine consciousness must be able to move rhythmically among paradoxical demands and between objective and subjective worlds. Interruptions must be met by a spirit that has learned through moments of illumination that an integrated self can swiftly go out to meet the moment and as swiftly return to its own center, for center and circumference are one.[25]

It may be that when she is following the thread of purpose through the intricate maze of daily demand, it becomes gray as a cobweb in an empty room; but she must hold it fast until a silver light touches it and it gleams, trembles with the weight of a moonlit premonition, grays again in predawn loneliness till a sudden light falls upon it and she knows it as the golden thread of Eros, which, transformed by the alchemy of love, has led her back to the center where she finds herself as woman.

Through keeping fast to this golden thread, she learns that to live one's own life is fullness of being, for every experience, however small, has depth and transpersonal meaning if it is lived in the beauty of spirit that is so close to earth wisdom. Slowly she learns that there is no experience really her own that will not bring her to greater understanding of life, *if* she will serve with devotion the eros who comes in so many forms. Jung says:

In our absorbing everyday life there is . . . little room for obvious heroism. Not that the call to heroism does not reach us. On the contrary that is just the damnable and burdensome part of it, our banal daily life makes demands on our patience, our devotedness, endurance, self-sacrifice, and so on, which we must fulfill modestly and without any heroic gestures to court applause, and which actually need a heroism that is not seen from without. It does not shine and is not praised, and it seeks ever again the disguise of everyday apparel.[26]

Her daily life demands this heroism of woman.

She learns to love, to hold and to let go. She discovers that it is not

---

[25] In Sotoba's line, "I am there and I am back," the Zen idea of immediacy is illustrated.

[26] In Jacobi, C. G. Jung, *Psychological Reflections*, p. 189.

that which has lived and gone from her that she secretly mourns, but the unborn potential, the unlived experience, the demand of life that she refused. Yet, even when she feels drained by regrets, she must make peace with them if she would keep them from stopping up the wellsprings whose waters must again flow and once more give life to the seeds of her spirit.

When she allows regret to move into regressive channels—speculations on what might have been, endless turning of the wheel of futile wishes—she can no longer apply love or thought to present realities and to the potentials that they contain. What *now is* must become the starting point of what is to be. One must reappraise one's part in disaster, but to continue to look back upon past destruction when a way opens to the unknown future atrophies feeling, and the fate of Lot's wife, whose backward glance turned her into a pillar of salt, may be hers. Yet, with paradoxical demand of the unconscious, woman cannot choose to await her own time of readiness, for the moment may come upon her, the treasure be revealed without regard to her personal preparedness. She must seize upon it or lose it. Like the old childish rhyme, "Ready or not, you must be caught," life thrusts upon her the moment when she may seize the treasure of involvement.[27]

Life, in its feminine aspects of creative receptivity, always contains a potential of new birth. Nietzsche has said, "Everything about a woman is a riddle and everything about a woman has one solution. It is called pregnancy." The urge to give birth to a child is the instinctive urge of the feminine being, and its fulfillment is a completion of her nature. It is her gift of life, not only to the child but to the man whose seed she bears. The biological level belongs to one phase or period of woman's life, and can be misused by the woman who desires to remain too long on the instinctual plane. Faced with a difficult inner problem or a problem of relationship which must be met if a new spiritual attitude is to be brought forth, she finds it

---

[27] There is a legend of Brittany that once in a hundred years, at midnight on Christmas Eve, when the cattle kneel, the cromlechs—the monolithic stones—go down to the ocean to drink. Buried at their roots is the stone without price. He who dares seize it in that moment before their return becomes possessor of the treasure. It is the moment of peril, for the cromlechs have power of swift return and may bury the despoiler beneath their weight. Yet if the moment is not seized, it is gone beyond the span of human life, buried for another hundred years.

easier to have another baby. Becoming pregnant may be woman's way of trapping the man whose nature has presented difficulties that she is unready to face.

If she moves from this biological level into the realm of spirit, she enters a new phase of pregnancy. She can bear and nurture the new idea, the creative concept. She can bear children of man's spirit as well as of his loins. In each phase of her life woman learns the meaning of pregnancy and of the "bringing forth" of the child.

The I Ching says of these children of her spirit:

The sons represent movement, the beginnings of movement, danger in movement, rest and completion in movement. The daughters are devotion in its various stages, gentle penetration, clarity and adaptability, and joyous tranquility.[28]

These children are not blood kin, nor are they spiritually related to the children of impatience and restlessness perceived in the dream of a ten-year-old girl:

I am walking down Park Avenue. All the women are pushing baby carriages. I think, "How nice." But when I look into the carriages, all the babies are radios playing jazz.

If this is the music to which woman listens and this the child whom she brings forth, eros will not remain with her long. For this child is the fruit of her ego eroticism, her demand that she shall be entertained by life. She does not even listen to the voice of this child of boredom and meaninglessness. She just pushes it along because there is nothing else to do. This woman's casements open not upon the magic world of imagination, of music, of poetry, of love but upon the wasteland of scorned reality. The instinctual rhythm does not awaken even a primitive response; it merely accompanies her aimlessness. How far this inert pleasure is from the joyous tranquillity in which woman gives birth to the child of love and joy!

How many are the ways of bring forth and how diverse the children woman must nurture.

> For it is surely a lifetime work,
> This learning to be a woman.
> Until at the end what is clear

---

[28] After R. Wilhelm, Introd. to the I Ching, Vol. I, p. xxxi.

Is the marvelous skill to make
Life grow in all its forms.[29]

Pregnancy as impregnation by logos or by the moon spirit is an
inner conception in which the seeds of knowledge, of creative idea, of
spiritual insight are implanted. To carry these seeds means to accept
and assimilate them, to transform them and be transformed by them
so that they may be brought forth as children of insight and wisdom.
They need the secrecy, the time of growth in darkness if they are to
come forth. In pregnancy, woman gives herself completely to the unknown, unpredictable natural force that is producing new life within
her. She must wait, she must accept, she must fulfill; then she must
serve and direct that to which she has given birth. This is also true
when she is bearing a seed of knowledge, of insight or of spiritual
wisdom. She is impregnated with the seed of the word; she accepts
it; she lets it develop within her. She gives herself wholly to the task
of forming and realizing, of nurturing and transforming, in which her
whole being is involved. So she learns the secret ways of love and can
look with clear-eyed perception upon the reality of that which she has
brought forth, be it an inner child or one born of a human father.

In the feminine psyche the need of knowing never loses its vital
connection with the paramount need of loving. Yet without the
conscious awareness that knowing brings, woman cannot truly love,
for she, as well as man, must "know [her] goal and [be able] to do
what is necessary to achieve it."[30] Yet the goal and the way are not
those of masculinity, for the feminine urge to consciousness arises
from her basic need to understand and live out in actuality all the
values that relatedness may contain, and her goal is a more complete
wholeness which reunites on a higher and deeper level that which
has been separated by the keen blade of perception and differentiation. This urge seeks to unite not only the fragmentary parts that have
become alienated by the struggles of two separate egos, but also to
bridge the chasm between conscious and unconscious so that the living springs of the unconscious may be released in their creative power
in herself and in the person with whom she is connected by the binding ties of love. The way is a road of mystery, and the perils of the
way often are not understood until they have been met and over-

---

[29] May Sarton, "My Sisters, O My Sisters," in *The Lion and the Rose*, p. 60.
[30] Jung, *Contributions to Analytical Psychology*, pp. 179–180.

come not only in those moments of dramatic climax of clashing opposites but in the even more heroic encounter of daily living which demands the true devotion of a deeply lived inner experience. This is the "secret that's never been told." "The Tao that is talked about is not the true Tao," and the way is the winding path of the serpent that comes continually upon the unexpected.

This way is a journey into the heart, and the heart, faced with its own complexities, asks, "Who are you? Who am I? What is the force that binds us together?"

Descending into her own heart in order to ascend unto the god, woman may find a creature who is caught in a dark web of desirousness, compulsive passion, fiery emotion and the tangled threads of unconscious love and hate. When woman is caught in this dark web of fate, she is indeed enslaved, her creative receptivity transformed into sensuous passivity and her consciousness devoured by the one who comes to her only in the "dark paradise"[31] of blind "inloveness." Truly "Eros is a mighty daemon," one who must be feared as well as loved. And yet again we find the paradox: If she seeks to evade the experience or to cut her way ruthlessly out of the entanglement and free herself by denial of her own feminine involvement, she may lose the chance to fulfill her destiny as woman. Only through understanding the nature of this experience in which both are caught can she find a way of disentangling the threads which bind them together in darkness, thus setting them free to face the reality of each other. Then the gates of the "dark paradise" are closed to her, and before her lies the mystery road of love whose goal is reunion with the beloved in a relationship in which they both accept the working out of a common destiny.

The first agent of liberation may be doubt—doubt of herself, doubt of the experience, doubt of the object who has been clothed in the image of the god. This doubt asks the fatal question, "Who are you?"

With this question she turns the light of conscious perception upon the object of her love and sees the man in his human reality—not, perhaps, as he wishes to be seen, nor as she has wished to see him. The old illusion is gone. A new reality may take its place if now she has courage to face what the light reveals.

---

[31] A term used by Neumann in his perceptive and masterly interpretation of the myth, *Amor and Psyche*.

Individual love dares this experience as an act of higher conscious-ness. Its light dispels the projection and reveals both the shadow and the light, the beast and the spirit, the cleavage and the wholeness. Now only love can save them, for love is the thread that binds nature and spirit together; and the love of woman claims the whole man, not just his masculine strength. Yet, this claim is not to possess but to set free, and in this freedom to achieve a conscious relation strong enough not only to sustain the inevitable difficulties and daily fric-tions of life, but also to meet the variable undercurrents of their un-conscious relationship which now must be understood between them. When consciousness reveals behind the image the man in all his human frailty, it may rouse in him a masculine desire to escape lest he be burdened with a conscious and responsible relationship to one who has heretofore accepted his own image of himself. If woman fears to face the truth of what she has seen and retreats to the old il-lusion, she may serve only the shadow, the selfishness, egotism, un-related sexual demand, or the anima in her form of petulant, power-loving child who has no desire for the transforming power of love lest it awaken and demand devotion. If in this light of consciousness she sees the god slumbering within the man, the light awakens real love within her heart and she knows that she must make herself worthy of this god. Only through her own awakening can she hope to find the god in him. Only by becoming woman can she find him as both man and spirit. For this she may have to wound in order to awaken, to risk the loss of the beloved rather than lose the truth of love itself. This may mean choice of a lonely way, for the journey into the self is a solitary one. But its aloneness is not the loneliness of an isolated ego, for the meaning of the search is ever present, and each step brings her nearer to a knowledge of love.

For this achievement woman must fall in love with love itself; only so can she know eros as an inner god in whose service her true self is made manifest. Only so can she receive and fulfill the purposes of love. Only so can her receptivity become truly creative and her noth-ingness become filled by the creative springs of the unconscious.

Again and yet again fullness returns to nothingness in order that it may be filled. Creation means to be created, being filled means to pour forth, to empty oneself in order to receive. Without this pouring forth the waters of the being become stagnant; without the influx

from the living fountain the soul becomes barren. Giving, pouring forth, emptying; accepting, receiving, being filled; waiting, awaiting, nurturing; created, creating, bringing forth—this is the spiral on which the feminine spirit ascends. And this feminine spirit seeks its life in every creative man as well as in woman.

CHAPTER 13

The Man in Woman

৩৪ ৪৯

The animus is a psychopomp, a mediator between the conscious and the unconscious.[1]

Even as creative man comes to know and revere the revelations of the anima who, as soul, liberates for him the creative springs of the unconscious, so woman, on her journey toward wholeness, must understand and value the inner man, the animus, who brings new levels of consciousness and interprets and defines meaning in her life.

As an inner personality, the animus is a composite of inborn masculine potentials, the innate image of man latent in the feminine psyche and the imprint of her early experiences of man—father, brother, friend, lover. His role is compensatory to that of the conscious attitude, but since his activities often disturb outer adaptation, awareness of them may be repressed from consciousness. As mind, he connects her with thought and willed purpose; as spiritual guide, he leads her into the unconscious and connects her in an increasingly meaningful way with the creative images. He is not only an entity but an inner process of development. In his negative form he destroys her power to love and sterilizes her thinking. As bringer of light, he connects her with the transforming forces of the unconscious through which she is herself transformed. His function changes with the process of her inner development.

"Man means mind to woman." But when woman has not achieved

---

[1] Jung, *Aion*, p. 16.

a conscious relation to the masculine principle as it moves within her, she frequently is at the mercy of what Jung has called the "natural mind of woman." This natural mind is far different from the logos mind—word, spirit; it is a purposive directive force that knows and makes use of the instinctive wisdom of Mother Eve and of Lilith. It speaks the creative or devastating word through an uncanny perception of what is happening, or may be made to happen, in the unconscious of another. It is subtly aware of what is coming into being in a situation or of what may be enticed into being and, through an irrational or apparently irrelevant word, can arouse emotional confusion and inject doubt and distrust into a human situation. Or it may cut across all logical argument with an unrelated, emotionally shattering statement that nevertheless produces the desired result. The play *Life with Father* illustrates the power of this feminine approach. Father is struggling to make Mother face the alarming discrepancies that her expenditures have produced in the family budget. He has all the reasonable arguments, all the damning facts. "But then you do not *love* me," wails Mother; and Father, in bewildered defeat, finds himself placating this lovely fragile creature whom he has, with clumsy masculinity, mysteriously wronged.

This natural mind may be "wise as a serpent" but that by no means guarantees that it will be "harmless as a dove," though it assumes a dovelike demeanor when it asks the apparently innocent question that poisons the creative idea just coming into being. A child or friend or "loved" one develops an unexpected interest or discovers a latent talent which the woman fears will destroy the ambitions that she has placed upon him "for his own good." With disarming appearance of childlike interest she asks, "Do you really think all this *means* anything?" "Does it?" the one questioned asks himself, and he may find he is caught in a morass of doubt. The greater the emotional tie between him and the inquisitor, the greater the confusion wrought by the question. Or woman may use the piercing deadly weapon of false praise. "That is really very well done—for a child"; or "On the whole it shows possibilities—for an amateur." By either of these methods the creative impulse can be aborted.

If woman's goal is power, she will be quick to see the weakness, the fault, and she will have swift intuition of how to make use of her perception in order to have her own way without apparently demanding it. If, on the other hand, she is oriented by love of life and gener-

osity of spirit, she instinctively speaks the word that awakens life in others. Such phrases as, "to create an atmosphere," "to create harmony," "to create a situation," mean, literally, *to create*. Such people bring to life in others dormant forces that have awaited the magic touch of intuitive perception. They are midwives of the spirit. They love life and are related to the outer happening and the inner movement. Their instinctive connection with the animus as inquiring mind makes them ask the question that awakens awareness of hitherto unperceived meaning. Woman must learn to understand her natural mind and to take responsibility for the effect it produces. Redeemed by the directive power of clear thought and consciously accepted purpose, the feminine mind still retains its instinctive wisdom. Conscious and unconscious mind are not at war but act in creative interplay, and the word that speaks itself through her is in the service of life.

As mind in its quickening power, the animus is the principle of conscious knowledge that brings order out of the chaos of undifferentiated emotions, irrational impulses and purely instinctive reactions. Intuitions which are often only impulses toward thought, must be disciplined into clear differentiated thinking if woman is to meet the problems that confront her in the modern world. The development of her logos mind enables her to think independently, to choose consciously and to work with integrity for the goal she has chosen.

When once this has been learned it is so obvious that it is never forgotten without a tremendous psychic loss. The independence and critical judgment gained by this knowledge are positive values and are felt as such by the woman. Hence she can never part with them again.[2]

Clarity of thought is necessary to woman. The muddleheaded woman does not even muddle through; she bogs down. It is only when thought, divorced from feeling, becomes intent on proving its own superiority that thinking destroys the free flow of life because it arouses antagonisms which prevent the impersonal exchange of ideas through which new concepts are awakened. When applied to questions of feeling and relatedness, thinking not only separates and discriminates, it illuminates the fundamental areas of need and possibility. Through perception of inherent differences and also of essential

---

[2] Jung, *Contributions to Analytical Psychology*, Harcourt, Brace edition, p. 180.

human likenesses, it clarifies areas of otherness as well as of to-getherness.

It would be as absurd to say that logos thinking has no part in woman's life as that man is incapable of feeling and love. A woman must be able, when confronted by a problem of the intellect, to think as clearly, as impersonally, as a man. Perhaps the most difficult task is to train herself to concentrate on the demands of her impersonal or professional interests during the hours when her heart is involved in emotional problems. Yet this discipline is necessary if the inner man is to mean mind to her in those situations that demand clear thinking. For there is the human pact which forbids our letting down any contract that we have made with life. What we have promised, that we must fulfill to the utmost of our ability, be it in relationship, in profession or in a mundane job by which we earn our daily bread. This, after all, is one of those paradoxical situations where eros and logos seem to contradict each other, yet really meet on levels above and below the immediate situation.

It is through innate knowledge of this paradox that woman can think like a man and yet, at the same time, *not* think like a man. Thinking may be her superior function. It may be natural for her to use it objectively and impersonally. But no matter what her type or superior function, she must train her mind if she is to have part in a world in which she is called upon to enter into the realm of ideas and impersonal interests. Whether her superior function is thinking or feeling, intuition or sensation, her education in this modern world is, unfortunately, often geared to suit the man's world into which she is so frequently pushed, willy-nilly. From kindergarten to college the curriculum is often a hand-me-down, patterned on what was formerly considered the proper training for the masculine intellect only. In this world the young woman finds herself competing with man and measuring herself by masculine standards. This training has pitfalls and may deliver woman over to an arrogance of thinking that can separate her from her life of feeling. Many a woman has gotten the best of an argument only to find to her dismay that she has gotten the worst of a relationship. The negative animus often regards as annoying intrusion the very situation out of which the woman could create a revealing and transforming experience which would far outweigh any intellectual achievement, for the animus as intellect divorced from feeling does not know Eros, the god who gives woman

"grace to meet the moment." When woman retains her central attitude as woman, her thinking is used in the service, not in the domination, of feeling. It is then that she learns the meaning of thought in the interplay of the opposites—the masculine and feminine principles within her own psyche. Modern woman, intent on self-realization, often has no notion of what the self really is and therefore falls into the trap of ego realization which cuts her off from her life of feeling and from the flow of images from the unconscious.

Jung says, "The intellect has indubitable usefulness in its own field but it is a great cheat and shaper of illusions outside of it, namely when it seeks to manipulate values." Then its light is that of an *ignis fatuus*, a will-o'-the-wisp, that leads woman into a bog of confused theories about the intellectual and spiritual life. This happened to a young woman who, at college, became infected with the concept of herself as a spiritual leader. Through her animus projections upon a brilliant professor and an eloquent cleric, both of whom admired her mind, she came to believe that the words she echoed were her own invention. Since she could repeat them—even rephrase them—convincingly, she became a welcome platform speaker in college groups. This led to a position as lecturer and seminar leader in women's colleges. Her dishonest mind told her that she had to choose between personal and impersonal relatedness since, quite obviously, she had no time for both. She was greatly in demand; her increased activities and the acclaim that they brought her testified, she was convinced, to the rightness of her choice and to her own superior powers as bearer of spiritual light. Caught by the effectiveness of her own arguments, she was often ruthless in driving home a point and scornful of her less intellectual opponents. Her impatience (for her time was limited) with stupidity or ignorance made her quite unmindful of the wounds she inflicted. Or perhaps one of her less intelligent sisters would fling a too-intelligent criticism into the discussion and she would find herself embroiled in an animus battle where, for truth's sake, her animus had to win, no matter what happened to the adversary. She was riding high, wide and handsome on a golden cloud of spiritual illusions when this dream intruded.

I am back home on the farm. I see the postman coming and I go down to the box at the foot of our road. It is full of mail—all for me, except one letter to my sister. I feel very superior, and a

little pitying at the meagerness of her portion. Then I see that all my mail is second class, but my sister's is a letter—a love letter—from the young man to whom she is engaged.

On waking, she found herself strangely disturbed. *She wanted that letter*. Platform words that she had so glibly used to illustrate the meaning of the spiritual life came back to her. "One thing is needful." How often she had quoted these words in her exhortation on the spiritual life—the impersonal life of godly works. "Martha, Martha, thou art careful and troubled about many things." She was careful; she was troubled; also she was very, very busy. Could this activity be second class? Could one be a Martha in the house of the spirit? "Mary hath chosen the good part." Today the words had a different import.

"Though I speak with the tongues of men and of angels, and have not charity"—*caritas*, love—but this was surely spiritual love, *agape*, not earthly love. A sudden stab of jealousy surprised her, for she had always looked down on her sister, the comings and goings of her sister's friends, and her evenings with her lover. Surely this was not "the good part." This was not the true light—and yet. . . . The question had awakened strange discontents. Could it be that spiritual love was grounded on earthly love? The dream in its directness and simplicity cast a new and different light upon shadowy processes in her own unconscious and drove her to seek help. Other dreams showed not only the poverty of her life as woman but also her own repressed feminine hunger for a woman's life of human relatedness, her thwarted capacity as woman. She saw the wounds that her assumption of superiority inflicted upon the very people whom she was instructing in the way of spiritual love. She saw the "unloveness" of arrogance and she came to know that "before the voice can speak in the presence of the gods, it must have lost its power to wound." It will not lose the power to wound except through clear eros thinking.

Further dreams showed that it was not her profession that was second rate but the way that she had allowed her false concept of spirit to dominate it. The postman—the simple everyday animus—had brought the message that revealed her poverty as a woman, namely, that the "cheat and shaper of illusions" had robbed her of her treasure, the power to love and to receive love—the love letter. She envied her sister that letter: this she admitted, though pride wished to deny

it. Her sister's fiancé had not a brilliant mind, nor was he versed in high spiritual concepts. He was warm, sympathetic, alive to personal needs. This then was what she envied her sister. This she not only must develop in herself but must value in others. In the end she found in her postbox a letter that was not second class mail.

If woman chooses, or is chosen by, a business or professional life, "the invisible sun" that lights her thinking must still be love. Her thinking must be clear, cool, purposeful, disciplined by long and arduous devotion to the tasks demanded. She cannot substitute emotion for reason and knowledge. She cannot act out of undisciplined good intentions, nor from intuitive perceptions based on momentary feelings; she must learn not only the disciplines of love but also the disciplines of thought so that her feeling may be based on clear perception of values.

A woman physician, whose vocational life had been dedicated to scientific research on occupational hazards, was asked how she could, when fighting for the passage of a better labor law, face fifty or more antagonistic men and hold clearly and decisively to her point without arousing those negative undercurrents that the animus never fails to awaken in the masculine psyche. She said, "I keep before my inner vision a scene I once witnessed—a thin tired bewildered child sitting with loving patience beside a father who was dying of lead poisoning. Then I remember the meaning of my research in terms of human life." Holding to her feminine center, she spoke as woman to these men. Her arguments were clear; the ground on which she stood was solid, for she knew, not only scientifically but factually and humanly, every phase of her subject. Her appeal was to their fair-mindedness and to their mutual search for truth. She gave rather than demanded. Had she met this male audience with only the strength of her well-trained mind or with a determination to outargue them she would have aroused only their animosity. Had she failed in her loyalty to scientific truth gained by years of devoted discipline and study, her love would have appeared as sentimentality and would have roused their contempt. She knew to the uttermost detail the importance and applicability of what she said. (Also her smile was very gracious, her eyes were very blue and instinctively she chose hats that matched her eyes!) She knew the meaning of transpersonal love and how knowledge could serve love. In the critical moment, the vision of the child brought together the clear cold logic of her logos thinking and

the eros thinking of her heart. In this way the child image, though invisible to the listeners, moved in their unconscious and worked its own magic of receptivity so that their minds were open to a consideration of her argument.

When the woman who has never submitted to discipline of mind or clarification of meaning becomes identified with the animus as word, she may feel herself called upon to save a benighted masculine world. Mrs. Moffatt, headmistress of a "finishing" school, lived complacently in this type of identification. Her noble attempts at world betterment are described by the secretary to whom her letters were dictated:

We might, and did, write to President Wilson to tell him of our Presbyterianism and to rejoice in his; or to Mr. John Galsworthy to tell him that the school had greatly profited by certain of his sketches; or to a prominent soap company to say that, much as we liked most of their products, we detected a certain vulgar scent in a certain soap and deplored its manufacture as below their standard of excellence. We wrote to statesmen, mayors, clergymen, and rabbis; financiers, actors, college presidents, and physicians; columnists, cartoonists, and wardens of prisons. We wrote to Mr. A. E. Housman to thank him for his poem on the cherry tree and to tell him that we recited this poem in chorus every spring. We wrote to Mr. H. G. Wells to take exception to certain of his educational ideas and to put certain pertinent questions to him. When Mr. Wells had neglected for some months to answer our letter, we wrote to him again. We wrote to Mr. Thomas Hardy to suggest a somewhat brighter point of view toward the universe, reminding him that, in our opinion, one held one's fate in one's own strong hands, and acknowledging that we should like his characters immeasurably better if they had more spirit in them to struggle on. Mrs. Alice Meynell, whose poems were in those days attracting attention, received word from us that, although we could not follow her religious thinking, we were grateful to her for her poem on thoughts as flocks of sheep, since we could use it in our character-building school. Our letters were thus admonitory, appreciative, advisory, as occasion demanded.[3]

This sublime ignorance of the real nature of her animus made Mrs. Moffatt unaware of how he interfered with her vision as a woman. She recognized only what she chose to recognize. This did not in-

[3] Mary Ellen Chase, A Goodly Fellowship, pp. 138–139.

clude "rats on the third floor in spite of our voluble terror of them," nor that "certain of her girls were mentally unable to pass college examinations," and that "other schools in Chicago were in every respect better than her own." Sitting contentedly in her armchair, with blinders carefully adjusted by the negative animus, she looked out upon a vision of a world she had constructed.

In both these women, physician and headmistress, the masculine and feminine principles had achieved an inner relationship. Mrs. Moffatt had not the faintest idea of what the inner man looked like nor how he appeared to others. So far as she was concerned he was nonexistent. Nevertheless he had achieved a secret marriage with her shadow, and the brats that he begot were self-complacency, egotistical opinions and ignorance of feeling values. In the physician he worked in the light. He showed her the relation between knowledge and transpersonal love and how the one served the other.

So long as the shadow seeks him out, the animus remains the invisible magician who can cleverly confuse good and evil, can make self-righteousness assume the form of righteousness and prejudice appear wisdom's self. He also tells the woman that nothing is needed but good intentions, even when she is complacently using them to pave the road to hell. If the woman is fortunate enough to be jarred out of this complacent relationship by some disaster that brings her face to face with her own failure, it may be that she will examine the creature within herself who has brought it about. This act of consciousness will bring the animus into visibility. She can then perceive his duality—light of conscious perception and shadow of chosen ignorance. "Ask and ye shall receive." If her shadow asks the gift of will to power that moves in ignorance, the gift will be given. If love asks power to will, to accept the discipline and to seek out the true form of the logos so that at each crossroad of choice she may see more clearly the destined way, that gift will be given. Yet the road on which she travels may be long and difficult before, through the white magic of love made conscious, the Magician becomes the Helper, the Guide.

When woman fails in the task of relatedness to the masculine principle within herself, she frequently looks for a man to live it out for her. The type of man she chooses depends in great measure upon the stage of development that she has herself reached and upon the archetypal image of authority constellated by early experiences.

It is natural for the adolescent or the young woman just emerging

into womanhood to project the animus upon a man of physical prowess. Any male who embodies physical strength or beauty can awaken instinctual forces deeper than thought or feeling which, since the nature of her sexuality is still unknown to her, she interprets as a divine fire kindled by the hero.[4]

Mere brute strength can arouse such responses not only in a young girl but in the woman who has lived too much above her instincts so that their primitive, even barbaric, elements have been covered over with layer upon layer of cultural veneer. A woman in pursuit of culture took a vacation from her "mundane marriage." She went to a city where she could attend lectures and frequent art galleries and concerts. But here, on the quest of "the higher life," she chanced to attract and be attracted by a stalwart young brute, a handyman in the house where she had taken an apartment for solitary meditation between the hours devoted to pursuit of culture. Unable to face as her own the emotional turmoil that he aroused in her, she projected all the qualities of the hero upon him and entered into what she euphemistically called an affair with him. When through bitter experience her eyes were opened to the reality of the man and the part that her own instincts had played, she discovered the disturbing fact that this experience had awakened her own sexuality. She could no longer treat intercourse as a marital necessity demanded by the animal in man. Sexuality was part of herself. With courageous acceptance of the part that her own instincts had played in the experience, she faced the full implication of her act. She acknowledged it to herself and to her husband. His unexpected understanding revealed deeply human qualities, unperceived while her image of her own superiority had clothed him in the garment of a prosaic businessman, a good provider. With newborn humility, she saw what her former barren attitude had done to her marriage and to herself as woman. She accepted the strange unacceptable way in which the awakening had come to her as an act of grace beyond her understanding. Through it, what might have proved a fatal choice brought her, after many struggles, into a new relation to the instinctual

---

[4] Naïve remarks give glimpses into the youthful feminine psyche. A young woman gazing dreamily at the lifesaver on the beach remarks, "But I do like a hairy man." Even more in point is a conversation between two young college women coming away from a lecture on philosophy. "Wasn't he simply *wonderful?*" "Y-e-s . . . but I didn't understand a word he said." "Neither did I, but he is such a big strong he-man."

woman in herself, to the animus and to her husband. She saw that fate had been kind.

The traits of the physical hero exist in woman as well as in man. In their positive form they endow her with strength, courage, energy. In their negative aspects they manifest themselves as ruthlessness, brutal disregard of others or primitive masculinity that invades instinctive life so that sexuality becomes divorced from feeling and functions with masculine aggressiveness or even with license, though in her heart, which she rarely consults, she knows that there is nothing so cold as loveless sexuality. For the truly feminine woman, sexuality is not a momentary experience, however ecstatic the moment may be, but an expression of love that seeks a personal relationship whose goal is a permanent and responsible union. If she violates this, she never discovers the meaning of sexuality as a transpersonal force uniting two human creatures in a way that leads to the development and fulfillment of each.

The man of simple deeds—a carpenter, builder, tiller of the soil—often carries the image of masculinity for the woman who has got too far away from her own instinctive roots. Such a man has a connection with earth and nature which the woman who lives in her head sorely needs. If she can make conscious these needs and accept with understanding love the gift he brings her, the relation can free her from snobbish or arrogant ambitions and bring her into contact with a side of herself that her intellect would never have chosen had she followed the dictates of her rational mind. Also, the woman deeply rooted in her earthiness may find rest and content in the life she shares with such a man. In that case it is not a projection but a true relation based upon a mutuality of nature and interest.

The woman of worldly ambitions may find her hero in the man who has accomplished deeds of significance and has attained power in the world. If her hidden motive is ambition and she succeeds in acquiring him, she may live in complacent identification with his achievements. Her husband's position is her position; his accomplishments are hers. One such woman said to me, "I feel so exhilarated, we have just been made vice-president of the business." Another woman dreamed:

I am riding in a high coach far above a crowd of women who look up at me with envy. My husband is by my side. I realize,

with pitying condescension, that all these women below me are only spinsters. No wonder they look up to me.

Such a woman, having achieved her purpose, is relieved of all the responsibilities of making a conscious relationship with the inner man who could arouse impulses toward individual action, or with the husband whom she has annexed as an exploitable possession.

When the authority image is placed upon the man of intellectual attainment or spiritual leadership—teacher, philosopher, priest—woman may appropriate the words and the husks of thought without letting the seed, the spirit contained within the word, enter and be born within her. For woman is fascinated by words—especially long abstruse words—and even the incantations of pseudospirituality can rouse her to enthusiasm and fill her with echoes of concepts that she re-echoes so often that she comes to believe they are her own. Thereby her ego is inflated but not nourished.

It is this fascination with words that gives the oratorical animus—intellectual or spiritual leader, quack or charlatan—such hypnotic power for good or evil over the woman. As an inner factor he is often manifest as a voice that utters infallible pronouncements. The voice, the word, is symbol of the masculine principle of creative energy; "the hearing ear" is symbol of feminine receptivity. When woman is under the fascination of the rhetorical animus, she has no power of discrimination in regard to the word that her ear receives. Any word spoken with the voice of authority can have dominion over her. This word then becomes crystallized in an opinion or an impregnable conviction which she applies indiscriminately to any human situation or to any new concept that seeks its own expression. She has a handy platitude to solve every crisis, an opinionated word that can act as a snuffer to any small flame of original thought.

Even when the animus projection is placed on a man of true power who intrigues her mind and quickens her thoughts, her worship of intellect may prevent her feeling from being touched. She will then use any contact with the man as means of pursuing intellectual and philosophical speculations about a human experience or a dream instead of letting the eros meaning penetrate her heart and spirit. Through such speculations she succeeds in separating herself from the emotion which might connect the experience with her personal problem as woman.

A brilliant intellectual woman, who used her mind to dispel the emotional message of her dreams, arrived at her analytical hour full of absorbingly interesting dream associations culled from many abstruse sources. Having experienced many such hours, Dr. Jung put out his large warm hand and smilingly asked, "Well, and what have we brought today, some more opinionated opinions of opinions not our own?" She burst into tears. "Good," he said as he put his hand on her shoulder. "Now we can begin together." Tears melted the ice that had frozen her feeling, for his act of human understanding had released the pent-up emotion that could now find an outlet in a new form of transference in which she did not fear to bring her neglected, hence inferior, feeling into the analysis. Through this, he released her from "the cheat and shaper of illusions," and her analysis became an emotional and spiritual experience. Until woman has a knowledge of her relation to the inner man who comes to her with a demand for consciousness and for mental and spiritual activity, the psychic energy which should be devoted to the development of her masculine potentials flows back into the unconscious and there activates the shadow side of her masculinity. Usurping this submerged energy, the animus may develop autonomous power so that he can decide the choices of her ego and even dominate her personality. A medicine man would say to such an animus-ridden creature, "Woman, you are possessed by the ghost of a man."

It may indeed be a ghost, for, though the original object of her projection may long since have died, his voice may still make pronouncements whose validity has never been tested in relation to special situations or been reappraised by conscious thought. Swallowed whole as absolute truths, they reappear as impregnable convictions or arrogant generalizations. Since she knows the truth, she is saved the trouble of finding it out. Instead, she is called upon to enforce it in the lives of other people. Such pronouncements call up every negative feeling in the man at whom the spurious thinking is directed. But it is not only man who is drawn into the battle; animus often answers animus in an argument between two women. Like calls to like; a wolf howl is answered not by a wood thrush but by a wolf, a ghost call by a ghost who answers from a dead past.

"If you die when God tells you, he takes you and cleans away all your ghosts." Release from this ghostly authority may be a long process of death of old convictions and birth of new concepts—birth

of the image of love through awakened understanding of the father image as creator of light and consciousness.

A woman had been rejected by her father because she was a daughter instead of the much desired son. "Only a girl," he had exclaimed at her birth and had turned from her. This she did not know until years afterward, and throughout her childhood she could find no reason for his repudiation of her except some unworthiness in herself.

Unfortunately, she was fascinated by him. He was a man of great charm—something of a Don Juan. A tenor voice, a facility in sketching and ability as a raconteur made him mysteriously attractive to the female sex, especially to the child who hovered on the outskirts of his attention. Occasionally she amused him by her feminine reactions, her enthusiasms and even her small coquetries, for she was very much a girl child. But his was only a momentary glimmer of attention, and he brushed aside any attempts that she made to interest him in her childish thoughts or her small ambitions. Usually he was unaware of her.

When she was hardly more than a child he died, and with death he passed into a world of silence, for his name was rarely spoken. In this silence he ceased to exist as a real personality, but in her unconscious he lived on as a governing image. Occasional overheard family conversations brought back memories of times when she had seen her mother draw back into remoteness and silence had been filled with strange hostility. Pitying comments of solicitous relatives about her mother's patience with his qualities that were "after all, so like a man," aroused in her intuitive fears of men, but did not destroy the image of the god who had rejected her. Even when, from the same family source, she overheard how he had greeted her birth, it only added to her confused picture of herself.

Then the relation to her mother, which reinforced her femininity but did not change her inner attitude toward masculinity, restored her sense of being loved, accepted and admired for being so essentially a girl child. As she grew older, this feminine self attracted and was attracted by men, yet when a particular man came too near, she retreated to the safety of promising "all things to all men" without committing herself to any one man. This seemed to work well until a man who possessed the charm and fascination of her father, as well as his undependability, fell passionately in love with her. Swept away

by his ardor, she had no awareness that his likeness to her father challenged her to wipe out the former experience of rejection. There was a period of paradise; then the enchantment broke. He betrayed both himself and her. But instead of seeing him in his destructive reality, the bewildered sense of repudiation present in her childhood returned. After he left her, she went back to life and succeeded in hiding the seriousness of the wound not only from other people but even from herself. Perhaps if her mother had still been alive, the wound might have been detected and she would not have been able to cover it over with interests and activities. She made "a marvelous adjustment," as her friends told her, but if anyone came too near, she retreated to her tower of safety and drew up the drawbridge. Yet, since she smiled down upon the would-be intruder, she felt his defeated withdrawal was another evidence that life was against her and her isolation was forced upon her by people and circumstance.

Problems entirely connected, she thought, with her job made her decide to ask analytical advice. But the unconscious took no heed of her professional quest. Dreams dealt with inner realities in a way that startled her out of her precarious security.

I am in a room with many doors but no windows. I know I have been here through a long winter. I yearn for sunlight and the sound of human voices. I start toward one of the doors, but a dark powerful man holding a key in his hands steps in front of me and turns the key in the lock. I go to another door; again he is there before me. At each door he blocks me. As we reach the last, I know something in me, unknown but compelling, is willing him to lock this last door. I hear the dull click as the key turns itself. I am imprisoned with my jailer. He has grown immensely tall, sinister and powerful. A strange drugged sense of peace comes upon me. There is now nothing I can do but surrender completely to whatever he may will. He comes toward me; something deeper than acquiescent despair awakens. It cries out for life, for deliverance. As if in answer, I hear a high clear note of music and a shaft of light pierces through the ceiling. Its radiance is blinding. It terrifies me: behind me is merciful darkness. Yet something within me chooses and, trembling, I step into the light. As though seized by the radiance, I am drawn upward out of my prison upon this pathway of light and sound and find my feet are upon the earth. The walls are gone. An open road lies before me. It winds up a hill and disappears into a forest.

The mystery of the dream was upon her when she woke. She turned toward the morning light as it streamed in her window, but again the windowless room enclosed her and the creature who had willed the turning of the key stirred within her. Deliverance was only a dream! There was too much against her. But dreams do not lie. If a creature in herself had willed her imprisonment, that creature must be faced. But this was not what the dream said. It had told her to call upon a power greater than the imprisoning darkness, and the unknown power had answered her wordless cry with the shaft of light and music that, falling from the heaven above, entered not through door or window but by cleaving the ceiling, making a pathway of release where no pathway was possible. She remembered the moment of agony when she had longed for deliverance from the light and from the freedom and the demand it offered. She could step back into the nondemanding darkness. In that midnight hour of her extremity, the choice was hers.

In the dream she had chosen the light and, with this choice, had been drawn *upward onto the earth*. Again the paradox: heaven above, heaven below: earth below, earth above. She had been drawn by heaven upward to earth so that in her own life she might find the light of truth and the music of love and, through living, find herself as woman. The winding road was before her; it led into a forest—into the pathless, the unknown, the place where fate comes to meet one. She must now affirm her choice, trusting the light.

She felt confident that coming dreams would, as messengers of light, show her the new way. Strange how the unconscious speaks! With complete independence of our conscious demand, it chooses its own symbols and brings its own message. This was the dream that came to her:

I am on a wet dreary road where long grasses entangle my feet. A man—is it B?—is with me.[5] Night closes in. We reach a lonely house and can go no further. We enter a dim bare kitchen where an old woman is seated in a rocker. A shadowy man moves about in the background. There is something strange, outworn, sinister in the place. The woman says, "I will make noodles for supper. Yes, that is what I will do. I will make noodles. Kitty shall have one too. Look at kitty—everyone loves her." In a

---

[5] A wealthy, shrewd, yet dull man who was at this time attentive to her. She enjoyed what he gave her and he found her amusing.

small crib is a kitten with a strange wizened look. She has on dolls' clothes and a nursing bottle lies on her breast. Her legs have straightened out like human arms and legs, but her hands and feet are paws. She lies stretched out straight, as a child might. The woman says, "You don't like our kitty. She is thirty-nine years old. Everyone loves kitty. She is so good. She has never tried to climb out of the crib." I see the shadowy man glance toward her. I think, "He has done this to her." I am repelled—yet feel compelled to pick her up. I must take her from this place. I feel horribly responsible for her. The atmosphere in the room is poisonous, full of a strange unreality. The woman and the shadowy man watch me silently but malevolently. I go out into the night.

She woke; Kitty—a miniature monstrosity—was still in her arms. She heard the woman's voice: "She is thirty-nine years old." That was her own age. "She is so good." She herself was good—good and terribly wronged—at least so people had told her, and so she had believed. "She has never tried to climb out of the crib." She felt the crib like an iron cage about her. She hardly knew whether she was kitty or whether kitty was her burden. She saw the shadowy man watching skeptically as she lifted kitty from the crib. She remembered the skeptical expression on her father's face when, carried away by enthusiasm, she had told him of some magnificent childhood plan.

A flood of self-pity overwhelmed her. This was what life had done to her. *She was kitty*—imprisoned in the crib. It was her father's fault. "She has never tried to climb out." Was she trying even now when, for so many years, her father had been gone even from conscious memory? Words of the analyst came back. "If one's failures are projected upon the parents, one is still in the nursery, a child refusing to grow up, refusing to listen to the voice of the self." She remembered voices that she had disregarded. Could they have been voices of the self? They had tried to show her realities that she did not want to face. The sinister man, father of kitty, her own father, the man whom she had married—all seemed to regard her with the same skeptical expression as she lifted kitty from the crib. Kitten! In moments of affection her lover had used this name and she had felt young, childlike, innocent, accepted. Had her feeling tried to remain on the kitten level till it had atrophied into this inhuman thing? Had she played this kitten role with B? was this why he had

vanished when she was brought face to face with the monstrous reality of kitty?

For days the dream haunted her. Then, again she chose. If kitty was herself, then she must carry the burden of herself into the forest of the unknown. One morning in active imagination she again stepped into the night with kitty in her arms.

I am on a lonely heath. In the distance a great fire burns. I go on and on endlessly. Kitty has grown very heavy, but I cannot put her down. She belongs to me. Now we are near the fire. I know what I must do. I hold kitty on my outstretched arms and step into the flames. Their hot tongues burn into my flesh. I lay kitty in the center where the heat is most intense. She is all I have. Yet I must not save her. The flames flare up, die down. There in the ashes at my feet is a baby girl. As I hold her in my arms I exclaim, "I must find her father."

Her conscious mind intervened and she tried to manipulate the fantasy, so, of course, as a creative product, it came to an abrupt end, and she was left trying to build up a satisfying image of the father of this living girl child. Instead, memories crowded in, words came back—"I trust you completely. I put my whole life in your hands." How noble she had felt over this magnificent gift of herself to the man upon whom she had placed the image of savior! Were these kitty's words as she evaded the responsibility of adult relationship and chose the safety of the crib, the parentage of the ancient crone who would keep her on a bland diet and the sinister man who would look on with skeptical amusement? Through the merciless, merciful fire which she had herself chosen, kitty had become a living child who must find an inner authority in a father who would teach her the meaning of womanhood. She knew that to find this father she must go forward into life remembering that in the divine interplay of conscious and unconscious the impossible is often the way. "The impossible!" She knew now that even though she had met many difficulties with courage, she had never, of her own free will, gone on to the end. Instead, when she had "done the best she could," she retreated to barren safety. Now she must take her chances in the unknown forest.

The way was long and there were many dreams that dealt with the

unexpected. Out of the many, I have chosen a few that deal with her search for the father.

> I am in the office of Dr. X. There are flowers on his desk. I know it is the anniversary of his mother's death. He does not speak of the flowers. He says, "If we could study the life of the tree and know its secrets, we would be able to tell the moment when new life is ready to start. We should not forget that in all spiritual development one thing grows out of another."

Dr. X was a friend whose advice she trusted. In his childhood he had been crippled by a bone disease that had made him dependent upon an overloving and devoted mother; but he had in early life cast off dependence for a relation of growing maturity. Out of pain and crippling, he had achieved courage to accept the limitations that cut him off from youthful activities as opportunities for research by which he could discover new beginnings and how "in all spiritual development one thing grows out of another."

Through this introverted search he had discovered interests within himself and had come to a knowledge of his own vocation. Suffering and pain had brought a desire to know more about the bodily and spiritual suffering. Rooted in the reality of his own experience, he had come to know how in spiritual development one thing grows out of another, and so he had learned the secrets of inner development and had come to a place where he could affirm the meaning and purpose of his life as a man.

As she pondered this dream, she saw how in her dreams the process of transformation was unfolding within her. That she must consciously choose that way is shown in the following dream.

> I am on a forest path. I hear two notes, one harsh and metallic, the other flutelike, clear as the single note of my dream. A young man comes toward me. He has two tuning forks in his hand. He holds them out to me and says, "Either is yours for the asking but you must choose to which you will tune the song of your life, for it is you who must strike the note."

She could choose the old harsh way of nonliving or the living note that she had heard in her dream of deliverance. She chose to go forward, and when her temptation was to retreat from life, she felt

kitty's stiff little limbs and knew that was the way back to the crib and to imprisonment. She must go the way of the child of new beginnings even though she did not consciously know that way. There were many dreams; then in the darkness of a midnight hour, this vision appeared to her.

I hear a voice. "And from thy navel shall flow wine, sweet like unto honey." Then I am in an old, old street, gray and narrow. In a rounding corner, in a niche of gray stone, is set a vessel shaped like an urn or a chalice. An old man leaning on a staff draws near. With him is a little boy. The old man gazes at the chalice with a look of almost incredulous joy. The child looks up at him trustingly. The old man reverently takes the chalice in his hands, and as he does so it fills itself with a glowing living liquid. He puts it in the hands of the child and the child offers it to me. I know a solemn sacramental choice is offered and again I am afraid, yet I raise the vessel to my lips. As the burning wine touches them, the vision fades, except for the gray niche where, in place of the vessel, is the naked body of a woman. She lies with one arm and her hair covering her face; across the navel is a deep gash in the form of a cross, and from the wound at the center of the cross flows a clear golden stream.

She feels again the burning touch of the wine upon her lips. She sees the "vessel shaped like an urn or a chalice"—urn of burial, or chalice of new life. She hears the words, "Father, if Thou be willing, remove this cup from me." She had accepted the cup and, with its acceptance, the wound of the cross had become the wellspring of new life, and "wine, sweet like unto honey" poured from its center. She had never heard of the navel as symbol of the fountainhead of regeneration and renewal, yet she felt that the wounding had, in a way beyond her comprehension, reopened a source of living energy. It seemed that the living symbol, arising from the depth of the unconscious, acted as transforming agent even though she did not at the time understand its symbolic meaning.

Jung says:

When the libido leaves the bright upper world, whether from choice, or from inertia, or from fate, it sinks back into its own depths, into the source from which it originally flowed, and returns to *the point of cleavage, the navel,* where it first entered the body. *This point of cleavage is*

called the mother, because from her the current of life reached us. Whenever some great work is to be accomplished, before which a man recoils, doubtful of his strength, his libido streams back to the fountainhead—and that is the dangerous moment when the issue hangs between annihilation and new life. For if the libido gets stuck in the wonderland of this inner world, then for the upper world man is nothing but a shadow. . . . But if the libido manages to tear itself loose and force its way up again, something like a miracle happens: the journey to the underworld was a plunge into the fountain of youth, and the libido, apparently dead, wakes to renewed fruitfulness. This idea is illustrated in an Indian myth: Vishnu sank into a profound trance, and in his slumber brought forth Brahma, who, enthroned on a lotus, rose out of Vishnu's navel, bringing with him the Vedas . . . This is a primitive way of describing the libido's entry into the interior world of the psyche, the unconscious.[6]

In the language of the symbol the navel is the place of regeneration. The return to the navel is a return to the fountainhead, the source, so that again the stream of creative energy may flow.[7] Introversion—sinking back into the unconscious, into the depth of one's inmost self—is a return to this primary source in order that again libido may flow into the emptied vessel of the self. The vessel had been empty when it was in the gray niche, but in the hands of the old man wine had flowed into it from its own source of self-renewal; and this was the wine that had been given her to drink. Then the wound became the place of regeneration. She knew intuitively that it was not inflicted by the outer world but self-inflicted. The cross, the symbol of suffering, of bearing the burden of one's self in the tortured descent into the hell of one's own inmost being, had to be endured before there could come the renewal. And the instrument—the sharp knife of tormented thought that brings one face to face with the cleavage between the ideal and the reality, with the conflict of instinct and spirit—was the sword of separation, discrimination, self-knowledge, with all its promises and its torturing possibilities! Nietzsche says:

> You sought the heaviest burden
> And found yourself.

---

[6] Both quotations and a picture are to be found in *Symbols of Transformation,* pp. 292–293, par. 449–450 and Plate XLVIa. My italics.

[7] A wooden carving of the Nootka Indians shows, through an opening in the navel, the face of the one who has returned to this cave of rebirth. *Ibid.,* Plate XLII.

One finds one's own life, one's own cross, the burden of one's own unfulfilled desires, of one's own unlived potentials—a burden that must be carried to the place of crucifixion and rebirth. One finds the necessity of reconciliation between the opposites which must be "brought together so that the navel as maternal center of nourishment becomes the creative matrix of the future."[8]

The wound is the reopening of the source which may release the creative stream or may destroy life at the source. One can, from the wounding, die the death of the soul, or one can die the death of crucifixion, rebirth and resurrection. She tried not to evade the suffering of the descent into the depth. She reviewed the past with honest eyes as shadow forms confronted her. The vision lived itself within her and new meanings unfolded themselves.

One night she saw the arches of the inner cloister of Santa Maria de Novello. Like flowering crosses they spread above her. Where they met at the center flowers unfolded. In their curves were the little Della Robbia bambinos; she was in the inner cloister of woman, of the mother and child, where the cross flowered into new life.

Then into her so dearly won peace came a dream that startled her into new awareness of how far she still had to go on her journey back to her feminine self.

Dr. Y comes to me bringing a basket full of the fruits of his harvest. I exclaim, "But these are only two-dimensional. They are perfectly good symbols of geometry or logic, but as symbols of life and maternity they are useless." He asks, "Did you say maternity or eternity?" I answer, "The one flows into the other." He says, "Can you make them into living symbols?" I tell him I will try. I take the basket from him, but I know I cannot do it alone and that I must find someone other than Dr. Y to show me. I leave him and go on this search. I see, coming toward me, a mature woman dressed in blue. We go together into a room like a cave. She kindles a fire and lays the patterns on the hearth. The firelight now fills the cave with ruddy glow. Every few minutes she touches these two-dimensional things softly. Then, as they begin to assume form, she holds them in the flame and the transformation takes place. They become living creatures, children of light and fire.

---

[8] *Ibid.*, p. 301.

Dr. Y was a psychiatrist whom she had known for many years. He was intrigued by the concepts of depth psychology but he studied the manifestations of the unconscious from a discreet distance, and the advice he gave to himself was, "Hang your clothes on a hickory limb, but don't go near the water." The dreamer had enjoyed his brilliant intellectual discussions and the way his intuition ferretted out the problems of other people, but when she had tried, also from a discreet distance, to discuss her own emotional difficulties with him, the interchange became lifeless intellectualization, two dimensional patterns untouched by the life-giving dimension of the living symbols. In the dream she sees this clearly. The fruits of his conscious mind are perfectly good symbols of geometry or logic, but as symbols of life and maternity they are useless. Maternity, eternity. Truly "the one flows into the other" when one descends to the region of the Mothers, the realm of

> . . . Formation, transformation,
> Eternal Mind's eternal re-creation.[9]

It is in this realm of the Mothers that she will find the creative power to give to these two dimensional concepts the added dimension of love. For this she must seek the help of the ever-living feminine maternal principle in the unconscious.

"Seek and ye shall find." Hardly had she set out on her search when the Mother came to meet her—a far-different mother from the one who had kept kitty on a bland diet. This Mother, who knew the transforming power of the flame lit by love, would help her find the father of the living child—the phoenix of the flame. So might she become liberated from the power of the projected image, the false redeemer, the trickster of intellectual rationalization, the father who would always permit her to remain a child.

With the dream of Dr. X a new father image had been revealed, one who revered the secrets of the tree and knew "the moment when new life is ready to start." Before she could come to a knowledge of this father, she had to find her own relation to the Mother as symbol of a never-ending process of renewal, for maternity and eternity flow into each other.

Again her vision returned and the child stood before her holding

---

[9] Goethe, *Faust*, tr. by George Madison Priest. The Second Part, Act I, p. 182.

the cup. She looked into the face of the old man in whose hands the empty chalice had filled itself with wine and saw the image of the Father who had said, "Let there be light." Knowing the meaning of the birth of light through the darkness of death and crucifixion, the Wise Old Man had put the chalice in the hands of the child, the carrier of the essential meaning of the old. This child of new beginning could offer her the choice between life and death.

This ever-living child (the *puer aeternus*) comes in new form when life offers, from the wisdom of the past, a way of new beginning. He comes as neglected child, as triumphant child, as the child who is herald of the dawning of a new day within the self. Always he asks the same question: Are you born? This eternal child stands in ever-evolving form at every crossroad of choice and asks, Are you born into this new life that I now offer you?

One last dream and we leave her.

The man and I are searching for a treasure. We are walking, hand in hand, down a white path near the edge of a swift-flowing stream. The stream broadens out into a lake. We go on to the end. There we find a simple square house whose door stands open. We go in. Behind a table sits the old man of my vision. In front of him are two candles, one white, one black. As we stand before the table, the candles bend down of themselves till their unlit wicks almost touch and a flame leaps between them. It rises in a spire of living light. From the flame a burning drop falls upon the table and becomes a blue jewel that is transformed into a radiant white stone. At the same moment I feel the fire leap between us as though our own energy had met and become one living flame. Reverently, we take up the jewel and go out together.

The candles, black and white, impelled by the will of this mana personality, the wise old man, bend of themselves. They choose submission to a will greater than their own. The flame leaps between them, and out of the fire the essential element is fused. It falls upon the table as a living spark, which is transformed into the stone—the jewel without price. The same flame leaps between the man and the woman, making them part of the mystery and inheritors of the jewel born of the flame that had arisen from the meeting of the opposites.

She went back over the long history of her inner journey. When

she had started, the inner voice of authority had been the ghost voice of the father who spoke in the silent glances of skepticism that made her distrust her feminine self as well as the image of masculinity. How had this voice become that of the wise old man? She remembered her first words when, after the sacrifice of kitty, she had taken into her arms the living child, phoenix of the flame: "I must find her father." She knew that in that dream she had indeed found him as spirit of wisdom and of inner authority, who, as guide and psychopomp, could show her the way to unite the feminine and masculine elements of her being and so lead her upon the pathway of the self.

The interplay of the masculine and feminine elements within the psyche are so vividly portrayed in the following dream that I cannot refrain from including it in this chapter. It is the dream of a woman who had early known mind as doubting thought and spirit as self-accusing judge. Through a perilous inner journey, she had come to see the animus in his true nature as interpreter of the images of the unconscious, yet at times he still appeared in his old dark form and weighed her down with a sense of the meaninglessness of her life. It was in such a period that this dream came to her.

I am in bed in what seems to be a high gallery in a vast, darkened, empty amphitheater. A monstrous black man is pressing down upon me, almost smothering me. I "know" that a performance is taking place on the stage far below us. I struggle to rise, but the giant weight is too heavy for me. I fight with all my strength. It is useless. The man puts his hand over my eyes. The blackness is now impenetrable, the weight intolerable. The feeling comes to me that he cannot help what he is doing. It is I who must in some way help him. I put my hand over his, gently and with reassuring pressure.

Now we are standing together, hand in hand, at the center front of the gallery. The stage below us is in twilight grayness; in its center is a black pear-shaped crystal. Outlined by its own darkness, it glows as though touched by light (moonlight?). As I watch, a small spark, a light seed, appears within it. It sends off sparks of light that come together in points of intense illumination and form patterns like stars in a cosmic dance. They concentrate into lines of living energy of varying luminosity. Some gleam like gold; some shine like silver. They intermingle in weaving patterns of light. This is the Dance of Life. Now the

strands of energy are all about us. I feel the movement of the dance alive in every fiber. In an instant of intensity, my whole being is vitalized as though an electric current had invaded me. I look up at my partner's face. It glows like living bronze. His lips are curved in a strange smile; his eyes, clear crystal green, look straight into mine. I see a living world mirrored in them. As I look into this green world, music fills the air as though "the morning stars sang together." I feel him sway to the rhythm of the dance. Trustingly, I follow his lead as we move in the vibrating interplay of gold and silver and sound. There is an instant when the current leaps between us; it enters my very being with a force like a lightning flash. I am trembling, yet vibrantly alive.

Waking, she lay listening to the music, feeling the pulsations of the dance move through every fiber of her being. Some force beyond her knowing had entered and possessed her. She was spent, yet vitalized, and she knew, in a way beyond conscious knowing, that the seed of the spirit had entered into her and that, as soul, she had conceived.

For many days she lived in the sense of wonder and awe. Then she re-entered the dream. Again she was in the dark empty amphitheater, struggling to free herself. Again she felt the impulse toward compassionate understanding. Whence had it come? Did some current even then pass between them when in the darkness she had touched his hand? Only by doing the little that she could as woman did the first transformation take place and the second scene of the dream become possible. Standing together hand in hand, the current flowed imperceptibly between them and her eyes were opened to behold the cosmic drama enacted on the vaster stage—the dark world-womb, its impregnation by the spirit, the birth of the eternal spark, a radiant center giving forth streams of energy, gold and silver intermingling, interweaving, coming together in stars of light. She knew the star as symbol of individual being, and she saw these stars as individuals, mana personalities perhaps, who accepted their part in this eternal dance of creation.

Then the energy flowed about them, penetrated and united them so they too were part of this movement of life, part of the purpose, part of the cosmic plan. She now sees her partner as the inscrutable god who will direct her steps in this intricate dance; yet yielding, following, she too directs their steps until, in the instant of lightning

flash, the energy leaps between them and the inner marriage becomes a living reality and as one they enter the cosmic dance.

Again she looked into the green eyes where she had seen a new world coming into visibility. In this world stood the image of the man who had offered her entrance into love. Again she felt the shock of the current, the lightning thrust, and she knew that she loved. She saw the difficulties, the demands of his complex nature, the necessity for full commitment. In that moment the negative animus again stood before her in his form of self-doubt and negation, and she chose love and trusted the power of yielding in order to transform this dark element of her own being. In that moment she again heard the music, felt the pulsations of energy and knew that, even as in the dream, she had entered into the Dance of Life, and the vast and empty amphitheater had become filled with its eternal energy.

It is through woman's relation to the transformed and transforming animus and through the intricate steps of a fully lived human relationship that she learns the varying patterns of this dance. In trusting herself to the movement of the guide, she discovers that no matter how intricately the dance moves, no matter how many its changes, interruptions and deviations, it never loses the vital thread of meaning that holds it connected with and that returns it to the center.

When a man and woman enter as partners into this intricate and beautiful rhythmic movement, it is the man who leads; and yet, most subtly, the woman vitalizes and also directs the pattern by her own yielding, for by this she communicates life. Woman must be aware of and responsive to man's every movement; yet man too must become aware of woman's response so that the current of life may flow between them in an act of creative beauty which follows the rhythm of a music to which they are both attuned. In this dance anima and animus act as guides and interpreters of the unconscious, and inner and outer become welded together.

CHAPTER 14

Interplay and Relatedness

✥

The meeting of two personalities is like the contact of two chemical substances: if there is any reaction, both are transformed.[1]

Let us return to our dreamer who saw the candles bend at the wordless command of the wise old man. She remembered an evening when she had sat by the fire with two old friends who had been married many years—a chance argument, a clash of opinions and then a look of complete acceptance of each other that wordlessly bridged over differences making them also a source of communication. They were so simply and effortlessly together. Another picture rose, a painting she had seen only once, a single spray of bamboo etched against a vast moonlit sky—the near branch, the distant moon, the serenity of the near and far brought together on a small strip of silken fabric. How simple it was! But what lay back of that simplicity? Long years of training of hand and eye, years of communion with beauty before vision and hand could meet in the few swift sure brushstrokes. Had such long travail lain behind the look of mutual comprehension that flashed between husband and wife when for a moment their innate differences had met in opposition? Was the look of understanding also born of years of discipline and of inner vision? In each instance the golden moment was given—bamboo and moon responding to a single instant of time, conscious and unconscious meeting in a flash of awareness—but the swift interchange of

---

[1] Jung, *Modern Man in Search of a Soul*, p. 57.

259

understanding and of humorous acceptance was the result of years of discipline, devotion and trust in the vision of something greater than the immediate.

An amazing yet convincing realization came to her: there was a region where the opposites did not cancel each other out; where feeling and thought, intuition and sensation could meet as equals; where love confirmed itself through clarity of concept, and thought reverently sought counsel of love; where rational and transrational could break bread together and be mutually nourished, mutually deferential to each other. This was the meaning of that look that held the years together. It had come from acceptance of the conflict of the opposites in two natures who, she knew, were originally at variance in their basic personalities. For the first time she perceived the inner meaning of "for better, for worse; for richer, for poorer" and realized that in the inner marriage of truth and love, of instinct and spirit, each experience might be better and richer, however tragic its suffering, if the ego learns to accept its own worsening and find in its own poverty the meaning of inner wealth. In the flooding up of new understanding she felt the peace of one who begins anew from where one really is. For each awakening offers the choice of a new beginning.

She looked back on her own experience and knew that she had once thought of marriage as a final goal, an achieved relationship in which one could rest assured and in which all one's doubts would be magically resolved because one was loved. Instead she had found her own marriage to be only the entrance to a trail of branching paths that led up a mountain of many difficulties. Could they have reached the summit together if she had been wiser in her choices of the way, more understanding of a nature so diverse from hers, more willing to listen to the voices that warned her when she blindly followed paths not really her own? This she would never know, for their ways had separated long ago and, should they again meet, there would be no trail through the unblazed forest of separateness that lay between them. Whence, then, came this sense of the peace of a new beginning? Was it from a newborn trust in life's eternal power of inward bestowing, a trust that had come to her when, through the transforming power of the living symbol, loneliness and self-isolation had changed to aloneness in which new meanings, like strange flowers, had unfolded?

She saw, in this illumined moment, that the depth-dark failure of her marriage was that it had confirmed both her childhood distrust of her own power to give or to inspire love, and her doubt of the integrity and loyalty or the hidden motive of the person who offered it. Distrust had permeated every form of relatedness: love, friendship, profession, and had even distorted her image of God. Bereft of trust she had drawn a circle of isolation about herself, all the time telling herself it was others—even the inward Other—who shut her from life. Then, through her experience of the transforming power of the symbol, loneliness had become aloneness in which she dared penetrate the darkness of the unconscious, companioned by the shadow who was becoming the friend. She remembered with gratitude the mysterious sequence of the dreams; she knew that something had happened so that she could now choose life with its manifold difficulties and opportunities and see them being interwoven in an evolving pattern. A yea-saying to life had displaced the old negative distrust; kitty's stiff little frame had become a living child and with this inner transformation, outer life had changed—seemingly of itself.

When a central attitude of goodwill toward man acts spontaneously in moments of choice, the response elicited is a movement *toward*; then "something happens"—that is, a potential of new relatedness is born out of the moment. One moves toward life and its responsibilities. This does not mean a loss of clear vision or of the perception of evil; the awakened spirit perceives danger as well as opportunity. It also perceives opportunity in danger and discovers that good may come out of evil in an interplay which brings to consciousness the varying elements involved in every form of relationship.

Nowhere is this more true than in marriage, with its drastic demands and creative possibilities, for here the opposites meet in all their constellating power of negative and positive polarities. The current may leap between them or be short circuited in darkness. The contrasexual tendencies that must be assimilated are constellated not only on the human but also on the archetypal level, for the unconscious enters, clothing the human in the garments of the primordial images. Goddess and hero meet in the magic of "inloveness" and face the inexorable continuity of a mutually accepted destiny bound to the future by children, those hostages of fate, and by the commitments not only to each other but also to society. For marriage is not

only an individual as well as a collective relationship, it is also an institution on which the structure of society depends.[2]

All this, however consciously considered, is, and should be, secondary in the magic moments of early love when each is convinced that never before has such an experience occurred except, perhaps, in the life of the gods.

Yet these two "whom God hath joined together" must enter the banal everyday life that makes innumerable demands upon their patience, their endurance, their understanding, their sense of humor and their power of intuitive perception.

The man must share his morning paper with the shining goddess who has taken on the guise of mere woman; the woman contemplates the hero's attitude toward the overboiled egg. The cloak of illusion may fall and the test of love begin in that heroic encounter with the ordinary in which all the unconscious elements of each of the partners play their unpredictable roles. The goddess is caught in trivial situations where she too seems trivial; the hero, confronted by the unexpected, finds he has mislaid his shining armor; and both discover that the contract "made in heaven" must be fulfilled on earth if it is not to end up in hell. Yet each of these banal situations may become a sacrament in the ritual of love.

Marriage has been called "the domestication of the Recording Angel." It is he who presides over the signing of the register. It is he who sees all the invisible signatures and knows that there are four leading actors who sign this contract: two egos whose signatures stand out for all the world to see, and two actors, animus and anima, who sign in invisible ink. Following these there is a host of invisible signers: shadow, secret motive, ruling ambition, who will play their parts in the ensuing drama. It is their acts that the angel records as well as those of the two egos who believe themselves to be the sole signers.

It is dangerous for either man or woman to identify with the Re-

---

[2] In the following discussion of the warfare and the reconciliation of the opposites in marriage, there will be no attempt to deal with those basic and fundamental problems of marriage as an institution on which our social fabric rests, or of that most important question, its effect on children. The problem of parent and child has been discussed at length in my book, *The Inner World of Childhood*, and an adequate discussion of marriage would need a volume to itself.

cording Angel, whose ledger of relationship records the triumphs of love and of the spirit, as well as all the shabby compromises, the evasions of noble promises, the open faults and the secret sins. If the woman tries to take over the record, she may read only the pages of the man's faults and her own grievances. She may assume the garment of patient Griselda (who must have been maddening to live with) or, like a gadfly with angel wings, take refuge in assumption of superiority and intolerably virtuous tolerance, which stings the man to outbursts of violence. If she is wise, she will concentrate on her own page first, and seek to understand and acknowledge her relation to her shadow, who has so many traits in common with the man's undeveloped eros—traits he is so ready to project upon her. If she understands, but does not accept these projections or secretly try to use his weakness to strengthen her power over him, she can become friend of this inner woman and so help the man to achieve a more conscious relation not only to herself but to his own unconscious. Seeing her shadow qualities enables her to bring understanding and, it is to be hoped, some kindly humor to the interpretation of his record. Otherwise the man answers her arguments with quotations from the pages of her own bad marks and feels righteous justification because, throughout many centuries, his identification with this particular angel was taken for granted. If the woman remonstrates, he may go off on a little trip with his negative anima, or walk out of the picture, taking refuge in his masculine interests. He knows a little absent treatment will usually bring the woman around. He hopes that by this method he can return to a type of domestic harmony in which all unpleasant truths are buried, and they can "forgive and forget" in decent well-mannered repression—till the next encounter. Or he discovers—inadvertently, of course—a woman whose understanding misunderstanding gives him happy unconsciousness of his own inadequacies. Wounded pride or vanity leaps out toward the woman who will misunderstand in a soothing way. Unconscious or semiconscious relationship, which may continue over the years, has no more frequent basis than a nondemanding misunderstanding in which the persona can preen itself in the illusion that its heroic sufferings are accepted with due admiration. Such search for admiring misunderstanding is not limited to the male sex.

Sometimes the conscious actors may succeed for years in ignoring the hidden signers of the register. They live within the framework

prescribed by church and society. The marriage moves along good conventional lines, the plot never getting out of hand by developing into dramatic or individual form. The egos play their roles as desired, neither one inquiring into the true nature of the other. These so-called happy marriages may be only a state of unconscious content-ment, far different from the rare and great achievement of two inte-grated persons who have learned both separateness and togetherness.

Many marriages never pass beyond the point where neither has knowledge of the buried potentials of the self or of the other. Both believe in the "sacredness of marriage": the woman because it gives her a sense of security and permanence in the personal relation and in her position in the world, the man because "his love of comfort and a curious sentimental belief in institutions prompts him to this faith, for with a man, institutions always tend to become objects of feeling."[3]

But it may be that in one of those private readings of the records of this still undomesticated angel, the secret activities of one of the in-visible signers leaps into visibility and a hidden antagonism stands forth in its stark reality. The fire of negative emotions flares up, and the hitherto discreet related persons find themselves embroiled in vulgar conflict where all sorts of things buried beneath well-bred silence leap out. If this conflict is faced, the emotional outburst may clear the air; or the invisible signers may break in, shouting all those things that have been whispered in secret, repressed lest they spoil rapport or virtuously denied in the desire to preserve the *status quo* of a respectable marriage. Anima and animus take over the leading roles; recriminations, barbed innuendoes, banal invectives are shot out like quills from a porcupine that enter easily into the flesh of the opponent and are as difficult to dislodge. And all this time the two egos are under the illusion not only that it is they who are talking, but that their words offer sensible solutions to insoluble problems. The scene is not a sudden happening, any more than a volcano's eruption is the sudden transformation of a peaceable mountain. The pent-up emotions have long been seething under the surface of what one "must of course feel," or of what is more expedient to ignore, or of what the family or the community expects of one or of what is best for the children. When the aroused emotions speak, both the man and the woman feel that they are confronted by some strange

---

[3] Jung, *Contributions to Analytical Psychology*, Harcourt, Brace edition, p. 174.

interloper, and that they themselves have been mysteriously be-witched. The tension must be endured until the energy released finds a way of transcendence, a point of view in which things are seen in new proportion.

In the anima-animus battle it is well to remember that truth should *not* be spoken at all times. In the hands of arrogance, scorn or will to power, truth becomes the most deadly of weapons; because it can-not be factually denied, it finds entrance into the vulnerable spot, the Achilles' heel of the antagonist. Yet both are wounded, for he who inflicts the wound has destroyed his chance to clarify the issue within himself and so to grow in understanding and in love. Victory leaves only the cold comfort of self-righteousness, a frigid bedfellow.

If the woman is not to fall into the trap of hostile argument, she must be clear as to her own feeling. She must also be aware of the relative importance of the subject under discussion and the rightness of the moment for bringing it up. The wise woman deals with contro-versial questions when the man is not preoccupied with his masculine interests and when his anima is at peace.

What happens to the relationship in these periods of opposition and tension depends, one could almost say, upon the god whom each envisioned when they were joined together—that is, upon the concept of the greatest value that secretly dominates each life: power, money, position, convention or the spirit of love and truth. Two contradictory gods cannot make peace in one menage.

Yet sometimes in these moments of antagonistic encounter, a blind force greater than personal emotion may compel this particular man or woman to break in violence something that the conscious ego has not had the strength to break, for each may fear to lose somnolent contentment or illegitimate power over the other, and to risk all in the game of love. In the Kundalini Yoga the place of the fire is also the place of the jewels. The flame of intense emotion may be needed to burn away the lethargy of *laissez faire* that has caught the man and woman in its grip and to bring them to a vision of reality. If they can endure this fire, they may find beyond it the place where fiery emotion becomes the pure flame of devotion—quiet, steady, and yet infused with all the magic of the unconscious—a love where tenderness or shared suffering is continually surprised by joy. This joy is the discovery of what each ordinary encounter may awaken, how the simplest act may contain the mystery of the god.

The essential differences of life do not end, but rather begin, with

marriage. Conscious acceptance of mutual responsibility brings with it suffering and an opportunity for true maturity. Impulse cannot sustain this responsibility and suffering. Habit or careless acceptance dulls eye and ear. A loose string vibrates to no touch, gives forth no music.

If there is fundamental love, patience, humility and a search for a clearer mutuality and understanding of oneself and of the other, even lines spoken in sudden bitterness can be used to bring clear consciousness of the nature of the buried oppositions. An admission of a mistake or hasty judgment can be accepted, and the one who admits frailty is, perhaps, even more loved because of these all-too-human qualities which enter into wholeness. Only Pooh Bah can say

> I never yet made one mistake—
> I'd like to for variety's sake,

and we do not recall him as a much-loved figure in the operetta.

When the inner intent is to clarify in order to strengthen the bond, criticism loses its sting; it becomes a mutual search for a truer basis on which the relationship can stand. In such an atmosphere neither one fears to admit vulnerability, for each trusts in the integrity and inner intent of the partner. Perhaps the woman is that rare creature who can sense what the man may become through the development of his own potentials and yet is content with his reality. She does not demand heroism beyond his capacity. He then is able to bring his tentative gropings and his undeveloped thoughts into the warm lovelit atmosphere where they can grow naturally, and often he finds that he can surpass himself as the wellsprings of life seem to open of themselves within him. A man is not afraid to expose the almost embryonic children of his psyche to the woman who has a creative maternal attitude toward young and undeveloped things; he feels her desire to help them grow in freedom in accordance with their own nature. In her the image of anima and mother are fused in a life-giving form. Even in her maternal aspects she still acts as soul, the seductress who draws him into life—his own life, with all of its paradoxical problems—where he must accept his burden of individual choice. Such a woman is both soothing and terrifying; she awakens his libido and leaves it free to choose its own goal. And the man willingly abandoning his solitary heights offers to the woman a companionship of mind and spirit which, unlike that blissful condition of

"two minds with but a single thought," stimulates her own thinking so that the spark of new awareness is awakened between them. Vistas are opened in which images of the unconscious move as messengers of new concepts. This is the true function of anima and animus—to open the doors to the unconscious so that each may become more complete in oneself and in the relationship.

The awakening to true consciousness of either of the partners may bring to life undiscovered values, longings, undreamed-of aspirations, creative potentials hitherto sacrificed to accepted demands or ego convictions; or it may awaken antagonisms that have been stifled by a desire for peace at any price. Each may ask, "Who is this person whom I have married, and what are we really doing to each other?" This question brings the unconscious factors to light, and their acts must be acknowledged. In the revelation of oppositions, the marriage may be wrecked; or new possibilities of understanding may develop which bring deeper values into each life and into the marriage so that both are transformed and meet on a higher level of consciousness. Through this process a new relationship may come into being, defying tradition and insisting on its own creative way. In accepting this, woman learns to submit to the laws of her own being and to love rather than to rely on being loved. Man finds his own relation to eros. No longer does he confuse his infantile "lust for freedom" with the true freedom to choose but to confirm his choice by his permanent commitment to a central relationship, doing "gladly that which he has to do" to sustain its essential values.

Yet if the man finds that through this conflict he has, with no small effort, won a needful insight into his own soul, he will not let it go again, for he is too conscious of the importance of what he has won.[4] And the woman, having found her relation to mind as the power of clear and independent thought and to spirit as the voice of inner truth, cannot return to a medieval form of relationship. Something deeper is demanded by each, for they cannot return to the old. The new has been awakened.

Love is a mighty force whose power reaches from heaven to hell; it can enter every aspect of life. It searches out the heart and demands its own sacrifices, bending only to its own truth. In opening the heart to this god, let man be sure he can stand the testing that will come,

---

[4] *Ibid.*, p. 186.

for unless he chooses commitment to an inner law which is far more exacting than any on the statute books, the end may be disaster. Yet the risk must be taken; one must stand unmasked in one's own reality.

The man may find that he can no longer meet the demands and ambitions of the woman because something within him is seeking a return to the creative springs of his own being, and this he cannot find with her. The woman may offer her own reality and find that the man refuses to accept her right to be herself.

Here again reality is the great awakener. The two may stand before each other almost as strangers. Will they accept a new covenant based on the right of each to be an individual self? Upon the answer to this question, marriage breaks, or "rises" to new depths.

When the crisis reveals essential inadequacies or innate differences that set limitations upon the development of either the man or the woman, it may be that the only honest answer is divorce, for to remain in a situation poisoned by secret hostility is a violation of the truth of the self. The outer law must not be broken except at the command of a more searching inner law, which cannot speak with authority unless, in integrity and truth, every effort has been made to fulfill the old. This effort involves a painful self-searching in order to discover the causes that have long been accumulating in the unconscious, for it is the slowly developing inner situation—not a sudden infatuation or discovery of unexpected difficulties—that produces divorce.

This self-examination brings the two egos once more face to face with the two who signed the contract in invisible ink. Man searches out his true relation to his anima; woman questions the actions of her animus. They see these signers not only in their unconscious manifestations but also in the creative possibilities of inner relatedness: man with his anima, who opens for him the creative springs of his own being; woman with her animus, who reveals to her the sources of mind and spirit. In this way an inner marriage takes place in the soul of each. If the inner marriage of each brings renewed love between them, the outer marriage becomes a quarternity—man, woman, anima and animus joined together in a new covenant which is a union of inner and outer forms of relatedness.

Here again is a risk, for these two individuals may find that in their newly discovered reality they have not found the answer to the problems that confront them in their marriage. But even here a new relation comes into being, for each is able to stand alone and also freely

and generously to admit the right of the other to find fulfillment in a way that inner truth demands.

Only in his innermost heart can a man or woman know the way that this truth of his own being must be fulfilled. Then "ask not what a man does, but who within him does it."

The qualities that make of marriage a living and vital experience are active in every relationship. Acceptance of reality, awareness of potentials of good and evil, openness to the voices of the unconscious, goodwill, loyalty, trust, respect for the uniqueness of each personality —all these are qualities that enter into every form of relationship. The same question is asked at every crossroads of choice. "What am I bringing to birth within myself and what am I arousing within the other person who is involved in this particular situation?" If one can face these questions with integrity, there is little danger that any form of relationship will be used by the ego for its own aggrandizement.

Even if a basic relation of love and trust is achieved, this does not mean that conflict ceases, for "the flow of life again and again demands a new, more comprehensive adaptation. Adaptation is never achieved once and for all."[5] Every continuing relationship means new development, progression from level to level. In each encounter with opposition, something is roused in the unconscious which has to be met as one's own inner problem. So one becomes more conscious and more understanding of oneself and of the other.

In every conflict, inner or outer, conscious and unconscious continually confront each other, for "the psychological transcendent function arises from the union of conscious and unconscious content [which] have a curious tendency not to agree."[5] Yet they need each other—the conscious to give form and reality, the unconscious to fertilize the conscious—in that interplay through which man becomes not only a creature of instinct and will but also a living spirit; for "instinct and spirit are indissolubly bound together." Only by acceptance of conflict may the opposites be transcended and the new attitude come into being.

Do we not all possess, buried, perhaps, under the rubble of daily existence, "the instinct for transcendence?" The urge to fulfill a destiny which we only dimly apprehend, yet which we know to be based upon a discovery of the reality of an eternal and spiritual en-

---

[5] Jung, *The Transcendent Function*, p. 5.

ergy, can act as a living presence within us if we will let it illumine the small self which it inhabits. Through this instinct we perceive the two faces of reality: the tangible, visible, touchable something called matter, and the vital, creative, invisible something called spirit—the two realities that must be fused into a new "somewhat" if the invisible is to become visible, the interior word to be heard, the new reality to appear. Through acceptance of this continuous interplay of conflict and relatedness, one moves not toward a finished state but toward a beginning: one enters upon the journey toward wholeness.

CHAPTER 15

Journey Toward Wholeness

❧ ❦

Here then stands the newly-awakened self, aware for the first time of reality, responding to that reality with love and awe . . . not merely to be thrust into a new world but set at the beginning of a new road. . . . That a quest there is and an end is the single secret spoken.[1]

And this secret spake Life herself unto me. "Behold," said she, "I am that *which must ever surpass itself*."[2]

"WHERE WAS I as *myself*; as the whole man, as the real man?" A strange question for Peer Gynt, the renegade,[3] to ask as he comes to the last crossroad and is confronted by the vengeful images of those life choices which were only evasions of conscious choice. Yet, in asking the question, he reveals a secret perception which he has excluded from consciousness, a knowledge that all the time this "I as myself," this "whole man," had existed as an inborn image of what the real man was intended to become. It was from this "I," this self, with its power of being and becoming, that the prideful unrelated ego had escaped in order to make defiant choices against the same self that now his question sought.

At each crossroad of decision, man may ask this question concerning any element of himself with which he has lost contact. "Where

---

[1] Evelyn Underhill, *Mysticism*, p. 238.

[2] Friedrich Nietzsche, *Thus Spake Zarathustra*, tr. by Thomas Common, p. 125.

[3] See Chapter 5, "Enemies of Choice, Part II," p. 69.

have you been when you might have been helping me?" the man seeking his lost power of relatedness asks of the anima, the soul, to whom he might have given reality. "Where have you been?" the animus-driven woman asks of her inborn power to love, and of the creative spirit that once quickened and gave meaning to her life as woman. The answer is always the same. "I have been inside you all the time." Peer, who stood "choice free," asks this question of the repudiated self. Could he have listened, he would have heard the answer, "I have been inside you all the time, waiting in the central place from whence you fled; I have surrounded you on every side, but you saw me only as darkness and, as you fled me, you plunged into deeper darkness, and so you knew me as enemy, not as friend."

Over and over throughout life this choice has to be made between the enemy and the friend for, behind the never-ending confrontation by the opposites lies a power, a dynamis, operative in the process of reconciling the split between nature and spirit, ego and non-ego, conscious choice and the creative unconscious, healing the psychic wound that severs man from the sense of completeness and from becoming that which he was intended to be—that which, below the threshold of ego consciousness, he *is*.

This undiscovered self, this "isness," is always, even in childhood, trying to make itself manifest through the life of the individual in a process of growing self-realization. To discover and live out the meaning of the self through choice of awareness of the hidden movement of non-ego forces is the journey into wholeness. It is a journey of change, rebirth, transformation on all the different levels of the being. It is a way that "goes onward and contains its own correction,"[4] for "only what is really oneself has the power to heal."[5] This self, Jung says, is "as it were a virtual point midway between conscious and unconscious," between ego and non-ego. It acts as a center of gravity that holds the fragmentary parts together. It is also a source of dynamic energy out of which consciousness is born. For the self is not only the source and groundwork of the personality but also the power that seeks to become manifest through the choices and experiences of that same ego to which it has given birth. In other words, this non-ego force needs the ego in order to fulfill itself in a

---

[4] Eugen Herrigel, *The Method of Zen*, p. 79.
[5] Jung, quoting from his writings in conversation with the author.

meaningful relation not only to the world but also to all the unborn or lost potentials of the whole man.

Human nature shrinks definitely back from becoming conscious. What, however, drives [man] onward toward consciousness is the self. . . . On the one hand to become conscious . . . is a conscious act of will on the part of the ego, on the other hand it is a spontaneous emergence of the Self which has existed forever.[6]

"My soul and consciousness, that is my self; I am encompassed in it as an island among the waves, as a star in the sky."[7]

The vast encompassing Self, "greater than the great," may become "smaller than the small" and enter each man's heart as seed kernel of his being. As seed, this "smaller than the small" is buried deep in the soul of the man, and consciousness must seek him out if the man is to find and make manifest in his life that which he was intended to be. That there is an awakening, "a single secret spoken," perhaps by an image that arises, perhaps by an experience vouchsafed, is all we know; yet the new road, "mist veiled, image filled," is there and the journey must be taken into the Self to find the self, into the unconscious to find new consciousness, into the darkness to find the light, into aloneness to find the Other—that "totally Other"—who is "nearer . . . than breathing, closer than hands and feet." Here, at every turn of the spiral, we find ourselves confronted by that inner friend or foe, and "whether he is friend or foe depends upon ourselves."

We shall find him in his oneness only when we have experienced him in his diversity; only when we have faced "with love and awe," with fear and conquest of fear, his various manifestations within our own psyche. For the self is wholeness. It contains all that consciousness has tried to ignore both in evil and in the demands of the spirit. Lao Tzu says, "The man who knows others is clever but the man who knows himself is illumined." He knows "the face that was his before he was born," that is, the face of the one he was intended to become when he discovered the meaning of his life.

"The descent into the self is not only a mythical or ritualistic withdrawal; it is a tormented exploration of the dark depth of the soul."[8]

---

[6] Jung, "Transformation Symbolism in the Mass," in *Spring 1952.*
[7] Georges Duplain quotes Jung in an interview, "On the Frontiers of Knowledge," *Spring 1960,* p. 11.
[8] Arnold Stein, *Heroic Knowledge,* p. 209.

When in this descent you come upon that which you have despised in the outer world and see its full malignity, you find that each man must see how this enemy, until now invisible, has entered into his life, furnishing the plausible excuses that led to evasion of responsibilities that were unrecognized opportunities, ensnaring him in that greatest deception, self-deception. All that is dark within himself arises and confronts him, and he knows that in himself exists a driving force of evil; the same evil that has done the horrible things, the evil that he contemplates as far removed in time and space, is existent in him as sleeping potential.

Man has done these things. I am a man who has his share of human nature; therefore I am guilty with the rest, and bear unalterably and indelibly within me the capacity and the inclination to do them again at any time. . . . None of us stands outside humanity's black collective shadow. Whether the crime lies many generations back or happens today, it remains the symptom of a disposition that is always and everywhere present—and one would therefore do well to possess some "imagination in evil" for only the fool can permanently neglect the conditions of his own nature. In fact, this negligence is the best means of making him an instrument of evil.[9]

A true man knows that his most bitter foe, or indeed a whole host of enemies, does not equal that one worst adversary, that "other self" who "bides within his breast."[10]

"All that is insignificant, paltry and cowardly in us cowers and shrinks from this acceptance."[11] All that is heroic goes out to meet it. For the true man knows that it is this brother to whom he must be reconciled if he would bring his gift to the altar and himself be received in his wholeness. The negative archetype is part of the dark aspect of the Self that is the enemy; but the Self as friend brings to us the vision of the redeeming aspect so that the "archetypes, awakened from their slumber within us, become visible images and effect transformation in us. . . . They rise up within us and become our guides."[12] As guides they show us that wholeness demands ac-

---

[9] Jung, *The Undiscovered Self*, pp. 96–97.
[10] Jung, in Jacobi, *C. G. Jung, Psychological Reflections*, p. 202.
[11] *Ibid.*, p. 33.
[12] Heinrich Zimmer, "On the Significance of the Indian Tantric Yoga," *Spiritual Disciplines*, p. 8.

ceptance of the light as well as the darkness. But do we want the light? *One day of complete awareness is more than most of us can stand.* For in the light all things are awakened and become alive within us and we are faced not only with original evil but with original goodness in all its infinite potentiality. Man does not want to be reminded of these possibilities when he is filled with the power of his own dark energy that can encompass for him so many things. He fears the light because it reveals a spiritual urge that would drive him to renunciation of those deeds that he can perform in the darkness that hides him from himself.

If he faces the challenge of the light as also present within himself, he penetrates beyond the small reaches of his personal unconscious into that region extending into the subhuman and suprahuman world of archetypal magnitudes where he is confronted not only by infinite evil but by infinite good, which calls upon him to become more than his small personal self. He faces the challenge of the living God.

It is dangerous for man to call upon the living God, for, as the light falls upon his heart, all that has slumbered, whether of good or of evil, awakens and pushes upward into the light, and he knows that all these things have been within him from the beginning and he is faced "by his own dualism to which he knows no answer." The terrible gift of choice is forced upon him and must be confirmed by his own will. Often he would choose the merciful undemand of darkness. Yet the risk of the light must be taken if we are to accept ourselves not only as we are but as all that we may become through choice of awareness. Self-acceptance is not a static act, for it includes awareness of the changing evolving factors within the personality. With each experience newly met the potentials are newly mingled, recombined, changed into a purer more refined essence or into a darker substance according to the nature of the inner choice. For "the self is not a reality that is given but a reality that seeks itself" and finds itself through man's own choice.

To find that reality,

> We must go down into the dungeons of the heart,
> To the dark places where the modern mind imprisons
> All that is not defined and thought apart.
> We must let out the terrible creative visions.

. . . .

Return to the most human, nothing less
Will teach the angry spirit, the bewildered heart,
The torn mind, to accept the whole of its duress,
And pierced with anguish, at last act for love.[13]

The terrible vision of eternal energy of good or evil, of man made in the image of a creative God, of the power of the spirit as it works within him to his destruction or to his redemption—these visions we release from the dungeons of the heart, and we release them in fear and awe as well as in love. The descent into the self is the most dangerous journey man can take, for to know the Self, the Self that dwells within one's self and encompasses one's self on every hand, is to arouse a hidden life of unforeseeable, unknowable creative possibilities. It is a discovery of the spark that becomes the fire that can quicken or consume. It is the terrible vision of the God in whom all things become manifest.

This is the journey, this the return, through which we may learn to know—to realize inwardly—that "the only way to ascend unto God is to descend into ourself,"[14] and the only way to manifest him in our small individual lives is to "return to the most human, nothing less."

It is a journey of continuous return from our human life to our inmost secrecy and from this secrecy back to "what is most human"—the breaking of bread, the simple giving of oneself in the knowledge that transcendence is manifest in immanence, manifest in our smallest act which is deified by love of God and man; to know love as an indwelling force, not as something we receive from an object but as something that, through inward finding and outward sharing, we make real in life.

This return "to what is most human" in ourselves and in our relations to our fellow men is a return to all of humanity, for the impulses and motives, the instinctual drives, the urgencies of the spirit, the loves, the hates, the fears and the faiths—all are contained within the circle of the Self. If we know our self, no human being, no human act, is wholly strange to us. We have met these things before because we have experienced them within ourselves; yet we have never met them before, because they have never before been

---

[13] May Sarton, "Santos: New Mexico," in The Lion and the Rose, pp. 28–29.
[14] Jung, in conversation with the author.

combined in exactly this way. Each experience and relationship is recognition, understanding and discovery. Accepting the mystery of the unknowable element, we learn to accept individual differences, varying viewpoints, typical and functional reactions of another. Such clarity in both subjective and objective realms enables us to penetrate beyond difference into that depth where the roots of human experience have their beginning.

The discovery of kinship is not born out of self-repudiation. If you say of your inmost thought, desire, emotion or act, "This is the unforgivable sin, I can never forgive myself," you will find the same sin in another and be unable to forgive the sinner, for you will confuse the sin with the man who exists behind the act. You will always be stumbling upon the nonunderstandable and irreconcilable in every human being whose life you touch, for you do not understand, nor are you reconciled to the same element within yourself. Without self-forgiveness, self-acceptance, self-love, we seek to imprison the recalcitrant elements in ourselves in the oubliette of solitary confinement, hoping that we have imposed a life sentence. But what of the imprisoned one? Is he transformed? Is he redeemed? And as we turn to the outer world, does our compassion seek to redeem through love, or do our self-hate and self-distrust seek to condemn and isolate?

Inevitably in this return the inner man will shadow the outer man, the reality will shadow the pretense. If this inner man has become the self-hating judge, he will speak through our voice, will act through our will, his mind and spirit will permeate our being, so that even in the idealism of our consciously willed charity he will condemn instead of understand and will exercise his conscience with the contemplation of sin until it grows in strength to condemn. This is why one must love oneself with a self-redeeming and self-transforming love.

The self, the inexorable judge whose eye discerns the reality behind the veil of illusion, pronounces the judgment of the self by the Self.[15] More and more, as man faces inner reality, the Self becomes the

---

[15] Man may be touched by pleas he has not known,
God may be merciful, all just, all wise,
Only before myself I stand alone
Daring no pardon, stripped of all disguise.

—Jane Bliss Gillespy, "The Perfect Judgment," in *The Eastward Road.*

judge; but if there is true self-love, the judge becomes the redeemer, and the sense of judgment is lost in the miracle of transformation.

"Thou shalt love thy neighbor as thyself." How shall we follow the commandment if we are taught, and inwardly believe, that self-denial is the way of righteousness? For self-denial is the first person of the blind negative trinity—self-denial, self-distrust, self-hate— those enemies of the self who forbid creative choice. When the ego dares not affirm the true choices of the Self, all that is spontaneous becomes suspect, tainted with undefined guilt. But the real guilt of living a lie in relation to the truth of one's own being does not become conscious. Instead, there is a vague, ghostlike, omnipresent sense of guilt that saps the energy and breeds suspicion and distrust. Through distrust the life of the self becomes a process of denial of the Self, and the ego is filled with nameless anxiety.

This anxiety comes from a hidden unacknowledged perception that he has yielded to a regressive force which makes him content to remain less than he might become if he would give life to his own potentials. Despair confronts the man who believes that he has forever lost the opportunity of becoming himself and of expressing the significance and meaning of his existence. Negation permeates his every act and an undertow of anxiety vitiates energy; guilt is generalized; hope of redemption is lost because there is no known sin to be expiated or transgression to be forgiven. Fear of life becomes fear of death because death of the spirit has already closed the door upon rebirth.

Yet always there is the gift of grace, for the Self, even in childhood, is showing glimpses of that other creative life-giving trinity— self-awareness, self-affirmation, self-acceptance—the three that become the four through a love of Self that opens out into love of God in man and man in God.

This, though a gift of grace, must be chosen and rechosen, affirmed and reaffirmed by the ego, for self-awareness grows from many choices, many acceptances of the unacceptable, many acts of loyalty to that which the Self has revealed in moments of deep experience. Through these experiences comes the knowledge that one is most free when all sense of freedom is lost in dedication, most oneself when one is not oneself but is consumed by the energy of the Self and the working out of its commands.

Meister Eckhart says,

God loves himself and his own nature, being, and Godhead, and in the love he has for himself he loves all creatures, not as creatures but as God. The love God bears for himself contains his love for the whole world.[16]

One must love one's own self enough to dare to let it take its intended form, enough to defy patterns not one's own, to take the lonely way when the self indicates its need so that aloneness becomes not an alienation or isolation but a privilege and a communion with the Self who, while encompassing us on all sides, yet abides in the innermost recesses of the being. This is the love that forever seeks true enlightenment in the Self and in every creature, an enlightenment that shows "the way that goes onward," and, having reached its center, of necessity radiates outward toward all life.

This radiant center is at rest, yet forever active. When the spark becomes the center, it can no more help giving forth emanations of its own essence than the sun can help giving light.

We recall the vision of Rabbi Levi, son of the Baal Shem.

Some time after my father's death, I saw him in the shape of a fiery mountain, which burst into countless sparks. I asked him: "Why do you appear in a shape such as this?" He answered: "In this shape I served God."[17]

The spark becomes active at the moment of intuitive perception when the truth that we have heard a hundred times awakens a creative response and becomes alive in us. Then it, in turn, creates sparks from its own radiant center. And through this radiant quality man gives testimony not only to the wholeness of the Self but to the essence of the man's being, so enabling him to manifest that which was given him to bring forth. He therefore must love and respect his own uniqueness and be content to serve the world through perfecting and sharing the special gift that is his inborn heritage.

In *The Legend of the Baal Shem*,[18] we find these words:

God never does the same thing twice. That which exists is unique, and it happens but once. It is because things happen but once that the in-

---

16 *Meister Eckhart*, pp. 224–225.
17 Martin Buber, *Tales of the Hasidim*, Vol. I, p. 85.
18 Martin Buber, "The Life of the Hasidim, Shiflut: Humility." In brackets are some condensations of the text by the author in an attempt to give the essential meaning of the section. Omissions in the text are not indicated, nor is the original paragraphing always followed.

dividual partakes in eternity. Uniqueness is the essential good of man that is given to him to unfold. And he who has become so entirely individual [totally at one within himself] that no otherness any longer has power over him or place in him has completed the journey. Only in his own way and not in any other can the one who strives perfect [become] himself. "He who lays hold of the rung of his companion and lets go of his own rung, through him neither the one nor the other will be realized." But as man seeks God in lonely fervour, there is a high service that only the community can fulfill. The uniqueness of man proves itself in his life with others. For the more unique a man really is so much the more can he give to the other [also the more can he receive through his own openness and humility. For he knows that the individual who is whole is but a part, and the more truly himself he is the more intimately] does he know that he is a part, and there stirs within him the community of existence.

"Every man has a light over him, and when the souls of two men meet, the two lights join each other and from them there goes forth one [new] light. And this is called generation." To feel the universal generation as a sea and oneself as a wave, that is the mystery of humility. But when one "lowers himself too much, [he forgets that he is] the son of a king." [The "young aristocrat"[19] who also dwells within, can, through love, redeem the dark brother. This king's son is brother to the world and one with all.]

[Not he who knows himself in his uniqueness and kingliness, but he] who contrasts himself with others, who sees himself as higher than the humblest of things, [is caught in the net of pride. He] rules with measure and weights and pronounces judgment. He who measures and weighs becomes empty and unreal like measure and weight. [And there is a heaviness in him, the heaviness of the ego burdened by its own possessions.] In him who is full of himself there is no room for God. But when a man rests in himself as in the nothing, he is not limited by any other thing, he is limitless, and God pours his glory into him [and he is exalted, yet humbled. This] humility is no willed and practiced virtue, but an inner being, feeling, and expressing, indivisible as the glance of a child and simple as a child's speech. "In each man there is a priceless treasure. One shall honour each man for the hidden value that only he has."

Living with the other as a form of knowing is justice. Living with the other as a form of being is love. Love is all comprehensive and sustaining. There is a great moving force therein. Love lives in a kingdom greater than the individual and speaks out of a knowing deeper than the knowing of the individual. [It is] life pouring itself into life. Thus first [does

---

[19] A term used by Meister Eckhart.

the individual soul] behold the soul of the world. [He who lives in this way realizes with his truth] that all souls are one; for each is a spark from the primordial soul, and the whole of the primordial soul is in each.

Thus lives the humble man mixing with all, untouched by all, devoted to [all, yet alone in his own] uniqueness; [on the heights of solitude] fulfilling the bond with the infinite and [in] the valley of life the bond with the earthly, flowering out of deep devotion and withdrawn from all desire of the desiring. He has no fear of the before and the after, of the above and the below. He is at home and never can be cast out.

His aloneness cannot become isolation or alienation; his oneness is one with the creative life of God.

If uniqueness is all that matters, it becomes idiosyncrasy and the individual becomes that travesty, the individualist. True uniqueness is an unfolding of the inborn meaning of the personality. Jung says individuation means becoming one's own "innermost, last, and incomparable uniqueness . . . becoming one's own self."[20]

Man realizes himself through his willing choice of vocation and his commitment to the essential task that has been given him to fulfill. This opens the wellsprings of his own creativity. God realized himself through manifesting himself in creative act. He realized his own divinity by becoming human, entering the world stream of joy and of suffering, accepting his own gift to vulnerable man—the gift of choice. In the solitude of the desert Jesus encountered his shadow, his own dark brother, Satan. Here choice was offered him, the choice between power and affirmation of the truth that he had come to manifest. And beholding the kingdoms of the world and the power thereof, and seeing the risks of this truth and the sacrifice thereof, he chose the truth of his own unique destiny, thereby affirming the uniqueness and dignity of each human being, of himself and of the humblest man. Through this choice he dared to proclaim, "Ye are all sons of God," and "The kingdom is within." This is the statement of a man who comes at last to peace beyond the descent into hell. It is the peace won by the risk of accepting the essential meaning of one's own life.

Jung says:

This apparently unique life has become a sacred symbol because it is the prototype of the only meaningful life, that is, a life that strives for the

---

individual realization of its own particular law, such realization being absolute and unconditional.[21]

"Imitation of Christ" is a purely symbolic concept.

Christ can indeed be imitated to the point of stigmatization without the imitator coming anywhere near the ideal or its meaning. For it is not a question of an imitation that leaves a man unchanged and makes him into a mere artifact, but of realizing the ideal on one's own account—Deo concedente—in one's own individual life.[22]

Jesus never imposed his way on others. His first miracle was changing water into wine at the marriage feast in Cana. His love went out to children and to the lost children of humanity. He did not denounce riches except where they stood between man and his own soul. He loved the still, small pleasures of life even while He followed the still, small voice as it spoke in Gethsemane, for He recognized that it was the voice that called Him to choose and to fulfill that for which He had been chosen. In true symbolic imitation man follows the still, small voice that speaks to him in the time and place where his individual life is set. He chooses that for which he was chosen, thus fulfilling his destined purpose. Only by following this voice of his own destiny can man say humbly, reverently, in his joy or in his agony, "For this came I into the world." Such acceptance leaves no place for inferiority. It is simple, direct. Yet it opens the way to crucifixion, rebirth and transformation—and to a faith in life as a force that must "ever surpass itself."

The Self as friend of choice urges man to take the risk of this choice of self-affirmation, for only through this can he fulfill his destiny and bring into world consciousness that which was entrusted to him to bring to consciousness that which was entrusted to him to bring to consciousness within himself. In this way man becomes a living testament to the truth that is vouchsafed him and, deeper than diversities of creed or ritual, he perceives the oneness of a universal truth in which they all have their being. He also discovers that "not only is human existence the area in which the symbols and sacraments are manifested: . . . the tangible existence of a human person can itself be a symbol, a sacrament."[23]

---

[21] *Integration of the Personality*, p. 298.
[22] Jung, *Psychology and Alchemy*, p. 7.
[23] Martin Buber, "Symbolic and Sacramental Existence in Judaism," *Spiritual Disciplines*, p. 168.

Let us look back over the way that we have come, recalling those moments when, even in childhood, the Self as friend vouchsafed a vision or glimpse into a world beyond the child's or man's knowing, and the small emerging ego was, however fleetingly, aware of a reality beyond its grasp. As we discussed some of these early experiences—with Twinkle and Pitch-Black Dark, the Golden Baby, the Starfish "with the eye in the middle of him," the blue flower that became the touchstone of reality, we saw how moments of awareness come and leave their mark upon the emerging personality.

The boy, alone on the wintry road, looking up at the star, was pierced by an awareness of something that was from the beginning steadfast, changeless in the midst of change.[24] As he stood there, silent, alone, he felt the star alive within him, distant and immediately present. The North Star, ruler of the compass by which the mariner charts his course, steers his way, was his star. He must never betray it. In the wonder and the stillness of the starlit winter night, he felt called to a purpose. Though the "single secret spoken" was that "a quest there is and an end," he knew intuitively, unmistakably, that the purpose had to do with giving form to beauty—beauty of line, of color, of sound, of inner vision. This, then, was his quest, his vocation. To this end he must trust the star to rule the compass of his will so that he might, in some way he could not yet envision, find his vocation, fulfill his destiny. He must, if he would make real the wonder of this moment, never betray the star within himself.[25] Throughout the years he gave himself fully to those moments of intensity when, touched by the finger of the creative spirit, he sensed a beauty to which he must, however crudely, give form; nor did he ever lose the sense of mystery that had touched him in that moment. In this way the early vision—often obscured by fears, doubts, conflicts as the ego pursued its way toward consciousness—came to its awakening. Many years afterward, on the long inner journey, his spirit was illumined by the knowledge that star and rose, truth and love were, from the beginning, one within the self. I was privileged to see how the childhood experence lived for more than half a century

---

24 This is the boy whose childhood experience was given in Chapter 6 above, "Childhood and the Friend of Choice." His latest return to that experience in a moment of illumination was described in Chapter 11, "The Woman in Man."

25 Much of this was wordless, yet these words are his own as nearly verbatim as I could set them down when, years afterward, he told me of the experience.

within the man and found life in the creative artist that he was to become. In childhood he did not know the star as symbol of individuation or know that, as an archetype, it slumbered within him awaiting his experience to give it form as image. Yet, when inner and outer symbol merged as one, the distant star became the inner guide in this journey into the Self to find the self.

The boy who sought counsel from the Hard Thinker Dragon[26] had this sense of "a someone" existing within oneself who can give direction in time of need. This Hard Thinker Dragon, who gave the surprising answers that you found you had better follow, lived not in the head or the heart but "in the cave of the tummy," the realm from whence the dynamic drive of the emotions arises. Such a phrase as "he cannot stomach it" means the rejection of the experience by the aroused emotions. To stomach it means inwardly to digest and assimilate the idea that has aroused emotion. The Chinese Zen Master, Takuan, says in his letter on Pranjna the Immovable, "It is better after all to keep the mind in the lower part of the abdomen just below the navel, and this will enable one to adjust oneself in accordance with the shifting of the situation from moment to moment."[27] To think with one's belly produces the immediate reaction in which something more fundamental than the intellect directs the response.

The dragon in Chinese philosophy is symbol of masculine dynamic creative energy, the arouser, the awakener. He lives in the fiery furnace of the emotions, yet he is not consumed by their fire. He therefore can speak from the fire yet from beyond the fire—that is, from the place where, through the "subduing of the affect," one goes with one's instinct instead of against it.

Would the boy have been able to go down into the cave of the tummy had he not first put the sister-mother in a cage and drawn about his own small ego the red circle that protected him from his own regressive longings and so gave his ego courage to go down into the place of the fire? It is interesting to note that this drawing (the E enclosed in the circle of red) came before the Hard Thinker Dragon made its appearance in the child's life and his small ego was able to go back and follow the direction of the non-ego, thus winning for itself a new integration through the incorporation of something won from the unconscious—the non-ego force.

The integration of the ego, through which it may maintain a con-

---

[26] See Chapter 7 above, "Return of the Image," p. 111 n.
[27] D. T. Suzuki, *Zen and Japanese Culture*, p. 105.

tinuing relation to the Self, is a life process, for without this com-munication between ego and non-ego the unsubdued affects may suddenly take over the field of consciousness and reduce the ego to "those bits and fragments that we call man." Yet, even in these early stages the Self can act as a magnet in reassembling the fragmented parts and make possible a reintegration of the ego on a new plane of conscious perception.

The dismemberment and rebirth dream of a seven-year-old girl shows how this mysterious power can act in the gathering together of bits and pieces of the fragmented ego.

I was on a crocodile's back in a Canada [cannibal] land. Then I felt something on my head. I thought it was a cannibal but it was a spear. I jumped off the crocodile's back but I felt I was burning up in a fire. Then they cut off my arms and legs and they threw my legs to the crocodile. And they pulled out my eyes and cut off my nose and they ate my eyes and my nose and all the pieces of me, but they threw my legs to the crocodile and he ate them. And then they put me together again. They put in my teeth one by one, but they could not find my eyes or my nose. I had to find them myself. So I did. And then the croco-dile gave me back my legs. And then Mother was there and she put me in a bathtub and washed me all over. And then I woke up and I was in my own bed and it was morning.

She is in a cannibal land, that is, in a place where she may be torn apart and devoured by those inner cannibals, the untamed emo-tions. Here she sits unconcernedly on the back of the crocodile—another devouring element, inertia, that can swallow the conscious energy that the ego needs in order to face a sudden situation that may arouse emotion. In this state of unconsciousness she fears neither the crocodile nor the cannibals. But something happens, per-haps in the outer situation, and a sharp spear (a penetrating dan-gerous thought) enters her head. She leaps off the back of the croco-dile and finds herself among the cannibals, the aroused emotions, and feels as if she were burning up in a fire. The cannibals have be-come real. They tear her to pieces and devour her. We speak, quite literally, of being torn apart by violent emotions, devoured by greed, cruelty, hate, love or desire—that whole tribe of untamed affects that inhabits the cannibal land inside oneself. They eat "all the pieces" of her except her legs. It is upon one's legs, one's own feet, that one

must stand firm when assailed by devouring emotions. The cannibals throw these to the crocodile; that is, they deprive the ego of *any* consciousness of the real situation or of how she can take a stand against it.

After the dismemberment she experiences a ritualistic restoration. "They" put back the pieces; that is, after the fiery emotions have had their way with her, she cools off and sees what has happened. But this does not show her the part that she has played in the situation. "They" do not give back her eyes and nose, the organs of vision and intuitive perception. These she has to find for herself: some power beyond the dismembered ego, a power that can come only through self-reflection, must come to her aid if she is to do the seemingly impossible task. Blind and without eyes, she must see her way to recover her eyes; deprived of her nose, her intuition, which gives her power to smell out the reality of the inner situation, she must find for herself this organ of instinctual perception. In fact, she must achieve the impossible if she would come together again and be herself—"*so I did.*" A power that can achieve the task impossible to the ego enables it to perform the miracle. Then, when she has done that which she had to do, the crocodile gives back her legs— the unconscious renders up what it has devoured, and she can stand on her own feet.

When she has attained this firmness, the mother appears; that is, when the ego, directed by the non-ego, has done its part in the act of restoration, it has become ready for initiation into new consciousness. Then the Great Mother appears in her cleansing restoring power. In the ritualistic bath the initiate is cleansed from his past and emerges as a newborn creature. She "washed me all over. And then I woke up and I was in my own bed and *it was morning.*" In other words, she wakes in the old familiar surroundings but wakes to a new day, a new beginning.

Who was the "I" who directed the ego in its search for the essential parts devoured by the cannibals? When the "I" as ego ceases to exist, the I as self-uniting and self-transforming power, existing from the beginning, takes over the direction of energy, and this apparently non-existent ego can do the impossible and, through this meeting of will and grace, become reintegrated, reborn into the next stage of life.

The child told me the dream as a strange happening, a mystery tale that had told itself, yet one in which she was the protagonist.

It was very real. *It had happened to her.* We did not attempt to probe into its imagery. That could have divested it of its irrational power to act within the psyche. Through the frailty of the barriers between conscious and unconscious, the child partakes of that subterranean awareness, deeper than conscious knowledge, that in dreams expresses a wisdom that the developing ego cannot interpret, yet which acts of itself in the process of inner growth. We cannot say of these childhood experiences that they bring about a transformation. There is as yet no formed personality capable of being transformed into a new wholeness. Such dreams are glimpses into the mysterious depth of the creative unconscious. Yet in the life of the child they are real, more profound than any experience of the day, for the child is at the mercy of both the inner and the outer world. How far such dreams work within the psyche in the process of integration we cannot say. Even in telling the dream this child was again enclosed within it and she lived in its mysterious reality. In recounting it she was back in its wonder as though she herself had taken part in a rite of initiation. The sharpness, the intricate details, indicate that it had a vital connection with her immediate and personal situation. Shortly after this dream she again "flew to pieces" and, in a quarrel with a playmate, tore up a picture the other child had painted. Instead of accusing the other child and justifying herself as was her wont, she looked at the pieces, gathered herself together and, seeing that she could not undo the action of her own violent emotions (the inner cannibals), said, "I guess when I get mad I have to do something about it." Who can say that this altered attitude was the dream working in her? Who could venture to deny it? Such a dream may leave its mark upon the psyche and continue its creative work—silently, secretly—even after its vivid impression has faded from consciousness. I was able to watch the child over many years and to see her growth in self-reliance, self-control, and self-recollection. I saw her struggles to understand her own uncontrolled moments, her growing powers of self-reflection. It seemed that the dream unfolded its meaning as the need of the child drew upon it.[28]

---

[28] The following lines appear in *The Tibetan Book of the Dead*, p. 204:

> May I recognize whatever appeareth as being mine own thought-forms,
> May I . . .
> Fear not the bands of the Peaceful and Wrathful, Who are [mine]
> own thought-forms

In the process of dismemberment and rebirth, the self acts as a magnetic center drawing together the fragments—the part souls. In this the self may act through the awakening of the hitherto despised function, or it may use the essential quality of the personality as agent in the reassembling.

In the Egyptian myth of dismemberment and rebirth, Osiris is murdered by the enmity of his dark brother Set. Isis, his sister-mother-lover, seals the body in a coffin of darkness and hides it away. Set discovers the place of hiding, opens the coffin and dismembers the body. Isis searches out the scattered parts and reassembles them—only the phallus, the organ of his own creativity, can she not find. This Osiris must find for himself, for he is the ever-self-creating god. Must even a god in his rebirth and resurrection find within himself the source of his creativity?

In a poem on the dismemberment and rebirth of Orpheus, Muriel Rukeyser uses the concept of the fragment that, as symbol of the essential element, becomes the agent of the reassembling.[29] The fragments of Orpheus, scattered upon the mountain, that have become only "wounds in their endless crying," are awakened by the groping severed hand that reaches blindly for the lyre. "The hand has risen . . . the four strings now sing: Eurydice." Love sings through the hand that has been the instrument of song, and that song draws together the parts dismembered by the furies, and Orpheus arises in his wholeness as a god.

Jung says:

The psychological equivalent of the [reintegration of the dismembered parts] is the integration of the self through conscious assimilation of the split-off contents. Self-recollection is a gathering together of the self.

". . . learn who it is that taketh possession of everything in thee, saying: *my* god, *my* spirit [nous], *my* understanding, *my* soul, *my* body; and learn whence is sorrow and joy, and love and hate, and waking though one would not, and sleeping though one would not, and getting angry though one would not, and falling in love though one would not. And if thou wouldst closely investigate these things, thou wilt find Him in thyself, the One and the Many, like to that little point, for it is from thee that he hath his origin."[30]

---

[29] Muriel Rukeyser, "Orpheus," in *Selected Poems*, p. 105.
[30] "Transformation Symbolism in the Mass," in *Psychology and Religion: West and East* (Coll. Works, 11), pp. 264–265 (quoting Hippolytus, *Elenchos*, VIII, 15).

The self, the little speck, the all-encompassing one, contains all the elements that must be separated, reintegrated, reborn. Throughout the whole span of life, dismemberment and reassembling are parts of a continuous interrelated life process as consciousness develops from out the matrix of the unconscious in the individuation process.

Our dismemberment is our journey through the hell of our refusals, the violations of our intended wholeness by our own conflicting elements. Yet in the essential element of the Self, if it has been chosen and developed as it was destined to become manifest, lies the power to reassemble the split-off parts into a newly transformed creature in whom

> . . . the exile of our music
> and the dividing airs are gathered home.[31]

When the ego co-operates with the self in this process, a step is taken in the journey toward wholeness. This the ego may refuse to do and through its attempts to achieve its chosen goal may disregard the demands of the Self, leaving behind the early visions, the promptings of the heart, the simple human claims, and forget that the soul is the one who acts as interpreter of the creative images that arise from the depth of our being. For a long time the loss of soul may go unnoticed, activities increase, acquisitions multiply, yet underneath the achievement nothing satisfies, nothing nourishes; there is only emptiness. To stop and look into the depth would reveal, not that nothingness of the void out of which all unborn things come into creation, but the bottomless void of meaninglessness. Still the ego presses on—one more step and the goal that consciousness has set will be reached and the restless ego can rest satisfied. Then will come plenty of time for enjoyment, for relatedness to his fellow men, for self-reflection, for inwardness, for the discovery of meaning. But instead, moments of depression increase, life slips away like sand through Time's hourglass and the man secretly fears that death may come before the moment of achievement when one may really begin to live. Questions arise. Who am I? What am I seeking? What dreams of the morning are now lost in the dusk of oncoming night? How can I find that sense of life that my youth once knew? Perhaps,

---

[31] Muriel Rukeyser, op. cit., p. 109.

in spite of the ego's disregard of all except its own efforts to pull itself out of the slough by its own bootstraps, these restless questions may penetrate below the surface and, from the ignored depths, the Self answers in a dream.

This happened to a man who became caught in the meshes of doing and acquiring, through which he thought he might find his being. Moments of depression came more and more frequently. At times a sense of loneliness overpowered him—even in moments when he had achieved something for which he had struggled. Aloneness disintegrated into lonely isolation. Loneliness is a greedy spirit reaching out for small satisfactions. One can be very lonely when the fountains of the heart are sealed by a multitude of things "and the lonely of heart are withered away."[32] Then one may begin to search for someone who will pour the waters of love, of relatedness, of irrational feeling and intuitive perception, into the waste places of the soul. In his concentration upon the fulfillment of his masculine choices, this man had ignored the feminine qualities that sought their life within his psyche. The drive for self-fulfillment is, however, present and, if not consciously met, finds its outlet in an obsessive demand that it shall be lived out by another. Such a man is very vulnerable to any woman who can awaken the anima image, the image of the soul that he has lost. This man found himself compulsively attracted to women who seemed to have magical power over him, who seemed, in fact, to have taken possession of his soul.

It is a dangerous thing to have anybody walk away with one's soul, but it is a tragic comedy to discover that it has been done quite inadvertently and that the new possessor desires only to get rid of the possession. Man cannot endure having the drama, which to him is a tragedy, prove to be only a comedy in which he is not the protagonist but has played the fool in the eyes of the world—worse yet, in the eyes of his inmost self. This discovery may drive him into isolation and self-alienation so that he again seeks escape into the ten thousand things that keep him from realizing the pitiful fact that the inner things once desired have withered and died in the rootless region of ego consciousness.

This man felt that life had failed him. But he had no realization

---

[32] Yeats, "The Land of Heart's Desire," in *Plays*, p. 156.

that he had failed life. This was the illuminating dream that showed him how he himself had chosen defeat:

> After a long and difficult ascent I have at last reached my goal—the summit of a towering mountain where I had thought to see the whole world stretched out below me. Instead I am on a sheer peak of rock that rises from a black craterlike place. Only bare pinnacles surround me. I hear a mocking voice, "Little man, little man, who are you?" Like derisive laughter, the words echo and re-echo from every bleak crag. Now each rock seems to mock me. "Little man, little man, who are you?" Fear comes upon me. Who indeed am I? My very name falls from me. It has no substance. Recalled and spoken, it too would taunt me with its meaninglessness. Fear becomes panic. I must find my way down from this empty height. I turn back to find the way that I have come. It is now blotted out by dark clouds, but the voices drive me on. I must go down, even though there is only a perilous way over crags that skirt precipices. The rocks tear at me; the mocking laughter follows me; the voices pursue me. After untold hours I seem to feel that someone is guiding me. As I follow I know not what, the voices fade into the distance. At last I see below me a green valley through which a still stream runs. As I enter the valley a woman, ageless, very fair with her own inward serenity, comes to meet me. She is carrying a lamb in her arms.

The imagery of the valley brings clearly to mind the Psalm of the Good Shepherd. Here are the "green pastures," the "still waters"; here is the promise fulfilled: "He restoreth my soul." The fair woman comes to meet him carrying a lamb in her arms, even as, in the eternal parable, the Good Shepherd tenderly carries the lamb that was lost. Is the fair woman bringing back to him the potential of innocence and childlike openness to life that he lost so long ago when he started on the way of the ego? "Except ye be converted, and become as little children, ye shall not enter into the kingdom of heaven."[33] To "become" a child through being "converted"—that is, *transformed*—involves a return to the simplicity and spontaneity of the child, to the immediate and direct grasp of reality, to the wonder, the acceptance of paradox, the direct experience of the opposites, to the reality of the dream, to the knowledge that he exists in

---

[33] Matthew 18:3. This quotation is also discussed in different form in Chapter 3, "Early Choices of Good and Evil."

both worlds at once. To this return the man must bring all that he has learned through facing the experiences of self-alienation and self-acceptance, through development of intellect and maturing of feeling. It is a return to innocence after the primary innocence has been lost—a higher innocence founded on the integrity and simplicity of that "true man of no rank" who has become free of the guilt of ego living or of nonliving and so has entered on the journey toward wholeness. On this journey he finds that certain childhood experiences have not been forgotten by the Self, the sage who lives within the being. These are words received by the sage who is existent within the child. In the flow of the years the child becomes the sage and the sage becomes the child. The innocence and simplicity of the child and the wisdom of the sage are, through steps of creative transformation, united in the divine harmony which is peace in action, and the word takes on meaning.

All this the fair woman knows, for the way to the kingdom is known not to the intellect but to the soul. The soul who comes to meet him is made fair by her own inward serenity. She is ageless, for she is, from the beginning, the interpreter of the Self.

While he has pursued his masculine way of conscious achievement up mountain paths to the bleak crags, she "has been there all the time" in the green valley of the sheep. When, driven by the frantic urge to escape the taunting voices of his own emptiness, he listened to the inaudible voice and allowed himself to be guided by the unseen presence, she has already come to meet him.

At the sharp urge of necessity he has dared the dangerous descent; but will he now accept all that the soul can reveal to him, the inner meaning of the life of the valley in its simplicity, its innocence of attained integrity, its power of transformation? Or will the dream, on his return to the outer world, become to him only a poetic fragment, a lyric episode? Or—even more dangerous—will he forget those heights of ego isolation and the inexorable voice that asked of him the question that each man must answer for himself and by himself, "Little man, little man, who are you?" To escape from this question is to escape into the empty fullness that is death of the soul.

From inner emptiness man climbs only to empty heights, but when the soul leads, he descends into the self to find the Self and discovers that the descent is the ascent to the valley of vision which is also the mount of transformation. In this valley he perceives that,

in the language of the soul, all that his ego has seen as high is indeed low, and that which he has rejected as beneath is indeed above. The dream shows him the reality of that region which he has called "depression." It is the summit of ego isolation where, in his effort to escape from the life of the Self, he has fled to this wall-less prison and is confronted by the inexorable question, "Little man, little man, who are you?" He finds no answer. Even his name falls away, for a name, though it may relate only to the persona, is still a way of communicating, of establishing one's sense of identity. The loss of this name produces panic, for it is in his name that he has trusted. He must escape from this place where his own meaninglessness confronts him. He will go back to the old life. But the old way is closed off. Then the voices become those of the Hound of Heaven. They pursue him, leaving him no choice of the way. They drive him into the unknown depths. In his extremity his ego pride falls away, and as he descends, he becomes willing to accept the mysterious guidance of an invisible presence; so guided, he comes to the valley of the Good Shepherd where the soul abides. Here he may find the answer. For the house of the soul—of the Wise Woman—is also the house of the Interpreter and she will show him many things—things forgotten, not yet known, to be awakened, to be lived in inwardness. She will show him also things moving in the depth of his own being which he now, for the first time, perceives in their unacceptable reality and in their neglected possibilities. She will also show him the way into the land where the greater images reveal the immortal truths to mortal being. She will lead him to the true aloneness that is found in "that infinite quietude in which all energies and relations are at play."[34] Will he take with him these things when he returns to his daily life?

Return he must to his human responsibilities, his family, his professional life. Here again is the paradox. Returning to his crowded world of many people, many activities, many so-called opportunities, may be only return to isolation, to hunger in the land of plenty, to joylessness in a world of joy; for again he will meet the old temptation to *have* instead of to *be*, to acquire instead of to create out of himself and his own abundance a life that brings him to oneness with nature and his fellow man. Whatever has been attained through inward confrontation cannot become real in a vacuum but

---

[34] From an essay by Heidegger quoted in Jacques Maritain, *Creative Intuition in Art and Poetry*, p. 178.

must be worked out in confrontation of the I and thou in the world of human relatedness. The release from the thousand and one things that collectivity demands of us can come only through a growing consciousness of the Self and its power of selecting that which is intrinsically our own, and through our creating in accordance with our own nature. This release brings freedom. If he accepts the dream, the soul will go with him into this new freedom and will show him the way by which, no longer driven by the former ego urge to acquisition and achievement but led by the new urge to self-realization, he will find the old made new.

Will he let this Self that has been revealed to him act upon him, permeate his being, so that, centered within him and yet encompassing him, it changes his relation to himself and to his fellow man? For all that is inwardly conceived must be brought forth and enter into life.

On his return he will find the old name waiting. It is a name belonging to the "little man" of many affairs. Will it now answer the question, "Who are you?" For in this "vale of soul-making" he has heard the promise, "And I will give him a new name and it shall be written in the Book of Life."

The decision is his. Will he risk it? Every decision is a risk; there is always a doubt to be overcome. It is an act of faith. He will lose much that he has held to be desirable, even indispensible. And the new way means he must listen to the inner voice even when his ego shouts defiance; he must follow, instead of ruthlessly pushing ahead. His conscious will must be enclosed within the greater will so it is converted, transformed; and as new man he receives the new name and comes to know who he is. If he makes this choice, he will have set out upon that most difficult journey, the journey toward wholeness.

> Everyman, I will with thee go to be thy guide
> In thy most need to be by thy side.

So speaks the soul.[35]

The instantaneous response of the physician confronted by the young intern's account of the irrational forces that had determined

---

[35] *Everyman.* In the old mystery play it is Knowledge who makes this promise which he fails to keep. This promise will be kept by the soul.

his ignominious failure[36] was the act of a man so at one within himself that, when the unexpected and unpredictable appeared, he could react without the intrusion of doubt or of intellectualization. All the damning factual evidence of the youth's record was in his hands, but the evidence of unconscious forces beyond ego control awakened swift perception of the essential meaning of the situation, and his own suprarational response (the destruction of the record, the words, "We start from here") came from a being whose consciousness and unconscious were in harmonious accord and who could trust the sudden direction of the inmost self and make it manifest through the act.

This revelation of the real man awakened an image that had lain unborn in the unconscious of the youth. He saw man not as the avenging father but as one who "through clarity brings deliverance." His own acceptance of and trust in this greater reality freed him from the dominance of the old invisible father image that had, in moments of crisis, taken over his power of conscious choice. He had, through failure, come to a *cul de sac* and was forced to seek an answer where his conscious ego believed that no answer could be found: to seek enlightenment within the confines of his own dilemma. This was beyond the power of the ego who sought in vain for reasonable solutions. Only by emptying his mind of rational thought, even of conscious conjecture, could he have made it possible for the new image to arise from that fountainhead of creative possibilities where all that is unborn, yet embryonically existent, awaits its moment of birth into consciousness. The old image was there, a shadow waiting to seize upon the moment, but the upsurge of newly roused emotion gave him back the power of love and loyalty that he had lost so long ago, and this gave power of transcendence to the new image of man suddenly released within him.

In that instant the youth not only perceived the spirit, the self, of the older man, but the spark, the unborn self, was also awakened in him so that he felt his own powers and abilities, his own courage and will to endure, spring up within himself. Physician and youth were both enclosed in the wholeness of the greater Self, each illumined in his own creative potential, and the young man himself experienced a moment of enlightenment, of rebirth.

---

[36] See Chapter 7, "Return of the Image," p. 131.

A sense of purposiveness reawakened within him. At first he thought it was to follow in the footsteps of the older man to whom he now felt a passionate allegiance. Then, as time went on, he realized that with the return of trust and loyalty he had also returned to freedom of choice—choice of his own way as it was revealed to him through the interests that sprang up as he continued his medical research and as his own unique potential developed. Through accepting the moment of enlightenment, his own way became clarified so that he chose, not in opposition to the negative father image that had theretofore ruled his life, but in the freedom of the son who chooses to claim his inborn, yet god-given, heritage.

He discovered that with the return of trust, love and loyalty as once more existent within himself, he could not only trust this man who had called them forth but could also trust the Self in which these powers were operative; and he could love and give loyalty to the truth of his own being. This is the true self-love—love of the Self beyond the self, trust in the indwelling spirit, loyalty to that which has been envisioned, faith in a power beyond the ego that can confirm and bring to pass that which the moment of illumination has brought forth within the soul. The newly awakened self heard the secret that life speaks to each man who has ears to hear. "Behold, I am that which must ever surpass itself." And the young man perceived that only thus can the life we live become also the life of the gods.

CHAPTER 16

Faith Beyond Fear

≈§≈

Where understanding is, where the mind is, where the power of investigating truth is, there God has his image.[1]

"THE SEAT OF FAITH is not consciousness but spontaneous religious experience which brings the individual's faith into immediate relation with God."[2] Such experience can come through acceptance of a message that arises from the unconscious, a reverent acknowledgment, "This is true, this has happened." The following simple dream wrought a miracle of faith in a woman who had long felt herself severed from God and man by a sin of her youth.

To understand the dream we must go back a little and discover the place where our dreamer was at the time the dream came to her. Reared in a rigidly pious community by a rigidly pious mother, she had been trained in meticulous adherence to duty in conformity to the law of a god of ten thousand thou-shalt-nots. Possessing an original warmth and spontaneity, an inquiring mind, a vivid imagination, she had been admonished that on the road to salvation all these gifts must be taught to conform. They must walk to heel on the pathway of righteousness; if she herself would walk thereon she must not allow her eyes to be distracted by beauty along the way. It was, indeed, a straight and narrow way.

And yet, from within herself arose the mighty wind that swept

---

[1] St. Augustine, quoted by Jung in *Aion*.
[2] Jung, *The Undiscovered Self*, p. 88.

her from this ordered path into sin against the law of a jealous un-forgiving God and of an equally jealous mother. The act itself was hidden from the community, but all her inner retreats were blocked by her own sense of its enormity, and she was shut away from her-self and from the fountains of her own being. Seized by the shadow, magnified by guilt, her sense of sin became an insuperable obstacle, blocking the way to rebirth of the spirit. The world is full of lights and shadows, of change and transformation, yet man can shut them from his vision with his own hand, which he mistakes for the hand of God. It is strange how an identification with a single act can lock the ego into its own past. An act of achievement may do this even more effectively than an act of sin, for pride takes over and writes, *Finis*, and the ego reads and rereads its own autobiography. In either case, achievement or failure, it is as though the small personal clock of time is stopped—it does not matter at what hour—and eter-nal time cannot move in the soul in the ever-changing process of transformation.

Guilt imprisoned this woman in the past of a single mistake, yet, even in this small prison, she did the best she could. Under the domi-nance of the god image in which she believed, she acted with integ-rity and faithfulness and tried to accept, without bitterness or re-sentment, the life she felt *ought* to be hers from now on. Misdirected integrity, doing the best it can with the bewildered moment, is mys-teriously ready for the awakening of grace when mistaken belief en-counters the moment of miracle in which a new image arises. Then choice is again offered: a choice between retreat into the known security, however tortured, or the leap into the unknown where an unknown God of tomorrow awaits birth within the soul.

This choice can come even to one self-imprisoned in a yesterday which does not open on a new tomorrow. Until the dream came, such was the state of this woman. Opportunities that her ego had desired were closed to her, but the real disaster was that she chose nonliving in the form of "sinlessness," and by this choice, spontane-ous impulse and desire became forever suspect. Guilt and conformity strangely seek to limit the power of grace within the soul. Neverthe-less, in spite of vigilant guard over her emotions, love again stirred within her and she married a man who knew all about her "sin" and was singularly unimpressed by it. Even this did not release her spirit. Her mind continued to police her feeling and laid down for her a

strange pattern of contradictions. She believed in forgiveness, but could not forgive herself. She believed in love, but could not accept her right to receive its warmth. She believed in freedom, but chained herself to a single act of the past lest she again stray into sin.

Within her self-imposed restrictions she achieved many things. She loved her husband and children and became a "good wife" and "good mother," though how much they all missed through her fear of gaiety and joy no one could appraise. She had a job which she performed admirably. It helped the family budget and left time for the home. She was an admired and helpful member of the community. Her well-disciplined thoughts and feelings were ready to serve life, but only in ways that kept her spirit safe from adventure. She was approved of; occasionally she even approved of herself. She did not realize how circumscribed her life had become, for her buried potentials were unborn children, unhappened things. At times vague longings, "improper" discontents, stirred within her, but she repressed them as childish rebellion.

Then periods of depression seized her. These too she tried to ignore, but they persisted. Inwardly she withdrew more and more from people though outwardly she appeared her same competent self. In one of her periods of perplexity and distress, she sought help, and life gave her the gift of this dream.

I am going to a gathering that I feel is a festive occasion. I have on a new garment, one that I have long desired. It is blue, simple, suitable. Then I see that in the front, at the hem, a large hole has been burned, as though by a white-hot iron. It can never be repaired, for the threads about it are so scorched that they will break away if I try to mend it. I am singularly undisturbed. There is something for me to do which may take a long time, but that does not matter. It is the "remedy" given to me if I will accept it. Then I am on a flight of steps with many other women who are all peeling potatoes. New potatoes are brought to me. I notice the others are old and one does not peel new potatoes, but since this is my share in the communal labor, I start to peel them. They have earth upon them, but I do not mind. If they soil my dress, it is all part of what I am given to do. Then I am aware that as my own hands are performing their task, invisible hands are reweaving the irreparable hole. Simultaneously my communal task is completed: my garment is made whole.

The dream changes:

> I am in my own house. A storm is rising. Clouds, ominous, forbidding, pile up in the sky. From them a hurricane will be let loose. My little sister Mary is missing. She has ventured out to meet the storm. I am in agony of fear for her, yet even in my terror I feel a rueful amusement at her adventurous joy in life that disregards oncoming storms. I search. I call her. She is gone. Now I am angry with her for being careless of the danger, but I know, with a sudden penetrating perception, that it is my mother who is really to blame. My mother has never watched over, or cared for, Mary. She has never tried to understand her or to make her realize that elemental forces are too powerful to be played about with. Anger at my mother, distress for Mary, tear through me. As I search for her I wake in terror.

At once the day's routine claimed her. It so often happens that with the coming of morning, that which has been known in the silence of the night is relinquished to the claims of many-voiced day. But today the early scene of the dream remained clear and distinct; it filled her with an irrational sense of release from the old dragging undercurrent of guilt. As she moved about her accustomed tasks, they seemed to be part of the dream, a communal task which she was performing with all the women of the world, a task of love. She was no longer alienated, apart, separated by a guilty secret. Could it be that the dream had a reality which she had inwardly accepted? In an hour of solitude, while her hands were busy with the familiar household tasks, she relived the dream. She sat on the steps with the women who were strangers and yet intimately one with her through their mutually shared task of preparing a communal meal. The humble service became a ritualistic act. She was Woman serving in the temple of the home. But why had she been given *new* potatoes to peel? "Thou shalt not peel new potatoes!" She had been taught this in her childhood. Was there a hidden meaning in the irrationality of this given part? Should she forget the teaching of what one shall not do? Was this part of the new release? The "new" had dirt on them. New things should be spotless. She smiled as she thought how little the "dirt," the touches of earth, mattered, even if they rubbed off on the new garment. Potatoes, *pommes de terre*, were earth apples! Their earthiness was part of their reality. It was while

she performed this earthy task, accepting both the irrationality and the dirt, that the garment was made whole. It was then that the miracle happened, and the miracle was true.

Again she saw the hole in the garment; it was at the hem. She remembered the woman who touched but the hem of His garment, and was healed of an issue of blood of which she had been diseased twelve years. The synchronistic figures arrested her attention. It was twelve years since her very womb had been pierced by an arrow of guilt, and ever since, the life blood of her vital energy had seeped away in continuous and uncreative repentance. She was healed; her veins were filled with new life.

And the dream said the new garment was *hers* and suitable for all occasions. It was a garment given her, not one that her conscious ego had chosen. What had been given her that she had misused? What had been restored by the miracle? She began to look on her present life with new eyes. It was her own. Her husband and children were hers. She had never allowed herself to enjoy them freely, for she felt she had no right to her happiness in them. She had stolen them in a moment when God was looking the other way. At any time He might punish her by taking them from her if she allowed herself to forget. This childish and primitive concept of God struck her in all its absurdity. She had never really been conscious of it before. Yet the old hidden concept had so great a hold on her that she looked up as if expecting to see this God in an ominous forbidding cloud. Instead, she saw the sunlight on a tree; the leaves, moved by an almost imperceptible wind, formed changing patterns against the impenetrable blue of the sky. This moment was a festive occasion, filled with the joy of one who

> . . . felt through all this fleshly dress
> Bright shootes of everlastingnesse.[3]

Her thought, that she had been taught should be held on the leash of discipline, walking to heel, following the footsteps of duty, ran back to a long lost memory.

She is again a nine-year-old child, the age of the dream-Mary, also of her own little daughter Mary. The child is on her way to school. She is going down a dusty road, meadowlands stretch away

---

[3] Henry Vaughan, "The Retreat," in *Poems*, Vol. I, p. 59.

on either side, but on one side a barbed-wire fence straggles from nowhere to nowhere, from anywhere to anywhere. The fence posts loll in indifferent leisure. Here the miracle may happen—the meadowlark may wing up from the silent grass and fill the air with song. He comes. The child stands immobile, not daring even to breathe. Will he! oh! will he sing? Then the cascade of silver sound, shining raindrops falling all about her! It is so short! Will he sing again? Fear rushes up in her. She will be late to school. Bright desire and dull duty contend within her. Now she is already late. As she runs, frightened and driven, the song comes from the distance—the song she dare not hear. She runs from joy, but she cannot run from pursuing guilt. She has stolen for private delight the precious time given her for dutiful work.

Memory becomes fantasy; she, the child, turns, choosing the song. Again she hears it, clear as in that long-ago morning. It pierces through her lethargy like a divine arrow. It wells up within her. Almost simultaneously, terror grips her, the terror of the night that she had lightly dismissed, and the second act of the dream drama returns to her, real and present. The hurricane is upon her. Mary is lost.

The old attitude of self-blame springs up in her and, forgetting the language of the dream, her self-condemning thoughts go, not to Mary her dream sister, but to Mary her own little daughter. Has she left this child in dangerous freedom? She has rejoiced in Mary's adventurous nature, her zest for living, her independence of spirit. She has looked with tolerant amusement upon small wayward impulsive acts. Should she have controlled them? Was her joy in Mary's freedom a secret self-indulgence? The dream says it is her mother's fault that Mary is lost. Her mother's fault! Irrationally, without any apparent connection with this dream-Mary, she was swept by a storm of anger against her mother. Other memories pressed upon her. She remembered the morning of sudden spring when she had opened her shutters upon an orchard turned to a blossoming sea. Watching the movement of foam petals against the sky, she had forgotten to dress, had forgotten to set the table for breakfast. Her guilty descent, her mother's cold implacable face! She was not worthy of love; she had forgotten duty. And the winter afternoon when the sun had dropped behind crimson cloud-mountains, its glory flowing to midheaven, she had lingered on the lighted road and been late for her music lesson.

"Wasted time ticks in hell." How horribly that clock of hell had ticked in her childhood. Tick, tock; duty, control; control, duty. Another hour. The tension of her mother's disapproval became unbearable, and her love for her mother burst out in an impetuous gesture. But such love was "uncontrolled emotion demanding unearned acceptance." Tick, tock; tick, tock. "Love is act, not impulse." Nothing that she ever could do seemed quite worthy of her mother's love.

Without warning, all these repressed emotions swept through her. She hated control, she hated her mother's black-and-white creed that deprived life of its color. She hated the cold certainty that stifled questions. She hated her beloved mother. For days this storm raged through her, a primeval chaos of love and hate. Her habit of control kept the outer pattern of her life unaltered, but she suffered the emotion to sweep through her. She did not deny it or feel guilty because of it. And then chaos took form in hate, and a strange release came with its acknowledgment: she was not bound by gratitude and service to something that she hated—something that hated *her*. Then she faced hatred and acknowledged it. Her mother must have loved her. She remembered sacrifices that her mother had made for her, sacrifices in order that she might "return to the ways of God." Who was this God to whom she must return? Did she hate her mother, or did she hate her mother's God? Suddenly, like a shifting of great winds, the hurricane swept her into another place of memory and became the fiery wind that had swept her into life—life that she had seen only as sin. Again swept by the fiery wind into a place of new understanding, she gave thanks for the sin and for the tempest of emotion that had swept her from the small cold place where her mother's righteousness and her own lack of courage would have kept her. What would have been her ego-chosen life had not the greater will seized her, swept her into the storm, broken her and defeated her ego choices? She saw the barren heights on which her conscious purpose had been fixed. Her ego had not intended love to defeat sterile righteousness or ego achievement. This was the choice of a Greater Will.

> Dreamer, it is I who am your dream—
> Would you awake, I am your will.[4]

---

[4] Rilke, *The Book of Hours*, tr. by Babette Deutsch.

She was awake now, awake to the dream. Who was the "I" who must become her will? Was it that I—the "I am that I am"—whom Mary was seeking in the storm, the god who was the will of tempest and fire, of love and of the meadowlark and his song? The dream said it was her mother's fault that Mary was lost. But who was her mother? Who was Mary? Even as she asked, she knew the answer. The mother who worshipped an old god whose final opus was the ten thousand thou-shalt-nots lived now within her and still feared that Mary would waste time in the forbidden joys of love and beauty. If she found Mary, would she find the god for whom Mary had searched in the hurricane?

Mary was lost. She must find Mary. A dream often holds the clue which can enable the dreamer to discover the lost parts of the individual self which must be recovered if the psychic wound is to be healed and the dreamer is again to find the pathway that leads to the intended wholeness. What had this little sister Mary, this sister self, possessed that must be searched for and found within the heart of the hurricane? Could it be the song of the meadowlark, the exultant joy in spring's awakening, the dreams of things to come, the perception of beauty that was almost pain? The dream said Mary was nine years old. Dreams do not use numbers lightly. They have a precise meaning. She was nine the year that she had started her solitary two-mile walk to the district school. It was then that she first became acutely conscious of the beauty of the shifting cloud shadows, the sunshine running in ripples as the wind moved through the long grass, the distant horizon that spoke of strange lands beyond envisioning. Again she felt the miracle of spring stir, and the morning of the orchard's blossoming was alive within her. Where had all these things gone—these things that she had believed dead and decently buried? Nine years old! It was then that her thoughts began to stray, and, touched by the mystery of life's beauty, she had forgotten duty. It was then that she had first met its inexorable demand. It was then that she became aware of her mother's disapproval and of the vigilance of her mother's vengeful God. It was then that joy and duty became, to her, irreconcilable contradictions. How could these oppositions be bridged? How could joy and duty cease to contradict each other? She went back now to the other Mary who had set the table a hundred times, who had followed duty often in a spirit of "wicked" rebellion, in fear of her own "sinful" nature. It was then

that her mother had taught her the meaning of original sin. But was there not also original goodness? This her mother had never believed.

Belief in original sin without belief in original goodness curdles the milk of human kindness most effectively. This was the milk on which her mother had fed her just at the time when her spirit was beginning to reach out for its own life and its own original experience. After those terrible sessions when her mother had shown her that "the heart is deceitful and desperately wicked," the conflict between duty and delight could not be resolved in her childish mind. They stood as implacable contradictions. How deeply this had been ingrained she was only now beginning to realize. She still feared original experience. She was still constrained to live under the law. Freedom to live above the law she saw only as license. She began to see, as she pondered the dream, that until one has been able to follow the law as the expression of a common good, he cannot safely break it to follow his own way; for impulse and sudden act, breaking through law's barrier without a sense of value to be achieved, may only put him outside law. All the fundamental disciplines are essential. Without them, any chaotic impulse may appear as free choice. But discipline, duty, conformity, unfed by the creative springs that arise within the self, bring death in sterility or deliver man over to the contradictory forces of chaos.

She began to see what Mary had been seeking in the hurricane. If her mother had not been so afraid! Afraid! The word surprised her; she had never thought of fear in connection with her mother. Now, since the word had been spoken, she must examine it. Yes, her mother had been afraid—afraid of breaking the law, afraid of life, of love, of original experience and, most of all, afraid of God—not with the fear that is the beginning of wisdom, but with the fear of a child for a vengeful father. She and her mother, imprisoned by the same fear, neither of them able to escape from the "jealous God who visits the iniquities of the fathers upon the children" if they dare to stray into joy! *And life had not given her mother the gift of a dream.* For the first time, compassion for her mother stirred within her, and she longed to share this gift; and as the still, small voice of compassion spoke within her, the chaos of hate and fear was stilled, and she dared look deep into her own heart where, forever, the energies of good and evil would await their awakening. After her own mistaken act, not only had she feared God, but also she had feared herself and those

fiery energies that could so easily come alive within her. And she had feared love; for had He not taken vengeance upon her because of her sin of loving? Had He taken vengeance, or had she taken vengeance on herself? She feared this wrathful God whose voice spoke out of the hurricane and out of the fire. But Mary had gone out to find him. Only this morning she had heard the voice of the hurricane as her own hatred. Only a moment ago she had heard the voice speak as a god of her being, who had delivered her over to chaos. Yet out of chaos, when faced, had come new form.

Slowly, as she pondered the dream, new awareness came to her. Impulses were not evil; only in their misuse were they destructive. If she had dared accept them, dared to follow through on what they had awakened within her, would they have turned upon her in devastation or would they have blessed her? Was her denial of their awakening power the greater sin, the sin against life? Insofar as she had accepted "the fruit of her sin" (her mother's phrase), she had been blessed, but she had feared to rejoice; she had sought to limit the power of grace within her soul and so had limited her own creative energy, even in her acceptance. Says Kierkegaard, "It takes moral courage to grieve, it takes religious courage to rejoice." To rejoice in the quickening power of the fire within the heart and in the power of weak and erring man to endure the agony of the flame till he knows its cleansing grace.

The "wasted moments" of her childhood returned as moments of revelation, whose meaning had been blotted out by fear. Such moments cannot return on ego demand. Never again might that sudden vision of eternal renewal come to her in the way it had that morning when the blossoming orchard, illumined by a joyous morning sun, had burst upon her wondering eyes. As the picture rose behind her eyelids, the revelation burst upon her. The moment still lived; a power greater than her own small bewildered ego had kept it alive until she could see it with newly awakened eyes. Reverence, awe, filled her spirit, and she gave thanks. Then, again perplexity touched her. Why had the sense of guilt blotted out the vision? Whence had the darkness come? Her mother's fault! Why? She saw again the unset table and her mother's face. There, in that far-away past, duty and joy had faced each other as irreconcilable enemies, and the implacable God of vengeance had triumphed over the God who, "knowing all, forgives." She could not tell her mother's God of the joy that other God had created. So, in her moment of fear her confused childish mind

had chosen the ancient God. Hence duty, instead of being the God-given way of expressing love and joy, became its enemy.

Then laughter came upon her. Duty—it had been her duty to peel new potatoes—had also been a joy, a preparation for "the festive occasion" to which her garment would be worn. The irreconcilable opposites were coming together. Joy and duty were being woven together in a pattern ordained by love. Only so could her garment be made whole.

In wholeness all that the ego has denied must be rewoven into the new pattern. She had denied joy; she had denied the laughter of the saints; she had denied the fire. She had acknowledged only grief, repentance and guilt. Therefore she must now acknowledge joy, redemption and rebirth.

She was come to the place where the three tenses meet: the past re-enters the present, and potentials of the future stir within. This was the meaning of the silent invisible weaving: the child she had been, the woman she was, and the mysterious self that she was intended to become were all woven together by the invisible hand, and the woof on which the threads were woven was love; for this, in spite of guilt and confusion, had been the guiding thread. It was not the continued consciousness of guilt that had made possible the weaving, but the fact that she had held, insofar as she was able, to the meaning of love in connection with her daily life.

Again she looked upon the world with Mary's eyes, a child's eyes, lighted by wonder. She saw "every grass blade fierce with meaning"—its own particular meaning as a single blade, its participation in meaning as "greenness"—the upward thrust of life. She listened to the stillness of the eternal that lives in the moment of the now. She lingered until, of themselves, her footsteps quickened, hurrying to that other beauty—potatoes to be peeled for dinner—an act "fierce with meaning" because it was part of the ritual of love. The true cleansing act of repentance is "a turning from and a turning toward," a turning from the mistaken act and a turning toward new life, a mingling of past and present from which a new future may be born. Old words re-echoed. "I am Yesterday, Today and Tomorrow and I have the power to be born a second time. I am the divine, hidden soul who creates the gods."[5] Could it be that the wasted moments were the saved moments, that the moments of joy in the wonder and beauty of life and

---

[5] Egyptian *Book of the Dead*, p. 211.

in its power of transformation had been kept safe by the hidden soul through the long winter of her self-imposed guilt in order that from them a new God might be created—a God who came to bring life and bring it more abundantly? With an uprush of newly awakened joy she chose this God whom the hidden soul had created and, with faith, accepted him. With the emergence of this faith, joy in beauty, in love, in life, was reborn within her. The past, in its essential meaning, was alive in the present and could go on into the future in ever-evolving form. For the past returns, not as the old objective experience, but as reborn spirit; love returns, not to the object of past love, except in the tenderness of recollection, but as an inner attitude that permeates the newborn being; trust returns, not as childish credulity, but as childlike trust in life and in a power residing in a Self greater than oneself; faith returns, not as a willed effort of consciousness or as imposed creed (Jung says, "Enforced faith is nothing but spiritual cramp"[6]), but as loyal commitment to the "spontaneous religious experience which brings . . . faith into immediate relation with God. . . . Yes he, [the Purusha,] is the whole world. He is the past and the future, he is formed by the urge for Wisdom, born from the world order, dwelling in fullness; he is Faith, true, great, above darkness."[7]

Dimly she perceived this faith, "true, great, above darkness," as faith in a God who can be born and reborn a thousand times in an ever-transformed and ever-transforming god image that dwells within the human heart. If we believe in that power of transformation and choose to let it work out its ever-changing form within us, faith in a power of grace is born within our soul, and that is a faith above darkness. Life really is the transformation of the god image within the soul of man, for "as each one's being, so is his faith. As he believeth, so is he himself."[8]

Again she was on the steps peeling new potatoes. They had dirt on them. Was the "new" an earthy thing that also had "dirt" on it—dirt that was part of the wholeness of life, part of a mystery that was the greater reality? "Here stands the newly awakened Self aware for the first time of Reality"—reality, the great awakener. Her daily life was real—real as the potatoes that she would peel for dinner, real as the spirit of love that moved through her as she did her task, real as the

---

6 "Psychology of the Transference," p. 172.
7 *Bhagavad Gita*, Song 17.
8 Upanishad in Hume, *Thirteen Principal Upanishads*.

darkness, the hurricane and the fire, real as the sunlight that streamed through the window, real as joy and sorrow, real as impulse and desire, real as sin and transformation, real as her every given talent, real as "the urge toward Wisdom," real as the spirit of God moving in the human soul. What was this mysterious spirit of God? He had come to her in the hurricane and the fire as well as in the still, small voice, and she knew that as the eternal energy of life she must fear Him as well as love Him. This, then, is Reality—to know "the One who dwells in him, whose form has no knowable boundaries, who encompasses him on all sides, fathomless as the abysms of the earth and vast as the sky."[9]

The moments when the soul awakens to reality are moments of "man's opportunity to be blessed." They are true experiences of rebirth. The "whole man," the "real man," is not the once-born or the twice-born, but the one continuously reborn in the eternal process of becoming and of being. Every moment of new awareness which is confirmed by the self in total experience is rebirth. Intellectual knowledge is conducive to change only insofar as it is also emotional knowledge, a knowledge that cannot be put into words but that infuses the whole being. When this whole man—"the true man of no rank," the man of "the everyday mind"—acts, there is no need, nor is there any impulse, to hesitate, for perception and action proceed from a personality that is freed from intellectual analysis and goes straight from the center to the center, enlightenment awakening enlightenment; for it is the unknown and unknowable Self that stands behind, above and within all the ego's reactions to inner and outer life. When the ego is in harmony with the Self in its wholeness, the immediate act springs from a source deeper than consciousness and is a spontaneous expression of the life purpose.

And "the newly awakened self, aware for the first time of reality, responding to that reality with love and awe," perceives a world of eternally creative energy where man, created in God's image, is "thrust into a new world, set at the beginning of a new road," knowing "that a quest there is and a goal," a quest in which his whole nature is involved. Through the choice of reality man is freed to make his decision of the way and to commit himself to it.

It is a long journey, this journey toward wholeness. On this way

---

[9] Jung, *Answer to Job*, p. 180.

man comes to know that the life of the self is the journey "from God the Void, to God the Enemy, to God the Friend."[10]

Out of the silence of the void, God the Enemy challenges man to separate himself from his unconscious undifferentiated oneness and to descend into his own darkness which is the darkness of God, where he may discover the spark of his own individual meaning. If man accepts the challenge, God the Enemy becomes God the Awakener who reveals himself as eternal change, creativity, becoming and being. Knowing this awakener as an inner abiding force, man knows himself as a creator who must ceaselessly give form and meaning to the formless that arises within him from the stream of eternal becoming. In this way comes to the knowledge of God the Friend.

This Friend he sees as "that non-temporal actuality that has to be taken account of in every creative phase."[11] For God remains a living creative force, though the aspects in which generations see him differ as his image is ever reborn in new transforming power. The religious attitude toward life remains as

the vision of something which stands beyond, behind, and within the passing flux of immediate things; something which is real, and yet waiting to be realized; something which is a remote possibility, and yet the greatest of present facts; something that gives meaning to all that passes, and yet eludes apprehension; something whose possession is the final good, and yet is beyond all reach; something which is the ultimate ideal, and the hopeless quest,[12]

hopeless because never ending, filled and illumined by hope because always on the pathway of the reality of transcendence.

This final good which is beyond all reach is born and reborn as the ever-transformed and transforming god image arising within the soul. Man must choose between the god image of yesterday and the new image that arises of a God who leads him into a tomorrow that challenges his sense of security in a known past. "One lives in images, thinks in them, creates them, is ruled by them, destroys them. All this is a matter of course, the course of natural life. When it is time for us to break the spell of something that we have lived by, it is a new god that informs us subtly, a new aspiration that impels us."[13]

---

[10] After Whitehead, *Religion in the Making*, p. 472.

[11] *Ibid.*, p. 500.

[12] Whitehead, *Science and the Modern World*, Ch. XII, p. 191.

[13] I found this in my notebook. I do not know whether or not it is a quotation.

It is this new god who offers man the never-ending choice, the choice of the leap forward, into the risk of an unknown tomorrow. This leap is an act of faith. It must be taken if choice is to become decision and if the will of God and the will of the newly awakened self are to meet as one. "Where there is oneness in the soul there will God's oneness dwell."

In this oneness the act takes on form as part of the living energy of that Self which, from the beginning has been both the goal and the dynamis that moves toward the goal. Faith as the urge toward transformation impels man toward this choice of the new god image in whom the mystery of immanence and transcendence meet.

Before this mystery, man knows himself as smaller than the small; yet, since God needs man in order that he shall become manifest in transformation, man becomes great in the process of God becoming man and man becoming one with God. Faith in this transforming process makes of all life a truly religious experience. "If you die when God tells you, you can come back and live all over again." Then again, "mountains are mountains and rivers are rivers." Again, Twinkle and Pitch-Black Dark are contained within the circle of the Self who is the Friend; and the commandment of the Rose and the commandment of the Star are one commandment and one promise; and knowing the Self, the world is known.

The inward choice of the transforming power of the spirit flows into the daily act, and the artist in life becomes the one who by faith makes the power manifest. Through this, man comes to an increasing knowledge of that greatest of all arts, the art of living, in which God the Awakener becomes God the Friend.

Bibliography

Adler, Gerhard. "The Logos of the Unconscious," in *Studien zur Analytischen Psychologie*, papers written for C. G. Jung's 80th birthday. Zurich: Rascher Verlag, 1955.

Adrian, E. D., *et al*. *Factors Determining Human Behavior*. Cambridge, Mass.: Harvard University Press, Harvard Tercentenary Publications, 1947.

Apocryphal New Testament, The. Tr. by Montague Rhodes James. Oxford: At the Clarendon Press, corrected edition, 1955.

Avalon, Arthur (Sir John Woodroffe). *The Serpent Power*. London: Luzac & Co., 1919.

Barlach, Ernst. *Der Tote Tag (The Dead Day)*. Berlin: Paul Cassirer, 1912. Quoted in Jung, *Psychological Types*.

Baynes, H. Godwin. *Mythology of the Soul*. London: Bailliere, Tindall and Cox, 1940.

Bible quotations are from the King James Version.

Bible of the World. Ed. by Robert O. Ballou. New York: The Viking Press, 1939.

Blake, William. *Poetry and Prose of William Blake*. Ed. by Geoffrey Keynes. London: The Nonesuch Press, and New York: Random House, 1935.

Book of the Dead. Tr. by Sir E. A. Wallis Budge. London: Kegan Paul, 1923.

Browne, Sir Thomas. *Works*. Ed. by Geoffrey Keynes. London: 1928–31, 6 Vols.

Buber, Martin. *The Legend of the Baal Shem*. "The Life of the Hasidim, Shiflut: Humility." Tr. by Maurice Friedman. New York: Harper & Brothers, 1955.

———. *Eclipse of God*. "Religion and Reality." Tr. by Norbert Guterman. New York: Harper & Brothers, 1952.

———. "Symbolic and Sacramental Existence in Judaism." Tr. by Ralph Manheim, in *Spiritual Disciplines*. New York: Pantheon Books, Bollingen Series XX, 1960.

_____. *Tales of the Hasidim.* Tr. by Olga Marx. New York: A Schocken Book. Farrar, Straus and Young, Inc., Marston Press, 1947. 2 vols.

Chase, Mary Ellen. *A Goodly Fellowship.* New York: Macmillan, 1939.

Coblentz, Catherine Cate. *The Blue Cat of Castle Town.* New York: Longmans, Green & Co., 1949.

Dickinson, Emily. *Poems.* Ed. by T. H. Johnson. Cambridge, Mass.: Belknap Press of Harvard University Press, 1955. 3 vols.

Dostoyevsky, Fyodor. *The Brothers Karamazov.* Tr. by Constance Garnett. New York: Random House, The Modern Library, 1950.

Eckhart, Meister, A Modern Translation. Tr. by R. B. Blakney. New York: Harper & Brothers, 1957.

Eliot, T. S. *Collected Poems.* New York: Harcourt, Brace and Co., 1936.

_____. *Four Quartets.* New York: Harcourt, Brace and Co., 1943.

Everyman. New York: Taylor & Co., 1903.

Frost, Robert. *Complete Poems.* New York: Henry Holt, 1949.

Gillespy, Jane Bliss. *The Eastward Way.* Privately printed.

Goethe, Johann Wolfgang von. *Faust.* Tr. by George Madison Priest. New York: Alfred A. Knopf, 1957.

Gospel According to Thomas. Coptic text established and translated by A. Gillaumont et al. Leiden: E. J. Brill and New York: Harper & Brothers, 1959.

Herrigel, Eugen. *The Method of Zen.* New York: Pantheon Books, 1960.

Hume, R. E. (tr.). *Thirteen Principal Upanishads.* London: H. Milford, 1921.

I Ching, or *Book of Changes.* The Richard Wilhelm translation rendered into English by Cary F. Baynes. New York: Pantheon Books, Bollingen Series XIX, 1950.

Ibsen, Henrik. *Peer Gynt.* In *The Collected Works of Henrik Ibsen.* Tr. by William and Charles Archer. New York: Charles Scribner's Sons, 1923. 6 vols.

Jacobi, Jolande. *The Psychology of C. G. Jung.* Tr. by K. W. Bash. New Haven: Yale University Press, rev. ed., 1951.

_____, ed. *C. G. Jung, Psychological Reflections.* New York: Harper Torchbook, 1961.

Jaffé, Aniela. "The Person and the Experience," from *Ghostly Apparitions and Omens.* Tr. by Veronica Ladenburg, in *Spring 1959, q.v.*

Jung, C. G. (Note: In this bibliography, the Bollingen *Collected Works of Jung* and earlier editions have been used. The editions consulted for this book are listed below:)

Aion. Researches into the Phenomenology of the Self. Coll. Works, Vol. 9, Part II. Bollingen Series XX. Tr. by R. F. C. Hull. New York: Pantheon Books, and London: Routledge and Kegan Paul, 1959.

Answer to Job. Tr. by R. F. C. Hull. London: Routledge and Kegan Paul, 1954.

The Archetypes and the Collective Unconscious. Coll. Works, Vol. 9, Part I. Bollingen Series XX. Tr. by R. F. C. Hull. New York: Pantheon Books, and London: Routledge and Kegan Paul.

"Commentary," in *The Secret of the Golden Flower, q.v.*

Contributions to Analytical Psychology. Tr. by. H. G. and Cary F. Baynes. New York: Harcourt, Brace and Co., and London: Kegan Paul, 1928.

Essays on Contemporary Events. London: Kegan Paul, 1947.

The Integration of the Personality. Tr. by Stanley Dell. New York: Farrar and Rinehart, and London: Kegan Paul, 1940.

Modern Man in Search of a Soul. Tr. by W. S. Dell and Cary F. Baynes. London: Kegan Paul, and New York: Harcourt, Brace and Co., 1933.

Psychology and Religion: West and East. Tr. by R. F. C. Hull. Coll. Works, Vol. 8. Bollingen Series XX. New York: Pantheon Books, and London: Routledge and Kegan Paul, 1958.

"Psychological Aspects of the Mother Archetype," in *Spring 1943, q.v.* (In Coll. Works, Vol. 9, Part I. Bollingen Series XX.)

Psychological Types. Tr. by H. Godwin Baynes. New York: Harcourt, Brace and Co., and London: Kegan Paul, 1923.

Psychology and Alchemy. Coll. Works, Vol. 12. Bollingen Series XX. Tr. by R. F. C. Hull. New York: Pantheon Books, and London: Routledge and Kegan Paul, 1953.

"The Psychology of the Transference," in Coll. Works, Vol. 16. Bollingen Series XX.

Psychology of the Unconscious. Tr. and introd. by Beatrice M. Hinkle. Poems tr. by Louis Untermeyer. New York: Moffat, Yard & Co., 1916.

"The Soul and Death," in *Structure and Dynamics of the Psyche.* Tr. by R. F. C. Hull. Coll. Works, Vol. 8, Bollingen Series XX. New York: Pantheon Books, and London: Routledge and Kegan Paul, 1960.

Symbols of Transformation. An Analysis of the Prelude to a Case of Schizophrenia. Coll. Works, Vol. 5. Bollingen Series XX. Tr. by R. F. C. Hull. New York: Pantheon Books, and London: Routledge and Kegan Paul, 1956.

The Transcendent Function (1916). Zurich: ed. & pub. by The Students' Association of the C. G. Jung Institute, 1957.

"Transformation Symbolism in the Mass," in *Psychology and Religion: West and East.* Coll. Works, Vol. 11. Bollingen Series XX. Tr. by R. F. C. Hull. New York: Pantheon Books, and London:

Routledge and Kegan Paul, 1958. (Also in *Spring 1952*, tr. by Monica Curtis.)

Two Essays on Analytical Psychology. Tr. by C. F. and H. G. Baynes. London: Bailliere, Tindall and Cox, and New York: Dodd, Mead & Co., 1928. (Also in Coll. Works. Tr. by R. F. C. Hull.)

The Undiscovered Self. Tr. by R. F. C. Hull. Boston: Little, Brown & Co., and London: Routledge and Kegan Paul, 1958.

"Woman in Europe," in *Contributions to Analytical Psychology*, *q.v.*

"Zarathustra." Privately circulated notes on seminars in Zurich, 1934–1939. Ed. by Mary Foote. Mimeographed, undated, pages unnumbered.

Jung, Emma. *Animus and Anima*. (Tr. of the passage in the Khandogya Upanishad after F. Max Müller by Cary F. Baynes.) New York: The Analytical Psychology Club of New York, 1957.

Keats, John. *Selected Letters*. Sel. by Lionel Trilling. New York: Doubleday Anchor Books, 1956.

Macnicol, Nicol. *Hindu Scriptures*. New York: E. P. Dutton & Co., 1944.

Maitland, Edward. *Anna Kingsford, Her Life, Letters, Diary and Work*. Quoted in *The Secret of the Golden Flower*, *q.v.*

Maritain, Jacques. *Creative Intuition in Art and Poetry*. New York: Pantheon Books, 1953.

————. *Poetry*. Bollingen Series XXXV:1. New York: Pantheon Books, 1953.

Meister Eckhart. See Eckhart.

Moore, Marianne. *Collected Poems*. New York: The Macmillan Co., 1955.

Neihardt, *John G. Black Elk Speaks*. New York: Wm. Morrow & Son, 1932.

Neumann, Erich. *Amor and Psyche*. Tr. by R. Manheim. New York: Pantheon Books, Bollingen Series LIV, 1956.

————. *Art and the Creative Unconscious*. Tr. by R. Manheim. New York: Pantheon Books, Bollingen Series LXI, 1959.

————. "On the Moon and Matriarchal Consciousness," in *Spring 1954*, *q.v.*

————. *The Origins and History of Consciousness*. Tr. by R. F. C. Hull. New York: Pantheon Books, Bollingen Series XLII, 1955.

Nietzsche, Friedrich. *Thus Spake Zarathustra*. In *The Philosophy of Nietzsche*. Tr. by Thomas Common. New York: The Modern Library, 1927.

Phillips, Dorothy B. (ed.), with L. M. Nixon and E. B. Howes. *The Choice Is Always Ours*. New York: Harper & Brothers, rev. ed. 1961.

Plotinus. *The Enneads*. Tr. by Stephen MacKenna. New York: Pantheon Books, 2nd ed., 1957.

Post, Laurens van der. *The Lost World of the Kalahari*. London: The Hogarth Press, 1958.

Rilke, Rainer Maria. *The Book of Hours*. Tr. by Babette Deutsch. Norfolk, Conn.: New Directions, 1941.

―――. *Correspondence in Verse with Erica Mitterer*. Tr. by N. R. Cruikshank. London: Hogarth Press, 1953.

―――. *Duino Elegies*. Tr. by J. B. Leishman and Stephen Spender. New York: W. W. Norton & Co., 1939.

―――. *Letters to a Young Poet*. Tr. by M. D. Herter Norton. New York: W. W. Norton & Co., Inc., 1934.

―――. *Sonnets of Orpheus*. Unpublished tr. by Ruth Spiers. Quoted in Neumann, *Art and the Creative Unconscious, q.v.*

Rukeyser, Muriel. *Selected Poems*. New York: New Directions, 1951.

Sarton, May. *The Lion and the Rose*. New York: Rinehart & Co., 1948.

Sayings of Jesus. In *The Apocryphal New Testament, q.v.*

Secret of the Golden Flower, The. Tr. by Richard Wilhelm. European commentary by C. G. Jung, English commentary by Cary F. Baynes. London: Kegan Paul, Trench, Trubner & Co., 1931, and New York: Harcourt, Brace & Co., 1932.

Sergeant, Elizabeth Shepley. *Robert Frost, The Trial by Existence*. New York: Holt, Rinehart & Winston, 1960.

Singer, Charles. *From Magic to Science*. New York: Boni & Liveright, 1928.

Spiritual Disciplines. Papers from the Eranos Yearbooks. Tr. by Ralph Manheim; paper by Jung tr. by R. F. C. Hull. New York: Pantheon Books, Bollingen Series XXX·4, 1960.

Spring. A periodical issued annually by the Analytical Psychology Club of New York, 1942–.

Stein, Arnold. *Heroic Knowledge*. Minneapolis: University of Minnesota Press, 1957.

Studien zur Analytischen Psychologie. Papers written for C. G. Jung's 80th Birthday. Zurich: Rascher Verlag, 1955.

Suzuki, D. T. *Zen and Japanese Culture*.

Tao Teh Ching. See Waley, Arthur, *The Way and Its Power*.

Thompson, Francis. *Works*. London: Burns & Oates Ltd., undated (1913). 3 vols.

Tibetan Book of the Dead, The. W. Y. Evans-Wentz. Bardos tr. by Lama Kazi Dawa-Samdup. London: Oxford University Press, 1957.

Underhill, Evelyn. *Mysticism*. London: Methuen and Co., 1911.

Upanishads, The. See *Bible of the World*.

Upanishads. Tr. by F. Max Müller. Oxford: Clarendon Press, 1900.

Vaughan, Henry. *Poems*. Ed. by E. K. Chambers. London: Lawrence & Bullen Ltd., 1896. 2 vols.

Waley, Arthur, tr. and ed. *The Way and Its Power*. London: George Allen and Unwin Ltd., 1934.

Whitehead, Alfred North. *Religion in the Making*. In *Alfred North Whitehead, An Anthology*. Sel. by F. S. C. Northrop and Mason W. Gross. New York: The Macmillan Co., 1953.

_____. *Science and the Modern World*. New York: New American Library, 1923.

Wickes, Frances G. "The Creative Process," in *Spring 1948, q.v.*

_____. "Three Illustrations of the Power of the Projected Image," in *Studien zur Analytischen Psychologie*, papers written for C. G. Jung's 80th Birthday. Zurich: Rascher Verlag, 1955.

_____. *The Inner World of Childhood*. Introd. by C. G. Jung. New York: Appleton-Century-Crofts, Inc., 1927.

_____. *The Inner World of Man*. New York & Toronto: Farrar & Rinehart, 1938.

Wilhelm, Richard. Introd. to the *I Ching, q.v.*

_____. *The Secret of the Golden Flower, q.v.*

William Sharp (Fiona Macleod), A Memoir Compiled by His Wife. New York: Duffield & Co., 1912.

Wodehouse, Helen. "Inner Light," in *The Choice Is Always Ours, q.v.*

Yeats, W. B. *Early Poems and Stories*. New York: The Macmillan Co., 1925.

_____. "The Land of Heart's Desire," in *Plays*. New York: The Macmillan Co., 1907.

Zimmer, Heinrich. "On the Significance of the Indian Tantric Yoga," in *Spiritual Disciplines, q.v.*

Date Due

DEC 18 2009			